THE STORY

OF

AN IRISH SEPT

THE STORY

OF

AN IRISH SEPT

THEIR CHARACTER & STRUGGLE

TO MAINTAIN THEIR LANDS

IN CLARE

BY

A MEMBER OF THE SEPT

LONDON: J. M. DENT & CO.

67 ST. JAMES'S STREET, S.W.

1896

This reprint would not have been possible without the generous sponsorship of the following:

Shannon Heritage, Bunratty, Co. Clare.
Roche Ireland Ltd. Clarecastle, Co. Clare.
Ennis Urban District Council.
Clare County Council.
Clare Archaeological Services.
Bill MacNamara, The Flowing Tide, Irish International Music School, Doonbeg.
Brigadier-General W. Donald Macnamara. Canadian Forces (retired).
Michael & Nollag MacNamara, College Green, Ennis.
John MacNamara, Maiville, Ennis.
Dr. Maccon J. C. Macnamara, Corofin.
John Rynne & Company, Solicitors, 13 Abbey St. Ennis.
Seán Spellissy, Ennis.
Peadar McNamara, Magowna, Inch.
Risteard Ua Cróinín, M.A. Dysert O'Dea.
Gemma Kelly, 25 Ashfield Park, Ennis.
Dr. Peter Harbison, M.R.I.A., F.S.A.(London), Dublin.
Patrick McNamara, Newgrove, Tulla.
Holmes O'Malley Sexton, Solicitors, 5 Perry Sq., Limerick.
Fr. Michael McNamara, Chairman, Clare County Board, Aiden Pk., Shannon.
Packie McNamara, Ballyminogue, Scariff.
Clune, Lynch & Co., Auditors & Accountants, 50 O'Connell St., Ennis.
Caroline O'Brien, The Celtic Bookshop, Limerick.
John O'Brien, O'Brien's Bookshop, Little Catherine St., Limerick.
Éamon de Búrca, De Búrca Rare Books, Castlebourke & Dublin.
John MacNamara, Admiral's Rest, Restaurant & Accom., Nature Reserve, Fanore.
Michael & Mary McNamara, Ballymaley, Ennis.
Michael McNamara, Newgrove House, Tulla.
Tom McNamara, Fortville House, Kilmaley, Ennis.
John McNamara, Supervalu, Kinsale.
Helen McNamara-Browne, Bruach na hAille Restaurant, Doolin.

ISBN 0 9519551 1 X

First printed by Ballantyne Hanson & Co.
At the Ballantyne Press. 1896.

This reprint was made in Ireland at
Colour Books Ltd., Dublin 13.   Feb 1999.

PREFATORY NOTE

The Sept, or group of families referred to in the following history were derived from a common ancestor, and occupied from the fifth to the seventeenth century a definite area of land situated in the centre of county Clare. These people were frequently assailed by Norsemen, Anglo-Normans, and by the English, but they successfully defended their lands and homes against invaders for twelve hundred years, and were then dispersed, but by no means exterminated, by Cromwell. Throughout this long period of time the members of this Sept remained an almost pure race; they were principally engaged in agriculture, and their surroundings varied but little, and that only with the lapse of time; until the reign of James I. they lived under the Brehon laws, and clung to the traditions of the Church founded by St. Patrick in Ireland. The history of a Sept placed in circumstances of this kind is not only an interesting study, but may teach us much concerning their character, and that of the Irish people, and thus help us to understand the hereditary qualities which to a large extent have moulded their career, and continues to influence the descendants of Celtic Irishmen as individuals, and collectively as a nation.

In preparing this story for the press I have to acknowledge the great help I have received from the researches of Mr. Standish Hayes O'Grady, especially for his work "Silvia Gadelica," and for his valuable translation of Magrath's "Triumphs of Turlough," and also for his generous assistance on many occasions. To my friend Mr. T. J. Westropp, I beg to return my sincere thanks ; his time and pencil have been placed at my disposal with characteristic Celtic sympathy, and as an archæologist few men have a more extensive or accurate knowledge of county Clare. Several of the plates in this work are taken from copies of Mr. Westropp's drawings which have already appeared in the pages of the "Journal of the Royal Society of Antiquarians of Ireland," and which the Council of the Society have kindly given me permission to reproduce. I have acknowledged in footnotes to these pages the authorities referred to, and as a rule quoted their own words rather than attempt to explain their meaning according to my ideas on the subject. Lastly, I must crave the indulgence of my readers for the imperfections of this work, which has been written during the few leisure hours of a busy, and often anxious life.

N. C. MACNAMARA.

GROSVENOR STREET, LONDON, W.
April 1896.

CONTENTS

CHAPTER I

CHAPTER II

CHAPTER III

CHAPTER IV

CHAPTER V

CHAPTER VI

CHAPTER VII

CHAPTER VIII

CONTENTS

CHAPTER IX

CHAPTER X

CHAPTER XI

CHAPTER XII

CHAPTER XIII

CHAPTER XIV

CHAPTER XV

CHAPTER XVI

CHAPTER XVII

CHAPTER XVIII

CHAPTER XIX

CHAPTER XX

CHAPTER XXI

ILLUSTRATIONS

CHAPTER I

ORIGIN OF THE SEPT

Locality in which the Sept lived—Boundaries of County Clare—Burren—Stock from which the Sept were derived—The Iberians—Their character—The Basques of Spain—The Celts—Their character—Sept derived from Iberians and Celts.

RIGHTLY to comprehend the history of the Sept,* whose fortunes we have to follow, it is necessary to know something of the locality in which its members dwelt, and of the stock from which they proceeded, for their surroundings doubtless influenced their mental as well as their physical character, and it is equally certain that their congenital qualities had an important share in shaping their history.† We shall find that the members of our Sept, from the early part of the fifth to the middle of the seventeenth century, dwelt in a well defined district of Clare, a county which until comparatively recent times was isolated from the rest of Ireland ; its southern and eastern boundary being formed by the river Shannon, which throughout this part of its course was only fordable at one place situated below the town of Killaloe. To the north, Clare is separated from Galway by a range of high hills (Echtye) running from the Shannon westward towards Galway Bay ; between the extreme western spur of these hills and the bay is a strip of low lying swampy land, through which the road northward from Clare passed ; this low land as well as the Echtye hills were in former times covered by a dense forest rendering them almost impassable. The geographical position of the county was such as to preserve its inhabitants from successful invasion, or from being occupied by foreigners until late in the sixteenth century ; thus not only did the people of Clare

* A sept consists of a group of families derived from a common ancestor.

† By congenital qualities or character is meant peculiarities, whether structural or mental, with which an individual is born. Important as these inherent tendencies are, our history will afford us a good illustration of the paramount power exercised by the law of selection, in crushing out septs and races of men who fail to keep abreast of the times in which they live.

A

retain their independence but also their old Brehon laws and customs for two, if not three centuries after much of the rest of Ireland had passed into the hands of Englishmen.

The county is divided by the river Fergus into east and west Clare, the greater part of the former being covered by low hills and bog land; but to the south-east of this part of the county there are a mass of lofty rugged hills which run down to the Shannon and the western shore of Loch Derge.   These hills in former times were covered with forest trees and were known as one of the best hunting districts in Ireland; it was here that Brian Boru lived, his place of residence being situated on a spur of the hills overlooking the Shannon as it passes out of Loch Derge, a spot of exceeding beauty, and commanding the ford of Killaloe, the only weak point in the boundary of Clare to the east.

The northern part of the western division of Clare is formed by the district of Burren, which Cromwell's general, Ludlow, refers to as not possessing water sufficient to drown a man in, wood enough to hang a man on, or soil sufficient to bury him in.   Burren is in fact little more than a series of bare hills, some of them rising a thousand feet above the level of the sea; the sides of these hills are terraced in a remarkable manner and are of a light slate colour, with patches of exquisitely green grass scattered over their surface; they are, however, intersected with deep valleys, forming some of the finest grazing lands in the country.* Burren, with all its barrenness, has singular charms: its northern boundary, formed by Galway Bay, is indented with creeks which run up to the foot of its hills for long the home of numerous smugglers.   To the west, the hills of Burren form perpendicular cliffs against which the Atlantic hurls its mighty waves, a coast which can hardly be equalled for the wildness or grandeur of its scenery, and which has been so well described by the Hon. Miss Lawless in her pathetic story of " Hurrish."

Up to the close of the sixteenth century there seems to have been only one road leading through Burren, and now, unless along the coast-line it is no easy matter to travel over this part of Ireland.   These highlands afforded a safe refuge to the pre-Celtic race, when they were driven westward by the more highly civilised Celt in his advance from the east.   How well these people defended their lands may be learnt from the investigations of my friend Mr. T. J. Westropp, who has discovered the remains of about two hundred pre-Celtic forts in this part of county Clare.   In close proximity with these remains some of the work of the earliest Christian settlers in Ireland still exist, rude in the

* "Memoirs of the Geological Survey," Sheets 114 to 123 (Ireland).

extreme, and said to have been built by the same hands as those which erected the forts above referred to; pagans and Christians dwelt side by side, the sentiments of the former largely influencing the people of this part of Ireland up to within comparatively recent times. For instance, in the middle of the seventeenth century we are informed that the Archbishop of Tuam had to cross over to the isles of Arran to destroy the oak figure of "Mac Dara," which the people then worshipped in spite of all the clergy could do to induce them to abandon the adoration of this idol.* At the present time Irish men and women living to the west of the Shannon are full of the folk-lore and ideas derived from their ancestors.

County Clare has no seaport town or bay of sufficient depth and magnitude to afford protection to modern vessels. Excepting Ennis, with its 6000 inhabitants, there are no important towns or many large villages in Clare; it is covered with hamlets, in which small farmers and tradesmen reside being essentially an agricultural district.†

Regarding the race or stock from which the inhabitants of Clare were derived. There are certain anatomical peculiarities which characterise various pure races of men; among these is the shape of their skulls. In some ancient burying-places in Ireland we find, with human remains, rude earthen vessels, flint arrow-heads, bone pins and shells, but no bronze or iron instruments, and we therefore conclude that these

---

* "Proceedings of the Royal Irish Academy," p. 813, third series, vol. ii., No. 5, August 1893.

† Ireland, as is well known, consists of a large, almost flat, central plain, which seldom rises more than two or three hundred feet above the level of the sea. This central plain is surrounded by ranges of hills or mountains, and is crossed by a number of sluggish rivers; it contains no less than a million acres of bog, the greater part of which lies west of the river Shannon. The central plain is composed of carboniferous limestone, covered to a large extent with layers of gravel or of boulder clay, forming a soil well adapted for the growth of grass. In former ages the surface of Ireland must have been overspread with extensive coalfields; but, with her characteristic cussedness, Ireland insisted on keeping her land exposed above the surface of the ocean; and so, in the course of ages, under the influence of rain, ice, and atmosphere, her rich coal strata was washed away together with much of her mineral wealth. During these long past ages England was submerged, and so her coalfields were buried beneath deposits from the ocean; and when the time came for her to appear above the waters her mineral stores were well guarded against the assaults of storm and frost, and have since yielded enormous wealth to her people. There can be no question that the loss to Ireland of her coalfields has vastly influenced both the social and political development of her inhabitants, compelling them to become agriculturists rather than manufacturers, and so to remain poor in comparison with their richer neighbours, the English.

articles were used by people who lived and died before the present era, because it was not long before Christianity was introduced into Ireland that bronze and iron instruments were freely exported from the continent into that country, and would have been used and buried in the graves of the people above referred to had they lived some time after the commencement of the Christian era. Together with the flint arrow-heads and bone pins we find the crania of the individuals who used these primitive weapons, and these skulls are characteristic in shape, being, in relation to their breadth, much elongated from before backwards. Skulls of a precisely similar form, together with the same kind of bone and flint instruments, have been found in many parts of Europe, including Spain, especially in the Basque provinces, where at present the inhabitants have not only traits of character similar to those possessed, so far as we can judge, by the ancient inhabitants of Clare, but the conformation of their skulls and features are believed to be identical with those of the pre-historic people of Ireland.* In this way we are led to think that the Basques of Spain, a remnant of the old Iberian race of Europe, are derived from the same stock as that which overran Ireland in former times; the pre-Celtic people of Ireland having been to a large extent Iberians, who probably passed over from Spain into Ireland.† Professor Boyd Dawkins observes that Erin, Ireland, the land of Erna, Ivernian, Ibernian, is merely a variant of Iberia, and that the name of the great island of the Western Ocean, and the south-western peninsula of Europe, is due to their having been occupied by the same race, a race so clearly marked off from all others as to be known by the same name.‡ Tradition refers to this long-skulled race as having been rather under the average height, with brown or grey eyes and curly dark hair, a type to be found in considerable numbers among the people of Clare at the present day.§ The ancient inhabitants of Ireland

* "Crania Britannica," by J. B. Davis and J. Thurnam, vol. i. p. 3. "Human Origins," by S. Laing, pp. 330 and 336; also "Kelt and Gaul," by T. De Courcey Atkins.

† It is quite possible that Ireland was inhabited by a race of cannibals before it was overrun by the long, flat-skulled race to which reference is made above. It must also be clearly understood that as one wave of people followed another from east to west there was an overlapping of one race by that which followed it. This was unquestionably the case with the Iberians and Celts. Nevertheless, the two races have left their characteristic mark on their descendants, which has remained up to the present day.

‡ "Fortnightly Review," p. 520, 1892; see also "Lectures on Welsh Philology," by Professor T. Rhys, p. 2.

§ "A Short History of the Irish People," by Professor Richey, p. 26.

from the earliest times were recognised as Iberians,* and, as we learn from the life of St. Senan, were known in central Clare as the Bascain tribe.†

The Iberian race, or Firbolgs, as they are called in the ancient records and traditions of Ireland, have left us something more than their bones; they lived on until long after the invasion of Ireland by the Celts, and many of their massive stone forts still exist in Clare. Mr. T. J. Westropp, in the September number of the " Journal of the Royal Society of Antiquaries of Ireland," has described, and given us the ground plan of two of these forts. Some of the most perfect and remarkable work of these people is to be found on the isles of Arran, at the entrance of Galway Bay. As the Celts advanced from the east, the Iberian chiefs of Ireland were driven westward. One of these chiefs, Aengus by name, took up his abode on the isles of Arran; his brother, Adhar, fixed his home in the centre of Clare, on the lands subsequently occupied by our Sept; this chief died, and was buried within two miles of the site of Quin Abbey; and the mound over his remains still exists in a perfect state of preservation. It is known as Magh Adhar, and will be frequently referred to in the following pages as being the spot on which the chiefs of the Dalcasian tribe were inaugurated kings of Thomond.‡

Our knowledge of the Irish Iberians is very imperfect; when we first have cognisance of their existence in that country, they had passed from their primitive state and developed into a people under the leadership of chiefs. Their consanguinie, near and remote, were classified into categories, and in conversation they addressed one another by terms of relationship, and not by personal names.§ At the time of the Celtic invasion of Ireland these people made a vigorous effort to resist the foreigners, and appear to have been led on more than one occasion by female warriors. One of them is referred to in a Celtic poem as follows:

> The valley where the lovely Fais fell,
> From her, as ancient Irish records tell,
> Obtained the name of Glean-Fais,

by which name it is known at the present time. Scota, the widow of a

* " Fortnightly Review," p. 528, 1892; also Holinshed's " Chronicles," vol. vi. p. 2; " Sylvester Geraldus Cambrensis," p. 121.

† " The History of County Clare," by J. Frost, p. 197.

‡ T. J. Westropp: " The Journal of the Proceedings of the Royal Society of Antiquaries of Ireland," p. 463, of 1891; also " The History of Ireland," by Abbi MacGeoghegan (translated by P. O'Kelly), p. 528; and O'Curry's " Lectures," vol. ii. p. 122, also vol. iii. pp. 74 and 65.

§ L. H. Morgan: " On Ancient Society," p. 387.

chief of Munster, was also slain in an engagement with the Aryan invaders.* Towards the end of the first century of our era the Firbolgs rose against the Celts; they had still a chief in Connaught who was of sufficient importance to receive the Celtic king of Ireland, but having invited the king and his attendants into his fort, the Firbolg chief slew the whole of them and then seized the government of Ireland. Their reign, however, was of short duration, for the Celts soon recovered their power, and slaughtered or drove out of the country great numbers of the old race. It was at this period that Aengus sought refuge in the isles of Arran.† From this history we learn that the Iberian stock were still powerful and numerous in Ireland at the commencement of the Christian era; and we shall find that in the district now known as county Clare, these people were not conquered by the Celts until the end of the fourth or the beginning of the fifth century.

In the isles of Arran the descendants of the old Iberian stock have probably existed with less intermixations of race than in most other districts of Ireland, except perhaps in parts of Burren, and within the past few years Professors Haddon and C. R. Brown, of Dublin, have visited these islands and reported concerning the people.‡ They state that at present the inhabitants of the isles of Arran (Galway), are still largely a peculiar and exclusive race, although mixed with Irishmen who have come from the mainland. The men are short and slight, but athletic in build; their average height is 5 feet 4¾ inches, whereas Irishmen average 5 feet 8½ inches. Their hands are small, with short span, and their forearm is often unusually long. The head is well shaped, long and narrow (cephalic index 75.1), but, viewed from above, the sides are slightly bulging, not flat, the height above the ears is considerable, and the top well arched. The forehead is broad, upright, and rarely receding, though not high as a rule, and the superciliary ridges of the brow, that is to say the bone over the eyes, are not prominent; the face being remarkably long and oval, the chin long and narrow but not angular. The eyes are rather small, close together, and marked at the outer corners by transverse wrinkles. The irises are mostly blue, or blue-grey; the nose long, straight, and pointed. The lower lip is rather large and full. The ears are not large, but stand well out from the head. In many of the men the length of nose and chin appears

---

* We learn from Holinshed's "Chronicles" (vol. vi. p. 2) that it was from this Scota, or Scotach, that the early Irish were known as Scots, a name subsequently given by the Iberian and Celtic settlers in the north of Britain to Scotland, the lands of the Scota.   † Professor O'Curry's "Lectures," p. 230.

† "Proceedings of the Royal Irish Academy for 1893," pp. 759 and 768.

decidedly great. The complexion is clear and ruddy, but seldom freckled; the hair is brown, mostly light brown, and the beard often reddish. On the whole, they are decidedly good-looking.

Their sight and hearing is singularly acute. Dr. Kean states that on a clear day any of them could discern, with the naked eye, a small black sailing boat at Black Head, twenty miles distant, before he could see it with his binocular. Some of them live to a great age, and the births exceed the deaths, but the population is decreasing, owing to emigration ; a tombstone in Killeany records the death of one who lived 119 years. They are exceptionally honest, straightforward, and upright in their dealings, and illegitimacy is almost unknown. Mr. P. Lyster, a magistrate of these islands, states that "The Arran islanders are, as a body, extremely well-behaved and industrious people. If there are disputes among them it is in connection with lands. There are very few cases of drunkenness. I have known two months elapse without a single case being brought before me ; for four years I have not sent more than six or seven persons to gaol without the option of a fine. There is no gaol on the island ; theft is very rare ; I only remember one case of positive stealing sent for trial."* They are singularly unmusical, no piper, fiddler, or musician of any sort being on the islands. Irish is their language, but English can be understood and spoken with strangers. Most of the weddings occur just before Lent. There is no courtship, the young man going straight to the house of an eligible girl and asking her to marry him. If refused, he goes elsewhere, and a man has been known to ask three girls the same evening before he was accepted. Wakes are held even for those who die abroad. At one time a funeral procession would be stopped on the road, and the mourners would raise small piles of stones. A corpse is always let out through the back door, for the Arranites believe in fairies, banshees, and ghosts. If at a marriage any one repeats the benediction after the priest and ties a knot on a string at the mention of each of the sacred names, the marriage will be childless for fifteen years, unless the string is burned. Pin-wells and rag-bushes are still frequented, and on the night before emigrating people will sleep in the open beside one of the holy wells, in order to have good fortune where they go. The Evil Eye is believed in, and certain days are counted unlucky, so that even burials do not take place on them.

Mr. Webster lived for many years among the Basques, who are the descendants of the Iberian inhabitants of Spain. He states that as a pure race they are only to be found in the mountain ranges of the Spanish Pyrenees ; that their skulls are long from before backwards, and flat from

* "Proceedings of the Royal Irish Academy for 1893," p. 802.

side to side ; that their faces are long and oval, with a good angle.*
The Basques have blue or blue-grey eyes, brown hair and fair com-
plexions ; the large majority of the young men are good-looking
fellows.   They have a remarkably upright carriage, what the French
call " une taille elancié ; " the Basque is under the average height, but is
a strong wiry creature capable of undergoing any amount of hard work.
If we compare this description of the Basques with that of many of the
people inhabiting the isles of Arran and Burren, we shall find that from
an anthropological point of view they are almost identical ; and in the
isles of Arran the most extensive works of the pre-Celtic people of
Ireland exist.   Mr. Webster observes that the Basque language has great
powers of assimilation, and freely takes vocabularies of other languages.
Max Müller is of opinion that it is one of the best representatives of the
Turanian type of language.

Until the year 1833 the Basques of Spain were an absolutely free
people, governed by their own laws and chiefs, who, with their Alcledes,
were elected by the people as their leaders and judges.   Every man's
home was his sanctuary, into which neither the law nor any other power
might intrude ; nor could any action be initiated against a man until he
had stated his case before constituted authorities ; it was then either dismissed or sent on for adjudication.   They levied their own taxes, and of
their free will granted a contingent of soldiers and sailors for the service
of the Crown of Castille, upon the distinct understanding that their
national customs and laws were to remain inviolate ; in fact, they
transferred their allegiance from the King of Navarre to Castille in the
twelfth and thirteenth centuries, because the former Sovereign attempted
to tamper with their " furors " or ancient rights.   These much prized
furors have not, so far as we know, been compiled or carefully studied,
but they related chiefly to the tenure of land, the Basques being essentially an agricultural people, living in hamlets scattered over their valleys
and mountains, and abhorring the idea of an approach to town life or
mercantile pursuits ; those of them, however, who resided near the coast
are excellent and intrepid sailors.

The third Earl of Carnarvon, who was born in the year 1800, and grew
up to be fond of adventure and foreign travel, being an excellent linguist,
states that he resided for some time in the Basque provinces before the
year 1833, when they were still a free people, and living under their
own laws and institutions.†   He observes that every man had a right to

* Rev. W. Webster: " Journal of the Anthropological Institute," vol. ii. p. 150
(" The Origin and Relation of the Basque Race ").

† " Portugal and Gallicia," by the Earl of Carnarvon, vol. ii. p. 219, 2nd ed.

state his own case before constituted authorities when accused, or as defendant; and that this was a right far more precious than even the *habeas corpus* is with us, and was thoroughly appreciated by these people. Lord Carnarvon states that in 1833 the Basques rose to a man against Queen Isabella of Spain, in her attempt to destroy their "furors," and so, he observes, they "were pronounced rebels by Her Majesty's Ministers; and the ancient law of their country was to be swamped and superseded by the common law of Spain; and this measure was carried by an arbitrary edict of a government of yesterday."

It is well to quote Lord Carnarvon's opinion regarding the character of the Basque people, because it seems that we are justified in maintaining that the pre-Celtic inhabitants, at any rate of that part of Ireland with which we are now concerned, and the Basques were derived from the same Iberian stock. Of the character of these ancient people we can only now collect dim rays of light; but at the present time we have many of their descendants with us, a mixed race to some extent in the case of the inhabitants of the isles of Arran, but almost pure, and allowed to develop under their own laws and institutions in the Basque province up to the time that Lord Carnarvon lived among them. He writes that they inhabited a free land and were men deserving freedom; and continues "the erect, not haughty carriage, the buoyant step, and the whole bearing of the men, spoke of liberty long enjoyed, well understood, and therefore not abused. Such men were the Basques, trained to habits of self reliance by centuries of self-government, fine men in spirit, not in name alone, drinking in with their mother's milk a love of justice and a reverence for law; in thought sober, yet independent, and wholly without fear, except the honest fear of doing wrong; models of ancient manners, and not unfrequently of manly beauty, faithful friends, generous hosts; following with fervour, but without intolerance, their fathers' faith, they were the Tyrolese of Spain, and, I might add, the flower of Europe. Lambs in the hour of peace, yet heroes in the field. With them the household charities and patriotism went hand in hand; in them the honest yet the kindest spirit, the mildest yet the proudest virtues were combined. Never, perhaps, existed a more perfect union of the qualities which should adorn a people; the idolatry of freedom so distinctive of the Swiss, and the unconquerable affection of the Tyrolese to his Princes, were, by a happy and most unusual combination, united in the Basques." * Lord Carnarvon continues: "They adhere with tenacity to the soil of their birth; no prospect of advantage or promotion can induce him to abandon his home; he is ready to make any sacrifice

* Vol. ii. pp. 220 and 338.

or incur any danger in defence of his home. The ties of kindred are peculiarly strong, nevertheless, the mother of a cherished family has been known without a summons to replace her lost husband in the ranks of Don Carlos's army by one, two, and even her third and only remaining boy."

There is much in this passage which reminds us of the character of the Irish west of the Shannon; from their history we shall learn that they likewise fought and strove for centuries to preserve their "furors," their ancient laws, government, and lands. It is true the Iberians of Ireland were conquered by the Celts, but it is equally certain that they were far from having been exterminated: the Firbolgs not only lived on in the West of Ireland, but they intermarried with the Celts, and the mixed race must have influenced to a considerable extent the social and political life of the inhabitants of Connaught, including county Clare.

The Celts passed over from the continent of Europe into Ireland and conquered the Iberian inhabitants of that country. I have referred to the elongated form of skull of the Iberian race; the crania of the Celts, on the other hand, was broad in proportion to their length from before backwards, and in the burrows containing such skulls iron and bronze instruments are found, which take the place of the bone weapons of the earlier inhabitants of Ireland.* Colonel Wood-Martin believes that iron and Christianity were introduced into Ireland within an approximately short period of each other; for although iron may, in small quantities, have found its way into that country, through the ordinary channels of commerce then open, at or just before the commencement of the Christian era, yet iron ingots or iron articles so acquired would be comparatively few in number.† It may be well to state that the Irish Celts belonged principally to the old Aryan or Goidelic type; they were a fair-haired, grey or blue-eyed race, tall, well-developed, handsome fellows.‡ We have the authority of Professor Zeuss for asserting that their language, together with that of the Greeks, Teutons, and Sclavs, belonged to the Aryan race—or, rather, they spoke a pure Aryan language. Subsequent to the invasion of England by the Goidelic Celts, a later inroad (Brythonic) of this race occurred, but these latter Celts did not pass into Ireland; there the old and pure Aryan stock remained, speaking a

---

* "Crania Britannica," p. 18.

† "Pagan Ireland," by W. G. Wood-Martin, p. 588.

‡ "Where Three Empires Meet." Mr. Knight states that the Celtic Irish west of the Shannon resemble much in appearance the Mussulman population of Kashmir (p. 24).

language the vestiges of which exist in the Erse, Manx, and Gaelic tongue.*

We hear of the Celts at one time as being a powerful nation in Europe, who pressed hard upon the Greek and Roman Empires, but who almost suddenly disappeared from the family of western nations, crushed by the Romans under Cæsar, and the Germans, who invaded their territory from the east. In England the Celt was driven back into Wales and the Highlands of Scotland, where he has dwelt and continues to live and multiply up to the present day. The German historian Mommsen, in his " History of Rome," concerning the Celts of Europe, observes " that in the mighty vortex of the world's history, which invariably crushes all nations that are not as hard as steel, such a people could not permanently maintain themselves. With reason, the Celt of the Continent suffered the same fate at the hands of the Romans as their kinsmen in Ireland suffer down to our day at the hands of the Saxons, the fate of becoming merged as a leaven of future development in a politically superior nationality." Monsieur Thierry, the historian of the Gaulic Celts, from an historical point of view gained an intimate knowledge of these people, and I have placed his opinion side by side with those of Mommsen regarding the congenital character of the Celt.

MOMMSEN.	THIERRY.
1. " The whole ancient world presents no more genuine knight."	1. " Personal bravery unequalled among ancient nations."
2. " Incapacity to attain or even to tolerate any organisation, either military or political."	2. " Marked dislike to the idea of discipline and order."
3. " Laziness in culture of the fields."	3. " Want of perseverance."
4. " Love of ostentation."	4. " Extreme ostentation."
5. " Extravagant credulity."	5. " Open to all impressions."
6. " Inclination to rise in revolt under the first chance leader."	6. " Perpetual dissensions."
7. " Irresolute and fervid."	7. " Extreme susceptibility; impetuous, and excessively vain."
8. " Clever."	8. " Remarkably intelligent."
9. " A delight in singing and a talent for poetry and rhetoric."	9. " A free spirit."
10. " In a political point of view thoroughly useless as a nation."	10. " As a nation the personal sentiment, the idea of self, far too much developed."

Mommsen adds that the Celt was remarkable for " his childlike piety,

* W. Boyd Dawkins: " Fortnightly Review," 1892, p. 521 ; see also O'Curry's " Manners and Customs," vol. ii. p. 188, and vol. i. p. 30; also Keating's " History," p. 115.

unsurpassed fervour of national feeling, and the closeness with which those who are fellow-countrymen cling together, almost like one family, in opposition to a stranger." *

Dr. Richey, who was Professor of Feudal and English Law in the University of Dublin, and to whose admirable "History of the Irish People" we are so much indebted for our knowledge on this subject, states that, in his opinion, the admitted failure of the Celtic race is not so much attributable to the inferiority of their organisation, as to the fact of their possessing a highly organised and sensitive disposition.   They are therefore extremely susceptible of emotions and perceptions, and apt to arrive at rapid conclusions, which are not always lasting.   They shrink against the staying power of the German race, the Celt's ideas being too often matured, before the Saxon has mastered even the premises on which his opinions are founded.   The stolid, persevering, and fixed purpose of the Saxon has and must prevail over the light-hearted, sensitive, and comparatively indolent Celt.   Dr. Richey, like Mommsen, dilates on the remarkably tenacious feeling which the Celt has for his fellow-countrymen, his family, and, when they existed, for his chiefs ; and the Rev. Dr. Todd, in his "Life of St. Patrick," observes that the "key-note of Irish history is the spirit of clanship among Irishmen, together with adhesion to ancient traditions."   Robert Knox, of Edinburgh, in his work on the " Races of Men," states that the Celt was made for the "game of war," and that herein lies the strength of his physical and moral character.   In structure and weight he is inferior to the Saxon ; in muscular energy and rapidity of action he surpasses all other European races.   *Cæteris paribus*—that is, weight for weight, age for age, stature for stature, the Celts are the strongest of men.   Zealous in point of honour, admitting of no practical jokes, admirer of the fine arts, his taste is excellent and his ear good.   Full of deep sympathies, dreamers on the past, gallant and brave, they are not more courageous but more warlike than other races.

Before leaving this subject we may refer to the closing history of a typical Celtic chief, drawn by Mommsen, who was not likely to flatter the Celt.   He writes as follows : † Cæsar having invaded Gaul from the south, and the Germans from the east, the Celts of Gaul were almost completely subjugated.   In the year B.C. 53 there was little left to them beyond Britanny, and there, under the gallant leadership of one

* "A Short History of the Irish People," by A. G. Richey (edited by R. Romney Kane), pp. 30-32.

† Professor Mommsen's " History of Rome," vol. iv. p. 280 (translated by the Rev. W. P. Dickson).

of their chiefs, Acco, they for some time resisted the Romans. But at length their last stronghold, Veneti, fell ; Acco was taken prisoner and executed by the Romans. This act was sufficient to rouse the whole Celtic people to revolt, and they elected Vercingetoria as their chief. He, despairing of defeating the Romans in the open field, determined to mobilise a large force of cavalry, and by its means destroy the enemy's supply of food, and to cut off his means of communication with Italy. Vercingetoria abandoned all weak places of defence and concentrated his efforts on strengthening those points he believed he could hold with success. In this way he defended Bourges, inflicting terrible losses on the Romans. For some time Cæsar's position in Gaul was extremely precarious. He failed to capture Gergoria, although he was himself in command of the siege operations. This defeat, the first Cæsar in person had ever suffered, gave great encouragement to the Celts. On the other hand, the Romans became disheartened, and, at a Council of War, Cæsar was advised to retire into Italy. This he refused to do ; and, by a rapid concentration of his army and enormous personal exertions, he at length succeeded in shutting up Vercingetoria and a large portion of his army in the fortified town of Alesia. The Romans invested the place for ten miles and completely cut off the supplies of the 80,000 men within its walls. Vercingetoria dismissed his cavalry, and they managed to make their way through the Roman lines, and, although 250,000 Celts collected for the relief of Alesia, the Romans had in the meantime rendered their position impregnable. Alesia fell, and with it the Celtic nation. The defeated Celts were allowed to disperse because Vercingetoria refused to take flight, but decided in a Council of War, that, since he had not succeeded in breaking off the alien yoke, he was ready to give himself up as a victim, and to avert as far as possible the destruction of his people, by bringing it on his own head. This was done. The Celtic officers delivered their chief—the solemn choice of the whole nation—to the enemy of their country for such punishment as might be thought fit. Mounted on his steed, in full armour, the Chief appeared before the Roman proconsul and rode round his tribunal ; then he surrendered his horse and arms, and sat down in silence at Cæsar's feet. Five years afterwards he was led in triumph through the streets of Rome, and while his conqueror was offering solemn thanks to the gods on the summit of the capital ; Vercingetoria was beheaded at base of the hill. Mommsen adds, "as after a day of gloom the sun breaks through the clouds at its setting, so destiny bestows on nations in their decline a last great man. The whole ancient world presents no more genuine knight than Vercingetoria, the Celtic Chief."

From the evidence referred to, we may form a fairly accurate idea of the congenital character of the people from which our Sept was derived. No question, their chiefs were almost pure Celts, being adverse to mixed marriages; the Iberians, however, were a comely race, and the marriage tie, if it existed in early times, was a very elastic one among our ancestors in the West of Ireland. There can be no question as to the extensive intermarriage of the Iberians and their Celtic conquerors, for in their ancient burying places skulls are found indicating a mixed race, and the same Iberio-Celtic form of skull is characteristic of the great majority of the crania of the agricultural population of Clare at the present time Nor have these people any reason to be ashamed of their ancestors, as the preceding pages demonstrate. The two races from which they have sprung possessed many virtues, and, doubtless, had their failings. Their combined qualities afford us the material on which to base our ideas as to the character inherent in our ancestors, and their history may lead us to reflect as to the paramount importance which their congenital qualities had in shaping their course through many generations.

In the two succeeding chapters, we must refer as briefly as possible to somewhat technical details, concerning the social and political conditions under which our ancestors lived, from the earliest times until well into the sixteenth century. Knowledge of this kind, however, is necessary to enable us to comprehend the life and subsequent history of the inhabitants of county Clare, or, for that matter, of any part of the South or West of Ireland.

CHAPTER II

The Brehon Code—Pre-Christian—Derived from Aryan Sources—Brehons, their office—Law of distress—Fasting on plaintiff—Homicide punished by fine—Bee judgment—Tribe, sept and chief of ancient Irish—Election of the chief—Conjoint family—Division of land among its members—Repartition of land—Parents and children—Fosterage—Guilds—Dwellings—Furniture—Dress—Food.

THE *Brehon Code* regulated the various ranks of society among the early Irish from the king to the serf, and in this code of laws we find the rights and privileges of each grade of society; the management of property, size of the dwellings, and rules and regulations governing the relations of the individuals concerned in every step of life from the cradle to the grave. Much of this work was elaborated before the commencement of the Christian era; it was committed to memory and handed down from one generation of Brehons to another.* These laws were not enacted by a legislative body; they were, as stated in the earliest compilation we possess of the Brehon code, the concensus of opinion of the people as to what was right and what was wrong in the conduct of human affairs; they are said to "contain the judgments of true nature; that is, what men might know and should be obliged unto by the mere principle of reason imposed by consideration and experience."† These laws were doubtless modified as the wants of society developed;‡ and from the earliest times until the reign of James the First of England

---

* "The Kelt or Gael," by T. de C. Atkins, p. 86.

† "Primitive Culture," by E. B. Tylor, LL.D., vol. ii. p. 356.

‡ *The law of nature* "is that which is so exactly fitted to suit with the rational and social nature of man that human kings cannot maintain an honest and peaceful fellowship without it; or, in other words, that which carries in it a natural goodness, or a usefulness arising from its internal efficacy, towards man in general. Though there be, also, a further reason of this denomination, inasmuch as law may be found out and known by the ordinary sagacity of man and from the consideration of human nature in common.

"*Positive law* is that which doth not by any means flow from the general condition of human nature, but from the sole pleasure of the lawgiver, though these laws ought likewise to have their reason and their uses in reference to that particular society for which they are enacted."—"The Law of Nature and Nations," p. 73, by Basil Kennett (done into English by Mr. Carew), 5th ed.

the Brehon laws remained in full force in Clare and other parts of the West of Ireland, and necessarily exercised a great influence on the social and political life of the people. There is abundant evidence to demonstrate the fact that these Brehon laws, derived from, or rather the product of the people, were not only just but were effective in administering to the evils they were intended to control, in a society such as that which existed in Clare until the close of the sixteenth century.*

Soon after the introduction of Christianity into Ireland, A.D. 432, by St. Patrick, it was determined to commit the Brehon laws to writing, expunging from them what was contrary to the precepts contained in the New Testament; otherwise these laws were confirmed by the Brehons and by St. Patrick, "for the law of nature had been quite right, except the faith and its obligations, and the harmony of the Church and the people." This was the opinion of the nine persons appointed to draw up this important work, which has come down to us in the form not long since translated into English under the authority of Government.† Dr. Joyce is of the opinion that this Brehon code consists principally of the legal rules in force among the Aryan race before its people migrated westward : they were preserved in their primitive form in Ireland because that country was never absorbed into the Roman Empire, and so they were elaborated there in a manner not found elsewhere.‡

It is beyond the scope of this work to attempt to review the Brehon code; but it is necessary briefly to refer to some of the principles laid down in these laws, because they directly influenced the life of the early Irish.§ The Brehon laws were in the first instance administered by Druids, who were likewise the schoolmasters and genealogists of the Celtic inhabitants of Ireland; but as these laws grew more complicated

* "View of the State of Ireland," by Edmund Spenser (A.D. 1596), p. 23; also O'Curry's "Manners and Customs of the Ancient Irish," vol. ii. p. 25.

† Nine persons were appointed to arrange and revise the Brehon laws: Patrick and Benen and Cairnech (three bishops), Laighaire (monarch of Ireland), Corc (King of Munster) and Daire, Mac Trechein (an antiquarian and learned in the dialects), Fergus (a poet), and Dubthask (Brehon, and poet to the monarch of the country). With regard to these persons Laighaire was never more than a nominal Christian, and his son was a pronounced pagan, as was also Daire, King of Ulster, and Corc, King of Munster. Fergus did not even profess to be a Christian, so that the revisers of the Brehon laws cannot have been highly charged advocates of the new religion.

‡ "A Short History of the Irish People," by A. G. Richey, LL.D., p. 54.

§ Mr. Laurence Ginnell, in his work "The Brehon Laws; a Legal Handbook," has given a remarkably able and clear account of these laws.

a class of men sprung up who devoted their lives to the study of the law and were known as the Brehons.

The Brehons had to pass through a course of twelve years' training to enable them to enter the lowest ranks of the profession. They attempted to meet all possible varieties of cases by rules, leaving no discretion to the Brehon as to the amount of damages to be awarded,* for the award rested either on a decision given in an actual or in a hypothetical case as laid down in the Brehon code. There was no appeal from the decision of a Brehon of one rank to another of equal rank, but there might be an appeal on the grounds of "sudden judgment," from the decision of a Brehon to a court or council of superior Brehons, for these officers were of different rank. A chief Brehon resided with the king of each province.

The Law of Distress forms a large and important part of the Brehon code; it defines the various steps by which a man who has been injured, or had to recover a debt, could compel the debtor to consent to appear before a Brehon to determine the merits of the case and award damages. It must be borne in mind that the early Irish had no law courts or judges who were able to enforce the law. The process consisted in the necessity which existed in a primitive society for the intervention of some extraneous influence, to arbitrate between persons who were otherwise unable to settle their own differences. And further that such disputes were not simply personal matters, individuals might disagree, but their action often implicated directly all the members of their family and of the sept to which they belonged. Individuals, as a rule, had no means of their own wherewith to pay a fine; it was from the family stock alone that a payment of this description could be met.

If the offender refused to submit his case to the arbitration of a Brehon, or declined to meet the award given against him, the injured person proceeded under the law of distress to seize a certain number of cattle or other effects of the defendant, after having given due notice of the action he was about to take. If cattle were thus seized they were placed in a pound and properly cared for. The parties concerned in the action then appeared before a Brehon with witnesses and all that was necessary to prove the claim. The arbitrator having heard the case on both sides, gave judgment in accord with precedence laid down in the Brehon code. This judgment was final, and unless the person against whom it was given or his family conformed to the decision, he was excluded from the family and sept to which he belonged; if a man low in the social scale

---

* "The Ancient Laws of Ireland," vol. iv.; Introduction, vol. vii.

he might be handed over to the creditor as a slave for a specific term of years, or for life.*

If the plaintiff happened to be a poor man who had a claim against a powerful landowner, it was possible the latter might take no heed of the demand. In cases of this description, after notice had been served by the plaintiff, if the defendant gave no pledges for appeal to arbitration, the former proceeded to "fast upon his more powerful neighbour," that is, he seated himself at the door of the rich man's house, and remained there without food until he received satisfaction. The Brehon law states that "he who does not give pledges to a fasting person is an evader of all ; he who disregards all things shall not be paid by God or man." This system of fasting by a plaintiff at the door of the defendant is still practised throughout India as a means of bringing a man to a sense of justice.† But in spite of a safeguard of this kind, under the law of distress the rich man had an advantage over his poorer neighbour, because the scale of damages awarded by a Brehon took account of the social position of the defendant. Beyond this, as before explained, in most cases the penalty of a man's crime did not fall directly on himself but on his family.

Homicide.—Under the Brehon laws, if a man committed murder, his family had to pay a fine to the relatives of the murdered man. The amount of the fine was such as the Brehon judged was sufficient to compensate the family of the murdered man for the loss they had sustained, and thus to remove their desire for revenge on the murderer. Cases of homicide were divided into two classes : the one committed without malice or forethought, the other with malice and premeditation ; in the former the fine imposed was one-half less than in the latter. Heavy penalties were added if the murderer attempted to conceal the body of his victim.‡ St. Patrick, when revising the Brehon code, insisted on the principle of life for a life being introduced, in place of a fine to satisfy the revenge incited in the mind of the murdered man's family. The saint soon had an opportunity of putting his precepts in force ; for his own charioteer was slain, and St. Patrick demanded the death of the murderer. The case was referred to the chief Brehon of Ireland, who, it seems, had previously become a Christian, and he decreed that the "murderer should die, or, as the saint promised, should pass to a new life in heaven."§ In spite of this assurance, the

---

* "Senchus Mōr" (Brehon Code of Laws), vol. i. p. 107.
† Sir H. Maine: "The Early History of Institutions," p. 297.
‡ "Senchus Mōr," vol. iii. p. 81.
§ "Student's History of England," by S. R. Gardiner, p. 32.

Irish declined to follow St. Patrick in this matter; and so murder remained punishable by a fine, and was one of the most serious charges brought against the Brehon code by the English lawyers of Queen Elizabeth's time.

Bee Judgment.—It may seem strange that a large part of one of the volumes of the Brehon code should be occupied with this subject; but bees were important beings in former times, honey being used by our ancestors in place of sugar until well into the sixteenth century. Under these laws, an owner of bees was obliged every three years to distribute a portion of his honey to his neighbours, because his bees must have gathered some of the honey from off their lands. One of the chief difficulties that arose regarding bees was with respect to swarms which had wandered beyond the land of their owners. It was assumed that the bees, to a large extent, fed on the farms to which they belonged, and that consequently a swarm, if it passed from its own grounds to a neighbours, belonged by right to the latter; but cases of this kind were very complicated, and gave rise to all manner of hypothetical and actual judgments, which fill many pages of the Brehon law tracts.

Tribe, Sept, and Chief.—In the Brehon laws the word "*fine*" is used for the family as we understand the term—that is, for the children of a living parent and their descendants. By the term "sept" (which is the same as the conjoint family in India), is meant the combined descendants of an ancestor long since dead, and who had been one of the sons of the original chief or head of the tribe.* The tribe consisted of a group or aggregate of such septs. To each sept a specific portion of territory or tribal and common lands were assigned. The number of families and septs forming a tribe were assumed to have originally proceeded from a common ancestor, and this relationship was the chain which bound all the members of a tribe to one another; † for, having been derived from a common ancestor, often a man of commanding qualities, his descendants were, to a greater or less extent, bound together by congenital dispositions, and so by modes of thought and character.

At the head of every tribe was a chief (flaith), who was elected by all the free-men of his tribe to office. In like manner each sept had its chief, who was also chosen by the free-men of the sept to office. For

---

* For instance, about the year A.D. 420 a Celtic chief called **Cas** settled in Clare. He became head of a tribe, the Dal-Casians (or tribe or people of Cas). Cas had many sons, the eldest, called Bloid, who was the progenitor of the sept of O'Brians. Cas's second son was called Caisin, and he was the progenitor of the sept of Macnamaras, and so on with his other sons.

† Sir H. Maine on "Early Institutions," p. 231.

example, the Macnamaras were a sept of the Dalcasian tribe, and in the year A.D. 1000 Brian Boru was chief of the Dalcasians and also monarch of Ireland. At the same time a person of the name of Menma was chief of the sept known as Clancuilein, or the aggregate of the various families of Macnamaras then living in central Clare. The members of the ᵣribe and of its subdivision into septs and families, bound together by congenital qualities formed a complete society, social and political; the tribe was the proprietor of everything, including the land, within its own territory; individuals as such had no property; even kings and chiefs held the greater part of their lands by virtue of their office, and not as individuals.

The chief was the recognised leader of his tribe during the time of war. He made peace or war without reference to any other authority; he led his men in battle, and as this often meant great physical exertion —fighting for hours together with a heavy battle-axe, sword, or lance— so the chief had necessarily to be in a perpetual state of training, and a great part of his time was occupied in athletics, in hunting, and such-like manly exercises. In Clare much attention was given to horse-breeding, which engaged the chief's time. Matters connected with the collection of revenue, hospitality, and chess-playing filled up the life of an Irish chief. A chief was elected to office by the free-men of his tribe, or of his sept, as the case might be, and was selected "next in blood that was eldest and worthiest" to the deceased chief. This principle must be clearly comprehended to enable us rightly to understand the history of these people: the title to nobility or leadership depended on the character of the man; neither birth nor wealth could raise an individual to be leader of the tribe or sept, but his fitness only—that is, his character as appreciated by thos⸱ who knew him. But it is obvious that under such a system the tribe r the sept might have been left in the midst of a battle or other eι ᵣgency without a proper leader. To obviate this difficulty, when the ᴄhief was chosen they elected a substitute chief, or tanist, as he was cᴀlᴇd.

Tanist, the eldest son of the cᴏief, was often elected as tanist to his father; but "he must be the mᴏst capable member of the family," no other claim was allowed. The ceᵣemony of inaugurating a chief and his tanist to office was little more thaᴎ the public ratification by his tribesmen of their choice; for the individual elected had invariably by his preponderating influence and chaᵣacter been virtually recognised as leader of the sept or tribe long befoᵣe the day of inauguration. If there were competitors for the office of chief an appeal to arms was most frequently resorted to in order to setᴛle the dispute; we shall meet with a notable example of this in the history of the family whose fortunes we have to follow. The chief of the tribe and of a sept had in proportion to their social position a certain quantity of land allotted to them which they held by virtue of their office ; they received tribute and certain cesses from the free-men of the tribe and sept of which they were respectively heads. The chief of a tribe like the Dalcasian thus became in time owner of large flocks which he received as the executive officer of his district, these he paid in part as tribute to the king of the province. He was bound to hospitality, to provide the means of war to a large extent, to repair roads, and so on, and it was his duty to supply stock for those who required it so that they might in their turn be able to pay tribute.

The Conjoint Family or Sept consisted of the kinsmen of a known ancestor who combined for social purposes. The members of such a family shared their goods in common ; their home was the centre of the family life, and was governed under a system of unwritten laws by an elected head or ruler, who was not only answerable for the safe keeping of the stock but also for the good conduct of the members of his family As there was no executive authority to enforce order in an household the head of the family was supreme within its precincts, from which, in case of necessity, a refractory number might be expelled to become an outlaw, or in most cases a serf.

A man and his wife living under such conditions would, with their children and grandchildren, soon overstock the parental home; it there-fore became necessary to make provision for the rising generation ; at the same time it was impossible to expand the lands allotted to the family so that an indefinite number of the parental stock might live upon that which it could produce. Provision had to be made to meet this difficulty. In the case of the founder of a family, each of his four eldest sons left the parental household and settled on tribal lands, which were allotted in such quantity as to enable them to maintain themselves in a position in society equal to that of their father. If the father had more than four sons, one of them remained in the home and took charge of it after his father's death. If there were more than five sons the others had to become retainers of their brothers, or had to shift for themselves, so that the family continued to exist, but there was a direct incentive to keep it within moderate limits. A new head was substituted for the former one, and if this individual had brothers, or there were other members of the family who were not in possession of sufficient lands to maintain them in their former rank, the head of the family was capable of acting for such persons as a witness in court, to supply bail, and was able to take the place of their father in all legal and public matters.*

On the death of one of the sept the chief made a re-partition of the land belonging to the family, every one receiving his share *per stripes* and not *per capita*. By the redistribution of the land, and by its allotment under the system of gavelkind, the descendants of the original head of a family claiming land were kept within due limits. This system was practically the same as that of the Hindoo joint family of the present time; in such a family all the property is held in common, and brought into a common purse; on the death of any one of the members of the family the deceased's share is divided among his kindred included in the family group.†

Parents and Children.—According to the Brehon laws a father was obliged to provide for his daughters either in their own home, or more commonly in the home of foster-parents, until the girls were of marriageable age, that is sixteen or seventeen years old. A father was bound to marry his daughters to men of equal rank to his own, and the son who succeeded his father as head of the house incurred similar responsibilities as regards his unmarried sisters. He was also compelled to support them, if necessary, in old age, sickness, or trouble. A mother in like manner had to provide for her sons; and they had reciprocal obligations.

The laws relating to marriage portions prove that under the Brehon laws the rights of women were carefully protected. Unlike the Roman law the Brehon code demanded for the mother of a family a position equal to that of the father, and when they possessed equal property the one could not enter into any contract concerning it without the consent of the other. We know little regarding the ceremony of marriage, if any, as practised by the early Irish; a divorce seems to have been a matter of mutual understanding even as late as the eleventh and twelfth

* "A Short History of the Irish People," by Professor Richey, p. 39; also O'Curry's "Manners and Customs," vol. i. p. clxxxiv.

† Sir H. Maine: "Early Institutions," p. 186. The practice of re-partition of the land in Ireland as in India was a re-partition according to existing shares, with a view of correcting the inequalities which might have crept in, and converting scattered holdings into more compact farms. The system of inheritance by gavelkind, or division among the sons, is uninterrupted. Every man has his fractional share as it has come by ancestral descent, and that share is represented by the land which is partitioned off to him. In the West of Ireland the system of redivision of the land has still its counterpart in the practice of "stripping the land," as it is called, carried on by landlords of the present day (Sir G. Campbell: "The Irish Land Question," p. 27).

centuries; for instance, Brian Boru took to himself a wife who had two other husbands, and when he found her too hot-tempered to be agreeable, he parted from her without ceremony.

Fosterage.—Our ancestors came to the conclusion that discipline, obedience to superiors, and the work which a boy or girl would have to follow in their future career, was best learnt away from home; they consequently sent their children, when about seven years of age, to a relative, or some one belonging to their own grade of society, to be nurtured and instructed for their calling in life. The person to whom a child was thus entrusted was called his foster-father, but he really stood in the same relation to the lad made over to him as an apprentice in after years did to his master. As the life of an Irish Celt was bound up in the soil and that which grew and fed upon it, so the cultivation of the land in its various branches was the chief thing a young Irishman had to learn, and, in addition, the use of arms whereby to preserve his home from enemies, human and otherwise. To enable the foster-father to fulfil his engagement, he was allowed, under the Brehon laws, when necessary, to chastise his foster-son, but it is strictly directed that in inflicting corporal punishment it was never to be carried to the extent of drawing blood or leaving a mark on a lad; heavy penalties were imposed on a breach of this law. In case of illness, inability to learn, or for gross misconduct, the foster-father was allowed to send the lad committed to his charge back to his parents. On the other hand, if a foster-father kept a lad until he was seventeen years of age, when he was always compelled to return home, and if it was then found that the lad had not become efficient in his calling, obedient and otherwise properly instructed, the foster-father was heavily fined, and the amount of the fine was made over to the lad, because, as the Brehon law states, it was "upon him the injury of the want of learning had been inflicted." * The fine to be charged in such cases was fixed by arbitrators appointed on both sides.

It is evident from the chapter on Fosterage which is contained in the ancient laws of Ireland, that the subjects which a foster-son had to acquire were immediately concerned with his material prosperity or calling, anything beyond this was learnt in schools to which the foster-father sent his charge. In these schools, before the ninth century, we have abundant evidence to show that the upper classes of Irish were taught Latin, history, and in some instances the Greek language.

According to the Brehon laws there were two kinds of fosterage, one

* "The Ancient Laws of Ireland," vol. ii. p. 155.

for payment, the other of " affection." If for payment, the foster-father received from three to sixteen cows as a fee for training a child; the number of cows depended on the grade of society to which the parent of the child belonged. The relations between a foster-child and the family of the person to whom he was entrusted were of the most intimate and enduring character. For instance, a foster-father was made responsible not only for the proper education but for any wrong done by a lad under his care. On the other hand, a foster-child was bound to aid and to support his foster-parents throughout life if necessary. Boys in the humbler classes of life were taught first discipline, and then how to perform the various duties of life they would subsequently have to undertake, such as herding cattle, the management of a kiln, dying and dressing wool, and forestry. The girls were instructed also in discipline, the use of the quern, kneading, and various other kinds of domestic work. The food of both boys and girls is prescribed by law, and consisted of stirabout (porridge) flavoured with salt butter or milk. Among the better classes honey was added. There was abundance of fish and meat to be had, but these articles are not included in the diet roll of young people in the days of old. The sons of the higher classes were taught horsemanship, chess playing, swimming, the use of arms, and other manly exercises ; they were "allowed a horse to ride in the time of races." * It seems that they rode their steeds bare-backed and with only a piece of rope in the animal's mouth to guide him ; girls were instructed in sewing, cutting-out, and in embroidery, as well as in all matters pertaining to the domestic arrangements of the household. It is certain that this system of fosterage did not weaken the tie between children and their homes and parents ; on the contrary, it seems to have developed an abiding love for the parental household and its surroundings. Beyond this, fosterage engendered an intense feeling of sympathy between various classes in Ireland, knitting high and low together by sentiments often stronger than those common to blood relationship, and so having a decided effect on the social and political life of the people.

Guilds.—There was evidently a tendency among the early Celts of Ireland to combine for mutual protection, and by co-operation to work the land for the advantage of the families who occupied it. The word " gial," or pledge, is of Celtic etymology, and from it is derived our word Guild.† The co-partnership was formed for working the lands held by several families ; in this way a large area of grazing land could

---

* " Senchus Mōr," vol. ii. p. xliv.

† O'Curry: " Manners and Customs," vol. i. p. ccxvi.

often be obtained which was easily accessible to the cattle of several homesteads. These guilds were established, under provisions laid down in the Brehon code, for "the mutual benefit and assurance between the co-partners." On entering a guild "each of the members turned to the others and pledged himself that the responsibilities of the united body should be the responsibility of each person."* The great advantage derivable from this institution of guilds was, that by combination or co-operation, persons of an inferior grade in society, and not therefore possessing land sufficient to qualify as witnesses, sureties, or to sue before the Brehons, could by joint action qualify one of the guild to act for them, and so obtain the full rights of citizenship. Artisans, and, in fact, all who lived by handicraft, could in like manner choose a member of their guild to act for them individually; so that practically no free-man was, under this ancient system, barred from the privileges of those classes of society which were above him in the social scale. It was through the guilds that villages first became established in Ireland, and subsequently developed into burghs. Of towns the Celtic Irish knew but little. They collected in places like Limerick and Galway ; but the trading community of such towns were largely constituted of foreigners, who carried on business with the agricultural population of the interior, exchanging hides and cattle, for wine, silk, brocades, and various other commodities. As early as the sixth century we hear of Gaulish merchants at Clonmacnois on the Shannon, and in the very heart of Ireland, selling wine to Saint Kiaran, who was at the time head of that flourishing establishment.† These early Irish, however, were excellent sailors, and enjoyed the perils of the deep, and still more the excitement and profit which frequently attended their maurauding expeditions on the coast of England, France, and Spain.

Dwellings.—These were for the most part circular in form, and constructed of wickerwork covered with clay or earth, over which hides dyed of various colours were frequently stretched. The roof was made of dried rushes, and sloped from the centre outwards. We have a curious reference made to a house of this description in a poem written about A.D. 570, and attributed to St. Baoithin. The saint, when a youth, was one day caught in a heavy shower of rain ; he took refuge under an oak tree, and seeing the drops falling from the leaves, amused himself by driving his heel into the damp soil, and thus making a small hollow, which was soon filled by the drops of rain from the tree. Baothin then said :

* Crith Gablash (" Senchus Mōr ").
† D. Hyde, LL.D.: " The Story of Early Gaelic Literature," p. 14.

Of drops a pond is filled ;
   Of rods a round-house is built ;
   The house which is favoured of God,
   More and more numerous will be its family.
Had I attended to my own lessons
   At all times and in all places,
   Tho' small my progress at a time,
   Still I would acquire sufficient learning.
It is a single rod which the man cuts,
   And which he weaves upon his house ;
   The house rises pleasantly,
   Tho' singly he sets the rod.
The hollow which my heel hath made,
   Be thanks to God and Saint Colman,
   Is filled in any shower by the single drop ;
   The single drop becomes a pool.
I make a vow that while I live,
   I will not henceforth my lessons abandon ;
   Whatever the difficulty may be to me,
   It is in cultivating learning I shall always be.*

Amongst the higher classes it was by no means uncommon to find several houses of this description enclosed within a fence, and occupied by various members of the same family. In such houses the hut inhabited by the females of the family was generally separated by a fence from that of the males. The smaller houses had no opening except the door ; the smoke from the fire, which was placed near the centre of the cabin, escaped as best it could through the roof. The head of the family, with his children and the retainers, all slept on the sand floor upon a bed of dried rushes.

Among the better classes beds were used and proper covering ; these were as a rule placed round the walls of the common room, in the centre of which was a dining-table surrounded with benches. The weapons and the leather or wooden jugs and platters belonging to the family were arranged on shelves or hung against the walls of the house. The distaff and spinning-wheel, and in many cases the loom, formed part of the household furniture. In the kitchen, which among the better classes was a separate hut, was to be found a kneading-trough, griddles, tubs, and other necessary wooden vessels, together with a cooking pot varying in size with the rank and requirements of the household.

A single house, or a nest of houses, as the case might be, was invariably surrounded by a well-made blackthorn hedge, and as a rule in addition, by a ditch and mud wall. This ring fence was directed by law

* " On the Manners and Customs of the Ancient Irish," by E. O'Curry, vol. iii. p. 33.

to be carefully constructed, for within the enclosure was the home of the family, and no stranger might enter it without the permission of its headman. In cases of crime the hand of the avenger was stayed at the gate of the fence surrounding the home, however poor the family might be to which it belonged; but the owner of the house was bound not to let a fugitive escape, for the law states that "he who lets a criminal escape is himself a culprit." Professor Sullivan is of opinion that the feeling thus engendered regarding the sanctity of the family home among the Irish was so strong, and existed for so many generations, that it has become a part of their nature, and accounts for the practice still prevalent amongst them of harbouring criminals who have thrown themselves on the protection of their relations.*

The law of trespass was remarkable as regards the household, and extended to the lower animals; for instance, the Brehon laws directs that on "the young pig that first goes through the fence, and shows the way to the herd, a fine is imposed on the owner equal to that of one animal. If a pig trespass a second or a third time the fine was increased to the sum of seven animals." † And so with dogs and other creatures. Precisely similar customs were established under the laws of Manu; in this code we find instructions given for the family to enclose its homestead "with a hedge of thorney plants, and to stop every gap through which a dog or boar could thrust its head." There is a curious reference in the Celtic Law Tracts regarding the construction of the fence; it was to be the work of the conjoint family, and to ensure the attendance of its members in the construction of the fence, it was enacted that "each of them shall give his victuals into the hands of others at night, so that he may remember to come in the morning to his share of the cotenancy work, and the victuals of the person that will not come may be safely consumed." ‡

The size of the precincts surrounding the house of a family was determined as follows. The owner of the premises stood at the door of his dwelling, and took a spear of a certain length, and so far as he could cast it did the precincts extend. This distance was doubled for each grade as it rose in the social scale. This practice again was similar to that enjoined in the laws of Manu, the distance there denoted for the precincts is according to the length which the owner could hurl a lance.

Dress and Ornaments of the Early Irish.—In a poem of the early part

---

* Introduction to O'Curry's "Manners and Customs of the Early Irish," p. clvii.

† "Brehon Law Tracts," vol. iv. p. 123. ‡ "Senchus Mōr," vol. iv. p. 123.

of the eighth century we have a description of the dress worn by a
retainer and also that of the poet attached to a large landowner; the
former wore a cape provided with a hood, and beneath this a woollen
tunic reaching from the throat below the knees, and confined round the
waist by several folds of a scarf.   This individual also wore tight-fitting
pantaloons reaching from the hips to his ankles; his feet were bare.
The poet had shoes made by himself "from brown leather of seven
doubles";* also a petticoat, or kilt, which descended to his knees; a
tunic such as that above referred to, fastened by an iron pin at the
throat; under the tunic he had a linen shirt.

Among the higher classes clothes such as those above described
were replaced by richer materials, such as silk, but in other respects were
of the same pattern, the brooch which confined the tunic being made of
gold or silver, and frequently the workmanship displayed in these
ornaments was of a high character; many of them have been preserved
until the present day as evidence of the skill and taste displayed by the
early Irish in metal work of this kind.   The apparel of the women
differed but little from that of the men, except that the kilt was longer,
their heads were sometimes covered with a veil, at others, with a hood.
Spenser states that after cutting their hair they wore "a great linnen roll
to keep their heads warme."   As a rule, in both sexes the hair of the
head was allowed to grow to its natural length.   This style of dress
seems to have continued in use among the people of Clare as late as
the end of the sixteenth century, for the poet Edmund Spenser, who
spent some time in Ireland as secretary to the Lord Deputy, writing in
A.D. 1596 in reference to the tunic above referred to, remarks that the
Irish, "when wandering in waste places far from danger of law, maketh
his mantle his home, and under it covereth himself from the wrath of
heaven, from the offence of the earth (for it is his bed), and sight of
men.   When it raineth, it is his pent home; when it bloweth, it is his
tent; when it freezeth, it is his tabernacle.   In summer he can wear it
loose, in winter he can wrap it close; at all times he can use it; never
heavy, never cumbersome; therein he wrappeth himself round, and
coucheth himself strongly against the gnats, which in that country doe
more to annoy the naked rebels, while they keep the woods, than all
their enemies' swords, or spears, which can seldom come nigh them.
Oftentimes their mantle serveth them, being wrapped about the left arm,
instead of a target, for it is hard to cut through with a sword; besides, it
is light to bear, light to throw away, and being naked, it is to them all
in all."   Spenser mentions other advantages of the mantle which we

* "Manners and Customs of the Early Irish," vol. iii. p. 105.

need not repeat, especially to the uses which he says the women were in the habit of employing this tunic; and so he states that the Government of Ireland came to the conclusion that the Irish mantle should be forbidden as an article of dress among the natives of that country.*

The Food and Drink of the Early Irish.—Among the poorer classes, oatmeal porridge formed the principal article of food, and when boiled in soup and properly seasoned, was thought to be excellent food. With this they eat flat cakes, baked on a heated iron and made of ground filberts, acorns, and barley-meal. But flesh and milk was largely eaten by all classes, for there was an abundance of cattle in the land. The extensive forests were full of wild pig, deer, and other game, and the rivers and sea contained an abundance of fish, and these were open to all. Watercresses were eaten as vegetables, and various kinds of seaweed. Beer was a favourite beverage, and mead made by dissolving fermented honey in water flavoured with aromatic herbs.

* " View of the State of Ireland," by Edmund Spenser, p. 88 (edition 1809).

CHAPTER III

Bards and poets of ancient Ireland—Their office—Schools conducted by—Fags in schools—Military system—The Fenia—Examination for admission into—Provision for poor and sick—The physicians and laws relating to—Land tenure—Possession of land all important—Constituted a freeman—The serf—Tribal lands—Private estates—Military retainers—System differed from feudalism—Social rank depended on amount of land a family possessed.

THE *Bards or Poets* played an important part in the early history of Ireland; from the monarch downwards all families of importance had a bard attached to them, and this individual filled the office of historian and genealogist; he also took a leading part in all matters connected with the social and political relations of his chief's household. Bards accompanied an army into the field of battle to watch and record the deeds performed by the members of the sept to which he belonged. This record, we are informed, was "made without partiality or affection, and with regard to nothing but merit." These records were compiled and revised once every three years by a council appointed for the purpose by the king of the province to which the bard belonged; not only were the deeds of valour performed by the Celtic chiefs preserved in this way, but the pedigrees of the families to which they belonged, so that, as Sir J. Mackintosh observes, "these records written in the Irish language date from the second century to the time of Henry Plantagenet, and are the most ancient European history in existence."* The accuracy of such of these records as have come down to us are confirmed by the researches of archæologists and of historians of the present day, and, beyond this, in these old annals reference is made under certain dates to eclipses of the sun and moon, the appearance of comets, hour of the rising of the sun, and so on, which astronomers assert must have occurred on precisely the days and hours referred to in the ancient annals of Ireland.†

We must bear in mind that, amongst the early Irish, soldiers received no titles or rewards from the State or from their chiefs for service

* "Sir J. Mackintosh: "History of England," vol. i. chap. ii.
† "A Short History of Ireland," by Dr. P. W. Joyce, pp. 26 and 32.

rendered in the field; their reward consisted in having their names honourably mentioned in the annals of their country. Their deeds were sung by their bards, and afforded a never-ending source of delight to the families and retainers of the chief to whom the bard belonged. The chiefs, it is true, were "assigned by the bards a distinguishing coat-of-arms, not as a mark of honour, but whereby they might be known from other chiefs, and recognised in the field of battle or at their place of residence."* The language of the bards, when translated into English, is often of an inflated, absurd style, but it was language appreciated at the times it was composed.

Education.—Irish bards, like the Hindu Gurus, had to study for a period of twelve years before being admitted into the lowest order of their profession. They were largely employed in the work of educating their countrymen; they taught their pupils by making them learn and recite a certain number of lines every day. Training of this kind not only developed the faculty of memory, but also of language, a power which would seem to have clung to not a few of their descendants. Schools conducted by bards and Brehons continued to flourish long after the introduction of Christianity into Ireland, and in many such schools Druids were also engaged as teachers.† These places of education, which in the West of Ireland were numerous, might be called secular schools, to distinguish them from those subsequently established by and immediately under the supervision of ecclesiastics, in which the Christian religion was taught in addition to the subjects common to both sets of schools. These subjects were history (especially that of Ireland), poetry, music, law, and military exercises. The secular schools were under the control of the supreme or of provincial councils. For instance, Professor O'Curry gives us the particulars of a council presided over by the ruler of Ireland in the year A.D. 574, which assembled to regulate the course of study and discipline to which students were to be subjected. Many of these Irish schools became so famous that students flocked to them from all parts of Europe. Keating states that he had examined the roll of Clonard, and found it had at one time no less than three thousand students. Dagobert II., King of France, was sent to Ireland to be educated; St. Senan, a native of Clare, states that in his time, fifty monks had travelled from Rome to study the Scriptures in Ireland.‡ The labour and exquisite taste shown by the Irish monks

* Keating's "History" (O'Connor), p. 143.
† Professor O'Curry : "Manners and Customs," vol. ii. p. 202.
‡ "Ireland and the Celtic Church," by G. T. Stokes, D.D. (third edition), p. 249; refer also to Dr. Ritches' "Short History of Ireland," p. 83.

of old in their copies of the Scriptures testify to the zeal and value which they set on work of this kind. Professor Westwood, of Oxford, writing on the penmanship of the Irish, remarks of the Book of Kells, that " it is the most astonishing book of the Four Gospels which exists in the world ; how men could have got tools to work out the designs I cannot conceive." He adds "I know almost all the libraries in Europe, but there is no such book in any of them."

In the larger schools, the students lived in small round cells, laid out in regular order, and according to the tribes to which they belonged. The authorities by no means neglected the care of their students' bodies. Physical training formed a part of their system of education ; beyond this, they encouraged horse-racing, honours were awarded for running, jumping, swimming, and other manly exercises. From the interest which not a few famous Celtic Irishmen took in after-life in their schools, it is certain that, on the whole, a student's career was far from an unhappy one in those early times.

In the life of St. Adamnan we meet with a curious story illustrating the fact that in his day fags existed in Irish schools. It seems that Adamnan, when a student, had been out early one morning to obtain supplies for those "noble students" upon whose good cheer it was his turn to administer. He was hurrying along the road with a vessel full of milk on his back, when a cavalcade overtook him, among whom was the King of Ireland returning at this early hour of the morning from hunting. Adamnan, in attempting to move out of the way of the king and his friends, fell over a bank and spilt his milk. The king, seeing the scholar's distress, said to him : " We will make thee happy again, thou shalt receive satisfaction from me for thy loss." Adamnan, not knowing the king, replied : " I have come to grief, for there are three noble students in our house, and there are three scholars of us wait upon them, and what we do is, one of us go round the neighbourhood to collect supplies for the other five, and it was my turn to do so to-day ; but what I have obtained for them has been lost, and what is more unfortunate, the borrowed vessel in which the milk was contained is broken, which I have no means to replace." *   This accident must have occurred about the year A.D. 660.

The Military System and Education among the Early Irish.—There are no accounts of military schools in Ireland ; it would seem that the sons of chiefs and landowners, as a rule, were placed as foster children at the age of seven years with some renowned soldier ; but so far as we know military training was only a part of a youth's education, he had

* Professor O'Curry : " Manners and Customs of the Ancient Irish," vol. ii. p. 77

also to devote a certain portion of time to study the history of his country, to poetry and music.

Although the famous Irish Militia, or Fenia, disappeared in the third century, we still have the standard of examination which a youth had to pass before he was admitted into that corps. A candidate, before he could gain admission into the Fenia, had to defend himself with a shield and hazel stick from javelins thrown at him from a distance of twenty yards. It was necessary for him to be a good runner, to leap over a bar up to his chin, and stoop under one as low as his knees. He had to be strong of arm as tested by the use of the sword, battle-axe, and mace. Having qualified in these subjects he had to give security that if he were killed none of his own family should attempt to avenge his death, "the affair of his death must be left wholly in the hands of his comrades, who would take care to do him justice."* Keating states that there were "four sacred injunctions binding the Fenia : the first was, never to receive a portion with a wife, but to choose her for good manners and virtue; second, never to offer violence to any woman; third, never to give a refusal to any mortal for anything of which one was possessed; fourth, that no single warrior of them should ever flee before nine champions."

The Fenia, like most of the Irish, were keen sportsmen, and after a successful morning's hunting, they sent the game to a convenient spot and roasted part of the venison on spits, the remainder they baked, after having bound it round with ropes of grass. The baking process was carried on in pits into which were first thrown stones previously heated in a fire. They ate but one meal a day; before feeding they stripped, bathed, and dressed their hair. "They then began to supple their thews and muscles by gentle exercise, loosening them by friction, until they relieved themselves from all stiffness and fatigue,† after which they took their meal, and then constructed booths and prepared their beds of brushwood placed on the ground, and over that moss and fresh rushes."

Provision for the Poor and Sick.—From the Brehon laws we learn that an officer was appointed to preside over the care of the poor and needy in the various districts of Western Ireland. Doubtless in after times, when ecclesiastical establishments had been planted over the length and breadth of the country, monks and friars were the chief

* Keating's "History of Ireland" (O'Connor's edition), p. 271; O'Mahony's edition of Keating, p. 349.

† In this description one recognises customs which at the present time are practised by the native sportsmen all over India.

C

agents in the distribution of charity. But in Clare such establishments were hardly operative until the fifteenth century. The Celtic relieving officer had large powers, for he was entitled to levy a rate in kind on the landowners of the district in which he resided for the maintenance of the "wretched and wandering poor." This officer is described as a "pillar of endurance," a truly Celtic idea of a relieving officer; he was further to suffer " the reddening of his face without insult to his tribe ;" in other words, he was not to consider himself disgraced because he was abused by beggars. Each tribe was chargeable for the maintenance of its own "sick men and women, and for the keep of those who were incurable." We also learn with "respect to sick maintenance " that it included the attendance of "a physician, and for providing food, bedding, and lodging, and in guarding the sick from things prohibited by the physician."* Amongst the things thus prohibited by law were "that the sick man be not injured by women, or by dogs (that is), fools and female scolds were not to be allowed to approach the sick person, or to offer him forbidden food."† Careful provision was also made for the children of lepers, or of those who were of unsound mind, of blind people and of orphans.

The Public Hospitaller was a recognised officer in Clare from the earliest times until the sixteenth century. The function of this individual was to keep open house on the part of his sept, and to receive distinguished strangers or officials passing through his district when the chief from any cause was prevented doing so. To enable the hospitaller to perform these functions he was allowed five hundred acres of free land, besides personal privileges. The hospitaller's house was in truth a kind of public hall, and in it assemblies were held in which various public functions were carried on, such, for instance, as the meeting of the heads of septs and the chief landowners to consult as to legislative or administrative matters concerning the interests of the sept—a form of County Council. The dwelling occupied by this official was built at the meeting place of cross-roads, and he was bound to keep a light burning over his residence throughout the night, so as to direct wayfarers to the house. The hospitaller was precluded from taking presents from persons who sought his hospitality, for he was supplied with stock for the purpose by the surrounding landowners. This official possessed magisterial powers over those who abode under his roof, so as to prevent them from damaging the place or its furniture, which was public property.‡

Physicians.—In the Brehon law tracts we meet with many curious

---

* " Senchus Mōr," vol. i. p. 134.   † *Ibid.*, p. 131.
‡ " Brehon Laws "(" Senchus Mōr "), vol. i. p. 47, and vol. iv. pp. 311, 313, 315.

regulations bearing on the position of medical practitioners among the early Irish. The services of the doctor were in those times so much appreciated by the Celts that it was by no means uncommon for the tribe to make a grant of land to a physician, so that in the words of the Brehon code, he might be preserved from " being disturbed by the cares and anxieties of life, and enabled to devote himself to the study and work of his profession."* A distinction is drawn in the Brehon code between the " lawful " and the " unlawful " physician; for instance, it is stated " if an unlawful physician remove a joint or sinew without obtaining an indemnity against liability to damages,† and with notice that he was not a regular physician, he is subject to a penalty with compensation to the patient."‡

If a man was maliciously or accidentally wounded he was removed to the house of a physician, who examined his wounds, and gave certificates as to their character, upon which depended the legal liabilities of the person who had inflicted the wounds. If the doctor thought he could cure the wounded man he gave security for his proper treatment, and in return received security for his fees ; these varied with the rank of the patient. If a bishop the doctor was entitled to forty-two cows, and so downwards through various grades ; for the " houseless, homeless man, a horse-boy, or a slave," the doctor's fee was two cows.

The Celtic physicians appreciated the value of cleanliness, pure water, and free ventilation in the treatment of the sick and wounded. The doctor's house, under the provisions of the Brehon laws, was the appointed place where the sick were to be treated, and as a matter of fact, until the fifteenth century, wounded men, including the chiefs of septs and tribes, were frequently taken to be healed of their wounds in the house of a physician. These houses were ordered to be built either on the bank of a running stream, or with such a stream passing through the precincts of the house. The building was to be provided with four doors, with the object " of allowing all that took place within it to be open to inspection,

---

* Keating's " History " (O'Connor), pp. 131, 138, 143 ; " Annals of Four Masters," A.M. 3922.

† " The lawful physician is exempt for blood-letting without taking guarantee, or giving warning of bad curing. The unlawful physician is bound to take guarantee only. This is the case when there was no wound upon the body before him (or when though there was, he increased the wound too much), if an impartial physician declares that it could have been cured lawfully. If there were wounds on the body before him, and if he did not increase them, and an impartial physician declares they could not have been cured more lawfully, he is exempt as regards them " (" Senchus Mōr ").

‡ " Senchus Mōr," vol. iii. p. 323.

and further to permit one door being left open which ever way the wind blew." The hot air bath was employed for the cure of rheumatism, and shampooing was highly extolled. There is much in the system of medicine as practised by the early Celts of Ireland which connects their ideas and practice with that contained in Sanskrit works on the healing art, and there can be little doubt that the Celts carried with them from their Aryan homes those notions of the practice of medicine and surgery which crop up in so curious a way in the Brehon law tracts.

In Keating's " History of Ireland " we have a reference to the resources of an Irish surgeon about the year A.D. 213, for the cure of his patient, who had been wounded by a spear in the thigh. The surgeon found on probing the wound that the rusty point of a spear head had broken off and remained deep in the flesh. He directed that a ploughshare should be made red hot in the fire ; this having been done, the doctor seized the heated iron, and with a " cruel countenance " brought it near the patient, at the same time ordering him to expose the wound. The patient, however, was so alarmed at these proceedings that he made a desperate leap off his couch and rushed across the room. This effort had the desired effect, for the piece of iron was forced by the contraction of the muscles towards the surface of the wound, and was then removed with ease by the surgeon. The individual treated in this way was a certain " Thady," a grandson of the progenitor of the Macnamara's, and ancestor of the O'Carrolls of Ely.*

Land Tenure.—The land question as regards Ireland is one which no one can approach with a light heart, nor is it my intention to do more than refer to the subject in a most superficial manner ; but the ownership of land among the early Irish was the centre around which their whole social and political life revolved. It was the possession of land and the means of cultivating it that constituted a freeman, in contradistinction to the landless person, who was a bondsman or serf, and possessed no social privileges or rights whatever beyond those conferred upon him as an appendage to his lord.

A certain tribe of Celts from South Munster early in the fourth century invaded that part of Ireland we now call county Clare ; after subduing the inhabitants of this territory, the Celtic chief who was in command of the invading force proceeded to divide the land, first, amongst his four eldest sons, and then to his other children and near relations. Lands apportioned in this way became what are known as " tribal lands," a tribute being charged on these lands by the chief of the tribe, who, as a matter of fact, had by conquest become possessed of

* Keating's " History of Ireland," p. 246.

them, and made them over to his tanist, sons, and near relations. The tribal lands, however, were simply lent to certain individuals who were nearest of kin to the chief; they were still the property of the tribe, and so at stated periods were redistributed amongst its freemen.* This principle is laid down in the Brehon laws as follows: "What a man had not bought he cannot sell." "No man shall grant land except such as he himself has purchased unless with the consent of the conjoint family; and he must leave his share in the land to the common possession of the family to which he belonged." It is further laid down in these laws that "a man was bound to keep his lands during his life perfect, and leave them with no greater debt than he received them with"; lastly, "persons are of equal rank when they have the same quantity of land."

It is, however, certain that, in the course of time, the descendants of the original chiefs came to occupy the same tribal lands for many generations, until such property passed into what we now understand as freehold, and was transmitted from one generation to another. Beyond this, the chief of the tribe reserved certain lands as mensal, or personal property; he took also the best of any subsequently conquered lands, so that in this way, beyond his tribal possessions, he accumulated private estates which he dealt with as his own. The same thing happened in the case of the chief men of a sept, and such private property was augmented from lands probably in the first instance in possession of the original occupiers of the soil, but which had not been included in the primary assignment of tribal lands.

No inconsiderable part of Clare was formerly covered with forest trees, bogs, and barren land,† all of which went to form the common lands; and these, under certain restrictions as to grazing, belonged to the freemen of the tribe. But as the forests were cleared off and waste lands brought into use, it was appropriated to a large extent by the existing landowners, and helped to build up the private property of these individuals.

The tribal lands were cultivated by the occupiers of the soil; about sixty acres were supposed to be sufficient to maintain a family in a fair position in the social scale. But the quantity of land was calculated by the amount of seed it required for cultivation and the cattle it could feed rather than by its area. A landlord having an excess of tribal lands beyond that which he required for his own maintenance and that of his family, handed over so much of the soil as he did not want to his relations. A landholder of this description did not pay tribute

* "Brehon Law Tracts," vol. ii. p. 345.
† O'Curry's "Manners and Customs," vol. i. p. cxxxvi.

for his land, but was bound to the landlord not only for military service, but also at stated periods to provide food for his lord's servants and family, and on certain festive occasions to grant him a specified quantity of food stuff.

There were, however, another class of landholders who were not only more numerous than those above referred to, but who in the course of time, as military followers, exercised the most important function in the State. These landholders occupied the private estates of landlords, to whom they paid tribute, either in stock, grain, or some other commodity. We can form an idea as to how this charge was liquidated, when we learn that in one instance, A, it amounted to "a calf, a salted pig, three sacks of wheat, three of malt, and a handful of rushlight candles"; in another case, B, to "a cow of prescribed size and fatness, a salted pig, eight sacks of malt, one of wheat, and three handfuls of rushlights." Individuals accepting the position of a landholder in these circumstances would hardly have been a Celt if, when taking the land, he had sufficient stock to work it; he was obliged, therefore, to turn to his landlord, who was in fact bound to supply his retainer with a certain amount of stock, in proportion to that which he had agreed to give for the land. For instance, in the case specified above, A, the landlord was bound to supply six cows to the landowner if he required them; in the case B, he had to supply twenty-four cows. But now came in the power of the landlord: every man accepting stock in this way was compelled to fight under his landlord whenever called upon; he became a military retainer, and had also to give his labour at all times in building forts, making roads, and other specified public works. It is true, no man was obliged to take stock, and he might return it to his landlord, and so be free from military service.* Beyond this, if "food, rent, and service" had been rendered for seven years by the recipient of stock, on the death of the landlord the landholder was entitled to the stock; on the other hand, if the landholder died, his family were to a great extent relieved from the obligation the deceased had incurred.†

But the provision for service covenanted for in the manner described was the keystone to the military system in Ireland, which led to so much bloodshed and trouble, for each chief had thus a body of fighting men at his beck and call. Over these retainers he had unlimited power, with no definite authority to control his actions. In fact, chiefs of this kind were as a rule absolutely their own masters, their power being limited, however, by the knowledge that if they attacked another chief

---

* " Brehon Law Tracts," vol. ii. p. 49.
† Sir H. Maine: "Early Institutions," p. 163.

they would not only be resisted, but might be worsted ; might was right in those days. Professor O'Curry has, however, clearly shown that this system differed from feudalism in many essential features. In the first place, the chief was invariably elected to his office, and his successor, or "tanist," was in like manner elected, by the freemen of the tribe. In the second place, the land in great part belonged to the tribe, and not to the chief or any other individual ; the tribal lands were governed through the instrumentality of the members of the sept who occupied the land.* The only resemblance which the Irish system had to feudalism was, that from the smallest landholder to the highest landlord, all paid tribute to the chief and received something in return ; this tribute was not vassalage, but a sign of allegiance to the landlord first, and then to the head of the sept, and tribe, or ruler of the province.

All landlords and landholders were freemen in consequence of their possessing land. This possession of land was all important, and it is the survival of this feeling which engenders that intense desire to possess land which is so marked a characteristic of Irishmen even at the present time. In days gone by the landholder was the freeman, the landless man the bondsman, because he had no direct lien on the soil. These bondsmen had no social position, they could neither appeal to a Brehon for redress, or appear to give evidence before him ; but in consequence of the law of tanistry and of gavelkind, it is certain not a few of the landlords' relatives must have been landless, and consequently bondsmen. This fact was of the greatest importance in the tribal system, for there was thus a strong hereditary feeling between the bondsman and the freeman of the same locality, and so a tie existed between the higher and lower grades of society which was of vast consequence from a social point of view. It is questionable if these Irish bondsmen were slaves in the way of being bought and sold ; doubtless slavery existed in Ireland until it was abolished by the clergy assembled in synod at Armagh in the year 1171 ; but the slaves of that period were for the most part English lads taken prisoners or sold to Irishmen by people of their own country. Even bondsmen, such as horse-boys, who were of the lowest class, herdsmen, labourers, and others who formed a part of a tribe, could by patient industry hope in the course of time to raise their families into the ranks of freemen.†

From the above statement it appears that from the earliest period of the Celtic invasion of Clare the land was held under two different systems ; under one, a portion of the tribal lands were assigned, on

---

* " Brehon Laws," by L. Ginnell, p. 136.
† " Senchus Mōr," vol. iv. p. 87.

certain stipulations, to members of the tribe, their title to the land resting on their consanguinity to the chief. The second class held lands as the retainers or landholders of individuals who had tribal lands in excess of the quantity they could themselves cultivate, or more frequently who possessed private estates ; these men were bound to the lord of the soil as military retainers, a state of things which continued to exist until the early part of the seventeenth century.*

Social Rank.—Landlords and landholders, as freemen, were divided into classes, according to the quantity of land and cattle they possessed, each class being entitled to definite privileges ; all such matters were carefully provided for under the Brehon laws. Thus, the head of a family could only claim admission into the lowest class of freemen if for three generations the family had possessed a certain amount of land and a plough, an ox and harness, a kiln, hand-mill, cooking caldron, and some other articles ; a larger amount of lands and stock raised a man a step in the social scale, and so he might rise to the sixth grade, in which class of society the landholder, among other articles, must possess " a head-bathing basin " and many other articles, all described with minuteness in the Brehon Code. And so with the landlords, they were likewise divided into classes, according to the quantity of land they owned. Among other articles such a person must possess furniture of the " highest order," beds and bedding, and a kitchen boiler, " in which a cow would fit, or a pig in bacon." †

A family might rise a step in the social scale if they acquired and held for three generations sufficient property to enable its head to qualify for a higher class. On the other hand, the loss of property entailed forfeiture of position and with it social privileges.‡ There was no hereditary claim to property, and every man was enabled by persistent application to help to raise his family in the social scale ; this was clearly the spirit and law of Celtic society in Clare as defined in the Brehon Code.

We may form some idea of a bondsman's position as a wage-earner in the ninth century from the following reference made to him in one of MacLonain's poems (A.D. 850). From this poem we learn that the wages received by a labouring man was " a cow and a cloak " per annum. In the story referred to by the poet, a certain labourer, whose home was in county Clare, having worked for a year under a landholder in Connaught, was returning home with his wages, and when crossing the hills of Echty he met MacLonain, and having entered

---

* Sir H. Maine : " The Early History of Institutions," p. 85.
† O'Curry : " Manners and Customs," vol. iii. p. 29.
‡ " Brehon Law Tracts," vol. iv. p. 227.

into conversation with the poet, the labourer told the poet that he belonged to the Dalcasian tribe. MacLonain evidently had a very high opinion of this tribe, and then and there composed a poem in their honour; the labourer was so delighted with this poem that he gave its author his year's wages, and returned home empty-handed but full of MacLonain's poem. This action and the gracious words contained in the poem so delighted the labourer's sept, that they made him a present of "ten cows for every quarter of the cow he had bestowed on the poet."

CHAPTER IV

Religious opinions of early Irish—The Irish Druid and his belief in a Supreme Being—Transmigration—Connac Mac Art (A.D. 227) his religion—Christianity among early Irish—St. Patrick—The Celtic Irish Church—Druidism long continued after Patrick's time—St. Patrick engrafted Christianity into Paganism—St. Columbia—Strife between monasteries—Cælestius (A.D. 370)—His opinions—John Scotus Erigena—Appendix.

HAVING briefly referred to some of the laws and social institutions of our ancestors; we may now consider the ideas upon which their religious convictions were based. With them Christianity was engrafted upon a long-established belief in a Supreme Being, the quickening Spirit of the universe.

Belief of the Early Irish in the World of Spirits.—The ideas held by the Irish Celt on this subject were in all probability derived from their remote ancestors, and have been handed down to us in the Sanscrit Vedas. From these writings we learn that the early Aryans believed in God, the Eternal Origin of all things, and in the immortality of the soul; their idea was that the spirit or soul of a being emanated from God and passed at the time of birth into man. God was the soul and the life.* The soul becoming contaminated by evil during its residence in a human being was incapacitated from reunion with God until purified by passing through other forms of living creatures. Everything that moved had life, or, in other words, was endowed with the divine nature. In this way our forefathers came to believe that the heavenly bodies, clouds, winds, the sea and rivers, including the vegetable and animal kingdom, were alive through the presence in them of the Spirit of God, which Spirit influenced their actions. Holding views of this kind we can readily understand the power which individuals would gain over their fellow creatures, if they could persuade them that they were able to influence the spirit which dwelt in the sun, sea, rivers and so on. The priests of old assumed this prerogative, asserting their power over Nature through familiarity with the spirit governing the universe. They studied medicine

---

* "Lectures on the Vedanta Philosophy," by F. Max Müller, vol. i. p. 477.

and the properties of plants, the seasons, and the heavenly bodies, and so came to learn something of the movements of the moon and planets, and grew to be astronomers, wise men, and teachers of their fellow-creatures.

The Druids seem to have held the same position among the Irish and Continental Celts as the Aryan Guru held in the East. Mommsen, in his "History of Rome" observes that the Druids, in whom the Celts had implicit faith, kept up the national feeling among the people, who believed that the Druids were able to influence the spirits presiding over the elements ; they were magicians or wise men who could propitiate both the good and also the malignant spirits. Druids in this way came to wield a vast influence over the affairs of their countrymen, in that they were held capable of bringing the elements and everything that moved to minister to the wants of man. Julius Cæsar informs us that in his day the Celtic Druids of Gaul believed in the immortality of the soul and in transmigration ; he considered that this was the key to their system. Cæsar states that the Druids were a privileged class, equal in rank to the chiefs ; they were judges in all matters of dispute. He adds that the Druids presided over schools of learning, to which youths flocked eagerly for instruction ; that they taught everything by verse, which was never committed to writing, in order to strengthen the memories of their pupils, and to preserve their knowledge from becoming popularised. Cæsar further states that the Druids were fond of discussing the movements of the stars, of the earth, and of the universe.†

If we turn to the accounts which we possess of the Irish Druids, we find that they were consulted, and their advice was implicitly followed in almost every step of life, whether relating to private or public affairs. Kings, chiefs, and the heads of families consulted their Druids on all important questions ; they acted also as arbitrators in cases of disputes. The head Druid of Ireland was hardly inferior to the monarch in dignity.‡ They did not attempt to control the morals of the people ; not that the early Irish Druids were immoral, but as Dr. Teylor observes they were unmoral, matters of this kind were beyond their province. The authority of the Irish Druid rested absolutely on the belief that he possessed a knowledge of the world of spirit which was not

* "The Origin and Growth of Religion," by T. W. Rhys Davids, p. 13 ; also Dr. Teylor on "Primitive Culture," vol. i. p. 477.

† "De Bello Gallico," vi. 13, 14 ; also see "Gratianus Lucius," cap. viii. p. 59, who confirms Cæsar's account of the Druids.

‡ "Professor O'Curry's "Manners and Customs of the Ancient Irish," p. 187, vol. ii. ; *ibid.*, p. 200.

granted to ordinary mortals, and further that this knowledge was only
to be acquired by long-continued contemplation and study. It would
seem, however, that any one who wished might become a Druid if he
chose to fit himself for this calling. Irish Druids were exempt from
paying tribute and from military service; they taught their pupils in
verse, and not only instructed them in religion, but also in astronomy,
and the laws of the country, and even in military accomplishments. For
instance, we find that the chief Druid of the province of Ulster, about
the commencement of the Christian era, presided over a school of this
kind; he limited the number of his pupils to one hundred.

The "Brehon Law Tracts" contain an introduction which there is
good reason to suppose is one of the most ancient records we possess
in the Celtic language; it appears to be older than the body of the work,
and in it is an account of the creation of the world resembling that given
in the Vedas.* Colonel Wood-Martin, in his work on "Pagan Ireland,"
remarks that from St. Patrick's Hymn we learn that the pagan Irish
worshipped and invoked the personified powers of Nature, and that this
is corroborated by passages from ancient MSS. For instance, a king of
Ireland received, as pledges that the sovereignty should for ever rest in
his family, "the sun and moon, the sea, the dew and colours, and all
the elements visible and invisible and every element which is in heaven
and on earth." Another monarch, having broken his oath, perished,
from sun, and from wind, and "from the rest of the pledges; for
transgressing them in that time used not to be dared." Again, in one
of the poems of the heroic age, Cuchulain called on the waters, on
heaven, earth, and the rivers to protect him, and the elements answered
his appeal.†

St. Patrick expunged much in the Brehon code which referred to
Druidical customs; nevertheless, in the preface to these laws, and in
various passages found in the "Senchus Mōr," we have references to
some of the practices of the Druids. For instance, we read that the
Druid was in the habit of "placing his rod upon a person, and through
means of the wand he could discover his history. In the same way he
could in a moment give an accurate answer to any questions put to
him.‡ He could reveal the time of a person's death, or of his own

---

* "Space being divided into the dark portion of the heavens and the starry
systems: the dark portion spirit-primary substance, the light portion the same
substance made tangible to the senses under the form of matter" ("Buddhism and
Christianity," by A. Lillie, p. 169).

† "Pagan Ireland," by W. G. Wood-Martin," p. 99.

‡ Professor O'Curry's "Manners and Customs," vol. ii. pp. 208, 209.

decease.* In another of these law tracts there is a reference made to sacrifices offered to evil spirits: demon feasts, as they are called, or provision for the "sons of death" and the spirits of evil men. Sacrifices made to such spirits were of a different kind to that offered to good spirits. In the very ancient book of "Invasions" we have the words supposed to have been used by the chief Druid who accompanied a large body of Celtic invaders into Ireland. A great storm having arisen, the Druid invoked the spirits ruling the elements, and so quieted the waves, after which he is said to have used the following language: "I pray that they [i.e., the Celts] reach the land of Erin, those who are riding upon the great sea. That they be distributed upon her plains, her mountains, and her valleys; upon her forests that shed showers of nuts and all other fruit; upon her rivers, lakes, and great waters." As Professor O'Curry remarks, there is nothing in the character of this very ancient record " to distinguish it from the prayer of any Christian of the present day, so far as the expression of the speaker's wants and desires are concerned."

The old Irish legends are full of wonders performed by Druids; but in all this literature we hear nothing of human sacrifices; they raised mists and storms to confound the enemies of the ruler of their country, and for other purposes. But one fails to obtain evidence of cruelty on their part; there is none whatever for imputing to them human sacrifices in the ceremonies they performed to propitiate the spirits ordering the course of Nature and the destinies of the human race.†

With reference to the idea of transmigration, it seems probable that it may have arisen in the minds of the ancient Aryans from their experience of the hereditary transmission of the disposition of parents to their posterity. The sins of the fathers had to pass through several generations before their effects were expunged from their descendants. However this may have been, transmigration was a belief accepted by the Aryan races and by the Celts of Ireland. In the ancient book of Balimote, which was a compilation of still older Celtic poems, the following verses refer to this belief in plain language. The poem alludes to the birth of a famous Irish hero, Cairrill, who, we are told,‡ for

One hundred years complete he lived,
He lived in blooming manhood;

* "Silva Gadelica," p. 98, by Standish H. O'Grady.
† "Manners and Customs of the Ancient Irish," by E. O'Curry, vol. ii. p. 228.
‡ See "Silva Gadelica," p. 267. After Christianity had come to Ireland we are told of Liban being turned into the form of a salmon, which she inhabits for three hundred years, and to pass to heaven after life prolonged beyond many ages.

Three hundred years in the shape of a wild ox
He lived on extensive plains;
Two hundred and five years he lived
In the shape of a wild bore;
Three hundred years he was still in the flesh
In shape of an old bird;
One hundred delightful years he lived
In the shape of a salmon in the flood.

Mongan, King of Ulster, as late as the seventh century, declares that he was not what men took him to be, the son of the mortal Fiachna, but of Manannan MacLir, and a reincarnation of the great Finn; he calls back from the grave the famous Fenian Caolite to prove this. In the same way the hero Tuan O'Carroll had also a second birth, and the warrior Cuchulain had his parentage ascribed to the god Lughea and not to his reputed father.* At the close of the tenth century the doctrine of transmigration would seem to have still lingered in the imagination of Irishmen.†

It is impossible to ascertain with any precision what the ideas entertained by the common people were upon these matters; we get here and there glimpses of the inner life of the more important actors in the drama, but of the lesser lights we know next to nothing. As an example of my meaning we may refer to the expressions used by the King Cormac MacArt, one of Ireland's greatest heroes, who flourished from A.D. 227 to 266; he was not only a distinguished warrior, but also a

---

* "Early Gaelic Literature," by D. Hyde, LL.D., p. 103.

† Maelusthain O'Carroll, the well-known author of the "Annals of Inisfallen" and friend of Brian Boru, had three favourite pupils who were so much alike that it was difficult to distinguish one from the other. They desired to perform a pilgrimage to Jerusalem. O'Carroll granted them their request, but foretold the death of the three friends in the East, and his request was that after their decease they should return to him and tell him how long he had to live and what were his prospects of heaven. The three students reached Jerusalem and died there. After death they met the archangel Michael and asked him to let them know the fate of O'Carroll. They were informed that to perdition he must pass because he falsified the canon, for his lecherous habits, and because he had abandoned the Althus. The three students passed into the bodies of three white doves, and in this shape appeared to O'Carroll: they told him what they had heard. O'Carroll excused himself on the ground that his son being sick unto death he sung the Althus round him seven times a day, but it was of no avail; and so he had given up the Althus, as it was evident God did not care for it. After a time the disciples again returned to their master, and were able to afford him more consolation than at their first visit; and so the story runs on, and like many others of the same class point to the idea of transmigration (O'Curry's "Lectures on Manuscript Materials," p. 77).

man of considerable literary attainments; the historian Keating has given us an account of Cormac's career, which need not be referred to in this place, beyond mentioning a characteristic anecdote of the young king. Cormac MacArt, when a boy, was one day present in his uncle's court at Tara. It appears that " certain sheep had strayed into and eaten up some vegetables growing in the queen's garden," the case was brought before the king, and he " adjudged the sheep to the plaintiff in lieu of the trespass." Young Cormac, hearing the sentence, came forward and remarked, the judgment " were more equitable were the shearing of the sheep given in damage of the green stuff cropped; for in the ground the grass will grow again, and so will the wool upon the sheep." *

Cormac having been actively engaged throughout a long reign determined, in consequence of an injury he had received to one of his eyes, to resign his throne in favour of his son, and to devote the remaining years of his life, as he stated, " *to meditation and the worship of God, the Creator of Heaven, and also of a place in which the souls of the wicked should be justly punished;*" these were Cormac's own words, recorded by himself in a work which existed in Keating's time, and from which the historian quotes. These expressions were made use of by Cormac before Christianity had spread into Ireland; he was brought up by a Druid and practised their art, for he undertook to cure one of his friends of leprosy by means of magic. It seems therefore probable that expressions such as those above quoted were not far removed from what was taught by the Druids before Christianity was introduced into Ireland; for in those days the Druids were the chief if not the only schoolmasters in Ireland. Cormac distinctly stated " that it was beneath the dignity of a rational being to adore anything in the form of an idol, but that his prayers should be directed to the living Supreme Being who created all things." * The following are some of his expressions which have come down to us through another Cormac of Cashel:

> Wilt thou steer my gloomy little bark,
> Upon the broad-bosomed foaming ocean?
> Wilt thou come, O bright King of Heaven,
> While my own will inclines to go to sea?
> With Thee the great, with Thee the small,
> With Thee the fall of hosts is but a shower.
> O God, wilt thou assist me,
> While coming over the boisterous sea?

* " Silva Gadelica," p. 357, by Standish H. O'Grady.
† Keating's " History of Ireland " (O'Connor's edition), p. 283.

There is much of the ring of the Vedic language in these lines; in fact, the mind of the early Celtic inhabitants of Ireland was essentially Eastern; they inherited no inconsiderable amount of the opinions, laws, and traditions of the old Aryan stock from which they sprung. General Vallencey gave many years' work to subjects of this kind; he came to the conclusion that "the established religion of the early Irish was a form of Buddhism." Much of the folk-lore of the Hindus at the present day is clearly identical with that of the Irish Celt; for instance, in the Irish romance of the Children of Lir, who were metamorphosed into swans, which, with the changing seasons, come and go on Lough Erne. These birds come and go scatheless; for in the mind of the Celtic peasantry they represent the souls of holy women who fell victims to Norsemen, an example of a pagan legend being completely Christianised.* Numerous old legends have in the same way been modified so as to fall in with the notions of Christian writers, and many of the old pagan institutions survived far into Christian times, such as the Fair of Carman.† In an appendix to this chapter I have quoted, from Mr. Standish Hayes O'Grady's "Silva Gadelica," a charge given by one of the ancient Irish Celts to his grandchild; advice older than our era, but containing much which many of us might take to heart and follow with advantage.

Christianity among the Early Irish.—Although Palladius preceded St. Patrick as Bishop of Ireland, it was not until the arrival of the latter Saint in the country, about the year A.D. 432, that Christianity took root among the inhabitants of Erin. Patrick, as a youth, having been carried a prisoner into Ireland, was employed by his master to look after sheep, he remained at work of this kind for six years, during which time he must have learnt the Celtic language, and much concerning the tribal and family system which then prevailed throughout the country. He subsequently escaped from captivity, and after some years returned to Ireland as bishop.‡ From St. Patrick's Hymn we learn that after " binding himself to many Christian virtues, which may be taken as confessions of his belief in certain Christian doctrines, he goes on binding himself to the elements, claiming thus, that not alone were the powers of Christianity on his side, but also the very elements that were

* "Pagan Ireland," by Mr. W. G. Wood-Martin, p. 140.
† "The Story of Early Gaelic Literature," by D. Hyde, LL.D., p. 14.
‡ "The Tripartite Life of St. Patrick," by Whitley Stokes, D.C.L., LL.D., published by authority of the Lords Commissioners of Her Majesty's Treasury Introduction, p. cxli.

worshipped by his opponents."* It is most interesting to follow the method adopted by this remarkable man in his efforts to convert the natives of Ireland to Christianity. Patrick was a born leader of men, and appreciated the importance in a society such as he had to deal with, in working from the fountain head downwards. No sooner had he arrived in the country than he went to Tara to demonstrate to the monarch that whatever powers Irish Druids might have over Nature, he possessed a power greater than theirs.† Having demonstrated this fact to the satisfaction of the king, he became a Christian, as also did his head poet or bard.‡ After accomplishing this task the conversion of the nation came as a matter of course. The Kings of Munster and Connaught soon followed the example set them by the monarch. St. Patrick was indefatigable in moving from one part of Ireland to another, baptising chiefs and their retainers, who seem to have accepted the new faith

---

* "Pagan Ireland," by W. G. Wood-Martin, p. 90.

ST. PATRICK'S HYMN.
" I bind myself to-day to the virtues of Heaven,
    Light of sun,
    Brightness of moon,
    Splendour of fire,
    Speed of lightning,
    Swiftness of wind,
    Depth of sea,
    Stability of earth,
    Compactness of rock."

Patrick having been called before the King, together with the chief Druid, they were directed to work miracles, and the Druid brought snow on the plain in front of them by "chants of wizardry and the arts of devilry." Said Patrick, "Put away the snow that has fallen." The Druid declined to do so till to-morrow. Patrick said " It is in evil thy power stands not in good." He then blessed the plain throughout the four quarters, and, quicker than speech, the snow vanished. The Druid invoked darkness, which Patrick removed by prayer to the Lord ; and so with water, fire, and so on ; the Druid appealing to the spirit influencing the elements and all moving matter ; Patrick by appeal to God obtaining aid directly from the Supreme Ruler of the Universe. We are told that Patrick said to the King, " Unless thou believest now thou shalt die ;" then the King went into the assembly-house of the people. " For me," he said, "belief in God is better than what is threatened to me that I be killed." " So then the King knelt to Patrick and believed in God, but he did not believe with a pure heart, and on that day many thousands believed." ("The Tripartite Life of St. Patrick," edited by Whitley Stokes, D.C.L., LL.D., part i. pp. 41, 61.)

† " The History of Ireland by the Abbé Macgeoghegan," by P. O'Kelly, p. 141.

‡ Ibid., p. 143, " He generally appealed to the great, convinced that the people would follow the example of the prince."

D

without question, but they did not, as a rule, discard their Druidical ideas ; in fact, we know that as late as the year A.D. 648, Marion, the wife of the King of Connaught, a "most compassionate and well-disposed lady, held to the ancient faith," and had "recourse to an eminent Druid, a retainer of the family, to reveal to her certain domestic matters." With regard to the mass of the people they may have absorbed a definite amount of Christianity, but it would be difficult to fix the point where their religion ceased to be Druidical and became Christian.†

St. Patrick never even suggested persecution as a means of enforcing the acceptance of Christianity by the people ; we have an example of his method of conversion in the case of the daughters of the King of Connaught. He met these ladies accompanied by their tutors, who were Druids. The king's daughters proceeded at once to question Patrick as follows : they inquired "whence he came, whither he was going, are ye men of the hills, or are ye gods?" To which Patrick answered : "It would be better for you to believe in God than to ask what race we are." The eldest daughter asked : "Who is your God, and where is He? Is He in heaven, or is He in the earth, or under the earth, or upon the earth, or in the seas, or in the streams, or mountains, or valleys? Has He sons and daughters, has He gold and silver? Is there abundance of all sorts of wealth in His kingdom?" To these questions the saint made appropriate answers. The king's daughters and their tutors were then baptised.‡

St. Patrick visited South Munster and was received by Angus, king of that province, at Cashel. This king was the great grandson of Cormac Cas, the progenitor of the O'Briens, Macnamaras, and other Dalcasian families. There is a curious story, referred to by the Abbé Macgeoghegan in his History (p. 146), regarding the baptism of Angus, "The holy bishop having leaned on his pastoral staff, which was pointed

---

* "Hibbert Lectures," 1886, p 579 : "The Druids of Britain were Brahmins beyond the least shadow of doubt " (the Archdruid, " Myfr Norganwg ").

† "Pagan superstitions seem to exist among some of these people up to the present day, for in the year 1895 we have a case reported of black witchcraft in co. Tipperary. A woman, aged 27, the wife of a cooper, has there been burnt to death under the supposition that she was a counterfeit or changeling who, being burnt, would disappear, whilst the real woman, held in hostage by the fairies or good people, would return. And so this poor creature was literally roasted to death by her fellow-creatures : fire being the great restorer and purifier ; showing that the same train of thought so long ago impressed on our ancestors still crops up among descendants in the nineteenth century." (Extract from the *Globe*, April 2, 1895.)

‡ O'Curry's " Manners and Cr...oms of the Ancient Irish," vol. ii. p. 202.

with iron, it pierced the king's foot, who suffered the pain without complaining, till the ceremony was ended.* The apostle hearing of the accident, asked his disciple why he had not complained. The king answered that he supposed the wound inflicted on his foot formed part of the ceremony."

From Cashel, Patrick proceeded across the Shannon to Cratlow, where it is quite possible one of the sept of Macnamaras resided, for it was there that we find them from the earliest records in our possession. However this may be, the saint is said to have journeyed through Clare to the mountains which separate that county from Galway.† Macgeoghegan states that the inhabitants of Thomond, many of whom at this time were of the old race, received Patrick; the Celts, in fact, had only conquered the Firbolgs of this locality some forty years previous to the visit which St. Patrick paid this part of the country.‡

In the life of St. Patrick, as given by Dr. Todd and other authorities, we learn that his success was so great that he soon found it necessary to make arrangements to meet the spiritual needs of the infant Celtic Church; this he did by ordaining natives of the country, who, being ignorant of Latin employed the Celtic language in the offices of the Church. Dr. O'Donovan states that nothing is clearer, than that Patrick engrafted Christianity on the Pagan superstitions with so much skill, that he won the people over to the Christian religion before they understood the exact difference between the two systems of beliefs, and much of this half Pagan, half Christian religion will be found not only in the Irish stories of the Middle Ages, but in the superstitions of the peasantry of the present day.

St. Patrick further adopted the customs and laws of the country in founding monasteries and other religious houses for the use of his followers. After having baptised a chief, he obtained a grant of land from him, upon which a church and surrounding houses were built, the whole being enclosed in a wall and fence forming the sanctuary. Here ecclesiastical and lay members of the monastery lived. At first

---

* "Usser Primord," cap. xvii. p. 863.

† "Silva Gadelica," p. 126.

‡ Macgeoghegan's "History of Ireland," p. 147 (P. O'Kelly's edition). "The fame of the miracles which the saint performed at Cashel, and the news of his coming to Thomond, reached Cathan, who called together all the nobles of his establishment, and crossed the river Shannon to come to the Apostle. Cassin was one of the number and received baptism by the ministry of St. Patrick in a plain near Limerick. Cassin died in the year 461, leaving his elder son, Carthan, who succeeded his father; he was the progenitor of our sept." (MS. in the Royal Irish Academy, 24 G. 20.)

they were all of the same tribe as the chief on whose lands they had established themselves, but in time they collected landholders and also bondsmen on their estate, who were in no way related to the members of the tribe ; they were, however, bound to do military service under the head of their monastery ; in fact, the monastical establishment was made a part of the tribal system of the country, its head and his tanist being elected to office by the community, and having all the rights and lands which belonged to the original head of the monastery. There was not unfrequently a temporal and spiritual superior, the latter being elected by the monks, the former by the members of the sept or clan to which the establishment belonged. The bishop had no judicial or administrative power over such establishments ; his function was spiritual. The Church thus established by St. Patrick consisted of isolated communities engrafted on-to the tribe of the locality in which they were founded.* The original home threw out branches, and so a monastery, like the conjoint family, spread. To all connected with such an establishment family words were applied signifying kinship and tribe.†

We may refer to the life of St. Columba as illustrating the working of this system ; he was born A.D. 521, and belonged to the tribe of O'Donnell. Columba was educated in the famous school of Clonard, and being destined for the Church was sent to Clomford to be ordained a "domestic bishop." On arriving in that place Columba found the bishop engaged in ploughing his land ; having been ordained, the saint devoted himself to missionary work among his countrymen. Columba was a distinguished scribe, and having borrowed a portion of the Scriptures from his friend the Abbot of Clonard, he proceeded to copy the work ; the owner of the book subsequently demanded not only its return, but also the copy Columba had made, but the saint refused to give up his copy of the work, and the friends not being able to settle the matter in dispute referred it to the King of Meath. The king decided that Columba must give up his copy as well as the original book to the abbot, upon the principles contained in the Brehon Laws, that "to every cow belongs her little offspring, so to every book belongs its copy." Columba gave up his MS., but he was "rash, passionate, and revengeful," and being a chief in his tribe as well as an ecclesiastic, in the year A.D. 561 he ordered out a large body of his tribesmen to attack the men of Meath, a battle ensued, in which some 3000 men are said to

* "Richey's "Short History of Ireland," p. 82.

† Sir H. Maine: "The Early History of Institutions," second edition, p. 236.

have been killed.* We need not follow the subsequent life of St. Columba in his home in Iona, or the wonderful work he performed in Scotland in converting the king and inhabitants of that country to Christianity.

It was not until the year A.D. 804 that the Irish monastic communities were exempted from military service. During the year 673 there was persistent war between the monasteries of Clonmacnoise and Durrow; and as late as A.D. 816, in a scrimmage between these establishments, some 400 men are reported to have been slain. The clergy in the eighth century went about the country and to synods armed, and "often fought pitched battles, in which many were killed with but very small provocation."

Although this state of things existed in Ireland, her monasteries were at the same time sending out missionaries whose devotion to their work in England and many parts of the continent of Europe has never been surpassed. The first rector of the School of Paris was a pupil of Bede, and the second rector of that great school was an Irishman named Clement.† As in the case of St. Columba, the better qualities of the Celtic missionaries were most conspicuously developed when serving in foreign countries; at home their warlike proclivities often predominated over the principles they professed. But we must not overlook the fact that it was due to the efforts of the early Irish Church that women were emancipated in that country from military service; and that slavery in its grosser form, that is in the traffic in human beings was abolished.

Before bringing this chapter to a close, we may refer to two famous Irishmen who in no small degree disturbed the minds of the orthodox in the fifth and eighth centuries. Cælestius, an Irishman, was born about the year A.D. 370, and therefore some sixty years before St. Patrick's time; he travelled to Rome to study law, and there fell in with a fellow-countryman, the theologian Pelagius. Cælestius struck up a warm friendship with Pelagius, and not only espoused his opinions, but, according to Archbishop Ussher, he became "the greatest depressor of God's grace and the advance of man's reason; he held that every one was governed by his own will, and received so much grace as he did merit." In fact, Cælestius, who was educated by Druids and Brehons in Ireland, adopted sufficient Christianity to efface the grosser ideas

* "Ireland and the Celtic Church," by G. T. Stokes, D.D., third edition, pp. 100-110.

† King Alfred is said to have been educated in Ireland. ("The Brehon Laws," by L. Ginnell, p. 2.)

contained in the system in which he had been brought up, and at the same time could not accept much of the supernatural in Christianity. Dr. Stokes observes that Cælestius was one of the most prominent figures in the religious and political world of his day. His activity was immense. He had developed, even in that early time a true Irish faculty for agitation, and realised fully that successful agitation can only be carried on by intense personal exertion. We find him disputing in Carthage, Rome, Constantinople, and in the far East. He bearded the Patriarchs in one place, and the Pope in Rome ; he was excommunicated by a Council at Ephesus. But what mattered that to Cælestius ; if the Pope and Patriarchs agreed with him, so much the better ; but if not, he did not care, but would seek redress in other quarters. There is reason to suppose that, with Pelagius, he ended his days in his native country.*

Another Irishman, John Scotus Erigena, of much the same cast of mind as Cælestius, flourished in the ninth century ; he was an eminent scholar, and was sent for from Ireland by Charles the Bald to translate certain Greek works. Dr. Stokes describes Erigena as a thorough Irishman : he was brilliant, learned, and a heretic ; so much so that the Pope Honorius III. issued a Bull declaring that the works of John the Irishman "abounded with worms of heretical depravity." Excommunication was denounced against him and all who should retain in their possession a copy of his works. He advocated the Pantheistic philosophy which many modern authors ascribe to Spinoza. Through the teaching of Johannes, the Irish school of the ninth century came to exercise a direct influence over the philosophic thought of modern times.† Erigena's principal work, "De Divisione Naturæ," is written in the form of a dialogue, distinguished for its Aristotelean acuteness and extensive information.‡ In this work he argues that, as before creation God alone existed, and in

* Pelagius held (1) that Adam had mortality in his nature, and whether he had sinned or not must have died ; (2) that Adam's sin was confined to himself ; (3) that newly-born infants are in the same condition as Adam was before the Fall : (4) that man may by his own exertions remain free from sin, the liberty of the will (law of Nature) being sufficient for that purpose, and to overcome temptation ; (5) that as the death and disobedience of Adam is not the necessary cause of death to all mankind, neither does the resurrection of the dead follow from the resurrection of the Saviour. Cælestius, however, passed from this line of reasoning into those of Pantheism, preceding in this respect his still more distinguished fellow-countryman, Johannes Erigena.

† "Ireland and the Celtic Church," by G. T. Stokes, D.D., third edition, p. 218.
‡ "History of the Christian Church," by the Rev. T. B. S. Carwethan, vol. i. p. 173.

Him were the potential causes of all future existence, so, too, in the end all created existence would return to God, for they were a portion of the universal life or divine nature, the idea upon which Vedantism rests, and which Erigena either produced from the depth of his own consciousness, or it was a resuscitation of the religious belief of his forefathers. A belief which Vedantists hold is summed up in a few words: "God (the Word) is true, the world is false, man's soul is God and nothing else; there is nothing worth gaining, there is nothing worth enjoying, there is nothing worth knowing but God alone, for he who knows God is God."* It is beyond my power to attempt to follow John Scotus Erigena or to explain his views; some of his opinions will be found in an appendix to this chapter.

It seems that the prominent feature in the religious belief of the Druids as given by Cormac MacArt, as also that of Cælestius, and of Johannes Scotus Erigena, was centred in the worship of God, the Creator of the Universe, and Giver of Life. God was life, and all things living therefore were for the time being the abode of God. At the time of death the life returned to God, as being a part of the divine nature; in this belief there was no need of human intervention between God and man. Cormac MacArt desired to be alone with his God, and by retiring from the world and all its cares to cultivate the spirit which dwelt in him and was destined to exist to all eternity. Cælestius harps on the same idea, and J. S. Erigena dilates on the subject, and endeavours to clear away the clouds of superstition which in his opinion obscured Christianity. In his work "De Divisione Naturæ" we have evidence that as far back as A.D. 850 Irishmen were well instructed in concerted music; for he dilates on the harmony produced by the combination of a number of voices taking different parts. These parts, he observes, alone are anything but melodious, but under the hand of the composer they are brought into unison. And so, he argues, it is with the apparently discordant elements by which we are surrounded, each organism is a part related to the whole universe which is moving on to perfection in God.†

---

* F. Max Müller: "Lectures on the Vedantic Philosophy," p. 172.

† See also vol. i. p. 550, "Manners and Customs of the Ancient Irish" (E. O'Curry).

APPENDIX TO CHAPTER IV

Mr. Standish H. O'Grady, in his "Silva Gadelica," has given us a translation from an old Celtic MS. contained in the "Book of Lismore," "The Colloquy of the Ancients." This is stated to have been taken from a still more ancient work, which is now lost, the "Book of Monasterboice." In this colloquy we have a conversation reported which was supposed to have taken place between St. Patrick and the last of the old Fenia of Ireland; and it is interesting as giving us some idea of the wisdom and philosophy of the early Irish Celts.

Cacilte the Fenia states that Finn the chief had given the following rules of conduct to his grandson, rules which, according to the narrative, must have been drawn up before the commencement of the Christian era:

"Mac Lugach! if armed service be thy design, in a great man's household be quiet, be surly in the rugged pass. Without a fault of his beat not thy hound; until thou ascertain [her guilt] bring not a charge against thy wife; in battle meddle not with a buffoon, for, O Mac Lugach, he is but a fool. Censure not any if he be of grave repute; stand not up to take part in a brawl; neither have anything at all to do with either a mad or a wicked one. Two-thirds of thy gentleness be shown to women and to creepers on the floor [*i.e.*, little children], likewise to men of art that make the *duans;* and be not violent to the common people. With thy familiars, with them that are of thy council, hasten not to be the first into bed; perverse alliance shun, and all that is prohibited; yield not thy reverence to all. Utter not swaggerish speech, nor say that thou wilt not render the thing that is right; for a shameful thing it is to speak too stiffly unless that it be feasible to carry out thy word. So long as in the universe thou shalt exist, thy chief forsake not; neither for gold nor for other valuable in the earthly world abandon thou thy guarantee [*i.e.*, him that places himself under thy protection]. To a chief utter not strenuous criticism of his people; for it is not a 'good man's' [*i.e.*, a gentleman's] occupation to abuse a great lord's people to their chief. Be not a continually tattling talebearer, nor a false one; be not loquacious, nor censorious rashly; be the multiplicity of thy chivalrous qualities what it may, yet have thou not the Irachts hostility inclined to thee. Be not a frequenter of the drinking-house, nor given to carping at old men; the conduct thou hearest recommended, that is right: meddle not with a man of mean estate. Deal not in refusing of thy meat, and any that is penurious have not for a familiar; force not thyself upon a chief, nor give a chief lord occasion to speak ill of thee. Stick to thy raiment, hold fast to thine armature, until the stern fight with its weapon-glitter be well ended; never renounce to back thy luck, yet follow after gentleness, Mac Lugach."

"Success and benediction," said Patrick; "a good story it is that thou hast told us there. And where is Brogan the scribe?" Brogan answered: "Here, holy cleric." "Be that tale written by thee." And Brogan performed it on the spot.*

J. S. ERIGENA.

Erdmann, in his work on the "History of Philosophy," vol. i. p. 291, observes that Erigena was "the Charlemagne of scholastic philosophy." He was born

---

* "Silva Gadelica," by Standish H. O'Grady, p. 115 (1892).

about 815, and was still living 877. He was a layman; his chief work is based on the idea propounded by himself that true religion is also the true philosophy and *vice versâ*. The idea that every doubt can be refuted by philosophy was so preposterous an idea that it was by the clergy declared to be insensate blasphemy. Erigena held that the Fathers taught what they learnt by reason; by reason is meant the common thought which reveals itself in conversation, where out of two reasons are made one, each speaker as it were becoming the other. The organ of this general thinking is the "intellectus" (also called "animus"), which stands above the ratio, which has below it the five senses and the life-force which belongs to the soul, because the latter is bound to the body. His speculative knowledge is unity of subject and object. He calls the whole investigation "physiologia," the totality of all being "natura," which is divided into four classes: the uncreated creating, the created creating, the created uncreating, the neither created nor creating. Of these, the first, the ground of all being, and the fourth, the last goal, fall in God; the second and third embrace the creation. Of his five books each describes a class. In the fifth book the return of every created thing into the source of creation is exhibited. The first four are Erigena's theology and physics, the last his ethics. The Scriptures are allegorically interpreted. He summons Origen, Ambrose, Augustine, and many of the Fathers to his aid.

First Book: God is the uncreated Creator ("summa bonitas"), and so the unity of three persons, "essentia," "virtus," "operatio." God is all in all, no being outside of Him. All exists so far as God appears in it. God, without ceasing to be above things, in them comes into being and creates Himself.

Second Book: First transition. The created creating nature, the "causæ primordiales," although created eternal, because God must always have created, or creation would have been accidental with Him, which is impossible. The chaos of Moses is referred to the primitive cause, by whom the brooding spirit is divided into genera and species. This is the only seed from which all proceed. Whatever is real in things is a participation in the creating truth.

Third Book: Physics. He looks on creation and preservation as one. God did all He had to do at once. The becoming cognisable is the highest existence of things; things are in man when he sees them.

Fourth Book: The goal is the return of man to God (also Fifth Book). Evil is the perverted tendency of the will, which is good. There is a restoration of all things at the final goal, even the demons. In death the elements are separated. All passes over into the "causæ primordiales," and the attainment of the full knowledge of God, in which the knowing and the known become one; it is not absorption, for the individuality is preserved.

CHAPTER V

In the preceding chapter I have endeavoured to give a brief account of the people from which the members of our sept were derived, together with the social, political, and religious conditions under which they lived until the middle of the sixteenth century: at that time certain arrangements were made between Henry VIII. and the leading landowners of Clare, whereby the tenure of the land under the Brehon code was for the first time disturbed; but in other respects the people living to the west of the Shannon continued to flourish under their old laws and customs until the reign of James I.

We may now proceed to learn from contemporary historians something as to the character of our ancestors, and to trace the influence which their inherited qualities had in moulding their career; for history is valuable in so far as it enables us to comprehend the causes which have led to the success or failure of the people to which it refers, and to probe the virtues and vices which, as links in the chain, their descendants are destined to pass on to their children. In the case of Irishmen, it seems that knowledge of this kind is of peculiar value: the government of that country has been, and still is, a vexed question, largely because due weight has not been given to the fact that the character of the Irish Celt and English Saxon differ, and laws and customs which to the latter appear to be unexceptionable, are by no means necessarily best fitted for the former people. Working on these principles, we must endeavour to discover from their actions in what the peculiarities of the Celtic Irishman consists, and if we come near the truth in this matter we shall have done something towards laying a foundation on which to base a system of treatment calculated to alleviate, if not to remove some of the social and political anomalies under which Irish Celts exist.

From an abstract of the registered pedigree of the Macnamaras, it appears that the family trace their origin in uninterrupted succession to "Cas, the son of Connal;" but we may go back farther than this, for there is historical evidence to show that Connal was the sixth in descent from a Celtic chief, who ruled over the province of Munster from the year A.D. 174 to 234; this chief's name was Angus.

Angus, or Olioll Oluim, as he was commonly called, was descended from the family of the early Celtic rulers of Ireland; he married the daughter (Sabia) of a renowned Irish hero known as "Conn of a hundred battles." Olioll, although a less distinguished warrior than Conn, was nevertheless a prominent character in Irish history; he was a scholar as well as a soldier; some of his poems still exist, and Professor E. O'Curry believes that these poems were actually the work of this king.*

Olioll and many of his successors lived at Cashel (Tipperary), within sight of the hills of Clare. From a strategical point of view, it was hardly possible for the Celtic chief of Munster to have selected a more advantageous position than the rock of Cashel upon which to take up his abode; this rock rises abruptly in the midst of a far-reaching plain, doubtless until comparatively recent times covered by a forest. The summit of the rock is flat, and like that of the Acropolis at Athens capable of affording space upon which to erect a considerable number of buildings, and above all having a deep well containing an abundant supply of water. On the summit of this rock Olioll Oluim built his habitation, constructed of wood and clay. We know but little of his life, and that little is chiefly derived from legends which have been handed down to us; among these is the curious tradition which explains why Angus was nicknamed Olioll Oluim (or docked-of-an-ear, as the name signifies).†

Angus had been engaged at some distance from Cashel overlooking a favourite stud of horses; night came on and the king directed his attendants to collect rushes and prepare a bed for him on the hillside, then he went to sleep "to the sounds of the grazing of his horses." In the morning, to the surprise of Angus, the grass, which on the previous night covered the hillside had disappeared; on a subsequent occasion in similar circumstances the same thing happened. As the king could in no way account for this phenomena he sent for his chief Druid to explain the matter to him. The Druid, on arriving at the hill, found that Angus was asleep, and he, therefore, took up his position near his

* O'Curry's "Manners and Customs of the Ancient Irish," vol. ii. pp. 57–58.
† "Silva Gadelica," by Standish Hayes O'Grady, p. 129.

master, and presently saw the side of the hill open and its denizens, headed by their chief and his daughter issue from the opening. As the hill chief seemed inclined to approach too near the sleeping king the Druid hurled a spear at him and killed him; "as for the girl, the king arose, caught and kissed her, but she resisted, and struggling to release herself from Angus she nipped off his ear, so that she left him neither flesh nor skin of the same, from which time never any such ear grew on him again"; henceforth, Angus was named Olioll Oluim, or docked-of-an-ear.*

Olioll had nine sons. Of these, Eoghan, the eldest, and six of his brothers were killed in a battle fought against their half-brother Mac Con, the son of Sabia's former husband, "nursed on the same knee as Eoghan, and at the same breast." Mac Con appears to have been a delicate, peevish child, and, when nothing else would pacify him, those under whose care he was brought the boy to Olioll's favourite wolf-hound, who was so tender and fond of children that young Mac Con and the hound became fast friends, so much so that he received the name of Mac Con (son of a hound). When Mac Con had grown to manhood he was entrusted with certain duties by his stepfather, and, having failed in his trust, he was banished by the king from Munster. He sought refuge with the King of Scotland without revealing his name and position, and was received on friendly terms. One day some Irishmen arrived in the Scotch king's presence while he and Mac Con were engaged in a game of chess; Mac Con questioned the strangers as to the state of affairs in Ireland, and then turned the conversation to that of his own family in Munster. "Oh!" said the strangers, "with them nothing goes well; they are under the bondage of women;" upon hearing this remark, Mac Con seized some of the heavy chessmen he was playing with and flung them at the strangers. "A fit of affection," exclaimed the King of Scotland; "it is evident to whom you belong." Mac Con then related his history to the king, and sought his help to regain his position in Ireland. The king accepted this obligation, and, having obtained help from Britain, they assembled "what there were of ships and galleys and barges in the coast of Britain and Saxonland, so that they filled the King of Scotland's ports." † The troops on board these vessels were placed under the command of Mac Con, and Beine, a Prince of Wales. The army landed in Ireland near the site of the present town of Galway. The monarch of Ireland, hearing of the invasion of his country, joined his forces with those of Olioll, King of

---

* "Silva Gadelica," by Standish Hayes O'Grady, p. 129.
† *Ibid* p. 352.

Munster, and the allies, led by Eoghan (Olioll's eldest son) and six of his brothers, marched to resist their step-brother Mac Con and his allies.* In the battle which ensued, not only was the monarch of Ireland slain, but also Eoghan and his brothers. So crushing a defeat was at once taken advantage of by Mac Con, who marched to Tara and caused himself to be proclaimed monarch of the country. He adopted the son of the former king, and this lad subsequently became the famous Cormac Mac-Art, to whose opinions reference is made in a former chapter (p. 47).

It was necessary to enter into the above details in order to understand the somewhat complicated system of succession to the throne of Munster. Olioll, before his death, appointed, with the consent of his tribe, one of his remaining sons, Cormac Cas, as his tanist. At the time Olioll made this arrangement he did not know that his eldest son had married the night before the battle in which he was killed, and that the result of this marriage was a son. So soon as Olioll was assured of this fact he revoked his former decision, and arranged that Cormac Cas should succeed him; but he decided that, as Eoghan had a son, he or his heirs must follow Cormac as King of Munster, the province being governed alternately by the family of Eoghan and then by the heirs of Cormac Cas, "without quarrel or dispute."† The descendants of Eoghan formed the tribe known as the Eoghanists, and the descendants of Cormac Cas the tribe of the Dalcasians.‡

Cormac Cas, therefore, son of Olioll Oluim, was, as Professor O'Curry remarks, " in a lineal descent the progenitor of the renowned tribe of Dalcas, which in the course of time subdivided into the O'Briens, Macnamaras, O'Carrolls, O'Gradys, and other septs. The Macnamaras were known also as the Sioll Aodha, Clan Cullen, Aodha and Cullen having been two famous chiefs of the sept."

Cormac Cas came to the throne of Munster A.D. 234, he married a daughter of the poet and warrior Ossian, who was in command of the Fenia of Ireland (p. 33), as his father and grandfather had been before

---

* We are told in this battle, fought at Mucramha, in Galway, that Mac Con, at the instigation of the Scotch, had deep pits dug in the field of battle, which were covered with hurdles and brambles. Before the fight the pits were filled with armed men, who, as soon as the Irish attacked, appeared in their midst from beneath the earth and produced great consternation among their enemies. Mac Con is also stated to have placed an " Albanach " and a " Briton " on either side of each Irishman he had impressed into his service to prevent the Irish from deserting.

† Keating's " History of Ireland " (O'Connor's edition, 1630), p. 234.

‡ O'Curry's " Manners and Customs of Early Irish," p. 387.

him. At this time the throne of Leinster was occupied by a king named Cormac, chief of the provincial King of Ireland. It appears to have been the custom for the ruler of Leinster, as monarch of the country, to summon the provincial kings and chiefs once every three years to a council at Tara, in order to regulate the affairs of the kingdom. On an occasion of this kind the King of Ulster determined to seize the sovereign power. Without warning he collected a large force and marched on Tara; Cormac was unprepared for this invasion, and had therefore to retire in haste from his capital. He then summoned a council of war, and inquired of his chief bard as to what steps it were best to adopt in existing circumstances. The bard replied: "O Cormac, unless that nearer to hand thou hast some battle-winning friend, then of Munster crave a champion, mighty hard-hitting, a lord that may relieve thee of all fear of enemies."* The king then consulted the chief Druid on the subject, and he concurred in the opinion expressed by the bard. So Cormac started off to the King of Munster, "the first of the Dalcasians," and at his hands received a hearty welcome. "The object for which we are come thither," the monarch said, "is to propitiate your good will," which, said the King of Munster, "thou shall right willingly have.' And so it was arranged that the forces of Munster should be placed at the disposal of Cormac, the Dalcasian chief, and his brother, Cian, being entrusted with the command of the forces. A desperate battle followed, in which the King of Ulster was slain, and Cormac restored to his throne, but the men of Munster suffered severely, Cian, their commander, the progenitor of the O'Carrolls of Ely, being killed. His son, named Tiege, was also wounded in this battle, and the surgical treatment which he received has already been described. Cormac Cas was wounded on the head, and for thirteen years, it is said, portions of his brain passed through the wound, but he continued to govern his province. Cormac Cas built himself a fort on the side of a hill, "in the midst of which was a sparkling translucent spring,† about which a royal house was constructed, and the king's couch so placed as to allow cold water being constantly poured over his head, which alone gave him relief from pain." In this place Cormac Cas died, he was buried in the hill where the remains of his father, Olioll, and his mother, Sabia, had already been laid.

From this history we can understand how the Dalcasians came into existence; they were a division of the original tribe, of which Olioll was

* "Silva Gadelica," by Standish Hayes O'Grady, pp. 359–68.
† *Ibid.*, p. 129.

head, into the Dal-cas, or sons of Cas, forming one branch, and the descendants of Eoghan the other branch. Of the Dalcasians, Keating, quoting from a very ancient Celtic work, remarks " this was a brave and martial tribe, and it was observed particularly of them that they always chose to be in the front of the attacking force when they entered an enemy's country, where they always distinguished themselves with signal courage ; and, when marching homewards, their place was to cover the army and to shield it from danger."* This passage was taken from the Psalter of Cashel, that is, from the official record kept at Tara, and revised by a council which assembled there every third year under the presidency of the king.

Mogh Corb, son of Cormac Cas, became King of Munster, A.D. 314; he reigned for twenty years. But, as before explained, the throne of Munster after Cormac's death was to pass to his nephew whose name was Fiachra. Some time before his decease Cormac Cas came to an arrangement with Fiachra to divide the Province of Munster, one part, to include what is now known as the counties of Kerry, Cork, and Waterford, were to form South Munster, and to be the patrimony of the Eoghanists. The other half of Munster, including the counties of Clare, Tipperary, and part of Limerick, were to form the Province of North Munster, or as it was called, Thomond, and was to form the patrimony of the Dalcasians. That part of Thomond, however, which was included in county Clare was claimed by the King of Connaught as belonging to his territories, and was inhabited by the Firbolgs or Iberian race. In the early days of their existence the Dalcasians were unable to occupy this portion of North Munster as they were not suffi- ciently strong to conquer the territory assigned to them from the people who occupied the land.†

Fiachra belonged to the Eoghanists, and it is unnecessary to refer to his history, but the legend connected with his birth is so remarkable that it is well to give it. We are told that Eoghan, the eldest son of Olioll, on his march with the forces of Munster to oppose his step- brother Mac Con, stopped, the night before the battle of Mucramha, at the house of a blind Druid called Dill. Eoghan demanded Dill's daughter Moncha in marriage, she was her father's charioteeress. The Druid predicted Eoghan's death on the following day but never- theless sanctioned his daughter's marriage with him, the result of which was a son, Fiachra as he was called, signifying a man of sorrows, " seeing that on the morrow of the day he was begotten his father

* Keating's " History of Ireland," p. 445.
† O'Curry's " Lectures," p. 209.

was slain, and that his mother perished on the day that he was born." * He was also called Broad-crown † for the following reason : Eoghan's widow, Moncha, being in labour, her father Dill told her that if the child were born on that day he must be a failure ; but if his birth were postponed twenty-four hours he would rule Ireland. " True it is," Moncha answered, " and for the sake of my child his birth shall be delayed." Whereupon she entered the river Sur and bestrode a stone in the mid-stream ; " maintain thou me," she cried to the rock, and to the hour of tierce upon the morrow," there she held fast. " It is time," her father said, upon which she loosed her hold of the rock and reached the bank of the stream, her child was born, but his mother fainted and died. The infant's head was flattened against the stone, whence the name " Muillethan, or broad crown, was imposed on him." ‡

To return, however, to Mogh Corb, son of Cormac Cas, who, after the death of his cousin Fiachra, came to the throne of Munster. His mother was the daughter of the commander of the Fenia, and her brother Oscar had filled the office of foster-father to Mogh Corb. After being elected King of Munster a quarrel broke out between Mogh Corb and the reigning monarch of Ireland ; the Fenia were at this time in revolt, and joined the King of Munster against the monarch, who in the engagement that followed was killed.§ Mogh Corb governed Munster for twenty years, and died A.D. 334 ; he left a son called Fercorb, and he a son Angus (Tireach, or the land grabber ‖), a name probably derived from the conquest which he initiated of that part of Thomond now known as county Clare.

Lughaid Menn was a son of Angus, and it was reserved to him to drive the King of Connaught out of Clare and to subjugate the Firbolgs who occupied that part of the country. Lughaid, therefore, was the first of the Dalcasian princes who was able to take full possession of Thomond, or North Munster, including Clare.

We are able to ascertain pretty accurately the date of this conquest of Clare by reference made to it in the " Death of Crimthan, King of Ireland."¶ From Mr. O'Grady's translation of this Celtic MS. we learn that, in Crimthan's reign, there was a great war, " and for a lengthened

---

* " Silva Gadelica," p. 354.   † In Celtic, " muillethan."
‡ " Silva Gadelica," p. 355.
§ See O'Curry's "Manners and Customs of Ancient Irish," vol. ii. p. 387, for account of battle of Gabhra.
‖ " Silva Gadelica," p. 378, also 174 ; O'Curry's " Lectures," p. 209.
¶ " Silva Gadelica," by Standish H. O'Grady, p. 377.

space of time, carried on by the Dalcasians of Munster to win the soil on which to this day they are still planted in Thomond ; and this matter was the efficient cause of all the future fighting between the Dalcasians of Clare and the King of Connaught"; the latter held this territory as part of his province. From the MS. above referred to, we learn that "Lughaid-menn was the first that violently grasped this part of Thomond," for which reason he is called Lughaid ; he is said to have made Clare "sword lands," or, in other words, lands taken and held by the sword. The historian adds, "the country which the Dalcasians acquired was taken by force ; not because they had any title to it ; it belonged by right to the province of Connaught."

Crimthan was foster-father to Connal, son of Lughaid, and died in A.D. 378.* At the time of the king's death, Lughaid seems still to have been engaged in military operations in Clare, so we may assume that this part of Thomond did not come into the possession of the Dalcasians until the close of the fourth or the early part of the fifth century.

Crimthan, King of Ireland, belonged to the Eoghanite division of Olioll's sons ; he was sixth in descent from Olioll, as also was Lughaid on the Dalcasian side of the family. Crimthan came to the throne of Ireland in consequence of his nephew, the rightful heir, being at the time too young to fill that office ; he was an intrepid soldier, and carried the Irish arms not only into Scotland and Britain, but also into the heart of France, and from all these he took hostages and great booty.† He left no children, and the succession to the throne was an open question, a fact which his sister hoped to turn to the advantage of her own son ; and to compass this end she determined to poison her brother, though "it should cost her her own life in doing so." Crimthan was invited to Connaught by his sister, and while there she poisoned his wine ; having first drunk some of this wine, she passed the cup to her brother. The king subsequently feeling that he had been poisoned, and his sister soon afterwards having died, he started for his home in Munster, but only reached Cratlow in the south of Clare, where he died in the year A.D. 378 ;‡ his success in arms and tragic death made a deep impression on the minds of his countrymen, so there can be no mistake as to the date of his decease.

* O'Curry's "Lectures," p. 498 ; see also the "Annals of the Four Masters" for the above date.

† "Psalter of Cashel," quoted by Keating in his "History of Ireland, O'Connor's edition, p. 295 ; also O'Mahoney's edition, p. 37.

‡ "Silva Gadelica," p. 375.

E

Connal being a foster-son of the monarch Crimthan, from his boyhood lived under his care ;* and the king became so much attached to him that when the lad grew to manhood Crimthan offered to assist him to gain possession of the throne of Munster. The men of that province, however, objected to this arrangement, or to accept a nominee of the monarch of Ireland as their king; they represented to Connal that he would thus be put into possession of that which did not belong to him; for although he was their kinsman, yet he had no claim to the throne which should as a matter of right pass to Corc, a wise and brave prince. Connal agreed to submit the question to arbitration, and the case being decided against him he resigned all claim to the throne of Munster and betook himself to govern his own tribe, the Dalcasians of Thomond. Crimthan had such implicit confidence in Connal that he handed over to his care the many hostages he had taken, because, we are told, he felt that he could "rely on the integrity of a prince who delivered up the possession of a crown that he was able to defend, for no other reason but because he had no right to it." In a poem contained in the "Psalter of Cashel," referring to Crimthan, it is said that :—

> Numerous captives he in triumph led
> And hostages, the bonds of true submission,
> These pledges and the prisoners of his wars
> He trusted in the hands of the brave Connal :
> Than whom a prince of more integrity
> And stricter justice never wore a crown ;
> This prince for arms and martial skill renowned,
> Enlarged the bounds of his command, and ruled
> With equity the countries he had won.

Probably this record is the earliest we possess as to the character of one of the immediate ancestors of the Macnamara sept. The poem refers to the conquest which Connal's father effected of a portion of the present counties of Clare and Tipperary. As Crimthan commenced his reign in A.D. 366, we may suppose he was then about five-and-twenty years of age. Connal, his foster-son, would hardly have been less than five years old at this time; probably he was seven years of age; and if he lived to be sixty years old he would have died about A.D. 419, at which time the Dalcasians were in full possession of Thomond.

We have, therefore, evidence from more than one source which agree in that Olioll Oluim died A.D. 234, his son Cormac Cas died A.D. 274,

* O'Curry's "Manners and Customs," vol. ii. p. 375.

and his son Morgh Corb in 334. Morgh Corb left a son, Fircob, who died A.D. 364, and his son Angus in A.D. 383. Angus's son Lughaid died . . . . and his son Connal about the year A.D. 419.* So that we have, in a direct line from Olioll to Connal, six generations, which, on an average, lasted thirty-two years; and this is about the time which, in Professor O'Curry's opinion, is the period to allot to a generation according to the teaching of early Irish history. Of these six persons, four were kings of Munster; but under Olioll's scheme of succession the elder branch of his family came into possession of the largest and richest part of Munster; moreover, they had not to defend their territories from the frequent invasion of a powerful neighbour as the Dalcasians had on the part of Connaught. Taking advantage of the weakness thus caused to the inhabitants of Thomond, the elder branch of the family gradually possessed themselves of the throne of South Munster, and for many generations became the kings of that province to the exclusion of the Dalcasians, who, however, exercised supreme power over Thomond.

Connal's eldest son was named Cais or Cas, and on the death of his father he became chief of the Dalcasian tribe; he had twelve sons who were the progenitors of the various septs of the tribe; and their descendants formed the families constituting the Dalcasian septs. The territory of Thomond was allotted to the chief, and in part to the heads of septs in proportion to their importance; a part of the territory was given to free-clansmen for their homesteads; another part to maintain the poor, old, and infirm members of the tribe; and a part was retained as common land which every member of the tribe was entitled to use under certain provisions (see p. 19).

We must bear in mind that, after Lughaid and his followers had conquered Clare the country was still inhabited by a brave and industrious people, the descendants of the old Iberian race (chapter i.). Doubtless many of the Firbolgs were killed, and those who remained had their lands taken from them by their conquerors and were therefore reduced to the condition of serfs; but they were good agriculturists, and we have reason to think a harder working people than the Celts, who could have formed but a very small percentage of the population for a considerable period after they had taken possession of the country.† The upper classes of Celts held aloof from

---

* The date of O'Connal's death is given by Sir W. Bentham, Ulster King of Arms, in notes to a pedigree he drew up for the late Colonel F. D. Macnamara of Ayle, as having taken place A.D. 434.

† H. D'Arbois de Jubainville: "Revue Celtique," vol. xiv. No. 1.

intermarriage with conquered races, but living in contact with the Iberians intermarriages must have been of frequent occurrence; and so an Iberio-Celtic population grew up in Clare side by side with one of purely Celtic origin, precisely as in Spain we have a large Celtic-Iberian population covering the peninsula; and in the Basque mountains there exists to the present day an almost pure Iberian race of people.

CHAPTER VI

Cas, chief of Thomond, the progenitor of the Macnamara or Clancuilein Sept—Their history from A.D. 455 to close of ninth century—Their tribal lands in Central Clare known as Ui-Caisin—St. Patrick—Macnamaras as Marshals of Thomond—Inauguration of Kings of Thomond on Magh Adhair—Attack by King of Ireland on Magh Adhair—He is taken prisoner by Sioda Macnamara, A.D. 877—Lorcain's character—Prosperity of Ireland and invasion by the Danes—Turgesius—Esida Macnamara appointed leader against Sitric—Brian Boru, Chief of the Dalcasians and King of Ireland—Battle of Clontarf—The Macnamaras led by their Chief Menma, A.D. 1014—Death of Brian Boru—Attempt to oppose return of Dalcasians to Thomond.

In the previous chapter it was explained how the Dalcasian tribe originated from Cormac Cas, and came to occupy the territory now known as county Clare, and that before these people could obtain possession of Thomond they had to drive out the King of Connaught and to conquer its Firbolgs inhabitants.

Connal, the son of Lughaid, died about the year 419; he left a son named Cas who became Prince of Thomond, and chief of the Dalcais. Cas had twelve sons, and from the eldest came the family of the O'Briens.

Cas's second son was called Caisin, and from him were derived the sept of the Macnamaras, or *Clancuilein*. It was not, however, until long after the time of Cas that the monarch of Ireland, Brian Boru, gave surnames to the principal families of Ireland with the object of "avoiding confusion, and that their genealogies might be the better preserved." * The family name given to the members of Clancuilein was Mac-con-Mara, or Macnamara.† Until Brian's time men's names, as a rule, were derived from some peculiarity of their features, not unfrequently from some marked trait in their character, as already described in the case of Olioll Oluim.

* Keating's " History of Ireland," p. 499.

† O'Hart observes that Cu, gen. "con," signifies a warrior; "muir,' gen. mara, the sea. Mac, according to Sir J. Ware, signifies the same thing as Hi, Sioll, Clan, and so on. It signifies, therefore, the branch of a family. So Macnamara is the family of Conmara.

At the time Cas became chief of the Dalcasians the tribe had obtained complete possession of Thomond, and as his sons grew up the four eldest were assigned lands according to their priority; Caisin, the second son of Cas, had a portion of land assigned to him between the rivers Fergus and Shannon; it extended some seventeen Irish miles from north to south, and sixteen from east to west. This territory is marked on all the old maps of Ireland as " Ui-Caisin " or the tribal lands of Caisin.*

Caisin therefore was the immediate progenitor of the sept of Macnamaras, in the same way as Cormac Cas was of the tribe of Dalcasians; from the time of Cormac the office of chief of the tribe had passed in unbroken succession through seven generations from chief to tanist; Cas being the last of the seven. The territories conquered by Cas's father and grandfather were of sufficient extent to allow him to divide them among his sons as tribe lands; and in this way the area we know as county Clare came to be subdivided among the members of this Celtic tribe. As time went on the four eldest sons of Caisin migrated from their father's house and had lands assigned them within the boundaries of Ui-Caisin, under the provisions of the Brehon laws.†

On referring to the pedigree in chapter xix. of this volume it will be noticed that from Caisin to Sioda the names of eight chiefs are given who respectively held the office of head of the Clancuilein sept. During the three centuries in which these chiefs exercised authority over their sept we hear but little of Clare; for this part of Ireland seems to have enjoyed a period of peace and prosperity, which was only seriously broken by the invasion of the Danes in the ninth century.‡ But it is evident that throughout the time county Clare had no history, the chiefs of Clancuilein maintained their position as second in rank to

---

* " Ui-Caisin."—The name and exact extent of this territory is preserved in the Deanery of Og-askin, which comprises the parishes "of Qim, Tullagh, Cloony, Doora, Kilraghtis, Templemaley, Kilmurry-na-Gall, and Inchicronan." After A.D. 1318 Ui-Caisin included, in addition to the above parishes, those of Killaloe, Aglish, Killuran, Kilnoe, Killokennedy, Tulla, Moynoe, Kilseely, Feakle, Kilfinaghty, Iniscaltragh, Tomgraney; in short, the whole of Upper and Lower Tulla (Frost's. " History of Clare," p. 35). † See chaps. ii. and iii.

‡ Carthan, the grandson of Cas, is said to have been baptized by St. Patrick about the year A.D. 455 (see chap. iv.). In an appendix to this chapter will be found the franslation of a legend by Professor O'Curry, from which it appears that another of the sons of Cas was not only a famous Druid but also held a prominent position in Clare at the commencement of the fifth century (" Manners. and Customs of the Ancient Irish," by E. O. Curry, vol. ii. p. 220).

the head of the O'Briens, who were successively kings of Thomond : for in the year A.D. 847 we find the chief of our sept filling an important post as Marshal of the Province, it then fell to the lot of Sioda (Macnamara) to inaugurate the head of his tribe as King of North Munster, or Thomond. The office of Marshal, we are told, "was a highly honourable one and was hereditary," * and so far as the province of Thomond was concerned was held for many generations by the head of our sept.

The ceremony of inauguration took place at Magh Adhair, situated within the Ui-Caisin tribal lands, upon the mound under which the last of the Firbolg chiefs of Clare was buried ; from a drawing made by Mr. T. J. Westropp, the existing appearance of this mound is clearly shown.† On the day of inauguration the heads of the various Dalcasian septs assembled around Magh Adhair ; the king-elect, his chief bard, and the head of the Macnamara sept then ascended the mound, the king-elect stood on a stone placed near its centre; his bard then recited certain laws which the chief promised to obey. The chief of Clancuilein then handed the king-elect a straight white wand, a symbol of authority and an emblem of what his conduct should be, straight and without stain ; the king promised to maintain the prestige and the customs of his tribe ; and having put aside his sword and other weapons, and holding the wand in his hand he moved round the stone so as to view his territory from all sides, which he promised to protect from invasion; the Marshal then in a loud voice proclaimed the chief's surname and declared him to be King of Thomond. Edmund Spenser states that the tanist was elected to office in the same manner as the chief, but only placed one foot upon the stone and then took the same oath as his captain.‡ It is stated in the "black book of Christ Church, Dublin," that the kings of Ireland were neither ordained nor anointed, but were kings by election and by the right of arms. §

In the year A.D. 847, a chief named Lachtna ruled over Thomond, and an individual called Flan was at the time king and also abbot and

---

* Joyce's " Short History of Ireland," p. 63.

† Mr. Westropp states that Magh Adhair " consists of a large, flat-topped mound, 20 feet high, surrounded by a low fosse, across which, to the west, leads an inclined way eight paces long (shown in the sketch) ; to the north side of the platform is a grave-like hollow lying east and west, while near the centre is a rough and weather-worn stone nearly level with the ground." See further account by Mr. Westropp: "Journal of the Royal Society of Antiquaries of Ireland " (second quarter of 1891), p. 463.

‡ " A View of the State of Ireland," by Edmund Spenser, p. 11.

§ Sir J. Davies (p. 14) and Edmund Spenser (p. 11).

bishop of South Munster.* Unmindful of the fact that the Dalcais were exempt from paying tribute either to the monarch of Ireland or to Munster, Flan nevertheless demanded payment and submission from Lachtna, which was refused, whereupon Phelim marched an army against Thomond and encamped on the eastern bank of the Shannon. Lachtna desired peace and assembled his chiefs, including Maolchuite, who at that period was the head of Clancuilein; they determined to resist the demand for tribute, and against the advice of their king wished to resort to arms in defence of their rights. Thereupon, Lachtna disguised himself and proceeding to Flan's camp he obtained an audience with the King of Munster, and came to an amicable agreement with him; the chief of Thomond then returned home; but in the meantime Phelim's mind had been poisoned by a sage he had consulted on the subject of the negotiations which he had been engaged in, and having been persuaded to distrust Lachtna he sent off a messenger in hot haste to recall that chief to his camp. On receiving this message Lachtna at once retraced his steps, "and when Flan saw his good faith he felt full confidence in the chief of Thomond, and as a token of regard gave him his own steed and robes." Flan, we are told, also gave his blessing to Lachtna, which, as Mr. T. J. Westropp observes, could hardly have been accounted of much importance, as this king and bishop had just previously attacked and robbed the churches of Clonmacnoise, Armagh, Durrow, and Kildare,† and put their clergy to the sword.

Lachtna was succeeded by his son Lorcain as King of Thomond; this chief was foster-son to, and tanist of Cormac McCullinan, who at the time was King of South Munster and Archbishop of Cashel. Cormac visited Lorcain, and amongst other good advice is said to have "impressed upon him the importance of religious education for children." Flan was at this period "Monarch of Ireland, and having demanded tribute from the Dalcais, which they again refused, he invaded Thomond and entered the Ui-Caisins' territory, A.D. 877. The monarch's bard, McLonain, warned him to be careful not to insult the Dalcasians": Flan, however, marched into Clare and pitched his camp on the sacred mound of Magh Adhair, and having challenged one of his followers to chess they sat down to the game, which he was hardly allowed time to finish, for Sioda Macnamara

* "Ireland and the Celtic Church," p. 199, by G. G. T. Stokes, D.D., Professor of Ecclesiastical History at the University of Dublin.

† "The Journal of the Royal Society of Antiquaries of Ireland," vol. ii. p. 400, part iv. 5th series; "Killaloe and its Ancient Palaces," by T. J. Westropp, M.A.

chief of Clancuilein, followed by Lorcain with a strong force, attacked Flan ; the king, however, escaped with some of his followers into the neighbouring forests ; but after three days' fighting he had to surrender to Lorcain and Sioda (Macnamara), who treated Flan courteously, fed his followers abundantly, and then escorted him on his way homewards across the Shannon.* After treatment of this kind it is no wonder that Flan's poet, McLonain, wrote in praise of the Dalcasians; a prose version of this poem will be found at the end of the chapter, and Professor O'Curry considers it as being authentic, among other reasons, because McLonain pays a particular compliment to Sioda-an-Eich-Bhuidh (that is, Sioda of the bay steed), the chief of Clancuilein, and to his son Esidia, who was young at this time ; they were two well-known personages in our sept, about the date of the poet's death, which took place in the year A.D. 918.†

Mr. Westropp refers to a trait in Lorcain's character which is worth preserving. As already remarked, the King of South Munster had made Lorcain his tanist, and the two were evidently on the most friendly terms. Upon a certain occasion, however, Lorcain proceeded to Cashel to visit his friend, but on arriving there he declined to enter the place until the king sent him a formal invitation to come and see him. It is by casual reference to incidents of this kind that we obtain a peep into the character of some of these early Celtic chiefs.‡

The historian, Keating, informs us that on a certain occasion Cormac MacCullinan had determined to hold a great feast at Cashel, and he sent messages to his chiefs to provide the necessary contributions, but they declined to comply with his request, "although many of them were near of kin to the king." The Dalcais hearing this " prepared with all possible speed what provisions were necessary, together with horses, equipages, arms, and jewels, and sent them to the

* T. J. Westropp: " On Killaloe " (" Journal of the Royal Society of Antiquaries of Ireland," vol. ii. p. 401, part iv. 5th series).

† Professor E. O'Curry: " Manners and Customs of the Ancient Irish," vol. ii. p. 101.

‡ Matthew Arnold remarks that Irishmen are distinguished by an " organism quick to feel impressions, and feeling them strongly; a lively personality, therefore, keenly sensitive to joy and sorrow. Quick and strong perception and emotions are to the soul what the senses are to the body; it means genius. But sensitive-ness must not be allowed with impunity to master the mind; balance, measure, and patience, are necessary, and these the Celt does not possess. He is ever chafing against the despotism of facts, straining under the effects of emotion; eager to enlist in the fray, but ' always to fall.' "

King of Munster.* Cormac received these presents with sincere gratitude which he expressed in verse.†

Keating, writing of this period, observes that the great prosperity of the people of Ireland towards the close of the eighth century led many of them to adopt " corrupt manners, vice, and profaneness—principally among the landowners "—from which they were suddenly roused by the cruel hand of the Danes.

The two first expeditions which the Danes made into the west of Ireland, took place in A.D. 795 and 801, and were both repulsed by the Irish.‡ But from 812 to 835 a vast number of Scandinavians flocked into Ireland, pillaging the churches and committing every conceivable cruelty on the inhabitants of the country.§ At this period, and for some time previously there had been incessant fighting among the ecclesiastics of Armagh for the office of Abbot ; the inhabitants of this monastery, of Clonmacnois, and Durrow, were also frequently at war with one another. Turgesius, the leader of the Norsemen, made short work of these ecclesiastics, for he drove them out of their establishments ; and we are told that the Abbot of Armagh fled, taking with him the shrine of St. Patrick to a district in Thomond east of the Shannon, which was inhabited by the Martini, a Firbolg tribe, who lived as a separate people under their own chief at Emly, county Tipperary, as late as the ninth century.

Turgesius was the acknowledged King of the North of Ireland, he hoped to establish a strong government and so to overcome the discord and anarchy which existed in the country ; he also desired to banish

---

* Keating's " History of Ireland," p. 449 (O'Connor's edition).

> † " May heaven protect the most illustrious tribe
> Of Dailgais, and convey its choicest blessings
> On their posterity. This renowned Clan,
> Tho' meek and merciful as are the Saints,
> Yet are of courage not to be subdued.
> Long may they live in glory and renown,
> And raise a stock of heroes for the world."

Archbishop Cormac MacCullen, King of Munster, was killed fighting against the forces of Leinster and Connaught, A.D. 908 ; he was driven to this action by the warlike Abbot of Scattery. Cormac was the author of the famous " Glossary," and was evidently a learned man ; and with his death the best period of Irish history passed away, for the country was soon after overrun by the Danes and subsequently by the English.

‡ We learn from Eginhard, Charlemagne's tutor, that " the fleet of Northmen arrived at Hibernia. After a battle had been fought, and no small number of the Norsemen slain, they basely took to flight and returned home."

§ Introduction to the " Wars of the Gaedhil with the Gail," p. xlv.

Christianity from Ireland; and he placed his wife to rule over Clonmac-nois: we are told that she was accustomed to preside at the high altar of the principal church of the monastery, and work the oracles of her religion from that position.* In the year A.D. 879 the Irish rose against Turgesius, and having killed him drove most of his followers out of Erin.†

The invaders soon returned in greater numbers than before, and over-ran the whole country. Kennedy, son of Lorcain, was at this time King of Thomond, and Ceallachan King of Munster. The Norsemen were anxious to obtain possession of these chiefs; but rather than attack Munster they hoped to entice Ceallachan to Dublin under false pretences, and then make him prisoner. Sitric therefore, who was leader of the Norsemen, entered into negotiations with the king of Munster proposing to give him his sister in marriage. Kennedy, King of Thomond, hearing what was going on and suspecting treachery, warned Ceallachan of the danger of leaving his province, and especially of withdrawing from it any large body of followers to swell his train in Dublin. Ceallachan therefore set out with a few retainers to bring his intended wife home, and among this force was Kennedy's son, Dun-chan. The cavalcade had nearly reached Dublin, when they were attacked by Sitric's soldiers and made prisoners. Directly Kennedy heard of this treachery, he assumed command of the forces of Munster as well as those of Thomond to revenge the insult offered to Cealla-chan and, if possible, to release him and also his own son from the hands of the Danes. Keating records the fact that " Kennedy resolved to prosecute his designs with the greatest despatch, and he raised in addition to his other forces a body of five hundred Dalcasians, and placed them under command of Esida (Macnamara), chief of Clancuilein." ‡

Everything being ready, and a fleet having started from Limerick for Dundalk, to which place Sitric had removed his prisoners, the army of Thomond marched for that port. On the approach of the Irish forces, Sitric took the prisoners on board his vessels which lay in the bay of Dundalk, so that when the Irish arrived they could do no more than stand on the shore and curse their enemies. Before long, however, they saw their own fleet, which had been sent from the Shannon enter-ing the harbour, and the Irish vessels at once closed with the Norsemen. The commander of the Irish ran his ship alongside that of Sitric's and

---

* Introduction to the " Wars of the Gaedhil with the Gail," p. xlviii.
† Keating's " History of Ireland," p. 440.
‡ *Ibid.* p. 470, O'Connor's edition; p. 539, O'Mahoney's edition.

boarded her sword in hand. He then endeavoured to force his way to the mast of the vessel, to which Ceallachan and Kennedy's son were bound; but he was slain. One of his followers, however, seized Sitric round the body and jumped overboard with him; they were both drowned. On realising what had occurred, the Norsemen became disheartened; Ceallachan and Dunchan were released, and arrived safely among their friends on shore.*

Ceallachan was succeeded by Mahon, son of Kennedy the Dalcasian chief of Thomond.

The west of Ireland, from the year A.D. 890, was overrun with Norsemen, who, we are informed, occupied the homes of the Irish, so that the owners had not even power to "give milk or eggs to a sick or infirm man; the foreigners claimed the right over everything." The Norsemen were far better armed than the native Irish, who at the time were utterly unable to withstand them.† It was in circumstances of this kind that Mahon and his brother Brian, the sons of Kennedy appeared on the scene. From its geographical position, and in consequence of the dense woods which covered its hills and plains, Clare was not so completely occupied by the Norsemen as other parts of Ireland. At any rate, from the account given in the wars of the Gaedhil with the Gail, we learn that Mahon and Brian, with the greater part of the Dalcasians living to the east and south of the Shannon crossed the river into Clare so as to escape from the invaders of their country; and they " dispersed themselves among the forests and woods situated between Loch Durge and the Fergus," or, in other words, over the Macnamara territories; from this locality the Irish proceeded to sally forth and kill all the foreigners they could lay their hands on. The effect of these tactics were to compel the Norsemen to concentrate their forces on the Shannon, where they built a fort in the district of Tradraighe, which at that time belonged to our sept and was subsequently the site of the Anglo-Norman castle of Bunratty. In these operations Brian Boru's forces suffered fearfully from constant fighting and want of food; and

* General Vallaney and some other authorities question the truth of this incident, but it is not only vouched for by Keating, who had exceptional opportunities for studying all that relates to the history of Munster, but the details he has given bear internal evidence of truth. For instance, MacLonain refers to Sioda and his son Esida in a poem I have quoted; and O'Curry states Esida about the year 918 was quite young. Consequently, we can easily understand how Kennedy might have chosen him in 954 to command a contingent of the Dalcasians in the army sent to release his son and the King of Munster from the Norsemen.

† " Wars of the Gaedhil with the Gail," p. 47.

Mahon, hearing of his brother's desperate condition sent for him, and at a meeting which took place between them Mahon argued in favour of submission to the Norsemen, for he had given up all hope of returning to govern in Cashel. From the old Celtic records we learn that Brian expressed great indignation at sentiments of this kind and even accused his brother of cowardice; he taunted Mahon by asking him if he thought their father or grandfather would have made peace while an enemy occupied Ireland. Mahon admitted all this, but argued that if they had not the power to resist the invader it was useless holding out against the foe; he asked Brian if he wished to see the whole of his tribe in the same state as his own followers. To this Brian replied "that such an argument was bad, because it was hereditary for him to die, and for the whole of the Dalcais likewise; as their fathers had passed away so must they; but it was not natural or hereditary for the Dalcais to submit to insult or contempt; their forefathers had never submitted to this, and no power on earth would make him do so."* The tribe on hearing this assembled to resist the invaders, and met them at Sulcoit in Tipperary. In this battle the Norsemen were defeated and fled to Limerick, which town Brian took, and destroyed its fortifications, inflicting great loss and injury on the enemy, A.D. 968.† This victory added so much to the prestige of the Dalcasians, that their rivals the Eoghanites grew jealous of them, and at the instigation of Malloy, chief of Desmond, they treacherously murdered Mahon, A.D. 976. Brian Boru was not slow to avenge his brother's death; he first sent a challenge to Malloy to meet him in single combat, and directed his messenger to add, that nothing short of the death of one of them would suffice. Receiving no satisfactory answer, Brian marched his forces into South Munster, and met Malloy; a battle ensued, in which the latter chief was killed by one of Brian's sons.

From the "Annals of Innisfallen" we learn that, in the year A.D. 977, Brian Boru, assisted by Aodh (Macnamara), chief of Clancuilein, stormed the island of Scattery, driving the Danes, who had found refuge there, to their ships, and completely clearing the district of Thomond of their enemies.

Brian Boru ‡ was now proclaimed King of Munster, but Malachy, who

* " Wars of the Gaedhil with the Gail,'" p. 61.

† " Annals of Innisfallen " (MS. British Museum).

‡ Brian received the name Boru or Boroimhe because he revived the payment of the tribute or tax known as the " Boromean Tribute " in former times, and which had been abolished since A.D. 680 (O'Curry's " Manners and Customs of the Ancient Irish," p. 231.

at the time was the King of Leinster, seeing the rising power of Brian, determined to demonstrate his own supremacy as monarch of the country; he therefore marched an army into Clare and pitched his camp on Magh Adhair; he uprooted the sacred oak-tree which grew on this mound * (A.D. 982). We can readily understand the indignation among the Dalcais produced by this act, for among other things the ceremony of inauguration of the King of Thomond on Magh Adhair demonstrated the fact, that the tribe had a right to elect their own king. It was therefore incumbent on Brian to retaliate on Malachy; after continued fighting it was determined by these chiefs to divide the sovereignty of Thomond; but constant feuds sprang up between the rival kings, and in the end Malachy solicited and obtained the help of the Danes of Dublin. The combined forces, Irish and Danish, met those under Brian Boru at a place called Glenmana; in the battle which ensued Brian was victorious; he then sacked Dublin, carrying off to his home at Kincora (Killaloe) a vast quantity of treasure.

Brian Boru now determined to rule Ireland; and Malachy ultimately went to his camp and submitted to him as being the more powerful of the two. Malachy retained his position, however, as King of Leinster, but Brian Boru, the Dalcasian chief, was acknowledged as supreme ruler over the whole country (A.D. 1002); the other provincial kings paying him tribute. Brian received tribute also from the Danes of Dublin in the form of one hundred and fifty butts of wine; from the inhabitants of Limerick a tun of wine per diem: he received a vast number of cattle from every part of the country; for instance, the chiefs of Burren and Corcomroe sent tribute of 2000 cattle and 1000 sheep; and so with other parts of Ireland. The order of the various kings and chiefs at Brian's table has come down to us and was scrupulously followed; behind the seat of each chief his arms were suspended.† The tables, we are told, were covered with gold-mounted cups; the food consisted of beef, mutton, pork, game, fish, oat-cakes, cheese, curds, onions, and watercress; wine, beer, and mead, together with the bilberry-juice, constituted their drink. The meat appears to have been cooked in the dining-hall.‡

Brian Boru in the year 1004 made a circuit through the whole of Ireland; and while at Armagh he confirmed its bishop as metropolitan of the country; the record of this fact, written by O'Carroll, Brian Boru's former tutor and

* " Annals of Innisfallen," and " Annals of the Four Masters."
† O'Curry : " Manners and Customs of the Ancient Irish," vol. ii. p. 127.
‡ " Killaloe," by T. J. Westropp (" Journal of the Royal Society of Antiquaries of Ireland," 1892, p. 404.

subsequent chief adviser,* was made in the presence of the king, and still exists in a copy of the Scriptures preserved in the Library of the Royal Irish Academy ; before leaving Armagh Brian laid twenty ounces of gold as an offering on the altar of St. Patrick.

After forty years of more or less strife Brian Boru at length found himself so securely seated on the throne of Ireland that he was able to turn his attention to developing the resources of the country. Kincora became its capital; its chief buildings being near the Clare side of the Shannon, at the head of the wooden bridge which then crossed the river. The houses were built of timber and clay and extended along the river bank for some distance ; near the river there were two churches, the one stone-roofed, which still exists to the north of the cathedral. On the summit of the hill above the bridge stood the palace surrounded by numerous buildings, which was the chief place of residence of Brian Boru and his descendants for many years. Brian's rest and Ireland's peace, however, did not long continue ; for political purposes he thought it wise to make an alliance with the Danes, hoping in this way to promote the harmony of the contending influences under his rule ; he therefore married the mother of Sitric, the leader of the Danes of Dublin ; this individual, whose name was Gormflaith, had previously married, first Sitric's father, and then the King of Leinster ; they both became weary of Gormflaith and turned her off, she then fell to the lot of Brian ; he also soon cast off his spouse but permitted her to remain in the palace at Kincora. To this place her brother Mailmoda came bringing with him a present for Brian, consisting of three masts for his ships ; these were carried on men's shoulders, and in crossing a bog the bearers came to grief, whereupon Mailmoda applied his own shoulder to the work, and in doing so tore off one of the silver buttons of his "gold-braided silken tunic," which had been presented to him on a former occasion by Brian. On the arrival of Mailmoda at Kincora he went to his sister Gormflaith and asked her to replace this button ; but she snatched the garment from his hands and threw it into the fire, reproaching him for wearing a garment which was a token of submission to Brian Boru. Mailmoda while stinging under this taunt happened to see Morrogh, Brian's son, playing at chess with another chief ; he suggested a move which lost Morrogh the game ; irritated by this, Morrogh turned on Mailmoda and remarked " that, like the advice you gave your friend at Glenmama, it lost the battle." Mailmoda replied, " I will give them advice now, and they will not be defeated a second time." To which Morrogh replied, " Have a yew-tree ready on that

* O'Curry : " Manners and Customs of the Ancient Irish," vol. ii. p. 177.

occasion." After the battle above referred to Mailmoda had been discovered hiding among the branches of a yew-tree. Mailmoda left Kincora next morning in great anger and made his way to Dublin; he was followed by his sister, who incited the Danes to revolt, and they were joined by a considerable force of the natives of Ireland and their countrymen from the Isle of Man, Britain, and Wales; Canute, King of England, was only too ready to help in the struggle hoping to establish his countrymen in Ireland as he had done in England. Sitric took command of the confederate forces.

Brian Boru, although in his seventy-third year of age was still vigorous enough to make the necessary arrangements to meet his enemies; and he determined to stake his cause and that of his country on the issue of the impending battle; Brian, however, felt it was beyond his power to do more than collect and take his army into the field; for a commander in those days had not only to lead his men, but also to fight hand to hand in the thick of the battle,* especially at weak points; Brian therefore wisely left the command of his army in the hands of his son Morrogh.

Every man of Brian's family marched with his army, among them his grandson Turlough, a youth of some sixteen years of age who was his father's standard-bearer.

These leaders were surrounded by Dalcasians; among them, Keating tells us, there marched with Brian to Clontarf "the children of Cas, son of Connal of the fleet steed; the Clancuileins (Macnamaras); around Menma, son of Aeodh, son of Endu, son of Esida, son of Sioda, son of Maelehuthier."† Keating, with his usual precision, identifies the leader of Clancuilein so that there can be no mistake about him, and on referring to the family pedigree we find that Menma was chief of the sept about the year 1014, when the battle of Clontarf was fought. From the "Annals of the Four Masters" we learn that "Menma, Lord of Ui-Caisin, died A.D. 1015, so that he was one of the few Dalcasian chiefs who survived the battle of Clontarf.

On the morning of Good Friday, April 23, 1014, the Irish army took up their position on the field of battle; they consisted of the Dalcasians in the van, led by Morrogh, the centre composed of the men of South Munster, and the rear by those of Connaught. The Danes under Sitric

---

* We are told that the night before the battle Aibhell, the banshee of the O'Briens, came to the king and told him he would die on the following day ("Wars of the Gaedhil with the Gail").

† Keating's "History of Ireland": O'Connor's edition, p. 506; O'Mahoney's edition, p. 572.

and their Irish allies formed a line extending along the shore of Clontarf with their backs to the sea.   Many of the Danes were clad in armour, but the Irish were dressed in their linen tunics and armed with their usual weapons—spear, sword, and axe.   No horsemen were engaged on either side, and each army numbered about 20,000 men.   There seems to have been no attempt at tactics, every man fought for himself, the rear taking the place of those in front who were killed.   The first to meet were the Dalcasians and the Danes, and so from early morning to sunset the battle was carried on without interruption.   Towards evening the Irish made a final effort and carried all before them, the Danes were completely vanquished, and with their allies fled from the field of battle.

The old monarch, Brian Boru, although unable to lead his army, watched its movements from a distance throughout the day.   We are told that his attention was constantly fixed on the standard of his son Morrogh, for so long as he saw it carried aloft he felt sure that all was well with the Irish.   Towards evening Morrogh's banner disappeared; at first Brian tried to persuade himself that it was his faulty sight and anxious watching that prevented him from recognising his son's standard, but when the truth came home to him the old man's grief was extreme, he could no longer watch the contest, but went into the tent his attendants had prepared for him, to give vent to his sorrow in secret. It is stated that his attendants urged him to retire from the scene, but Brian replied, "Retreat becomes us not, and I know that I shall not leave this place alive, for Aoibhel of Cragliath appeared to me last night and told me that I should be killed this day."   Soon after this the Danes fled in all directions, and Brian's servants seeing this left the old king and joined their comrades in pursuit of their enemies.   The king was thus alone, and at this moment a party of fugitive Danes came upon his tent; Brian was recognised, and though he did his best to defend himself the old man was soon overpowered and killed.*

Morrogh after fighting throughout the whole of the day, towards the evening found his hands so swollen that he was unable any longer to grasp his sword; when in this condition he was attacked by a Dane, and the two closed with each other.   Morrogh is said by main force to have pulled the armour off his antagonist, and then to have felled him

---

* The account of the battle of Clontarf, as given in the "Icelandic Sagas" (vol. iii., translated by Sir G. W. Dasent), is as follows : " When the Earl Segard came to Ireland he and King Sigtryg marched with that host to meet Brian the King of Ireland, and their meeting was on Good Friday.   Then it fell out that there was no one left to bear the raven banner, and the earl bore it himself and fell there, but King Sigtryg fled.   King Brian fell, with victory and glory."

F

to the ground ; the Dane at this moment drew his dagger and inflicted a wound in Morrogh's side from which he died on the following day.

Young Turlogh O'Brien fought by his father with great vigour, and after Morrogh was wounded Turlough seems to have pursued a Dane who rushed before him into the river, where the lad's body was found, his hands entangled in the long hair of his enemy.

There is reason to believe that not less than a quarter of the Irish army were left dead on the field of Clontarf, and among their number were included very many Dalcasian and other chiefs. The result of this action, however, was the complete annihilation of the power of the Danes in Ireland, a power they never again attempted to regain.

Donogh O'Brien, another son of Brian Boru, who previous to the battle of Clontarf had been directed by his father to proceed with a body of troops into Leinster, returned after the battle and took command of the remnant of the Dalcasians. Wounded and worn, these men were not to be allowed to return home in peace, for the King of Ossory, having a grudge against the Dalcais, refused to permit them to cross his territory. Donogh determined, nevertheless, to march on into Thomond, and drew up his men to resist those of Ossory. He directed the wounded to be sent to the rear, but they begged to be allowed to die fighting with their comrades. So weak were many of these Dalcasians that they were unable to stand without support ; Donogh, therefore, had stakes driven into the ground, against which his wounded warriors might lean for support, and, with a sound man on each side of a wounded one, they stood prepared to receive their enemies. We are told that the King of Ossory when he learnt what was taking place in the Dalcasian camp, thought it imprudent to further resist men of this stamp, and so the Dalcasians were allowed to pass on into their own territory. As already stated, there is every reason to believe that Menma (Macnamara), who had survived the battle of Clontarf, was one of the chiefs with Donogh O'Brien on this memorable occasion.*

PROSE VERSION OF MAC LONAIN'S POEM (A.D. 877).†

Lorcain of Loch Derg, in whom there is no shadow of deceit, generous and hospitable to all.

Flan (King of Ireland) said, "Fortunate it is Mac Lonain that thou hast arrived ; reach me the chessboard." Flan, with warlike purpose, had come to Magh Adhair:

---

* Keating's " History of Ireland " (translated by O'Mahoney), p. 581.

† See p. 27. Dr. Douglas Hyde informs me that this poem is written in the Deibhidh metre, which was the official metre of the Irish bards. The Gaelic text at my command is imperfect, and it seems, therefore, better to attempt to translate it into English prose, rather than into the metre in which Mac Lonain wrote.

on the fertile plain he had arrived. I forthwith despatched my foster son to Lachtna's son, and to his heroes, rehearsing to them our demands and conditions of peace. They, in reply, despatched their cavalry, so great was their number that earth trembled, and the clouds of heaven reverberated with their shouts, and their greatness. Our followers fled, there was not one of all the horses of our cavalry left on the fair plains of Adhair.

Sioda * of the bay steed took two hundred horses per man, we thought it a hard case, that he, single-handed, took all from us; he surrounded us from the south, and did us much mischief. He came round us from the north and set us trembling so that our forces gave way.

Flan from Tara's halls, the king of banquets, said, "O Mac Lonain for friendship's sake claim from Sioda his bay steed." Forthwith I went, and addressed Sioda, the free and pure. "Wherefore dost thou come Mac Lonain," said Sioda ? I replied to the Prince, the fierce warrior of the Gael, "To solicit the bay steed, Sir, I have come." "Hearken [said Sioda] O Mac Lonain, since thou art a man of verse, the bay steed of handsome crest have I long ridden ; it has [before now] been my lot to put in a good year on foot ; I shall do brave deeds without him [the horse]." "For Sioda be the black horse saddled," cried the poet, in great excitement ; "Flan will make an exchange for a bay a black one." Bay were all their steeds after that, the horror of death was in their weapons, though all the world had been at stake, yet Sioda maintained his friendship for me.†

Three days and three nights was the host westward on chilly Magh Adhair, without food, sleep, or store, neither resting nor departing. "Ask protection for us, Mac Lonain," said Flan, "from the men of Dal-Cas, from the men of Limerick ; surely they are generous and will grant our request." I rise up and reach the despoiling Dalcasians, and forthwith I recite a poem to the best men on earth. After that I urge my petition on the Dal-Cas, to the people of Limerick, to allow Flan and all along with him to go in safety. Righteous protection was given us, and guides to show us the way until we reached the Shannon, and from its fords to Tara. The Dalcasians, the best of all people in the land of Alba and of Erin. It was by them, without fail, that quarter was given to their enemies. To the Dalcasians of the clans has been granted the bounty, the valour of Erin, and every good between heaven and earth has been bestowed on the chief, Lorcain.

---

* Sioda and his son, Asoda, are the two "well-known chiefs of the Clancuilein or Macnamara of Clare " (" The Manners and Customs of the Ancient Irish," by Eugene O'Curry, vol. ii. p. 101). Professor O'Curry makes this observation in connection with this poem, written, by Mac Lonain, some time before A.D. 918.

† Dr. D. Hyde is of opinion that the meaning of this is " that Sioda's men appear to have said to those of Flan, when given the bay steed by Sioda, that there must be an exchange, a black horse to be given for the bay one, but Sioda would not withdraw from his promise."

APPENDIX TO CHAPTER VI

Lugardh Delbaeth (the fire-producer), who was a Druid, had six sons and one daughter called Aeifé, and she married Trad, who was a kingly chief and Druid, but without much land. After a time this pair found themselves the possessors of a numerous family. Accordingly, Trad said to his wife, " Go thou and ask a favour of thy father. It would be well for us and our children to get more land." Aeifé therefore went and asked her father to grant her a favour. Then Lugardh consulted his oracles, and said to his daughter, " If thou should order any one to leave his country now he must depart without delay." " Depart thou, then," said she, "and leave us the land thou inheritest, that it may be our property." Whereupon we are told Lugardh her father immediately complied, and with his sons left the lands and assigned them to Trad and his daughter. Professor O'Curry remarks: " I may add that this territory, even at the present day, retains the name of Trad, forming as it does the Deanery of Tradraighe in the present barony of Bunratty, co. Clare, a tract which comprises seven districts in which there are the ruins of five churches built by the Macnamaras. It was in this district that Rathfolan and Ballinacragga were situated, which were subsequently owned by the ancestors of the writer of this history.

To proceed, however, with the story of the Druid Lugardh. Having been thus deprived of his property, he crossed the Shannon with his sons and cattle and passed into the south-west of Westmeath. On arriving at a certain carn, we are told he built an altar, and on it placed wood, which " he ignited by his Druidic power. From this fire there burst five streams of flame, in five different directions; and the Druid commanded his *five* elder sons to follow one each of the fiery streams, assuring them that they would lead them to their future inheritance. One of these sons remained near his father ; his name was Nos, and he possessed a field on which his swine fed, and on this spot was subsequently built the famous monastery of Clonmacnoise (Cluain-mac-nois, the field of the hogs of Nos). In the fifth century, therefore, we find the people continued to believe in " oracles " or soothsaying, and in the production of magical fire by the Druids,* who, as will be observed by the references made in the legend, were not an exclusive caste, but formed a part of the Dalcasian tribe. This legend is, moreover, valuable in that it gives an idea of the social conditions under which these ancient members of Clancuilein came into possession of their tribal lands ; and, further, bears witness to the firm belief which still existed among them regarding the influence possessed by the Druids. The legend is in itself not more marvellous than those related of St. Kieran, who was a neighbour and contemporary of Lugardh.

Of this saint we are told that he was born in Ireland ; he preceded St. Patrick as a missionary, and lived to be one of his most intimate friends. It is related of his mother that in a dream she saw a star which fell into her mouth, and on referring the dream to the Druids for interpretation, she was told that " the child she should bear would be famed for virtue to the end of time." In after-life St. Kiernan renewed life in a dead man ; he went to sea on a rock which he caused to float, and so on, the record of his life being a continuous series of marvellous stories of this description.

* Professor E. O'Curry's " Manners and Customs of the Ancient Irish," vol. ii. p. 220.

CHAPTER VII

Aodh Macnamara, A.D. 1019—Teigue, A.D. 1044—Discontent due to bad harvests,
A.D. 1064—Lanfranc's Letter on Irish Church, A.D. 1070—Mac Conmara, death
of, A.D. 1090—Cumara-Mor-Macnamara killed by Chief of Desmond—Cumara,
A.D. 1143—Invasion of Kerry—Cumara Beg Macnamara, A.D. 1151—Battle of
Moinmore—Dunhual Macnamara, A.D. 1159—Conditions under which the
Sept lived.

AFTER the death of Brian Boru the Dalcasians elected his eldest son,
Teigue, to be King of Thomond and Munster; but a younger son of
Brian's, Donogh, who had married a sister of Harold, King of
England, claimed the throne. Teigue was murdered A.D. 1023, by
some, it is affirmed, at the instigation of his brother, but there is
no evidence whatever of fratricide in this case, although it is true that
Donogh succeeded to his brother's position. Teigue, however, had left
a young son, Turlough, who, had he been old enough, would have
succeeded his father. This youth was foster-son to Melachlin, King of
Leinster, and the close intimacy which sprang up between these two
individuals led to a combination which ultimately obliged Donogh to
resign the throne of Thomond in favour of his nephew Turlough, grandson of Brian Boru.

Aodh (*Macnamara*).—From the " Annals of the Four Masters " under
the date of A.D. 1019, we learn that " the son of Aodh, chief of Ui-Caisin,
attacked Donogh, son of Brian," and with a sword wounded him
severely on the head and right hand. " The son of Brian escaped, but
the son of Aodh was slain." It is difficult from the records at our
command to discover the cause of this attack on Donogh; probably it
arose from some personal quarrel between the two chiefs, or it may be
that Clancuilein had espoused the claims of the rightful heir to the
throne as against his uncle Donogh; whatever the cause of the quarrel,
the heir to the chieftainship of the Macnamara sept was slain, in consequence of his attack on the king. Ui-Caisin extended to within a few
miles of Kincora, in fact was only separated from it by the hills of
Bernagh, so that the O'Briens and Macnamaras must have been in

constant communication, and, as we shall subsequently learn, were closely connected by marriage.

Donogh having been recognised as King of Munster and Thomond, determined to follow his father's example, and endeavour to bring the whole of Ireland under his rule. With this object in view he marched with his army to Dublin, returning to Clare through Ossory and Meath, and receiving hostages by way of submission from the chiefs of these districts. Donogh speedily reduced the South of Ireland, but Connaught and Ulster resisted his claims, and with the King of Leinster made an attack upon Thomond. Whatever the views of Clancuilein were with reference to the claims of Donogh and his nephew Turlough to the throne, and notwithstanding that the latter was allied to the King of Leinster, they were bound to resist the invasion of their province. The whole of the tribe, therefore, prepared to support Donogh against the confederates who were banded together to destroy their influence.

Teigue (Macnamara) was at this time, A.D. 1044, "chief of Clancuilein, and next in rank to Donogh ; he was slain by the King of Meath." But his sept rose to a man to revenge his death, and "pushing on, burnt Ferns," the chief town of Meath, and killed the king's brother. During this incursion the monastery of Cluain-mac-noise was plundered by the Dalcasians. The King of Leinster, however, held his own, and his province for the time being remained independent under the rule of Melachlin, Turlough's foster-father.*

The next year Donogh O'Brien again invaded Leinster, looting the " great Church of Lusk " on his march, and carrying away captive those who took refuge in it.† While he was thus engaged the King of Connaught invaded Clare by way of the Shannon, and then, striking inland, he passed into Ui-Caisin and to Magh Adhair.‡ On this occasion Turlough O'Brien seems again to have accompanied the invading forces. After a fierce encounter with Macnamaras and other Dalcasian septs, the invaders had to effect a hasty retreat, to reappear, however, before long with the King of Leinster. The confederates advanced to Limerick, which the Dalcais being unable to hold, burnt before retreating into Clare.§ Donogh was now growing old and worn out by this constant warfare ; he retired, therefore, to Rome, where he died in the monastery of St. Stephen, A.D. 1064. Donogh had indeed been beset with difficulties, for we are informed that in consequence of "much inclement weather in Ireland, its corn, milk, fruit, and fish were

* " The History of Clare," p. 79, by the Very Rev. J. White, P.P., V.G.
† " Annals of Four Masters," A.D. 1051.
‡ *Idem.*   § " Annals of Innisfallen."

destroyed, and the people grew dishonest, there was no safety for any one." In these circumstances a council was assembled at Killaloe, and we are told that laws were then enacted "to restrain every injustice, great or small, and in consequence God gave peace and favourable weather."

Turlough O'Brien now became King of Munster and Thomond, and after the death of his foster-father he assumed the sovereign power over the whole of Ireland ; Ulster at first held out against him, but ultimately paid him tribute as a mark of submission. Turlough would appear to have had no great reverence for the Church, for he not only plundered the rich monasteries of Clonard and Kells, but he also removed from Clonmacnoise the skull of one of the former kings of Meath, and took it with him to Kincora. It is reported by the annalists that a mouse came out of the skull and ran under Turlough's mantle. The king was at once seized with " a sore disease, so that his hair fell off, and he was like to die, until the said skull, together with a certain amount of gold, was restored to the church, when the king began to recover." * In spite, however, of Turlogh making free with church property, Lanfranc, William the Conqueror's Archbishop of Canterbury, addressed the Irish king in A.D. 1070 as "the magnificent King of Ibernia, to whom God was mercifully disposed, and also to the people of Ireland, in giving him royal power over the land." Lanfranc proceeds to bear testimony as to Turlough's "pious humility, severe justice, and discreet equity." This letter was sent to Turlough O'Brien through the hands of Patrick, who had been elected Bishop of Dublin by the Danes, and passed over to England to be consecrated by Lanfranc ; Dublin, a Danish colony, having before this period placed her ecclesiastical affairs directly under the Roman Pontiff.

We find a similar condition of things existing in Waterford, where the Danes petitioned Anselm, Archbishop of Canterbury, to consecrate a monk of Winchester to fill the office of bishop in their city. It was not so, however ; with the rest of Ireland, the Celtic Church up to the eleventh century depended on their own bishops, natives of the country, to administer the affairs of their Church, which, as before explained, was instituted by St. Patrick and his immediate followers upon the tribal system. The constitution of the Irish Church led to many irregularities : bishops were changed without order or regularity, and multiplied to such an extent that at one time, it is said, there were 700 bishops living in Ireland. Many other irregularities had sprung up in the Church, and the Irish monks, like their tribal chiefs, were constantly at enmity and

* "Annals of the Four Masters."

war with one another.   Lanfranc referred to some of these irregularities
in his letter to Turlough, and also in an epistle which at the same time
he sent the Pontiff Alexander II., in which he complained that the Irish
had extremely loose ideas on the subject of matrimony.   Lanfranc
states that in the eleventh century men in Ireland left their wives without any canonical cause, married others, although near in blood to
themselves, or to the deserted wives.   They even exchanged wives.
Holy orders, he states, were given to Celtic bishops for money ; infants
were not baptised, or matrimony or consecration performed according
to the Roman canon.   The archbishop affirms that all this wrong was
done in Ireland because the Celtic Church was then independent in
matters of discipline of the Roman Pontiffs.   St. Malachy, some fifty
years before the arrival of the English in Ireland, describes the Irish
as " unbelieving in religion, Christians in name, but Pagans in
reality." *

There is a curious entry in the annals of Innisfallen for the year 1078
to the effect that " in this year five Jews came to Ireland, and gave rich
presents to Turlough, but they were sent out of the country beyond
the sea."

Turlough O'Brien died, at the age of seventy-seven, A.D. 1086, and
was buried in the cathedral church of Killaloe ; he was succeeded
by his second son, Mortagh.   The annalists inform us that " he was
installed by the chief of the Macnamaras at the royal rath of Magh
Adhair, near Tulla."   The chief of our sept at this period was
Mac Conmara.   His death is referred to as follows by the " Four
Masters " : " There died, in the year 1099, Cumara, son of Donall, Lord
of Clancuilein." †

The commencement of Mortagh O'Brien's reign was occupied, as that
of his father had been, in war with Connaught and Ulster for the
supreme power over Ireland.   At length he seems to have wearied of
strife, and in A.D. 1090 he met the various other kings of Ireland to
consult as to the means best calculated to bring these conflicts to an
end.   It was determined that the northern prince should be acknowledged
as the superior King of Ireland, and as such received hostages from them.
The meeting appears to have been a most amiable one, and the chiefs
" parted in peace and tranquillity,"‡ to commence, however, the old
game of war on their return home.   Mortagh seems to have been on
friendly terms with William Rufus, King of England, whom he supplied

* Morrison's " Life of St. Bernard," p. 242.
† " Annals of the Four Masters," A.D. 1099.
‡ O'Brien's " Historical Memoir," p. 53.

with Irish oak, it is said, to form the roof of Westminster Hall. The
Irish king's sister married a brother of the Earl of Shrewsbury; another
sister married Sigard, the son of the King of Norway. This king stayed
with Mortagh at Kincora for upwards of a year to enjoy the hunting
and fishing for which that part of Ireland had always been famous.
Mortagh fell into bad health during the latter part of his reign; he
died A.D. 1119, and was buried at Killaloe. He was succeeded by
Connor, as King of Munster, his brother Turlogh becoming King of
Thomond; so that Munster was again divided, as it had been previously
to Brian Boru's time, into South Munster or Desmond, and North
Munster or Thomond. After Connor's death in the year 1143 he was
succeeded as King of Munster by Turlough O'Brien, his nephew Mortagh
becoming King of Thomond.*

Cumea Mor Macnamara.—During the year 1134, Connor O'Brien,
King of Thomond, being absent from his territory, Macarthy, chief of
Desmond, invaded the province, "and in an engagement with the
Dalcais, headed by Cumea Macnamara of Ui-Caisin,"† that chief was
killed. His death is referred to by the annalists as follows: they state
"it was a just judgment on Cumea for having plundered, during the
previous year, the great cathedral church of Tuam." Macarthy, after
having slain the chief of Clancuilein, was returning with great booty to
South Munster, but was overtaken by the Macnamara sept, who
recaptured their property and slew Macarthy. It was during Connor's
reign that Cormac, Prince Bishop of Cashel, built the beautiful chapel
which still exists on the rock in that place, a very gem of massive
architecture, which, together with the wonderful missals and other
penmanship of the time, demonstrate the fact that, amidst all the
fighting and turmoil going on in Ireland, the arts were not neglected;
the work of the twelfth century in iron, gold and silver, not only
shows taste in design but skill in workmanship.

Turlough O'Brien determined to subdue Connaught, and on his march
from Clare had to "cut his way by clearing a path for his followers
through a densely thick forest" which covered the route which he took
along the line of country between the existing towns of Gort and
Atheney. He destroyed the "red birch tree" under which the O'Hynes
were elected chiefs, and, having taken the chief of the O'Kellys prisoner,
returned *via* Leinster into Thomond.

"*Cumara Macnamara*, son of Mac Conmara," we are informed, was
at this time "chief of Clancuilein. He was Turlough O'Brien's second

---

* "Historical Memoir of the O'Briens," pp. 63 and 66–68.
† "Annals of Innisfallen" and "Book of Munster," A.D. 1135.

in command, and, having made an incursion into Kerry, in an encounter
with O'Connor, king of that territory, this chief was killed by Cumara,"
A.D. 1143;* so that while the King of Munster was regaining his
power over Leinster, Cumara Macnamara was fighting for him in the
south, both having the common object of restoring an O'Brien to
supreme power in Ireland. In this purpose Turlough was thwarted by
his brother Teige, Prince of Ormond, who entered into a league with
the chiefs of Connaught, Meath, and the MacCarthys of Desmond.
Turlough, however, determined to make a desperate effort to overcome
the combined forces opposed to him, but failed to hold his own at the
battle of Moinmore (A.D. 1151).

Cumara (Beg) Macnamara seems, with his sept, to have taken a
prominent part in the battle of Moinmore, and to have fought with
great bravery, but towards the close of the day he was overpowered and
slain, a fate which also befell many of his clan.† Turlough O'Brien
escaped with difficulty from the field, and fled to Limerick; he was
compelled, however, to give the King of Connaught two hundred ounces
of gold as a ransom, as well as Brian Boru's drinking goblet, A.D. 1151.

Dunhual Macnamara, "chief of the Ui-Caisin, was drowned in the
Shannon," A.D. 1159. This notice appears in the "Annals of the Four
Masters," but we have no further record regarding this individual, who
must, however, have been a chief of some importance, or he would not
have figured in these annals, collected as they were from the official
records of the various provinces of Ireland.

After Turlough O'Brien's defeat he applied to the Prince of Aileach
for help on the condition of giving hostages, and through his aid
King Turlough was restored to his position in Thomond. South Munster,
however, was made over to the MacCarthys, who thus displaced the
O'Briens as chiefs of Desmond. Turlough's health gave way under
all the hardships and trials he had to undergo; he died in the year
1167.

We have now arrived at that period in our history when the Anglo-
Normans appeared on the scene to add to the discord and turmoil already
prevailing throughout Ireland. The social position of our sept and the
privileges of its members had for five centuries rested on consanguinity
and the possession of land as described in previous chapters of this work.
There can be no question as to the fact, that society among the early
Irish was also largely influenced by the hereditary qualities which existed
between the various members of a sept.

---

* "Chronicle Scotorum," A.D. 1143.
† Keating's "History of Ireland" (O'Mahoney), p. 606.

During this period a freeman was a man who held a certain portion of land, and being a freeman it was in his power to appeal to the law for redress, and to appear as a witness before the Brehons : his social status was absolutely ruled by the amount of land and cattle he held. Neither king nor chief could raise a member of the sept in the social scale, for it was the unalterable right of the humblest freeman by patient industry to raise himself, and his family from one grade of society to a higher one by acquiring land, and cultivating it to advantage ; but this industry and perseverance had to be the work of more than one generation, the process was to be a gradual one ; thrift and industry were consequently the stimulants, the road and only way to success or advancement in life. Crimes were considered as wrong committed by one individual against another, and might, therefore, be condoned by the person who was judged to be the aggressor, giving compensation for the damage he had inflicted on the injured party.

It is not difficult to picture to ourselves the circumstances of our sept, from the time they gained possession of their tribal lands in the early part of the fifth to the eleventh century. These lands were in extent about as large as the county of Middlesex. In this area (of Ui-Caisin) the sept of Caisin, son of Cas, were absolute masters, the Firbolgs, who occupied the country previously to the advent of the Celts, having been dispossessed of their lands they passed into the position of bondsmen. The members of the sept increased, but they were all derived from a common ancestor ; so that we can realise the influence which consanguinity had upon these people, and how their social life, their most cherished ideas and feelings were bound up in the soil ; it was through means of its produce that they lived : it was through the possession of land, and according therefore to the means of living that they held their position in society ; and this position with them was a different thing to our idea. With the early Irish each grade of society had its corresponding privileges, and raised its members a step up the social ladder. At one end of the ladder was the chief of the sept, who with the headmen had the power of making war or peace, of controlling the redistribution of the tribal lands, and, guided by his Brehons almost unlimited freedom of action over the sept. At the other end of the social scale was the bondsman, who, so far as freedom was concerned was on a par with the cattle he tended. But still numerous serfs were related to landholders, and most of them were derived from the common ancestor ; all were endowed, therefore, with the same congenital disposition ; consequently the bonds which united the members of the sept to one another were exceedingly strong. Unless we appreciate this fact it is impossible to comprehend the ancient or modern history of these people. Their hereditary qualities, and dependence on the soil, were in these Irish Celts of far greater antiquity than that of their history, they were probably qualities carried by their remote ancestors through numerous generations from their Aryan home, in their migration through the South of Europe and Spain into Ireland; these qualities had grown to be as much a part of the people as were their hands, feet, or any part of their bodies.

There is one other point we must refer to in connection with the history of our sept, and that of many other Irishmen of the period; it is that, although they lived in wattle and clay houses, rode horses without saddles, and allowed the hair of their head and face to grow to its natural length, they were nevertheless far from being mere barbarians. One of Ireland's most famous seats of learning was at Clonmacnoise, in close relation to Clare, and in that part of Ireland there were not only several well-known schools, but from this district some of Ireland's distinguished historians proceeded, and there can be no question as to the remarkable development of the intellectual powers of numerous Irishmen of this period. It is impossible that men of this stamp could have been produced in a society consisting of barbarians; in fact, Irishmen were more cultured than almost any other people in Europe from the fifth to the tenth century. No question the development of their civilisation was checked during the time their country was overrun by Norsemen, and subsequently by the invasion of the Anglo-Normans. In proof of this idea we may refer to the evidence afforded us by the history of Irishmen, such as Johannes Scotus Erigena, and many other distinguished scholars of this period (p. 54).

Mr. Lecky observes, that before the English conquest of Ireland civilisation had advanced in that island to so great an extent, that it enabled Irishmen "to bear a great, and noble part in the conversion of Europe to Christianity. It made Ireland, in one of the darkest periods of the dark ages, a refuge of learning and of piety. England owed a great part of her Christianity to Irish monks who laboured among her people before the arrival of Augustine; and Scotland, according to the best authorities, owed her name, her language, and a large proportion of her inhabitants to the long succession of Irish immigrations, and conquests between the close of the fifth and ninth centuries,"* Much of the energies and time of the chiefs and upper classes of society were in Clare, and other parts of the country devoted to military training and to hunting. Many of

* "A History of Ireland in the Eighteenth Century," by W. E. Hartpole Lecky, vol. i. p. 2.

their retainers were also employed in a similar way, especially in a sept like ours, who formed one of the chief supports of the Dalcais the most famous soldiers of the West of Ireland. Habits of this kind, however, developed the best qualities of these people; for to ensure success it was not only necessary for each man of the sept to be strong of arm, fleet of foot, and quick of eye, but he had over and above this to learn self-reliance, implicit obedience to the command of his superiors, and power to endure all manner of hardship and privation in the cause of duty and for the protection of his home and lands.

CHAPTER VIII

Ireland, on account of her sins, made over by the Supreme Pontiff to Henry II. of England—King of Leinster invited Anglo-Normans to conquer the country and made the Earl of Pembroke his successor, A.D. 1172—Henry II. visited Ireland and received submission of chiefs—Divides the country among his barons to take possession by conquest—Resistance of the O'Briens and Macnamaras—Attack on them by the Lord Deputy effectually resisted, A.D. 1192—Henry III. assumed right to govern Thomond, but had no power to enforce his rule—The Macnamaras and other septs refuse to submit to English rule—Niel Macnamara, A.D. 1242—His daughter married Conor O'Brien, King of Thomond—Importance of alliance—They defeat the English, A.D. 1257—Meeting of provincial kings for combined action futile—Magrath's " History of Wars of Thomond"—Sioda Macnamara inaugurates Brian Roe, King of Thomond, on Magh Adhair—Turlough O'Brien's revolt joined by the Macnamaras—Brian Roe seeks aid of Earl de Clare—Turlough and Clancuilein (Macnamara) gain a victory—Brian Roe murdered by De Clare—His son, Donogh Brien, succeeds his father and joins De Clare—Death of Sioda Macnamara at Quin, A.D. 1277—Succeeded by Covêha or Cumheadha—Mac Carthy of Desmond declines to give Covêha up to De Clare—Covêha defeats the Anglo-Normans—The Earl de Clare killed, A.D. 1287—The O'Briens and Macnamaras retain their lands and homes—Burning of fort at Quin by Covêha Macnamara—His death, A.D. 1306—Donchard Macnamara succeeds—His victory over other Dalcasian septs and his murder.

MATTHEW PARIS saith, that "in the year 1155 Henry II. cast in his mind the conquest of Ireland, for he saw it was commodious for him, and considered that they were but a rude and savage people, whereupon in his ambitious mind he sent to Adrian, Bishop of Rome, one John Salsbury with others, delivering his sute to that effect. Adrian, being a man of English birth, heard England's ambassadors the more willingly, and granted the king his request, as follows : after the usual mode of salutation the Pope wrote to Henry that he had 'been very careful and studious how he (Henry II.) might enlarge the Church of God here on earth—as for Ireland and all other lands where Christ is known and the Christian religion received, it is out of all doubt, and your Excellencie well knoweth, they do all appertaine and belong to the right of Saint Peter, and of the Church of Rome—you have advertised and signified unto us that you will enter the land and realme of Ireland to the end to bring it to óbedience unto Law, and under your subjection, and to root out from among them their foul sinnes and wickednesse, as also to yeeld and pay yeerly out of every house, a yeerly pension of one penny to Saint Peter, and besides also will defend and keep the rites of those Churches whole and inviolate. We, therefore, well allowing and favouring this your godly disposition and commendable affection, doe accept, ratifie and assent unto this your petition; and doe grant that you (for the dilating of God's Church, the punishment of sinne, the reforming of manners, planting of virtue, and the increasing of Christian religion) doe enter to possess that land, and thereto execute, according to your wisdom, whatsoever shall be for the honour of God, and the safety of the realme; and further also we doe strictly charge and require, that all the people of that land doe with all humbleness, dutifulness, and honour, receive and accept you as their Liege Lord and Soveraigne, reserving and accepting the right of holy Church to be inviolably preserved: as also the yeerly pension of Peter's pence out of every house, which we require to be truly answered to Saint Peter, and to the Church of Rome.'" * From this document we can comprehend the nature of the transaction by which a foreign Power made over Ireland to another foreign potentate; the remarkable circumstance in the transaction being that neither of the Powers entering into the agreement had the slightest right to the country they thus disposed of; the Celtic Church had in matters of discipline been independent of Rome; but even supposing this had not been the case, we fail to understand the grounds upon which Adrian IV. annexed Ireland to England.†

When Henry II. received the sanction of the Supreme Pontiff to take Ireland he was engaged in Normandy, and had neither men nor money with which to enter on the conquest of Ireland; but in the year 1166,

* Dr. Hanmer's "Chronicle," p. 216.

† Mr. King ("Church History of Ireland") gives a tradition connected with Tulla which is said to have influenced the famous Bull of Adrian IV., as follows: "The sale of Ireland by the Pope to the King of England was brought about, partly at least, under the influence of revenge for injuries inflicted on a papal officer by the Irish, worried as it would seem to resistance by his extortions. The account is as follows: O'Annoe and O'Chelchin of Cilmor O'Sluaiste from Cill-o-Sluaiste, or O'Slattery's (see Frost's "History of Clare," p. 218). These were they who stole the horses and the mules and the asses of the Cardinal who came from Rome to the land of Erin to instruct it, in the time of Dornhuall Mor O'Brien, King of Munster; and it was on that account that the successor of Peter sold the rent and right of Erin to the Saxons, and that is the right and title which the Saxons follow on the Irish (Gaedhil) at this day, for to the successor of Peter in Rome used to go the rent and tribute of Erin until then." (Dwyer, p. 536.)

having been asked by MacMurrogh, King of Leinster, to help him to regain the throne from which he had been expelled by his subjects, in consequence of his licentious mode of life, Henry at once recognised the advisability of taking advantage of the King of Leinster's appeal for aid, and so of gaining a pretext for interfering in the affairs of Ireland. The King of England, therefore, issued orders from Normandy conferring powers on certain Anglo-Norman barons to aid MacMurrogh to regain his throne; among others Robert Fitzstephen responded to this call, and in the year 1169 passed over to Ireland and landed near Wexford. Fitzstephen on arriving in Ireland was joined by MacMurrogh; one of their early feats was to burn the large ecclesiastical establishment at Kells, Slane, and Clonard, a remarkable way of furthering the object of religion, which was the ostensible reason advanced by Adrian IV. for making over Ireland to Henry II.

It is unnecessary to describe the slaughter which followed in the steps of Richard de Clare, Earl of Pembroke (Strongbow), who landed in Ireland in the year 1170. The provincial kings of Connaught, Ulster, and Munster were then fighting with one another, and far too intent upon their own objects to combine and defend their country from invasion.

At a synod of all the clergy of Ireland, which met at Armagh, the state of the country and its invasion by foreigners was the subject of serious discussion. It was agreed that the divine vengeance had fallen on Ireland because of the sins of the people, especially in that they were wont to purchase many of the natives of England as slaves. The synod decreed that all Anglo-Saxon slaves should be restored to freedom.* The clergy would appear to have realised the danger that threatened their country, and to have done their best to rouse the provincial kings and chiefs to a sense of their duty, with the effect of drawing a large force of Irish under the command of the King of Connaught to invest the town of Dublin, within the walls of which place the English of Leinster had to withdraw. No attempt was made to storm the walls of the town, and when the English cavalry and well-armed footmen sallied out of Dublin they took the Irish by surprise; the latter fled without making any resistance.

Dermot MacMurrogh died in the spring of 1171, and the Earl of Pembroke, who had married Dermot's daughter, according to English law succeeded to the title and estates of the King of Leinster. This, however, was going rather too far. Henry II. had no idea of seeing one of his barons become King of Leinster, and he therefore recalled Strongbow to England, and determined to visit Ireland himself. King

* Giraldus Cambrensis: "Conquest of Ireland," book i. chap. xviii. (Bohn's ed.).

Henry arrived in Waterford (in November 1172) accompanied by Strongbow, De Burgho, and other barons; he was met by MacCarthy, King of Desmond, who was the first Irish prince to swear fealty and subjection to the King of England. Henry proceeded to Cashel; he was visited by most of the Irish chiefs, including Donald O'Brien, King of Thomond, who made submission to the king and engaged to hand Limerick over to him. Donald, however, returned to Kincora, and seems not only to have overlooked the matter of tribute, but he carried on the government of Thomond exactly on the old lines, the King of England having no power whatever over the country.

Molyneux states that the princes, both temporal and ecclesiastical, of Ireland not only did homage to Henry, and swore fealty to him and his heirs, but he also received letters from them with their seals pendant in manner of charters, testifying they had ordained him and his heirs their king, after which he returned to England, in April 1173. This author also states that Henry II. introduced the laws of England into Ireland in a public assembly of the Irish at Lismore, and allowed them the freedom of Parliaments to be held in Ireland as they were held in England.* Without questioning the validity of these documents, the fact remains that, before leaving the country, Henry II. gave away the whole of Ireland to some ten of his Anglo-Norman barons, who were to take possession of their lands, if necessary, by conquest.†

Henry took no steps whatever to maintain authority in the country over which he assumed the sovereignty, and he made no effort to establish the English laws in Ireland; "neither left he behind him," as Sir J. Davis observes, "one true subject more than he found there at his coming over, which were only English adventurers."‡ Before leaving Ireland, King Henry convened a synod at Cashel, at which it was decreed that "the universal Church of Ireland should be reduced in all things

---

* "The Case of Ireland," by W. Molyneux: edited by the Very Rev. John Canon O'Hanlon, P.P., pp. 44.

† Five years later Henry II., at a Parliament held at Oxford, created his younger son, John, a lad twelve years of age, King of Ireland. Prince John went over to Ireland, but seems to have given offence to the native princes, and he speedily returned to England. Until his brother Richard's death, when John ascended the English throne, he was in the habit of granting charters to his Irish subjects, in which he styles himself Lord and not King of Ireland. Molyneux argues that if King Richard had not died and John succeeded to the throne of England, that John's progeny would have remained Kings of Ireland with an independent Parliament ("Case of Ireland," p. 36).

‡ Sir J. Davis: "A Discoverie of the True Cause why Ireland was never Subdued," p. 110. Giraldus Cambrensis, book i. chap. xxxiv.

G

to the order and form of the Church of England" (A.D. 1172). "Near kinsfolke were prohibited from marrying, children were to be baptised, and the bodies of dead Christians buried within the precincts of the church."*

Strongbow, finding that Donald O'Brien openly scoffed at the idea of the King of England having power over Thomond, marched with a strong force (A.D. 1174) as far as Thurles, intending to pass on into Clare; but he was met by O'Brien, who "defeated the earl and slew one thousand seven hundred of his men."† Strongbow, however, having received reinforcements and found an ally in Donald, chief of Ossory, who was a mortal enemy of the O'Briens‡ (p. 82), they attacked Limerick and carried it by storm. O'Brien seems to have had good reason to suspect treachery in this matter; he immediately afterwards seized two of his own family residing near Limerick, whose eyes were ordered to be put out, and a guest in their house was beheaded. Acts of this description would only have been perpetrated by the Dalcasian chief upon persons who were unfaithful to their tribe, as these individuals had probably been.

In the meantime the King of Connaught (Roderick O'Connor) had sent an embassy to arrange a treaty with Henry II. at Windsor (A.D. 1175), by which the King of Connaught was to retain his position in the west of Ireland, and to rule the whole country as Henry's vassal; through him the other kings and chiefs were to pay tribute to England; the Brehon laws were still to continue in force. O'Brien at once repudiated this treaty, and not only refused to pay tribute to England, but declined to give hostages in token of submission to the King of Connaught; the only present he would receive from that king was Brian Boru's drinking goblet, which had been taken from his family as ransom (p. 90).

In 1192 the English determined to subdue the Dalcasians, and so concentrated their forces and entered Clare at Killaloe; turning westward along the Shannon, they then struck north, intending to overrun the Ui-Caisin territories; but they were here met by the Dalcasians under command of the O'Briens and Macnamaras; the English were completely defeated and had to retreat in hot haste across the Shannon.

In the year 1221, we learn that King Henry III. made a grant of the province of Thomond to Donough O'Brien on the understanding

---

* Holinshed's "Chronicles," vol. vi. p. 163.
† "Annals of the Four Masters."
‡ Holinshed's "Chronicles," vol. vi. p. 193.

that he should pay a hundred and thirty marks to England as tribute ; and six years after the grantee's death, Henry, under a patent given at Westminster, granted the district of Tradree, co. Clare, to Robert Musegros, in this way encroaching dangerously near Ui-Caisin and some of the Macnamaras' most fertile lands.   King Henry also gave permission to this Anglo-Norman nobleman to build castles on his lands, one of which was probably that on which Quin Abbey now stands ; the king directed that Musegros was to have two hundred good oaks from the woods of Cratloe for the purpose of building this castle. It is evident, from the entries in the Patent Rolls of England and Ireland of this period, that Henry III. assumed not only a right to govern the province of Thomond, but beyond this he took upon himself to dispose of the land in this part of Ireland ; it was therefore certain, if the members of Clancuilein, and the other Dalcasian septs intended to preserve their ancient tribal lands and homes intact, that the time had arrived for them to rise in defence of their position.   They speedily showed their determination to resist the encroachments of the Anglo-Normans, and they rose, therefore, against Donough O'Brien "because he seemed to be favourably disposed to their enemies," and drove him out of Limerick ; he then took refuge at Clonroad, near Ennis, co. Clare, where he built a strong fort in which he might live.   If any of Robert Musegros' followers had settled in the south of Clare they were at this time expelled from their holdings ; nevertheless, it would seem that they retained one or more forts in the district, such as that of Quin and Bunratty.

The inhabitants of Clare subsequent to these events remained for some years free from foreign interference, and on the whole enjoyed a fair amount of peace ; although, we are informed by the "Four Masters," that in the year 1223 the chief of the O'Shaughnessys, one of the Dalcasian septs, was killed by the Macnamaras in spite of a solemn compact between the two to keep the peace.   This compact was ratified on the crozier of St. Colum, which is still to be seen in the Museum of the Royal Irish Academy, Dublin.*

* We have various references in the Calendar of the Papal Register of this period relating to Ireland, for instance :—A.D. 1225 : Canonization of St. Laurence (O'Toole) by Pope Honorius III., in which document the statement is made "that St. Laurence was son of the King and Queen of Ireland.   As to his miracles, the deaf, the dumb, and sick are healed ; he restored seven dead persons to life " (vol. i. p. 104). A.D. 1219 : "Mandate to the Bishop-elect of Norwich, papal legate " to compel the Justiciary of Ireland, if he has, as is asserted, condemned a former papal mandate, to come before the king and give an account of the rents and other goods of the king which he had received (Cal. Papal Reg., vol. i. p. 64).

Donough O'Brien was succeeded by his eldest son Conor, who was inaugurated on Magh Adhair (A.D. 1242) King of Thomond, by Sioda (Sheeda) MacNeil Macnamara. The territory of Thomond then extended from Loop Head to Cashel, thence to Parsonstown and the Bay of Galway; but no longer included South Munster, which had passed to the MacCarthys and other chiefs of Desmond. Conor O'Brien married the daughter of Niel Macnamara, who at the time was chief of Clancuilein, an event which had an important influence on the disturbed state into which Thomond was plunged by two rival sections of the O'Brien family who claimed the leadership of the Dalcasian tribe. By the marriage of the head of one of these factions with the Macnamaras, the most powerful septs of this famous tribe were intimately united, and through many years of terrible strife they maintained their supremacy, although the rival section of the O'Briens was supported by the Anglo-Normans under De Clare, who so soon as he could conquer its chief had been granted possession of Thomond by the King of England.

The first appeal to arms which Conor O'Brien was called upon to consider was at the request of Henry III., who summoned him, A.D. 1252, to cross over to England and aid in his proposed expedition against the King of Scotland; before Conor could ascertain the feeling of the Dalcasians as to taking part with the King of England in a war of this kind, Henry came to terms with Scotland and so the negotiations between him and Conor O'Brien fell through.

A sister of Conor married the King of Connaught, and having thus gained the aid of that chief and of Clancuilein he felt himself sufficiently strong to attack Limerick; he captured this town from the English and also Cork, and then overran the whole of Munster, so that,* as Magrath states, "he did not suffer one of the English nation to inhabit the size of the meanest hut in this part of the kingdom." Conor's further progress was thwarted by an outburst of rivalry between the Dalcasian and Desmondian tribes, forced into action by

A.D. 1213: Pope Innocent III. sent a notification to the King of Limerick, Connaught, and Meath that he was about to convoke a general council for the recovery of the Holy Land and the reformation of the Church" (vol. i. p. 38).

A.D. 1245: Mandate from Pope Innocent IV. to "the Bishop of Annadown and Clanfort to restrain the Archbishop of Cashel from molesting the Bishop of Killaloe, reported by him guilty of simony by reason that D. Carbrech, Lord of Thomond (Tuadomonia) in that diocese, had, contrary to the bishop's inhibition, paid a sum of money to R. de Burgo, Justiciary of Ireland, to restore the temporalities to the See (vol. i. p. 212).

* Standish Hayes O'Grady's translation of "Triumphs of Turlough," p. 2.

William de Burgho, who had gained large possessions in Galway, and so, through the weakness caused by the rivalries of the Celtic chiefs, an opening was again effected for the Anglo-Normans to force their way into the west of Ireland. Conor O'Brien, however, determined to face the foreigners in the field of battle, and in A.D. 1257, aided by Clancuilein and other Dalcasian septs, he met the English, and not only defeated them, but again drove them out of East Thomond, and also from Galway.

The fact seemed at length to dawn on the four provincial kings of Ireland that, if they were to retain their position, it was necessary for them to act together against the common enemy; and so it was determined they should for the second time meet and take steps to ensure concerted action (p. 88). Conor O'Brien was represented at this council by his son and tanist Teige. The council met (A.D. 1258), but when it came to the point of settling which of the four kings was to be supreme, the choice lay between O'Neil and O'Brien, neither of them would yield; the council, therefore, broke up without arriving at any decision on the matter for which they had been assembled; and so terminated the last hope of effective union between the native Irish chiefs to combine and work together for the good of their country. Teige O'Brien died soon after the termination of the council, and his father, Conor, seems to have been crushed by this blow; "he refused to drink, rejoice, or take comfort, and to such a depth and for so long was his grief prolonged, that his tribe rose against him;" his sorrow they respected, but when it passed into settled gloom they led their chief to understand that he must make way for some one else, if he desired to indulge in inordinate grief.

We have now arrived at that period in the history of our sept in which they were to be engaged for nearly half a century, together with the O'Briens, in resisting the efforts of the Anglo-Normans to obtain possession of Clare, and we have a work of singular interest to guide us in our history of this period : it is known as the " Triumphs of Turlough," which was written in the year 1459 by John, son of Rory Magrath the hereditary bard of the Dalcasian tribe. Our author states that he wrote his history from information given him by persons who had witnessed the scenes he describes, and from the contents of the work there can be little doubt that this statement of Magrath's is correct. Professor O'Curry remarks that the " Wars of Thomond " " stands unrivalled— the style of the composition is extremely redundant; nevertheless it possesses a power and vigour of description which, independently of the exciting incidents it describes, will amply compensate the reader's study."*   Mr. Standish Hayes O'Grady has quite recently added to the deep obligation which those interested in the early history of Ireland are already under to him, by having given us an admirable translation of Magrath's "Triumphs of Turlough," or the "Wars of Turlough." In the following pages I have made free use of Mr. S. H. O'Grady's translation, and, in fact, in places where it describes members of our sept have transcribed whole paragraphs of his work, which is a literal rendering into English of Magrath's original work written in Gaelic.

We are informed by the " Four Masters " that during the latter part of Conor O'Brien's reign, Thomond was not only at peace, but that the seasons were favourable and the people consequently prosperous. Magrath confirms this statement, and states that Conor O'Brien had amassed great wealth in his fort at Clonroad, and that a large proportion of the inhabitants of the province had " grown over-rich and in consequence had become turbulent, refusing to pay tribute to their king." In these circumstances Conor directed his brother-in-law, Sioda Macnamara, to muster Clancuilein, and the Kineldunal led by Anselis O'Grady, and to proceed into Tipperary to quell the insubordination which had sprung up in that part of Thomond.   Sioda seems to have speedily and effectually accomplished the duty he had been called on to perform; but in the meantime Conor had started off on a similar expedition into Burren, and having penetrated that part of his territory as far as the valley above Ballyvaghan, he was attacked, and we are told that "Conor O'Brien together with his third son and a daughter were slain." The body of the king was carried to the neighbouring Abbey of Corcomroe, and was there buried; Conor's tomb is still to be seen in good preservation in the north side of the chancel of this abbey.

Conor O'Brien had at one time gone near to rival his ancestor Brian Boru in the success of his military operations, as Edmund Spenser observes " in a short space he possessed all that country beyond the river of Shannon and near adjoining : whence shortly rushing forth like a sudden tempest he overran all Munster and Connaught ; breaking down all the holds and fortresses of the English, defacing and utterly subverting all corporate towns that were not strongly walled : for those he had no engines or other meanes to overthrow, neither indeed would

* Professor E. O'Curry's " Lectures on Manuscript Materials of Ancient Irish History," p. 235.   There is an English MS. translation of this Celtic work in the Egerton Collection, British Museum Library.   Mr. T. J. Westropp, M.A., has drawn up an able summary of the wars of Thomond in his papers on " The Normans in Thomond," to be found in the " Journal of the Proceedings of the Royal Society of Antiquaries of Ireland for the year 1890-91."

he stay at all about them, but speedily ran forward, counting his suddenness his most advantage, that he might overtake the English before they
could fortifie or gather themselves together."* One of the recent historians of Clare confirms this idea regarding Conor's tactics, and observes
that his success was largely due to his close alliance by marriage with
the chief of the Macnamaras, and the loyal support he consequently
received from that clan.†

Conor O'Brien was succeeded by his second son Brian Roe, who was
inaugurated King of Thomond, on Magh Adhair, by his uncle Sioda
Macnamara, but his eldest son had left as his heir a lad named Turlough,
nine years of age, and consequently too young to succeed to the government of Thomond. Brian Roe, therefore, reigned at Clonroad for nine
years, " and fought the English, governing with a strong hand ; " but in
the year 1277, Turlough revolted against his uncle, Brian Roe ; aided
by the Clancuilein sept, who were related to him, his grandmother
having been the daughter of Neil Macnamara, they drove Brian Roe
out of Clonroad. And after a conference with his supporters Brian determined to seek the aid of the Anglo-Normans ; so he went to " Thomas,
the Earl of Clare's son, who was of English race, a man of great consequence, then residing in Cork," who undertook to assist Brian with all
the English in Munster, if Brian would grant him possession of all that
part of Thomond between the Shannon and a line drawn from Limerick
to Athsollus." ‡ These terms having been agreed to, De Clare obtained
the help of the Fitzgeralds, the Butlers, and other Anglo-Norman barons,
and together with Brian Roe's followers they sallied forth from Limerick

* Edmund Spenser's " View of the State of Ireland," p. 24.
† Rev. P. White: " History of Clare."
‡ Thomas de Clare, Governor of London, was the second son of Richard Earl
of Gloucester, and he (Thomas), having borne arms against the king at the battle
of Lewes, eventually came over to the king's side, and with his brother Gilbert
arranged a plan by which Edward the king's son escaped from custody. This
brought them pardon, and Henry III. made Thomas his secretary ; Gilbert was
married to the Princess Joan of Acre, and Thomas de Clare got licence to settle
in Ireland (1269), but he did not go there until after Edward's return from the
Holy Land. He married a daughter of Lord Desmond, and got a grant of his
lands in trust from Prince Edward. De Clare had a nominal right to part of
Thomond, for Robert de Musegros, a former grantee, had surrendered Tradree to
the king (p. 99). The king subsequently granted Thomas de Clare in fee the
province of Thomond, including Tradree. Thus De Clare was established, so far
as Edward King of England could secure him, in the south of co. Clare, in the
angle made by the rivers Fergus and Shannon, north of which lay the Ui-Caisin
lands (T. J. Westropp's " Normans in Thomond ": " Journal of the Royal Society
of Antiquaries of Ireland," 1890, pp. 285–286).

to attack Turlough O'Brien with the intention of placing Brian Roe at the head of affairs in Thomond.   And so we have a repetition of the old story, mutual jealousy between Irish leaders, one of whom to strengthen his position called in the aid of foreigners to assist him in overcoming his adversary.   The Anglo-Normans were better armed and more highly trained soldiers than the Irish, but in a country like Clare their armour was an impediment to them, for the land was at this time thickly covered with forest, there were few if any roads.   Their Irish opponents were unencumbered with implements of war, their light shields, bows and arrows, with their favourite weapons the lance and spear, were all they carried ; half naked, with their matted hair tied with thongs over their eyes; fleet of foot and enduring as the beasts of their forests, such were the men the Anglo-Normans had to contend with in Clare.

At the time of De Clare's advance from Limerick to Clonroad, Turlough O'Brien was away to the west of the Fergus receiving the fealty of the MacMahons, and De Clare therefore entered Clonroad unopposed ; the Macnamaras were not prepared to meet him single-handed, and they retreated, with their cattle and goods, into the dense forests north of Clare.   Several of the Dalcasian septs, however, joined Brian Roe and the Anglo-Norman forces, and he strengthened and garrisoned the fort which before Conor's time seems to have been erected at Quin (p. 99), an important strategical post in the Macnamaras' territory ; in fact, it was only separated from the residence of the chief of our sept by the river Rine.   There was a church in this place dedicated to St. Finghin, which De Clare converted into "a church and a fortress."   This edifice still exists, with its massive walls and narrow lancet windows ; but De Clare's fort was on the opposite or eastern side of the stream.   It consisted of a courtyard some 120 feet square, with walls nearly 10 feet thick, and round towers 40 feet broad at three of its angles.   The lower part of these towers and the walls of this fort still remain ; it was within these that De Clare subsequently (1280) built a strong castle,* which has since made way for the beautiful Franciscan abbey erected on the site occupied by the castle within the fort of Quin.   In fact, the walls of the old castle and of the fort constitute part of the existing abbey.   De Clare at this time also built the castle of Bunratty at the "clear harboured mouth of the River Raite."   Part of this building is inhabited at the present time by the Irish constabulary.

* "The Normans in Thomond," by T. J. Westropp, M.A., ("The Proceedings of the Royal Society of Antiquaries of Ireland"); also "Annals of Innisfallen," 1280.

Turlough O'Brien passed from the MacMahon territory into Burren, and then northward into Galway ; and, having secured help from William de Burgho (Bourkes), he proceeded to join Clancuilein in the woods of Echty, and the combined force then commenced offensive warfare against De Clare, and the other Anglo-Normans who had settled in the district of Tradree.   So constant were these attacks that the foreigners constructed a wall and trench across the northern part of their lands, in hopes of preserving them from the Irish ; but defences of this kind were useless as means of protection against a race of active light-footed creatures like the men of Clancuilein.   Turlough soon felt himself strong enough to attack De Clare, and, with Sioda Macnamara, passed first to the north-east and ravaged the O'Grady's lands and other septs who had joined Brian Roe and De Clare ; he then led his forces southward, and met his Anglo-Norman adversary in the open fields of Mongressan (A.D. 1277).   De Clare was completely beaten, and his brother-in-law and other knights were slain.   Brian Roe and De Clare escaped to Bunratty, where the earl's wife denounced Brian of treachery and as having been the cause of her brother's death.   The unfortunate Irish chief was seized and brought into the castle-yard, where he was "bound to a stern steed" and dragged to death, and his body was then suspended by its feet from the gallows.   This murder was perpetrated by De Clare notwithstanding he had entered into a sacred alliance with Brian, upon which occasion they swore by the most solemn oaths to support one another, and mixed their blood in token of friendship.   The details of this crime are recorded by the " Four Masters," and were also transmitted by certain Irish chiefs to Pope John XII.

After this battle De Clare endeavoured to come to an arrangement with Turlough, but the latter declined so much as to listen to words of peace after what had happened to his relation Brian Roe, although he was his enemy.   Turlough proceeded with his victorious army to Magh Adhair, and was there inaugurated King of Thomond by Sioda Macnamara : Magrath states " that the septs of Thomond were delighted to receive their rightful ruler."   It is remarkable that in this and other references made by Magrath to the inauguration of the O'Briens as kings of Thomond, that no mention is made of any religious ceremony on these occasions ; if we turn to the " Icelandic Sagas " (vol. iv. p. 332) we find, in the year A.D. 1261, how different was the service performed at the coronation of King Magnus, the archbishops, bishops, and clergy being prominent personages in the ceremony (A.D. 1276).

De Clare having failed to come to terms with Turlough, felt that the charter he had received from the King of England granting him possession of Thomond, was of about as much value as the paper on which it was written ; but he still considered his wisest policy was to incite the jealousy of the Irish chiefs, and through their mutual destruction step into the position he so much coveted in Clare ; his next move, therefore, was by flattering and hypocritical messages sent to Donough, the son of the Brian Roe, to induce this young man to throw in his fortunes with the Anglo-Normans ; and, surprising as it may seem, Donough actually consented to co-operate with his father's murderer, in order to gain his own ends. The confederates started off on a raid through West Clare, attacking the MacMahons and other chiefs who had supported Turlough O'Brien ; De Clare then turned east and suddenly appeared before Clonroad ; Turlough O'Brien had to escape from this place, and he again sought refuge in Ui-Caisin and threw himself on the protection of the Macnamaras ; he was followed by a portion of De Clare's force under command of Donough, who that night encamped at Quin. We are informed by Magrath (quoting from O'Grady's translation of the " Triumphs of Turlough " (p. 11), " that the sheet anchor of the people, Sheeda (or Sioda) Macnamara, excellent with the spear," at the first dawn of the morning, with but a small company of retainers, determined to attack Donough Roe's force, hoping that during the confusion produced by a sudden onslaught he might be able to penetrate to Donough's tent and engage him in single combat. So desperate was this attack that Sioda penetrated into the midst of the camp of his enemies. These, however, converging from all sides encircled the chief, and most of his followers were killed. Sioda, however, never for an instant allowed an enemy to get a stroke home on him. " And so far now from desisting, the lion in this his solitary position in the hostile centre the more provoked him to mow down and clear his enemies, till at last he and Donough Brian Roe met face to face. Then he thought to have avenged himself on that chief, but Sioda was overborne by numbers and the valiant chief fell, pierced with many wounds." In bewailing Sioda Macnamara's death the poet wrote the following quatrains :

> It is sad, O cheerful Sioda, whom none dare oppose in war,
> When you came to Limerick, and when Brian fled before your cavalry,
> None could gainsay your fame, nor King Turlough's,
> Deadly thy blows, and red thy dart at Magh Greasain,
> I count for ever and cannot tell the number of thy deeds.
> Many in Quin's battle of swords, in the fight were laid supine,
> Thy coming into Quin without thy host, I cannot but greatly lament.*

* " Wars of Thomond " (T. J. Westropp's " Normans in Thomond," p. 289).

After the death of Sioda, Magrath states that Clancuilein assembled at Magh Adhair and elected his son Cumheadha (Covêha) Macnamara as their chief; the historian remarks that in "the choice of Covêha as their head, Clancuilein had not exchanged a stone for an egg, but had taken gold in place of silver";* "for now the *Cu* or Wolf-dog's rabies rose against those that bordered on his confines, towards his opponents he exalted his humour, and he made his martial deeds to be illustrious throughout neighbouring counties and provinces." Covêha was married to Sheilia O'Carroll, daughter of the chief of Ely.† It seems quite certain that the author of the records from which Magrath compiled his history had a strong feeling in favour of Covêha Macnamara, his son Lochlain, and grandson MacCon; he is never tired of detailing their prowess and feats of arms, although he is by no means sparing in his commendations of other Dalcasian chiefs. Covêha, soon after taking command of his sept, went to visit MacCarthy, chief of Desmond, in the hopes of obtaining his help in the cause of peace; De Clare having received intimation of these negotiations sent to MacCarthy to offer him a large bribe if he would surrender Macnamara to him. No, replied MacCarthy, MacConmara I will not surrender, the wolf-dog, he does not belong to me, and shall not go against his own will.‡ Covêha, however, finding his mission in the cause of peace was useless and that a large reward was offered for his life, made his way back to Ui-Caisin with all secrecy and speed.

From Magrath we learn that King Turlough and Covêha now came to the decision that they must depend entirely on their own resources if they were to be rid of the Anglo-Normans in Clare; they consequently set about organising their forces, over which Donald, a brother of the king, and Covêha Macnamara were chosen leaders. De Clare was not behind them in warlike preparations, and the opposing forces met on the plain near Tulla; the Dalcasians by a dexterous flank movement broke in upon the main body of the Anglo-Norman forces and completely overcame them, they fled from the field of battle in all directions; Covêha ordered the arms of the enemy who had been killed to be collected and sent to the King of Thomond, who at the time was occupied to the east of the Shannon; but the "gold spurs of the knights and their shields and armorial bearings he directed should be defaced and returned to De Clare." Turlough followed up this victory by marching through Tradree up to the walls of Bunratty Castle,

---

* "Wars of Thomond" (T. J. Westropp): Mac-con, or son of the wolf-dog.
† Pedigree in the Ayle Collection.
‡ "The Triumphs of Turlough" (Standish H. O'Grady's translation), p. 15.

and he there compelled De Clare to banish Donough Brian Roe into Desmond. In the following year the King of Thomond agreed for the sake of peace to divide county Clare with Donough, who was to rule over that part of the territory situated between the river Fergus and the sea, with its "endless forests, the sea-shore, and the defensible valleys of Burren"; while Turlough was to retain eastern Thomond with its fertile soil, its lakes abounding in fish, and the natural strongholds of its mountains to the north and south-east.* This arrangement between the two rival O'Briens was hardly likely to lead to permanent peace, and in fact complications soon arose between them, and led to endless fighting, in which, Magrath states, "that the poet and eye-witness of these scenes affirms that it was Clancuilein that maintained " the cause of Turlough O'Brien.

In 1284 it was agreed that the contending chiefs should meet and try and settle their quarrels. Donough Brian's coming was after this fashion : "He was sufficiently well drunken with mead to make him noisy, and when he came to the river's opposite bank, he thence gave Turlough O'Brien to feel the rough side of his tongue." † At his violent and bitter words Turlough's face grew red, and the chiefs who had been Donough's friends were so outraged that they passed over to Turlough, and they determined to attack Donough in one or other of the places in which he was sure to sleep that night. Donough hearing of this, mounted his beautiful horse and, followed by a few retainers, attempted to escape from his enemies, but they were too numerous for him. Wounded, he reached the river Fergus and plunged into it, "then it was that Donough, fervently adoring the true God, in hurried act of penance lifted up his hands, and so, with good courage, sank under the river's surface away from his enemies."‡

Turlough O'Brien was left the undisputed King of Thomond, or rather of Clare, with the exception of that part of it known as Tradree.

In September 1284, Thomas de Clare left Ireland for England, and he had no sooner turned his back on Clare than the Dalcais entered Tradree in order to occupy the lands upon which several Norman families had settled. In the Calendar of State Papers for Ireland of A.D. September 1287, we have a list of these people, and the amount of rent which they paid De Clare for their lands. Some twenty-seven different Anglo-Norman families are mentioned, among them a certain Patrick de Layndperun was in possession of *Rathfolan ;* Peter Kingsat, near Quin, paid as rent for his lands a pair of gilt spurs and a pair of white gloves

---

* The Normans in Thomond " (T. J. Westropp), p. 289.
† Standish H. O'Grady's translation of " Triumphs of Turlough," p. 24.
‡ *Idem,* p. 25.

at Michaelmas.* De Clare on his return to Bunratty was much enraged with Turlough O'Brien for his incursion into what he considered to be his own lands; he therefore gathered his followers together, and on the 29th of August 1287 met Turlough and Clancuilein within the borders of Tradree; the latter were again victorious, and Thomas, Earl de Clare, was killed, as also were some of his principal knights.† De Clare's eldest son Gilbert at the time of his father's death was only six years of age; he was made a ward of his uncle's wife, a daughter of Edward I. This lad only lived to the year 1308, he was succeeded by his brother Richard de Clare, who we shall subsequently find played an important part in the affairs of our sept.‡

After the death of Thomas de Clare, Turlough O'Brien with Clancuilein and other of his allies marched forth (A.D. 1304) "with his colours in the centre, and gilt shields outside," and cavalry in the rear; and passing through Cashel ravaged the country as far as Thurles, and then turned north, reaching Nenagh. At this point in his career he was persuaded by his friend the Earl of Ulster to give up the idea of further conquest and to return to Clare.

As Turlough's army moved along the lovely wooded banks of Loch Derg, Magrath informs us that "they were met by a lone woman who approached them, fair of face she was and of modest mien. From her strange aspect and beautiful form, the whole of Turlough's followers took heed of her: a maid with red lips and taper fingers, long and wavy flowing hair; her whole being commanded respect." She spoke to the king as follows: "My name is Ireland's sovereignty, and if strangers had not caused thee to turn back, the sovereign rule of the whole of Ireland would have been yours." Such delight had the army in listening to her that they pressed close on her; but she disappeared in the semblance of a bright cloud, repeating as she passed away a long poem which Magrath has given us in detail. Turlough then deeply repented having followed the Earl's counsel; nevertheless he ruled the whole of Munster and Thomond as his ancestors had done before him. For no less than nine-and-twenty years Turlough reigned over this province, during which time we are told there was exceeding abundance in the country and "every man was able to attend to and to perform the office of his station."§

* State Papers, Ireland, No. 459, A.D. 1301.
† *Ibid.* No. 1301; see Westropp, "The Normans in Thomond," p. 292.
‡ "The Normans in Thomond," by T. J. Westropp, M.A. ("Journal of the Royal Society of Antiquaries of Ireland," p. 383, vol. for 1891.
§ Standish H. O. Grady's translation of the "Triumphs of Turlough," p. 30.

In the following year, Magrath states that the Norman garrison of the "towering strong-walled castle of Quin, the capital and nursery of the English forces," had a quarrel with some of the neighbouring chiefs, and in a skirmish which ensued some of the Irish were killed, upon which Covêha Macnamara stormed the fortress, "broke in its mighty gates," and plundered all its armour and horses, finally breaking down its flanking walls and burning it, "and a dreadful black furnace it was." Covêha was then joined by Turlough O'Brien, and they proceeded to Bunratty, and destroyed the town. It was then that " Turlough contrived a piece of work such as in all Ireland never before had been set a-going : a plank-bridge, with edges accurately fitted, which [from the Bunratty side of the river below the fortress] spanned its sea-channel to the opposite shore [and cut off its water-borne supplies]. By these measures the garrison of the castle were tired out: and its fall impended when again the Earl of Ulster's instructions overtake Turlough who, from the hour in which the Earl undertook to counsel him, let the castle be." †

Turlough built and endowed the beautiful Abbey of Ennis, the ruins of which still exist in good preservation ; he died on the 10th of April 1306, and was buried in the church he had so lately completed. Turlough O'Brien's son, Donough, was chosen king, and was inaugurated by Covêha Macnamara at Magh Adhair, and " they wished him God's luck and man's luck."

King Turlough O'Brien was speedily followed to the grave by his trusted friend and supporter Covêha Macnamara, who was buried near the remains of Turlough in Ennis Abbey.‡ Magrath states that the following was the dirge sung over his body :

The royal fortress of the house of Tal falls to the ground, no more to be set up.
Covêha's wars deprived the foe of strength ; from Chodhna e'en to Cashel swept
    the land.

* " The Normans in Thomond," T. J. Westropp, p. 382.
† Standish H. O. Grady's " Triumphs of Turlough," p. 31.
‡ Magrath in his " Triumphs of Turlough," writing of Donough Brien, observes: " At last there fell on him a visitation of long-enduring consequence by which the country was ruined in its tuatha—which is that the lord by whom the citadel of state was held *in situ;* the thread by which each iracht's edges were in concord pieced with their adjacent neighbour's borders—I mean Cumea (Covêha) Moir Mac Namara took a sickness which attacked him suddenly. In the mild month of August—one thousand three hundred and six.—On the one day of the year it was that to join her Son sweet Mary went up to His City, and that Cumea likewise (his time being now run out), after purgation and (as was fitting) use of pious words, beyond all doubt attained to heaven " (Standish H. O. Grady's translation of " The Triumphs of Turlough," p. 33).

Covêha's peace gave wealth and corn and milk, strength to the Church, asylum to the poor.

At early dawn after the fight of Quin, that mast-like chief we chose—dweller in towers—

The conqueror, who rolled the battle back on Fertain's host, and from the field of war.

Chased Donough, and from end to end reduced the fields of Dubhglen and sea-washed Tradree.

Covêha of the swift steed won the crown for Turlough and repelled the English host.

Strong Carconlish, Bregha, and blue-streamed Grian, with Latteragh, and Hy Mongain, he destroyed Moynalbh, and Inis Amhlain felt his storm.

The great Covêha of the angry frays stormed Quin's strong castle, though the fight was fierce, till the proud Galls in clouds of smoke were burnt.

Covêha of the fierce steeds spoilt Tradree, Bunratty's town of high-built houses sacked;

He burnt with fire Bunratty's level plain till proud De Clare agreed to leave the land." *

Magrath observes that the latter years of Turlough's and the commencement of that of his son's reign might be considered as the golden age for Clare ; the poet declares that even the elements appeared to take a share in the happiness of man, the yellow fields vied with each other in the weight of the grain they bore, there was abundance for all, but no excess among the landowners: all were contented and happy.

After the death of Covêha Macnamara the sept of Clancuilein assembled and confirmed his son Donchadh as his successor. Magrath states that the sept had determined in favour of Donchadh before Covêha's death, so that his public election by the whole sept was really a matter of form. Our historian observes that there could be no difference of opinion in the selection of the chief, considering the acknowledged prowess of Donchadh, his tried loyalty to his king, his boundless liberality, and many other high qualities.†

* T. J. Westropp's " Normans in Thomond ": " Journal of the Royal Society of Antiquaries of Ireland for 1891," p. 383.

† Mr. S. H. O'Grady gives the following translation of Magrath's description of Donough (Donchadh Macnamara). The historian observes that gentlemen of his sept " were well affected to his flawless integrity, which with watchful readiness would maintain any man [whose cause was good]; because also no hardihood could show performance such as his valour had accomplished ; no beauty equalled his grace and symmetry ; no honour came up to his perfect chivalry; no sound was sweet as his clear words. And again : because for deference to his arch-chief, for openhandedness to his own subordinate captains, no man was [Donchadh's] peer. In generous donation to the hospitallers, in honourable consideration of the poet, he was pre-eminent : and who but he was gentle and winning with women, sweet-natured to young lads, cheery with them of his great household, a handsome purveyor of the wine-feast " (p. 34).

Thomas de Clare was killed in August 1287, and until A.D. 1310 the peace and prosperity of Clare was almost undisturbed, and then the jealousy of the Irish septs amongst themselves was the cause of a small war which broke out in the north-eastern part of the district. The truth was, the Hy-Blood, the Kennedys, Connings, and other Dalcasian septs, had for some time envied the position and importance which Clancuilein had obtained in the affairs of Thomond. This feeling seems to have been rankling in their breasts for a considerable time, and was brought to a climax by the foolish rollicking conduct of two of the younger members of the Donchadh-Macnamara family. These individuals had been on an expedition into Galway, and having fallen out with De Burgho's steward he was killed. Fearing the earl would speedily retaliate they sought protection in the ecclesiastical establishment of Moynoe, some of them resting in the great church ; but they seemed to think they were not properly entertained by the religious community of the place, and they proceeded, therefore, to help themselves and to pillage the neighbourhood for food. Conduct of this kind created an outburst of indignation, and Sioda's foster-brother was killed in the turmoil which ensued. Upon this Donchadh, the chief of the sept, took up the quarrel and laid waste all the lands of Moynoe, sparing only the church. The badge of war being thus thrown down, the Hy-Blood and other Dalcasian septs of East Clare were not slow to accept the challenge given by Clancuilein.

Magrath has left us some curious details of these proceedings (A.D. 1307) : he states that when Clancuilein learnt the extent of the coalition against them, "these gentlemen came together and brought their chief to reassure his clansmen, and to explain to them the nature of their difficulties." We are told that Donchadh Macnamara addressed the people as follows : Whether in this our necessity God will help us, who can say ? it may turn out to the damage of our enemies. A mere over-casting of the sky implies not of necessity that rain will fall in torrents. I will have recourse to the king and explain to him the jealousy and malice of these our tribesmen.* And so Donchadh went to O'Brien's camp and related all that had passed; he set forth the consanguinity of those opposed to him, and therefore their wrong-doing. O'Brien required the Macnamaras to give hostages for the performance of the conditions of peace; fourteen of Clancuilein's best gentlemen, and among them Donchadh's own son, were consequently placed in the hands of the king. But in the following year O'Brien sent word to Clancuilein that he could no longer hold back the Hy-Blood from

* Standish H. O'Grady's translation of Magrath's " Triumphs of Turlough," p. 37.

attacking them. Peace, however, having been declared, Donchadh had dismissed his forces, and his hostages had been given, so that he was deprived of their help ; we are told on hearing this news " his brow lowered and his face flamed with anger. He gathered his household and sped messengers after his scattered warriors to recall them." His sept were, however, disturbed by what appeared to them to be " fickle counsels," first peace and then war, in spite of the precious hostages they had given. " And in all this they saw the destruction of the amity of the Dalcasian tribes, a beginning of Munster's confusion, an end of the kingdom built up by Turlough (O'Brien) and Covêha (Macnamara), the peacemaker."* Nevertheless, the members of the sept in their families hurried in to the call of their chief, and " all craved to be led against the enemy ; they advanced to the dewy, grass-clad hill of Ballycullen." This force was composed of the sept of Clancuilein, and only a small contingent of the O'Dorcons. Donchardh said to his followers : My brave people, whose courage is unquestionable, although your numbers are few ; ye are loyal each to each ; the bond that unites you is a chain of love, and your charge is that of the squealing litter of one sow. Woe to them at whom ye shall let yourselves go—you have the advantage of being led by one head who knows what he is aiming at, while your enemies have many heads, and no one knows which of them to obey. Donchardh then set to harness himself for battle. The first piece brought to him was a trusty, well-made acton, dense, close-ridged ; easily did he assume it, and the extent to which it protected him was from his throat to his knees. Over which he was invested with a loose mail shirt of hard rings, close of texture and with gilded borders. A fighting belt, moderately thick and fitted with a chased buckle, this he drew tight over his mail, and in it hung his dirk ready to hand ; it was strong in the point, wide in the blade, thick-backed, and fixed in a decorated wooden haft. Over his shoulders he wore a fine-textured white tippet of proof. He set his strong plated, conical helmet on his head, took his broadsword, deeply fluted, having a golden cross hilt and a tracery-embellished scabbard, which he girded to his side. In his right hand he took the handy dart, to hurl among the enemy ; in his left he grasped the thick-shafted, solid-riveted, great spear that he bore with which to charge the enemy.†

* S. H. O'Grady's translation of " Triumphs of Turlough," p. 38.

† This description of Donchardh Macnamara's war dress is given from Mr. S. H. O'Grady's translation of the " Triumphs of Turlough," for it affords us an excellent idea of an Irish chief's preparation for battle in the early part of the fourteenth century.

"At the same time great was the tribesmen's commotion as they required their crimson-broidered actons, bright mail, flashing blades, and far-reaching spears; as they handed over to their horseboys their horses to lead them to the rear, pursuant to their resolve that never would they desert their chief; and as they chose out their other arms too: the young men, taken with the beauty of them, holding to the gilded and otherwise embellished weapons; veterans picking rather the old, with which many and many a time before they had triumphed in the fight, while soldiers sewed colours to their staves, and standards' edges were fastened to their spears.

"Then with loud clear voice of command Donchardh said: ' Let your soldiers give ear ! govern your anger; moderate your clamour; instruct your raw lads; exalt your spirits; your standards rear aloft so that under them the colours shall show plain; and of your battle let there be there three columns made.' At the chief's behest the movement was executed, and three columns were formed: one under Donall Mac Maccon's and Lochlain Mac Namara with their rising out; another, Maccon's and Sheeda's; the third, (Donchardh's*), together with his chieftains, hospitallers, and household.

"To speak with his noble lord [his brother] Maccon then came, and the stripling, addressing his chief, said: ' Sheeda and I in very deed are the authors of this dissension; wherefore seeing that by our rash and ill-considered act we have started the war, be it this day granted us that we two give the first onset. For we being they whom those fierce battalions will the most ravenously seek to come at, and the fair mark of their leaders' displeasure, our army would but suffer loss all the greater for their being found in immediate proximity to us.' In answer to which (Donchardh) returned: ' As regards leading off in this battle your three divisions shall be favoured equally. The centre I myself will take, in order that on me the main fight's brunt shall fall; let you, the other two columns, as wings support me one on either side, to pierce the enemy's flanks in case that ye and they now meet on the field.'

"(Donchardh's) brief monition ended, presently they made out a glare of fire that revealed the presence of hostile scouts. Nor was this a bidding that failed of hearty response; for at once Clancuilein pushed on to the green-fenced marches of Kilgorey, whence they saw three strong corps (made up of many kindreds), gay and gallant, foes worthy of gentlemen, that with sword and spear in haste moved towards them. Yet again (Donchardh) spoke to his people: ' Until they shall have crossed the mearing, rise not !' Short then was the pause before Hy-Blood crossed it, and desperately charged Clancuilein's station. These with alacrity rising stood fast and firm to meet them, both sides set breast to breast upon the place and the A B C of the business was begun. On either hand continually they poured their darts into each other, sent the eager deadly javelins whistling on their way through shield and mail, and from their slings mutually a quivering cloud issued to fall in rain upon their heads and helmets, on their crests and weapons.

"Upon finding the ground to be thus stiffly disputed with them, Clancuilein after a time (as was but prudent) in good order retreated from their position; but when Hy-Blood saw the move, with one accord the whole body of them, from high to low, used such profitless tactics, luckless, and big with future

* In Mr. O'Grady's translation the name is Donough not Donchardh.

penitence, as by some famous and all-triumphant enemy they might have been induced to adopt : in other words, they renounced all pursuit and turned back again, thus throwing away their half-won victory.

" When Hy-Blood had voided the field, Clancuilein as claiming the advantage sent up a mighty shout ; (Donchardh) the chief made up his mind to stand, and from that instant again and again his battalions launched themselves on the enemy ; clan-Teigue overlapped them, clan-Sheeda stuck to them, clan-Donough laid into them, clan-Melachlin slaughtered their gentlemen, deftly clan-Lorcan maimed them, clan-Anerhiny slew them." *

After this " most notable feat of war which Clancuilein had executed," O'Brien having learned that they were not guilty of the late commotion, returned their hostages. But the other septs of Thomond took compassion on the cantreds of Hi-Blood, " who had been riddled through and through, their leaders fallen and their hospitallers thinned off," and so they combined to attack Clancuilein, a severe battle was fought and the Macnamaras were beaten, and many of their leaders slain. " As the gallant Donchardh with but a few about him to keep his retreat after that engagement, some of his people took counsel to fall on him, in pursuit of which evil resolve he was killed by them ; " an instance of treachery which, so far as the Irish records go, is unique in the history of our sept.

* Standish Hayes O'Grady's translation of the " Triumphs of Turlough," pp. 40 and 41.

CHAPTER IX

Anglo-Normans under De Clare and allies attack the O'Briens and Macnamaras, A.D. 1311—Lochlain Macnamara, chief of his sept, treacherously seized by De Clare and executed with his nephew, A.D. 1312—Mac-con (Macnamara) succeeds as head of Clancuilein—Robert Bruce invades Ireland—Appears on the Shannon—Skirmish with Clancuilein—Mac-con (Macnamara) and sept at battle of Corcomroe, A.D. 1350—Richard de Clare defeated and killed—The Anglo-Normans completely driven out of Clare, A.D. 1332—Extension of Clancuilien territory from Fergus to Shannon—Mac Con died, 1365—Cumedha succeeded, followed by Lochlain Mac Con, whose daughter married Brian O'Brien, King of Thomond, A.D. ? 1364—Appeal of Irish Chiefs to the Pope to establish English laws in Ireland or else leave her alone—Edward III.'s opinion regarding Ireland—Duke of Clarence sent over to subdue country—Successfully resisted by O'Briens and Clancuilein—" Mear Irish "—Kilkenny Parliament, A.D. 1367—Gerald Fitzgerald sent his son to be brought up by O'Brien and Macnamara in place of the English Court—Second Mac-con (Macnamara)—The most powerful Irish families united in marriage through the Macnamaras, A.D. 1370—Alteration in tenure of land as shown by Macnamara's rent roll and other documents of the fourteenth century.

THE Anglo-Normans living in and around Bunratty, were not slow to avail themselves of the weakness caused by the strife that was raging among the Celtic septs of Clare ; Richard De Clare at once formed an alliance with Dermot Brian Roe, who before De Clare assumed the head of affairs at Bunratty, had been defeated by King Donough O'Brien and Clancuilein, for the latter, notwithstanding their struggle with the other Dalcasian septs, appear to have joined Donough against the common enemy. The Macnamaras, after the murder of their chief, had elected his brother Lochlain Mac Cumea Macnamara in his place, he being, as Magrath states, " a favourite with the chiefs for his bravery, with his hospitallers for his good-natured deference, with the clergy for his justice, and with little children for his mildness, with ladies for his affable sweetness of temper ; " he married a daughter of Donough O'Connor, chief of Corcomroe.*

Donough O'Brien, in conjunction with the De Burghos of Galway, in May 1311 attacked Bunratty, but De Burgo was taken prisoner, and

* Pedigree in the collection of the late Col. J. D. Macnamara.

Donough O'Brien was compelled to flee into Burren; he was closely followed by De Clare. Mr. Westropp remarks that treachery is infectious; and the same fate awaited King Donough O'Brien as had befallen Donchardh Macnamara; he was slain by one of his own followers, and his army then dispersed over the country. There seems to be no other theory by which we can account for the assassination of the leader of Clancuilein, followed by that of the King of Thomond, unless it be that both these chiefs had been defeated, and seem to have brought disgrace on their followers. It may be that they were considered to be unfit to lead their forces, and that the penalty of defeat was death to men in their position. Richard de Clare and Dermot Brian Roe were now supreme rulers in Clare, and the latter, with the approval of his Anglo-Norman friends, was declared chief of Thomond. Dermot, however, did not long enjoy his honours. The De Burghos and Clancuilein favoured the cause of Turlough O'Brien's son, Mortogh, in opposition to that of Dermot : the former therefore invaded Clare, and met the lately chosen king, who, we are told, with all the Dalcasian septs, "except Clancuilein," offered De Burgho and his allies battle; after a short and sharp skirmish Mortogh and the Macnamaras were victorious, and Dermot was again compelled to seek shelter in Bunratty Castle. Mortogh O'Brien was then conducted to Magh Adhair, and inaugurated King of Thomond, by Lochlain, chief of Clancuilein.*

Magrath informs us that Sioda Macnamara, younger brother of Lochlain, while on an expedition into Burren caught a miserable sickness, from which he died, " his body he willed to St. Brendan, and his soul to heaven's high King—none ever thought that the descendant of Mogh Corb would have died save on the field of battle." In St. Brendan's churchyard in Burra his body was laid to rest, and "his household mourning for him raised three loud cries of sorrow."

Dermot Brian Roe, in the year 1312, seems to have overrun the greater part of Thomond, except the Ui-Caisen territory, which held its own under Lochlain Macnamara ; many a time attempts were made to gain access to their lands, but never once did any captain from such an attempt return, unless altogether penitent.† Throughout the winter, with its cold, its blast, and sough of boisterous gales, this contest was carried on; and then Lochlain's clansmen exhorted him to set out for Bunratty, he having a safe conduct from De Clare. But this was a trap

---

* S. H. O'Grady gives his name in full, " Lochlainn mac Cumea mac Conmara."

† "Triumphs of Turlough," by Rory Magrath, translated by Standish H. O'Grady, p. 54.

set by Dermot Brian Roe to capture Lochlain, his object being to separate him from his followers, and De Clare joined in this act of treachery. Lochlain Macnamara was seized, laid in hold, and bound with iron fetters; urged on by " chorister-canons," Lochlain was taken from Bunratty to Loch Coolmen, and there beheaded, together with his nephew, and their bodies were thrown into the lake. " Clancuilein's poet expresses himself in commemoration of their barbarous death," as follows:

" I mourn two horsemen of the verdant Adhair; two branches of the cooling
    Slieve Eachty,
Two hearts that can no more defend us; two graceful bowers sprung from one
    soil;
Ah! Coolmen's lake! harsh is thy fearful tale, the dismal death of Lochlain is our
    ruin;
Maolsechlain our lion, fell in secret beneath the hill; may these verses like stones
    guard their graves.
' Woe to the abettors of those who slew Lochlain; he fell like a deer among
    hounds.' " *

The following spring, Dermot Brian Roe was taken seriously ill; Magrath states that " after he (as a matter of habit) had been let blood, he never nursed the infirmity, but rashly persisted to run, hunt, ride, and wear armour. All of which combined oppressed the chief greatly, and the ailment grew exceedingly, until, for its intensity, he took to his bed." At this time, he was visited by Melachlin Macnamara, nephew of Lochlain, and it was then he was seized and executed as above stated, with his uncle. Dermot Brian Roe rapidly grew worse, and died.†

Immediately after Lochlain's murder his sept assembled, on the 1st of June, 1313, and elected his son Maccon Macnamara as chief of the sept. Maccon married a daughter (Mary) of O'Brien, of Inchiquin.‡ Mortough O'Brien, King of Thomond, being engaged with the septs west of the river Fergus, De Clare sent a trusted embassy to urge Maccon Macnamara to join his forces with those of the Anglo-Normans, and so effectually to dispose of Mortough, and ensure peace in the country. The sept of Clancuilein, however, on the advice of Maccon,

---

* "The Normans in Thomond," by T. J. Westropp, p. 387 (" Journal of the Royal Society of Antiquaries for 1891 "). The poet refers to the Hi-Blood and other septs who had risen in arms against Clancuilein.

† " Triumphs of Turlough," Standish H. O'Grady's translation, p. 55.

‡ We learn from Mr. S. H. O'Grady's translation of the " Triumphs of Turlough " that the sept " chose their lord, and he on whom their election fell was Maccon, nor did they use ceremony other than barely to style him ' Mac Conmara ' " (p. 56).

declined to listen to these overtures, or to be tempted by De Clare's offers of an increase of their territory to give up the cause of their elected king and relation, Mortough; and the agents of De Clare had consequently, after much excited speech, to take himself off to Bunratty.*

Soon after this attempt to allure Clancuilein from his cause, Mortough O'Brien came into the heart of the Ui-Caisen territory. The sept were right glad to welcome their lord and foster-brother; and with him they marched eastward to punish the Hi-Blood clan, who had taken an active part in the events which led to the execution of Lochlain; this deed, in fact, had been perpetrated in the Hi-Blood territory. Mortough O'Brien and his forces were well-nigh coming to grief in this expedition, for the Hi-Blood managed to out-manœuvre the king, and suddenly appeared in his rear. Maccon Macnamara instantly divided his men into two parties, ordering one to appear as if in flight, while the rest of his followers were to pretend to be in pursuit; the enemy were thus deceived, and taking those in flight for Mortough's force and their pursuers as a party of their own followers, rushed down in confusion on the rear of Maccon's men, who instantly turned on their enemies, and before they could re-form cut them to pieces. This kind of warfare was carried on throughout the years 1314 and 1315, Maccon and his sept always being in the thick of the fray.

In the following year Donough, who had been elected to succeed Dermot Brian Roe, having been defeated by Maccon Macnamara's sons, fled into Ulster, and in conjunction with some of the chiefs of that province entered into communication with King Robert Bruce, urging him to come over and conquer Ireland. Bruce was willing to accept this invitation, hoping thereby to weaken his enemies the English, and so he despatched his brother, Edward Bruce, with a well-equipped army, into Ireland. The Scotch army, with Donough Brian Roe and his allies, passed southwards from Ulster, ravishing and burning the whole country; as Magrath states, "like a black cloud with vaporous-creeping offshoots and dark mist, hard to meet."† Edward Bruce ultimately fought his way south as far as Cashel, where he was joined by King Robert Bruce. Donough Brian Roe urged them on to attack Thomond and sack Limerick, and, so our historian informs us,‡ "the Scots reached the Shannon's banks, with intent to attack them of Thomond gathered on the opposite bank, the Scots lying at Castleconnell; and between the parties ensued some skirmishing in the river vicinity. As for such as were hurt of the

* "Triumphs of Turlough," p. 64.   † Ibid., p. 83.   ‡ Ibid., p. 83.

Albanachs, they are not the gentry we bemoan; but on this hither side was wounded a noble scion of the Thomond host, one that was stuff of a captain, an imp of the genuine orchard Hugh mac Donough Macnamara, I mean, who, however, recovered from that peril." *

At this critical moment a meeting of English and Irish chiefs was summoned in Limerick, and it was determined with all speed to collect an army to resist the Scotch.   Mortough O'Brien was unanimously selected, both by the Irish chiefs and by all the Anglo-Norman barons who were present, to command the united forces.   The Irish and their allies seem to have been rapidly brought together, and they at once advanced against the enemy's position.   The Bruces, however, thought it prudent to retire.   Soon afterwards King Robert gave up the idea of conquering Ireland, and returned home; his brother Edward being subsequently defeated and killed in an engagement with the English at Dundalk.   The "Four Masters," referring to the Scottish invasion of Ireland, observe : " Edward Bruce, the destroyer of the people of Ireland, both English and Irish, was slain by the English.   No achievement had been performed in Ireland for a long time before from which greater benefit had occurred to the country than from this; for during the three and a half years Bruce spent in Ireland a universal famine prevailed to such a degree that men were wont to devour one another." It is impossible to add to the force of this account of the misery produced by this invasion of Ireland ; the progress of the Scotch throughout the country was followed by a fearful outbreak of the plague, which cut off a vast number of the famine-stricken population.   We cannot overlook the fact that the English, who had assumed the right to govern Ireland, practically stood on one side for three years, while the Scotch destroyed the inhabitants of the greater part of that country.   County Clare escaped much of this suffering, for we are expressly told that neither the invaders nor the plague reached the people of that province.

Richard de Clare, at the close of the year 1316, went to Dublin, hoping to persuade the Council to recognise his friend Donough Brien as King of Thomond.   Magrath observes that De Clare not only spoke several languages, but was also graceful in his address, and had remarkably fine teeth ; a remark not likely to have been made unless by some one who had seen the man.   Mortough O'Brien, hearing of these proceedings, hastened to Dublin, and laid before the Council his position in Clare, and the fact that during the recent advance of the Scotch to Limerick, he had been acknowledged as king and leader for the Anglo-Normans, as well as of the Irish tribes and septs of Thomond : the

* " Triumphs of Turlough," Standish H. O'Grady's translation, p. 84.

Council could not pass over this service, and Mortough was recognised as King of Thomond. It is well to observe that Henry II. and subsequent Sovereigns, in their charters and letters, always addressed the O'Briens as " Rex Regi Thomond." According to our ideas, it appears somewhat ridiculous giving the title of king to the chief of a portion of one of the provinces of Ireland ; it was probably difficult to know what other title to give him, for he was more than a chief; at the same time, although he received tribute, he certainly could not be said to govern his dominion, for the lesser chiefs made war on one another independently of their king.

Donough Brian Roe, who had already brought such trouble on his country and to the inhabitants of Thomond, having received intimation that De Clare had failed to persuade the government in Dublin to recognise him as King of Thomond, determined again to try what he could do by an appeal to arms ; he therefore threw himself on his former supporters and the chiefs west of the Fergus ; most of these chiefs rallied round him and assembled on the hills of Burren above Ballyvaughan.

Dermot O'Brien, in his brother Mortough's absence in Dublin, issued a summons to the chief landholders of his territory to meet him in council ; and having come together they discussed the means by which they might best assail their enemies. Magrath reports that Mac-con-Macnamara was one of the members of this council, and said, "if the sept of Clancuilein alone were called upon to meet the enemy it would be impossible to keep them from doing so.' But the Clan Mahons, Clan Teigue (a branch of Clancuilein), the O'Conors, O'Deas, and many other septs were full of enthusiam to join their chief ; and after drawing up their plans the council broke up, "without a shadow of misgiving," and its members returned " to their homes to get on with all that was needed for the emergency of that formidable encounter on which, towards the recovery of their patrimonial rights, they were resolved ; and the place of meeting which they appointed for the last muster before the march was Ruane, of the grass-clad caves." *

All preparations having been completed, these devoted "Gael of the true breed, with new standards and with burnished arms—with a sound appetite for the fray, they covered the distance to Ruane, where cheerily the contingents welcomed every one the other. Not a man of those crowded irachts but longed to fall to, and among them cordial words of welcome passed—without a failure they kept that tryst, and were moved as it were by the spirit of one man." †

Maccon Macnamara, prudent and with few words, addressed the

* " Triumphs of Turlough," S. H. O'Grady's translation, p. 88.   † *Ibid.*, p. 88.

assembly; he said : I am a prophet that is, endowed with genuine science, and to you all now will e'en declare some portion of my forecast. A hard and mortal battle ye will have this time : one such as for long has not been fought, but one which will end in the final triumph of our cause. The head and chief of our enemies will fall, among them Donough their leader, and far-famed Teigue of Limerick. My favourite mailshirt, which Donough now holds, I will bring home again. In order to back up which good forecast I will be the first to join battle ; for in the hour of onset a chief utters truth only, as Meave said to her spouse :

" Announce that which is pleasant, persevere to declare all that is most favourable, for every true prince is a prophet too." *

With these words the host was rejoiced, and northward as straight as a pole urged their way towards the enemy, until they arrived at the Abbey of Corcomroe, in Burren, close to the shores of Galway Bay ; within the precincts of the monastery they secured their cattle. During that night many of them slept on the floor of the church, others in the most comfortable cubicles, where they enjoyed soft luxury and secured deep sleep ; others passed the night in mirth, although on the morrow they might die or lose the soul of some dear friend.†

Donough Brian Roe and his force in the meantime had assembled on the hills to the west of Corcomroe ; he told his men to remember that the purpose with which they had come on this perilous expedition was to gain the battle, and so make an end once and for all of the long discussions (of our tribe), either by your antagonists' destruction or your own death one and all. Magrath repeats that Donough explained to his men that their opponents were children of Cas as they were, of the same blood, " with whom your close embrace of kinship will be that of steel to steel." Then he ordered the advance steadfastly therefore : " children of Cas, now steady be "—and so they came to the shore of Loch Rask, and while all were looking at the shining mere " they saw the monstrous and distorted form of a lone, ancient, hideous hag, that stooped over the bright loch's shore. The loathly creature's semblance was this : she was thatched with elf locks, foxy-grey and rough as heather, long as sea-wrack, inextricably tangled ; that had a bossy, wrinkled, foully ulcerated forehead, every hair of her eyebrows was like a strong fishhook, and from under them, bleary dripping eyes peered with malignant fire between lids all rawly crimson-edged. . . . . The crone had a cairn of heads, a pile of arms and legs, a load of spoil, all of which she rinsed and diligently washed, so that by her labour the water of the lake was covered with hair and

* S. H. O'Grady's translation of " Triumphs of Turlough," p. 89.   † *Ibid.*, p. 89.

gory brains. The army, hushed, intently and long gazed at her, but the chief spoke to the beldame : 'What is thy name, what people are thine, or whom are kin, these the so maltreated dead on this moist shore?' she nothing loth replied : 'The Dismal of Burren I am named always, 'tis of the *tuatha dé Danann* I declare myself, and, royal chief, this pile stands for your heads, in their midst thine own head : which now thou carriest it, yet no longer is thine. Proudly as thou goest to battle, the time is not far from you when all to a very few ye must be slain.'"

By the perverse wretch's bitter forecast the host was startled, and with javelins straightway would have cast at her ; but on the rushing wind she rose above them and, being well aloft, delivered herself thus defiantly :

"Ill betide all that march here! a baneful trip 'twill be, an effort big with wrath! the combat will be rude ; till Doom 'twill ring how such an host rushed into fight ; there will abound both pointless spears and swords [shivered] to the bone [hilt], sighs, moans and grief for clan-Cas slain, a woeful tale ; the Red Chief's clan ; 'tis they must fail, must sink at last ; their prince shall fall ; thou comely Donough thou com'st not back ; smooth Brian of Berra shall supine be left ; Murtough More though fierce is stricken his body pruned. I tell you all your march bodes ill, your eastward course will breed much woe ! " *

But to his good host Donough cried : "Never heed ye the daft thing's rambling prophecy ; for in yon miserable being ye have nought but one that is a warlock leman to Brian-descended clan-Turlough-More, and in dread of their destruction at your hands, seeks thus to turn you back. For all that, let her not bring your gentles' natures to recoil ; but 'heads down' (like charging bulls) valorously achieve the onset which against your enemies ye have decreed."†

With Donough's incitement their temper rose and undeviatingly they strode on.

As Mr. Westropp observes, remarkable as Magrath's account of the appearance of this supernatural being is, no one who has heard the stories of people living in Burren at the present day can be surprised at his description. In this district circumstantial statements are common as to the visits of Banshees even in recent times, often told by people who had themselves seen such apparitions ; it is no wonder therefore that an author of the thirteenth century should indulge his readers with myths of this description.

We must, however, return to our historian's account of Dermot O'Brien's force which, as before stated, passed the night before the battle in the Abbey of Corcomroe. At the dawn of day they were awakened by reports of the advance of the enemy with standards displayed, with

* "Triumphs of Turlough," p. 93. † *Ibid.*, p. 94.

colours flying, and with gilt spears." Dermot, and Maccon Macnamara issued from the abbey, and Magrath observes, "a strange sight it was to see those Clancuileins come tumbling out and wriggle on their harness as they ran; nor ever, out of any monastery whatsoever had there streamed an order more grimly bent on fighting for their lands." We are informed that "the septs ranged themselves each under their own individual lord apart, and they then closed order under Dermot." Magrath states that Maccon Macnamara got himself into his armour, hard mail of proof, over which was a tunic, in which garb, as the chief was a-harnessing, his attendants in haste put it back in front upon him; he bade them return it carefully, and said: "We shall all the better be for this oversight, which portends some gain" still [even greater than that looked for]. Now steadily hook on the tippet and clasp the mail, fasten my helmet on my head, for this armour I will not change until as its price from yonder folk I win a better set.

"Here Clancuilein's phalanx fell in about their lord, and the leading gentlemen of the attack were Nicol Mac Cumea Macnamara, extreme particular spear point on all onset, special shield of deadly retreat; he was a ruddy youth of open countenance and handsome features, red-lipped, close-bearded, stalwart, and staunch, whose lot it was in this affair to take his brother and chief's right shoulder; nor surely may we pity one that at this juncture hath a shoulder prop such [as this of Maccon's] in battle; young Hugh Macnamara also, bushy and curly-headed, a genuine heir of Clancuilein, who stepped to his kinsman's other shoulder to be his guard."* And so Magrath continues, evidently describing as an eye-witness only could do, the words and characteristics of the men who fought in the year 1317 at Corcomroe.

They advanced with spears to the fore, and colours flying. Magrath informs us that Maccon proclaimed: In this field we will, if it so please you, have no precedence of kindreds, but every man that wishes to be to the fore let him for the first onfall race even as I will race; he that prefers the centre or is satisfied with the rear, according to his fancy, let him hang back and do such service as he may. Maccon further called on the chosen one hundred of his sept that had vowed to fall with him to come to the fore; but these words were hardly uttered before the "whole of Clancuilein answered with one voice, and rushed to surround their chief." †

And so the opposing forces reached the plain, whose face was scored with irregular seams; the foremost ranks let fly their stones and javelins,

* "Triumphs of Turlough," translated by Standish H. O'Grady, p. 96.
† Ibid., p. 98.

darts and arrows. The two sides then met hand to hand with ringing cheers, and spears well to the fore. Magrath gives a detailed account of the battle and of the valour shown by the chiefs of the various septs engaged, which may best be read in Mr. O'Grady's translation of Magrath's history.* As regards Clancuilein, he states that on Macnamara "fell the task of keeping the battle braced together; there he stood rooted and held the key of the position, dealing death to his enemies. For out of the West hardly was there come champion or great chief's son, chieftain or noble captain of Clan Brian Roe but continually and wildly cried out for Macnamara"—and in response to them his chiefs, one after the other, sprang to meet his challengers. Maccon had no easy game to play, as he found himself planted in the centre of the fight, encircled with a trusty band of his sept, who parried many a blow for him—among these, Nicol Macnamara fought desperately—and the feats that he performed, which, but for his shield, that proved his salvation, could never have been carried through. Hugh mac Donough Macnamara likewise did doughty service, though but a stripling, and so on with other members of the sept.† At length Donough Brian Roe was slain, and his followers were completely defeated by Dermot O'Brien and the Clancuilein and other septs of the Dalcasian tribe under his command. Dermot addressed his soldiers, urging them not to be overcome by the grief for the friends that had been slain. His words are reported as follows :

"Good army, children of Tal, now play the men ! no soldiers' work soft grieving is ; shake off your care and ours ; our remedy exceeds our hurts ; ye have before you labours which it were right that ye performed efficiently : all that by you on this ground are fallen of Brian-of-the-Tribute's clans, to honour them with tomb and sepulture ; from among those heroes to seek out and to set aside your own dead friends ; to count the spoils and heads ; to bind wounds stricken home to the quick ; to enter into possession of the principality ; at any cost to keep up your spirits. In God's name then, play the men and do it well ! " ‡

The sept of Clancuilein suffered most severely. Twenty-one of their principal leaders were killed, and among their slain chiefs was the lad above referred to. Magrath reports that Maccon lamented Hugh's death, who, with eight other of their chiefs, were buried in one trench, and the chief, bewailing them, said :

"Both good and bad this hosting has turned out : many as are our losses, the onfall to which we treated our enemy was a proper one ; good restitution we have gotten : our noble foe's best gentles ; for all that, alas, that I have not Hugh :

* Standish H. O'Grady's translation of " Triumphs of Turlough " (by Rory Magrath, A.D. 1459), p. 101.   † Ibid., p. 102.   ‡ Ibid., p. 204.

my heart's gentle darling, sense and intelligence of my soul! our far-ranging hunting hawk the athletic dark-browed stripling was, and shepherd of our irachts, swift, and the well beloved of our fighting men! after Hugh of the golden weapons, sad is our solitary singleness!" *

The bodies of Donough Brien and his chiefs were carefully buried by the Dalcasians side by side of their own dead "branches of the parent vine who had ceased to strive for the chiefry" (Magrath). After this office had been completed, "and hastily binding up of their wounds, fathers, with weak and faltering steps, were engaged in tending their sons, or sons bore their fathers to their abiding places of clayey mould; so that, with the numerous graves, the precincts of the abbey was ploughed up." Magrath's account of what followed is so characteristic that I have taken the liberty of appropriating it at length from the translation by Mr. Standish H. O'Grady. Our historian states:†

"So the army after their toil and travail had respite: some of the gentlemen triumphing over the foe and counting their own successes [how many and whom they had killed]; others bewailing their own losses and discussing those they had inflicted; others equitably dividing the strippings and totting up their gains; some shaking their actons and washing their mail, while others moaned and hoarsely groaned for the fresh wounds that made them like to swoon.

"It was but a short time that they had been devoted to these strange occupations when there came to them a hurried messenger, and: 'let your gentlemen arise to fall you in,' he cried, 'and your chiefs to get you into position; with all speed armour your champions, bustle up your kerne; in silence but resolutely, promptly, come forth of the monastery; for to attack you comes on a very torrent of enemies, a battle-armed flag-flying array, and smooth-panoplied over-numerous formidable mass, of anything but friends.'

"By these words pleasurable feelings were evoked both in leaders and in men, and they [the former] answered: 'not for a mere random while, not for a brief spell only, fortune escorts and follows you, from the day when good luck has conveyed your enemies to fall on you here. And whereas on this field many a one of you fought hard without preconceived special enmity to your opponents, now on the contrary not a man of you but feels for them abiding rooted detestation because of your companies fallen by their captains; [while they regard us in the same light] because of their supreme chief and foremost notables perished at our companies' hands. Neither in this present strait should we find coming against us "heads of battle" equal to the chiefs of a while

* Standish H. O'Grady's translation of "Triumphs of Turlough," p. 105.
† Ibid., from p. 109 to p. 112.

ago [whom we have buried]; hold ye therefore fast and maintain the triumph ye have won, and your kith and kin save ye that they be not beheaded. For your mangled are a multitude indeed, and to defend them we must make a dogged stand.' And the poet of the host went on :—

' Let your battles in their numbers rise . . . .'

"At which bright words, proudly they strode towards the enemy to meet him. Even their injured rose and in rough-and-ready fashion stanched their wounds: first, with moss they plugged the holes in their skins, then clapped on the rigid surface of close-fitting armour and the flat of their broad belts, to close the lips of their live cuts and gashes.

"With this coarse treatment they came away, cheerily saying : ' we verily being they to whom this coming bout promises the more advantage, all for the best it is that this godsend of our foemen's present menacing advance is granted to us; for our tribesmen have no interest to spare us, that on our enemies we should not spend our strength's last remnant.' Then their superiors strove to turn these damaged ones back to their sick beds again, but they said : 'nay, not so; this your design is not conceived aright; for of you all there is not a band whom more than us, this crippled company, it should become now to do battle valiantly. For this reason : both that we the least are able to elude it; and that, by our immediate forcible extinction, we shall be to you a loss the more trifling that already we stand in so near jeopardy of our doom. Neither in the result would it bring us honour that we tarried here behind you, which would but involve our decapitation by the enemy. Wherefore a just thing it is to use us up in the battle's first shock, and in the opening passage of the handiwork; for our ability to fly has abandoned us, our swift motion is disabled, nor have we possibility of escape from them, although our courage and skill at arms continue unimpaired.'

" After this debate it was but a little time (which they spent in nursing fierce inclination, in wrathfulness and impatience) until they saw hasty runners that from the other party came in, and advised them that the crowded phalanx they perceived to draw towards them was Conor O'Dea, the messenger adding : ' to sue for friendship, that he may come and speak with you, such is the motive of our advent.'

" At which hearing, disappointment overtook the gentlemen and petulantly, with small reticence, they said that to Conor they would give no amity : ' rather (quoth they) take him our curse; no good bodes this essay of his to get at [spy out] our invalids.' Here now their condition was pitiable : such as the most proudly had worn their armour to the place of that lively scrimmage which [as the thing turned out] they

never had, were they that from their standing posture in the ranks fell
fast and lay along. The mail being taken off them, ruddy jets came
redly spirting and spouting through their wounds, at their angry hurts'
slant open portals, and wide apertures of slashes dealt into the life, so
that with those brave men's blood the softly green-grassed spot which
they had taken up was all bedabbled and defiled. Never was heard
muffled sound more lamentable than their diverse companies' confused
hum as they lighted on their friends, carefully tended the infirm and
called to their leeches; into their fresh wounds stuffed pledgets,
expedited their confessions, and tenderly carried off their generous
comrades. For now that they found themselves defrauded of the
battle, of that brilliant host great plenty that in the very front readily
and briskly [for this second time] came out of the monastery all eager
to encounter, into the same were lifted back speechless and weak and
torpid.

"Now this made the third summit of high emprise and genuine
honour of the far-westerns, achieved [in the interval extending] from the
day in which first from blue Spain's rugged coasts the Gael arrived in
Ireland, until [this in which] the great battle of the Abbey [was decided].
And it cannot be but that to them of all Erin, besides it is a mischief
[grievance] that one and the same noble stock should have ambitioned
and attained to said three pinnacles of renown. The first occasion then
on which Brian's clans made their own of victory so imperishable was
the day of Clontarf's battle, by which both Gael and fresh-come Norse-
man thickly were exterminated ; but by obstinacy of the Gael it was won
after their leaders all were fallen with Brian and his son Morrough.
When the white Danes however, quite fresh, and their city's whole garrison [of Dublin] as well [by way of reinforcement], came upon the scene
to fall on the freeborn but enfeebled residue which [before they themselves died] the Norsemen had left of the Gael, a fine tale of slaughter
there would have been to tell had not the Dalcasians (cut up as they
were) risen and put the black Galls to instant flight

"The second turn at which again the Clancassians took the honours
was when, as Brian's son Donough returned from his preyings and with
the remnant of his gallant companies was on the march, Ossory in force
gathered against the Dalcasians to require hostages of Donough mac
Brian. Heart's torment to *clanna Chais* were these expressions: that
by reason of their fewness and debility their own continued and ex
origine natural servitors would have pledges of them. Therefore in their
weak ones anger rose, valorous disposition in their injured, and in their
dilapidated a flame was kindled, when they heard them whom the

natural fitness of things disqualified for such presumption, demand to have superiority over the children of Cas. Out of the order of battle in which they had stood to make their demand, headlong in spite of them they hurled Ossory; who being fled, many of the [wounded] Clancassians (after the effort of screwing themselves up for the fight) died.

"The present turn was the third at which the Dalcasians scored even such another signal triumph; but for outsiders in general [all Ireland] it was far from a triumph that above all Erin's tribes *clanna Chais* should have had this success, no matter how creditably they (as we have seen) carried it.

"Their heavy burthens they raised accordingly and bore into the abbey, where abundant wounded were in extremity, soldiers mutilated, leaders in dead faint, and where young men made lamentation."*

"A baneful scare ye had . . . ."

Magrath tells us that in the battle "a spear was put through Mac-con Macnamara's foot, which was the only part of his body not covered with armour." He adds that "if this was done to pin him to his place there was but little need to so severely harm it; for always in all battles and affrays his step was as deliberate as bold, solidly maintained no less than lively taken. Fine command he had of his strong fast-striking arm and polished long blue Danish blade, that shore and rent and laid about whenever any measured swords with him. In all phases of war his heart was firm, daring, hardy to undertake; never fear nor anxiety assailed his nature for enemy's numbers that he saw drawn up against him; and it was to expound all this that the poet made these quatrains :—

"A hero's qualities has Maccon . . . ." †

Mac-con went to Clonroad to be healed, and his nephew was brought to Ennis, where "his body, though it recovered not, yet his soul's cure was the result"; which means that he was at peace with God. The other wounded were borne to their homes; the whole host, sound and lame, scattered to their dwellings, and then it was that the poet uttered a lay :

"Victorious, O progeny of Tal . . . ."

In the summer following the battle of Corcomroe, under guarantee given by De Clare's wife and son, Mac-con Macnamara, as Mortough O'Brien's representative, went to offer De Clare terms of peace.‡ Sir·

* Standish H. O'Grady's translation of Magrath's "Triumph of Thomond," pp. 109–112.

† "Triumphs of Torlough," translated by Standish H. O'Grady, p. 115.

‡ *Ibid.* p. 120.

Richard, however, rejected these proposals; and on his own account tried to lure Mac-con into accepting terms granting him (Mac-con) "all sorts of privileges, and great wages" if he would only now turn and join the Anglo-Normans, who would protect him and his people. Macnamara at once replied that he could not listen to such proposals but only those which had Mortough O'Brien's approval, "seeing (he said) that whether for peace or war by him he would stand." Mac-con then took his leave of De Clare and went home to confer with O'Brien and the chiefs of Thomond. Magrath records that he said, "at the hands of yonder abominable perverse English gang, cruel and insatiable, overbearing, surly, sullen, full of spite, malevolence, and ill design, never (except as by virtue of bravery and of conduct in war, and by the strong hand generally you shall expel them) will ye have freedom or truce, peace or goodfellowship. Hence it behoves us stoutly and by main force to hold our countries against De Clare."*

In the following year it was decided to hold a conference in Limerick, to again endeavour to arrange terms of peace. De Clare and Mahon Brien attended this assembly, as well as the head of the Butlers and Bourkes; Mortough O'Brien and Mac-con Macnamara also came to the council, and propounded terms and guarantees of peace to the barons; but they were not acceptable. De Clare determined, therefore, to make a last effort to overthrow the Celtic chiefs of Clare; he had played one faction against another for years without success, and it seemed to him necessary now to rally all the Anglo-Normans he could collect, and, in conjunction with such of the Irish as chose to follow him, to do his best to crush the chiefs who had for so long stood between him and the possession of the territory now known as county Clare. De Clare was aided by Brian Bane, grandson of Brian Roe.† He marched to Quin, where he rested for a night, and then he passed over the Fergus westward. While crossing the river, a strange female apparition is said to have appeared to De Clare. Magrath states that she spoke Gaelic; and so De Clare asked his Irish followers to tell him who she was' and what she meant in washing a quantity of such blood-stained robes in the river. The banshee stated she was "Bronach, and abode in the fairy hills of the land, but that her permanent residence was among the dwellers of hell, from which place she had come to invite De Clare to follow her." Sir Richard scoffed at the creature, and passed on; his object being to attack the stronghold of the O'Deas. That chief was on the look out, and placed a number of his followers in some woods near a causeway and

* "Triumphs of Turlough," p. 120.
† "Historical Memories of the O'Briens," p. 126.

ford, over which it was necessary for De Clare to advance. On the following morning, De Clare, having detached a part of his troops to make a flank movement, so as to attack O'Dea in the rear, advanced with his main body on Dysert. Its round towers rose boldly over the trees and crags, little more than a mile westward.* O'Dea sent a number of his retainers to appear as though engaged in driving cattle over the ford. De Clare attacked them; and as they turned to defend the causeway De Clare, with his bravest knights, rode to the front. The O'Deas retreated, and were followed by De Clare over the ford, and so were separated from the main body of his troops, when he was suddenly set upon by the Irish previously hidden among the bushes on the sides of the road leading from the ford; and before his men could come to his aid Sir Richard and sixteen of his best knights were killed.

"Too late to save their leaders, the main body of the English force made their way with difficulty across the stream, and beset the survivors of the O'Deas in the wood. Just then O'Conor and his troops appeared on a hill above; they charged down the slope, and over the lowland, and fell on the English. These stood their ground bravely, headed by De Clare's son, who fought hand to hand with O'Conor; but the brave youth was at length overcome, gallantly dying on the field of battle, as became the heir of so noble a race as the De Clares.

Lady De Clare, directly she heard of the death of her husband and son, placed her belongings in boats, and passed over the Shannon; before leaving Bunratty, she ordered the place to be set on fire. This was the last of the Anglo-Normans in Clare; they had absolutely failed, after fifty years' fighting, to obtain possession of a single acre in that part of Ireland. The O'Briens, and Macnamaras had resisted them manfully, and succeeded in preserving their lands from the intrusion of strangers; a condition of things they maintained until as late as the year 1654.

It is true the English, after the battle of Dysert-O'Dea, assigned the castle and estate of Bunratty to Matelda, wife of Robert de Wells, and another sister of De Clare's, and appointed R. Sutton to hold the castle as a safeguard to the traders of Limerick, but in 1332, eleven years before Mortough O'Brien's death, the place was attacked and taken by Mac-con Macnamara, and so the king lived to see his power established from Limerick to the cliffs of Moher.†

Our sept had taken a leading part throughout the long years of warfare in Clare, so that we are not surprised to hear at the termination of the struggle they annexed the territory of the Hybloids and other septs who

* T. J. Westropp's papers in "The Normans in Thomond," p. 470 ("Journal of the Royal Society of Antiquaries of Ireland for 1891").   † Ibid., p. 472.

during the thick of the contest had attempted to crush Clancuilein, and who had put to death their favourite chief, Lochlain Macnamara. The lands of our sept were therefore, with King Mortough's full approval, extended so as to include almost the whole of that part of Clare situated between the rivers Fergus and Shannon, an area occupying some twenty miles from east to west, and eighteen miles from north to south.

Brian Bane, who had fought for De Clare at Dysert, fled from the field, and, with the consent of King Mortough O'Brien, was assigned lands in Ormond. He here came in contact with the English of the Pale, and entered into an alliance with them such as that which had existed between himself and De Clare. With the aid of his new friends Brian Bane first attacked De Burgo, who was supported by the Macnamaras and O'Briens; but the latter were defeated, and in the following year, A.D. 1328, Mortough and Mac-con Macnamara were again worsted by Brian and the English. After this, until the time of Mortough's death, which took place in the year 1343, the inhabitants of Clare seemed to have enjoyed comparative peace. We unfortunately lose the assistance of Rory Macgrath at this period of our history, for his work was brought to a close with the death of Mortough O'Brien. Macgrath, however, mentions Mac-con Macnamara as being alive in the year 1343, and we have good reason to believe that he continued as head of his sept certainly as late as A.D. 1365.

Clancuilein had not only been much weakened by the fighting they had passed through, but they were at this time invaded from Connaught, the king of that province he "marched into the Macnamara's territory in Munster, from whom he took hostages, and thus forced the sept to submit to Connaught."* In consequence of this state of things, on the death of Mortough O'Brien, Clancuilein was not in a position to support his brother Dermod to obtain possession of the throne, in opposition to Brian Bane, who at length found himself able to take by force the office of King of Thomond, which his father and grandfather had so long striven to obtain. Brian, however, only enjoyed his honours for a few years, for in 1350 he was assassinated by one of his own family.†

Dermod O'Brien, Mortough's brother, succeeded and died without issue; he was followed as chief of Thomond by his nephew, who died in 1360, and he was succeeded by Brian O'Brien as King of Thomond. Mac-con Macnamara lived on through all these changes; his son, we are informed by "The Four Masters," was slain in the year 1356, and, they add he "was the best son of a chieftain of his time; a youth of great

* "Annals of Ulster," A.D. 1331   † "O'Brien Memoirs," p. 130.

eminence and worth. " He met with his death through internal dissensions."

Mac-con therefore was succeeded by his Tanist, Cumedha Macnamara,* and he was followed by (Lochlain) Mac-con Macnamara, a grandson of Lochlain who had been executed in A.D. 1312. This man was twice married; by his first wife he had three sons, Sioda,† Tiegie,‡ and Mahon,§ and a daughter Slaine; by his second wife, one son, called by some authorities Hugh, by others John. (Lochlain) Mac-con Macnamara's daughter, Slaine, married Brian O'Brien, King of Thomond.‖

The Macnamaras had taken possession of Bunratty after the departure or rather expulsion of the Anglo-Normans from the castle, and in the year 1353 one of the few cases of " ecclesiastical discipline " recorded in the history of Clare overtook two members of the Macnamara sept. It seems these two men denied the doctrine of the Holy Trinity, and of the Incarnation, and rejected the authority of the Holy See. Rather than renounce their error they were burnt to death at Bunratty, by order of the bishop.¶

The opinion of the best informed Irishmen as to the social and political position of their countrymen during the early part of the fourteenth century is to be found in a document which they drew up and forwarded to King Edward the Third of England. In this document the leading Celtic chiefs of Ireland urged the king to adopt one of two courses : either to govern Ireland by English law, which to them appeared what should be done ; or else to leave the country to govern itself according to her own laws and customs. King Edward referred this petition to his advisers in Dublin, and they came to the conclusion that no action should be taken in the matter. Sir John Davies, Attorney-General for Ireland in the time of James the First, in his able work on the " True Cause why Ireland was never entirely subdued," refers to this appeal of the Irish chiefs. He observes : " I note a great defect in the policy of England ; in that for the space of many years after the so-called conquest of Ireland, the English laws were not communicated to the Irish, nor the benefit and protection thereof allowed unto them, though they earnestly desired and sought the same." Sir

---

* Frost's " History of Clare," p. 36.

† Sioda was killed in Limerick, A.D. 1369.

‡ Tiege, killed by his half-brother Hugh, A.D. 1378 (see Annals of Ulster and also of Clonmacnois).

§ Was an ecclesiastic of some kind, and whose family we shall subsequently find possessed of property in Tulla.   ‖ " O'Brien Memoirs," p. 135.

¶ Hon. R. O'Brien : note to " Dineley's Tour " (" Journal of the Archæological Society, vol. vi. 1867, p. 88).

John remarks that no true idea can be formed of Irish history unless full weight is given to this fact.

The Irish chiefs having been repulsed by King Edward, turned for help to the Supreme Pontiff (A.D. 1316), and forwarded to Rome a petition containing a summary of the grievances under which they and their countrymen suffered. This letter to the Pontiff commences with a recital of the early Celtic history of Ireland, and then passes on to the invasion of the country by Henry the Second, and to inform the Pope that the English "are incessant in their pursuit after us, endeavouring to chase us from among them; they lay claim to every place in which they can discover us—they allege that the whole kingdom belongs to them of right. From these causes arise the implacable hatred and dreadful animosity of the English and the Irish towards each other. We had once our laws and institutions; the Irish were remarkable for their candour and simplicity," but from the cruelty of the English they had "become artful and designing." * This memorial to the Pope states that the system established by the English in Ireland may be summed up as follows :

1. " Every man who is not Irish, may, for any kind of crime go to law with any Irishman, while neither layman nor ecclesiastic who is Irish can under any cause of provocation resort to any legal measure against his English opponent."

2. "If any Englishman kill an Irishman perfidiously and falsely, noble or plebeian, innocent or guilty, including the clergy, the crime is not punishable before our English tribunal."

3. " If any Irishwoman marry an Englishman, on the death of her husband she becomes deprived of one third of the property and possessions which he owned."

4. " If an Irishman fall beneath the blow of an Englishman, the latter can prevent the vanquished from making any testamentary deposition, and may likewise take possession of his wealth."

The Sovereign Pontiff was sufficiently impressed by these and other usages complained of, to forward this document to King Edward III., with the observation that, having " considered the matter maturely, we behest your majesty that you remove the cause of these misfortunes by fulfilling the duties of lord and master you may afford no subject for complaint, by which means the Irish, guided by a wise administration, may obey you as lord of Ireland ; " advice which, unfortunately, King Edward neglected, although he was distinctly warned by the Pope that " *those complaints should not be neglected in the beginning, lest evils increase by degrees, and the necessary remedies be applied too late.*"†

Wiser advice was never given, or more conspicuously neglected, until it was indeed " too late."

---

* " The History of Ireland," by the Abbe Macgeoghegan, translated by Patrick O'Kelly, p. 324.

† Macgeoghegan's " History of Ireland," p. 326.

Sir John Davies, writing two and a half centuries later than the Pope, regarding the state of Ireland, observes that "so long as the Irish were out of the protection of the law, so as every Englishman might oppress, spoil, and kill them without control, how was it possible they should be other than outlaws and enemies of the crown of England ? If the king would not admit them to the condition of subjects, how could they learn to acknowledge and obey him as their Sovereign ? When they might not converse or trade with any civil man, nor enter into any town or city without peril of their lives, whither should they fly but to the woods and mountains, if the English magistrate would not rule them by the law which doth punish treason, and murder, and theft with death, but leave them to be ruled by their own laws and lords, why should they not embrace their own Brehon laws which punisheth no offence except by an eric or fine ?"

It was to preserve their tribe and people from the untold misery created by such a state of society as that described by so able a lawyer as Sir J. Davies, that the O'Briens and Macnamaras fought so obstinately and so effectively during the twelfth, thirteenth, and following centuries, their object being to maintain their lands and laws, and to this end prevent the English from gaining possession of Clare. The Anglo-Norman families in the West of Ireland had, together with the native Celts, become so convinced of the misery caused by the action of England in Ireland, that the former preferred to throw in their lot with those Irish chiefs into whose families they had married. Ulick de Burgho (Clanricarde) and Sir E. Bourke, ancestor of Viscount Mayo, declared themselves independent of England, and "on the banks of the Shannon, in sight of the royal garrison of Athlone, threw aside their Norman dress and arms and assumed the saffron robe of Celtic chieftains." * So completely did these and other Anglo-Norman chiefs become fused into the native population that they are described as having become more Irish than the Irish themselves. No doubt the proclivities of these noblemen were towards the freedom of action enjoyed by Irish chiefs, who exercised not only the power of life and death over their tribemen, but could also command their services to a man in any military undertaking which they and their clan approved.

Edward III. has left us his views as to the condition of Ireland. He stated that his dominion in that country had "been reduced to such utter devastation, ruin, and misery, that they may be totally lost if our subjects there are not immediately succoured." "Our subjects" meant the English of the Pale ; and to succour these he sent his son,

* "The Story of the Nations—Ireland," by the Hon. Emily Lawless, p. 111.

the Duke of Clarence, over to Ireland; * on arriving in the country one of the Duke's first acts was to "publish an order to the effect that none of Irish birth should be allowed to approach him or his army, nor be employed in service of the warres." † (A.D. 1361). Lionel, Duke of Clarence, then commenced his march on Thomond, intending to break the power of the O'Briens, but his heavily armed men soon got mixed up in the bogs, and lost their way in the forests for want of guides. O'Brien was thus able to cut them off in detail; and the end of it was the expedition had to be abandoned, and so Clare was again preserved from an invasion by the English. The Duke of Clarence in the year 1367 met his Parliament in Kilkenny; and they then passed the famous Act of that year. In the preamble of this Act it is affirmed that whereas at the conquest of Ireland, and for long after, the English had used the language, mode of riding, apparel, and had lived under English law, now many of them had forsaken these customs and laws and usages; they live and govern themselves, according to the manners, fashions, and language of the Irish enemies; and also have made divers marriages and alliances between themselves and the Irish enemies aforesaid."

The meaning of the expression "Irish enemies" is explained in a letter of Richard II. to the Duke of York.‡ He remarks: "In Ireland there are three kinds of people, wild Irish, *our enemies;* Irish rebels, the English who had thrown off their allegance to the crown; and obedient English."§ King Richard adds: "To us and our Council it appears that the Irish rebels have rebelled in consequence of the injustice and grievances practised towards them, for which they have been offered no redress, and that if not wisely treated and given hopes of grace they will ally themselves with our enemies":‖ language very similar to that which the Pope used to King Edward, and with as little result. To return, however, to the Act passed by the Kilkenny Parliament in 1367:

By section 2 it was provided that "no alliance by marriage, compaternity, fostering of children, concubinage, or by amour, nor in any other manner, be henceforth made between the English and Irish of one part, or of the other part; and

---

* The Duke of Clarence had married Elizabeth, daughter of William, Earl of Ulster, whose mother, Hodiera, was wife of Richard de Burgho, and so traced her descent back to Roderick, King of Connaught, who had, in A.D. 1175, as "Rex Hiberniæ," entered into a treaty with Henry II. It is by Elizabeth of Ulster, and Lionel, Duke of Clarence, that Her Majesty the Queen, through hereditary descent, is brought into relation with the Celtic ruler of Ireland, the last *Ard-Ri,* or High-King of all Erin.

† Campion's "History of Ireland," p. 135.   ‡ Spenser's "History," p. 23.
§ Joyce's "Short History of Ireland," p. 326.
‖ Richey's "History of Ireland," p. 216.

that no Englishman, nor any person, being at peace, do give or sell to any Irish-man, in time of peace or war, horses or armour, nor any manner of victuals in time of war ; and if any shall do the contrary, he shall have judgment of life and member, as a traitor to our lord the king."

Section 3 : " Every Englishman do use the English language, and be named by an English name, leaving off entirely the manner of naming used by the Irish ; that every Englishman use the English mode of riding and apparel ; and if any Englishman, or Irish living amongst the English, use the Irish language amongst themselves, his lands and tenements shall be seized into the hands of his imme-diate lord ; if he have no lands he be committed to the next gaol ; that beneficed persons of holy Church living amongst the English shall use the English language."

Section 4 provides : " No Englishman, having a dispute with another English-man, shall henceforth make capture, or take pledge, distress, or vengeance against any other ; that no Englishman be governed in the termination of their disputes by Brehon law, being a bad custom, but shall be governed by the common law of the land ; and if any do the contrary he shall be adjudged a traitor."

By section 15 " it is agreed and forbidden that any Irish agents, that is to say, piper, storyteller, babblers, rimers, shall come amongst the English, and that no English shall receive or make gift to such. If he shall do so he be imprisoned."

Much of this Act was doubtless intended to apply to the English within the Pale; beyond that region the Government felt that it had really no power. Dr. Richey rightly states that the passing this Act was a retrograde step, and admission of defeat; for Henry II. had assumed power to rule Ireland, not one of its provinces only.

Brian O'Brien (p. 132) had hardly come into possession of Thomond when he was attacked by the Earl of Desmond (Gerald FitzGerald), but with the aid of Lochlain Macnamara, the English Earl and his allies were thoroughly beaten, and Desmond, together with several other noblemen, were taken prisoners by O'Brien and Clancuilein. " On this occasion Limerick was burnt by the Clancuilein, upon which the inhabitants capitulated. Sioda, son of Lochlain Macnamara (by his first wife O'Dwyer) assumed the wardenship of the town, but the English who were in it acted treacherously towards him and killed him." A.D. 1369.*

Sir William Wyndsor had been sent over from England as Lord Deputy of Ireland, and he took advantage, as his predecessors had done, of the fighting propensities of the Irish ; which he considered might, in the interests of England, be expended in slaughtering one another rather than against his countrymen. It was not difficult to sow discord among the sept of Macnamaras after the death of Lochlain. We have seen that this clan had nearly doubled the extent of their territory at the expense

* " Annals of the Four Masters," A.D. 1369; also " Memoirs of the O'Briens," p. 134.

of some eleven Dalcasian septs, on whom they imposed tribute, and thus converted them into bitter enemies. To protect themselves from local disturbances the Macnamaras therefore built many strong castles over the newly acquired district, and no doubt ruled with a firm hand. The ruins of many of the Macnamara castles still exist in Clare, and Mr. T. J. Westropp has kindly sent me pen-and-ink sketches of some of these buildings, which I am thus able to reproduce.

At the time of Lochlain Macnamara's death, A.D. 1365 (or 1373), Teigie, the son of his first wife (Sioda, his elder brother, was killed at Limerick 1369), and Hugh, the son of his second wife, came to an agreement by which they divided Ui-Caisin. The former family were to retain possession of the original tribal lands or West Clancuilein, and Hugh was to be chief of the recently acquired territory, and so become lord of East Clancuilein. But difficulties arose between these chiefs, and in the year 1377 we find Teigie Macnamara supporting the De Burgos, while Hugh had thrown in his lot with the English, who were commanded by the Lord Deputy. In an engagement that ensued the latter were successful and the Clanricardes (De Burgos) suffered severely. In the following years, we are informed by "The Four Masters," that "Teigie, the son of Lochlain Macnamara, was slain by the son of the daughter of O'Kelly," that is by his half brother. We have further official reference to the part which Macnamara took in these transactions in a close roll, 48 of Edward III., dated May 1374.*

On the death of Teigie, his son Mac-con Macnamara succeeded as chief of West Clancuilein; he married Oona Winfreda, daughter of O'Lochlain, chief of Burren, and in this way the branch of the family we have more especially to follow first came into immediate connection with that part of Clare which was ultimately to form the home of some of them. Mac-con was a firm ally of his uncle Brian O'Brien, king of Thomond, and notwithstanding the severe losses to which Clancuilein had been subjected, we find that their chief, in conjunction with the Clanricardes and O'Briens, made an expedition through South Munster, and compelled the English to pay tribute to the King of Thomond.

Soon after the termination of this expedition, Brian O'Brien's son married Ulick De Burgos' daughter, and in this way the O'Briens, De Burgos, and Macnamaras became intimately united by marriage, as they had been for long past by the closest friendship.†

* " O'Brien's Memoirs," pp. 135, 138, and 479, quoting from the "Annals of Ulster," and "The Four Masters."

† " Annals of Ulster and of Clonmacnoise " ; see also " Memoirs of the O'Briens," p. 136.

In the year 1370 the "Four Masters" notice the death of Joan, the daughter of Macnamara of Quin, and wife of MacCarthy of Desmond. These annalists also inform us that Philip O'Kennedy, Lord of Ormond, and Ainé his wife, daughter of Macnamara, both died within one week.* The four most influential chiefs in the west of Ireland were thus brought together by marriage through their connection with the Macnamaras, viz., the King of Thomond, the Earls of Desmond, Ormond, and Clanricarde. Marriages of this description were not confined to the upper classes ; and, for the most part, the married people adopted the language, dress, laws, and customs of the Irish. One cannot help feeling that if these marriages had been allowed to develop, Ireland would now have been in a different position to that which she occupies ; for there is no finer race than that formed by an amalgamation of the Celt and Saxon ; and of such people the inhabitants of Ireland would have now consisted, had it not been for the action of the English Government, who did all in their power to prevent the blending of the two races. They drove those who had formed connections by marriage with the Irish Celts outside their sphere of government and laws, and, together with the native Irish, regarded them in the light of enemies, to be hunted down and killed whenever they were met with. The Government then proceeded to bestow the vacant estates created by this policy upon young and untrained Englishmen, who bound themselves to live under such rules and regulations as were prescribed for them by English authorities.

Gerald Fitzgerald, Earl of Desmond, had been taken prisoner at the battle fought on the 10th of July 1369 ; he was conducted to Clonroad and must have become well acquainted, therefore, with the inner life of the establishment at that time under the supervision of Brian O'Brien and his wife Slaine Macnamara.† Desmond was at this period the representative of the King of England in Ireland, and was versed in the manners and customs of the English Court.‡ It is a remarkable fact that we find this nobleman some years later (1388) forwarding a petition to Richard the Second, requesting the king to allow him to send his son James (subsequently the famous Earl of Desmond) "to be brought up

---

* Frost's "History and Topography of Clare ; " also "Annals of the Four Masters," A.D. 1381.

† "O'Brien's Memoirs," p. 134.

‡ Fitzgerald, Earl of Desmond and Kerry, was granted the County Palatine, formed of nine counties and called the Pale. The lord who ruled over the Pale had power of making peace or war ; he held royal courts, created barons and knights, and appointed judges and administered laws.

and educated" at Clonroad by O'Brien, King of Thomond.* This
request was granted, and the lad was reared in the Celtic chief's household, in the middle of county Clare, a region which, if we are to believe
the accounts given by some historians, was in the fourteenth century
inhabited by a set of inhuman, bloodthirsty barbarians; this was evidently
not the opinion of the Earl of Desmond, who knew them well.

We have some important evidence connected with the latter end of
the fourteenth century, demonstrating the fact that although the Brehon
laws were still the only laws known in Clare, that the tenure of land
was undergoing change; there was then no question as to buying,
selling, and mortgaging land; indeed, we have a title-deed dated a
century earlier (A.D. 1251), which indicates a change in this direction.
From this document we find a certain Aodh Macnamara assigns lands
to John Macnamara, on condition of receiving thirteen milch cows, or
rather the right to pasture them on these lands.† Another deed, bearing
date A.D. 1365, enters into details as to debts due to Teige Macnamara's
children; reference is made to debts due for twenty years, with interest
on the same; and we have also the decision of the Brehon respecting
this mortgage.‡

We have a still more important document given in the original Gaelic,
and an English translation by Mr. Hardiman.§ It is the amount of
tribute of the several lands held under the "Lordship of Macnamara, that
is, of Mac-con (Lochlain), the son of Cumedha, the grandson of Con (Mac-
con, see 'Triumphs of Torlough'), the son of Lochlain (beheaded), the
son of Cumedha More," at the time of the division of Clancuilien into
two parts, about A.D. 1375. This rent-roll was made by "the stewards,
Philip O'Rodan and Conor O'Rodan, descendants of the red steward."
Then follows a description of about one hundred and thirty-five townlands which paid tribute to the Chief of Clancuilein and to his lady; for
it seems that his wife received her tribute "exclusive of the lord's rights."
This tribute amounted to about one thousand eight hundred and twenty
ounces of silver, which in practice was paid in cattle. This tribute did
not include rents or profits arising from the chief's own estates. Beyond
this the head of the Clan had the right of "food in these town lands
once a year," which, as before explained, means that he could billet
himself and his servants free of charge on those landholders who farmed
or occupied the lands above referred to. In this way the chief of a sept

* "O'Brien's Memoirs," p. 139, also Patent Roll, dated 1388, of Richard II.'s
reign.   † Frost's "History of Clare," p. 182.
    ‡ "Transactions of the Royal Society of Antiquaries of Ireland," vol. xv. p. 20.
    § *Idem*, p. 45; also Frost's "History of Clare," p. 36.

such as that of Clancuilein would not only have possessed a large income, and his powers over his tribesmen was technically without limit, but practically, unless he was strong enough to lead, he had to follow in the stream of public sentiment, for he was elected to office by his tribesmen, and they would have speedily got rid of him if he attempted to work contrary to the customs or spirit of his people as embodied in their code of laws. There is no reason to believe that the Irish chiefs abused their right to " coyne and livery," or billeting their retainers on their land-holders, as their English neighbours within the Pale certainly did, for in the preamble to a Bill passed by the Parliament in Dublin, 1449, we read that " in the time of harvest, companies of English soldiers were in the habit of going with their wives, children, servants, and friends, sometimes to the number of hundreds, to the farmers' houses, eating and drinking, and paying for nothing." They " many times rob, spoil, and kill the tenants and husbandmen, as well by night as by day," and their horses were turned out to graze in the meadows and in the ripe corn, ruining all the harvest, and if there was any show of resistance, they burn, rob, spoil, and kill, and for the most part the land is wasted and destroyed.* We have no evidence whatever of practices such as these in that part of Ireland which was governed by the native chiefs under the Brehon Laws.

* "A Short History of Ireland," by P. W. Joyce, LL.D., p. 337; Gilbert's " Viceroys," p. 355.

CHAPTER X

Richard II. in Ireland—Receives submission of chiefs, but no provision whatever made to govern the country, A.D. 1394—English rule confined to neighbourhood of Dublin—Inhabitants of Clare flourished—Quin Abbey founded by the Macnamaras—Death of chiefs of Clancuilein, A.D. 1428 and 1444—The English defeated by O'Briens and Macnamaras—Lands of Clare still preserved from invasion, A.D. 1499—Torlogh, King of Thomond, married to daughter of Rory Macnamara—Desperate battle of Knocktow, between natives of North and South of Ireland—Dalcasians defeated—A.D. 1510 the O'Briens and Macnamaras for the last time defeat the English and drove them out of Thomond—Firearms introduced and put an end to former method of warfare—Henry VIII. declared King of Ireland—His policy—The O'Briens and Macnamaras meet the Lord Deputy and Parliament at Limerick, and agree to become vassals of the King and adopt English land tenure, A.D. 1537—Agreement made between Henry VIII. and Sioda Macnamara on behalf of landlords of Clancuilein—Sioda Macnamara recommended by Lord Deputy to be created "Baron Clancuilein," A.D. 1543—Gavelkind existed in Clare at end of sixteenth century.

RICHARD THE SECOND having determined to cross over to Ireland with the object of subduing that country, landed at Waterford, in October 1394 with an army of 34,000 men ; the O'Brien and the other chiefs recognised the hopelessness of resisting a force of this kind, and they met King Richard at Drogheda and promised obedience to his rule ; this was all that was demanded from them by the English king, with the exception of the King of Leinster, who, together with the entire native population of the province were ordered to leave their homes and lands by a certain date so as to make way for English settlers. Richard soon afterwards left the country and returned home, as Sir J. Davies observes, " having spent huge masses of treasure, yet did he not increase his revenue thereby one sterling pound, nor enlarge the English border the breadth of one acre of land ; neither did he extend the jurisdiction of his courts of justice by one foot further than the English colonies wherein it was used and exercised before." *

Brian O'Brien after visiting King Richard at Drogheda, and subsequently in Dublin, returned to Clonroad ; he died in the year 1399. " Brian had by Slaine, daughter of Lochlain Macnamara, three sons.

* Sir J. Davies' "Historical Tracts," p. 51.

The eldest was too young at the time of his father's death to take his place as ruler of Thomond, so that Conor, their uncle, was elected to that office." * Brian's three sons, however, one after the other, subsequently held the office of Chief of Thomond. During Conor's rule, we are informed that peace and plenty flourished in Clare; "The Four Masters" state that Magrath died in A.D. 1425, "a prosperous and wealthy man."

Throughout the first half of the fifteenth century nothing happened which affected the position of the Macnamara sept. After Conor O'Brien's death, Torlough, one of Brian's sons, succeeded to the chieftainship of the Dalcasians. He married Catherine Bourke. Teige his son, was the ruler of this province from A.D. 1459 to A.D. 1466 ; he was married to a daughter of Clanricarde,† and his eldest son to a daughter of the Earl of Desmond, so that the ruling family of Thomond from and after the first half of the fifteenth century, were no longer pure Celts.‡

The War of the Roses was at its height when Teigie O'Brien became the ruler of Thomond ; and the attention of England was so completely absorbed in her own affairs that Ireland was entirely abandoned by her, unless in a small area of the country surrounding Dublin. In these circumstances the Macnamaras, under the orders of Teigie O'Brien, collected, as MacFirbis informs us, a host " such as we have not heard of with any of their name or ancestry since the days of Brian Boru." It would seem as if the intention of Teigie had been to emulate the deeds of his ancestor and to drive all foreigners out of Ireland ; he marched with his forces through Munster, compelling both Irish and English to pay him tribute. He then returned to Clanroad. Whatever Teigie O'Brien's intentions may have been, his career was cut short by death ; he expired at Inchiquin after a few days' illness. The inhabitants of Clare continued to flourish after the death of Teigie O'Brien, for we learn from "The Four Masters" that a certain MacGorman was at this period "the richest man in Ireland in live stock." This individual lived in the Baronie of Ibrickan in county Clare.

In connection with the history of the Macnamaras during the first half of the fifteenth century we must not overlook the work they did in founding and endowing the Abbey of Quin (about the year A.D. 1402) as a Franciscan monastery. The remains of this fine building are still in an admirable state of preservation, and are likely to remain so, having been included among the historical buildings to be kept in repair by the Board of Works under Sir John Lubbock's Act. The tomb of the founder of the abbey still remains, and the cloisters and walls enclosing

* " Memoirs of the O'Briens," p. 138.   † *Idem*, p. 177.   ‡ *Idem*, p. 187.

the precincts of the abbey are full of monuments erected to deceased members of our sept. In the year 1433, we are told by Wadding, that the Supreme Pontiff Eugene IV., issued a Bull to " Dilecto filio nobili mio Mac-con Macnamara. Duci de Clan Cullen," granting powers for the Franciscan order to take possession of Quin Abbey, and there they remained until it was occupied by Cromwell's soldiers.*

The " Four Masters " state that in 1428 " Macnamara, chief of Clancuilein, died ; a charitable and truly hospitable man, who suppressed robbery and theft, and established peace and tranquillity in his territories."

In A.D. 1444 these annalists have another entry, to the effect that Sioda Macnamara died. " He was the chief protector of the men of Ireland," and he is also referred to in the annals of Ulster, and of Munster as having been renowned for his hospitality.

The fifteenth century, so far as Clare was concerned, was not destined to close in peace. Sir James, a natural son of the sixth Earl of Ormond, arrived in the West of Ireland, claiming to be the heir to the title and lands of his father. Sir James was received by the O'Briens and Macnamaras, and also by the Clanricardes, these three families being closely related in marriage with the late Earl, were glad to support an Ormond, in opposition to the Earl of Kildare, who since Ormond's death had assumed paramount power over Ireland, and had been appointed Lord Deputy of that country by Henry the Seventh. Kildare, however, had been recalled to England by the king, and while there married the sister of the lawful heir to the Ormond estates in Ireland. On the Lord Deputy's return to Dublin he raised a pretext for quarrelling with the O'Briens, his real motive being to punish them for the support they had afforded to Sir James Ormond. Kildare marched with his forces into Clare and surprised the strong castle of Ballycullen, which

---

* Wadding, x. 525. No record of the Bull of Eugene IV. can be found in the Vatican, nor have I been able to discover a copy of any such document as that referred to by Wadding. Mr. W. Bliss has kindly sent me extracts from the records of the Vatican to the following effect: "To the Abbot of the Monastery of Clare, in the diocese of ' Laonien,' on behalf of Mathew Macconmara, priest of the same diocese, upon the perpetual vicarage of the parish of Cluony, vacant by the surrender of Henry O'Grady against Mathew Maccuilean, June 4, A.D. 1431 " ("Roman Transcripts Regetta Pontificum," 1431, an. i. lib. 13, fol. 119, Eugenius IV.). From the same source we learn that a communication was forwarded from the Pontiff on November 10, 1432, " To the bishop of ' Laonien ' on behalf of Tathidu Mac-conmara and Dubcoblaid Inymccma that with them a disposition may be made concerning the contracting of a marriage." Like permission is given to Maurice Mac-conmara and Raynyld Inymettomarra, dated November 1432.

belonged to Finn Macnamara. Leaving a garrison in this place, he moved on to Quin, where he was met by Conor O'Brien, who had hastily summoned the Macnamara and other Dalcasian septs to his aid, in order to oppose the progress of the Lord Deputy. After a fiercely contested battle Kildare was utterly routed by the Irish, and with difficulty made good his escape with the remnants of his troops across the Shannon. This battle was fought in A.D. 1499, and in the same year Conor O'Brien died, and was succeeded by his nephew Torlogh, who married Finola, a daughter of Rory Macnamara, by whom he had five sons, the two eldest respectively became rulers of Thomond ; the second son, Morrogh, however, resigned the chieftainship of the Principality, and became Earl of Thomond during the reign of Henry VIII.*

Torlogh O'Brien had hardly been appointed chief of the Dalcais before he was attacked by the Earl of Ormond, who was driven out of Thomond with considerable loss. Torlogh was destined, however, together with the Macnamaras, to be engaged in more serious military operations, in consequence of their relationship, by marriage, with the Clanricardes. The chief of that clan was at this time Ulick Bourke, whose first wife had been a daughter of Sioda Macnamara ; she died in A.D. 1498.† Ulick subsequently married a daughter of the Lord Deputy Kildare ; but he is accused of having illtreated this lady. At any rate, she left him, and so angry was Kildare that he determined to be revenged on his daughter's husband ; and at the same time he hoped by weakening the Bourkes' power in the West of Ireland, to enable the English more effectually to humble the O'Briens and other septs of Thomond. Kildare persuaded the chiefs of the North of Ireland to espouse his cause. On the other hand, Clanricarde and the O'Briens obtained the aid of the southern chiefs ; so that the whole of the Irish of the northern part of the country were brought into battle array against the natives of the southern half of the island. What is more remarkable, the commander of the Irish of the northern part of the island was an Englishman, the Earl of Kildare, and the commander of the southern forces was Clanricarde, of Anglo-Norman descent. It is hardly possible to conceive a more desperately hopeless condition of things than this ; that the Irish, or any other people, should thus have been divided and brought into the field of battle by commanders of a different and hostile race, whose object was to urge on the natives to destroy one another, so that the English

---

* Joyce's "Short History of Ireland," p. 348 ; Harris's "Wars of Ireland," vol. ii. p. 161 ; "Memoirs of the O'Briens," p. 161.

† "Annals of the Four Masters."

K

might profit by this act of national suicide.   Kildare no doubt to some extent made Clanricarde's treatment of his daughter the ostensible cause of the conflict; but in the hour of battle he withdrew his English troops from the field, and allowed the Irish of the north and south to tear each other to pieces; which they did in a most effectual and satisfactory manner, according to the idea of those who stood on one side to watch the conflict.*

The armies under Clanricarde, and Kildare, met at a place called Knocktow, near Galway, on the 19th of August 1504. "The Four Masters" record that a victory was gained over Clanricarde and the South of Ireland, and that of nine divisions which were drawn up in battle array in the army of the South, there survived the action but one broken battalion.   The northern Irish also suffered so terribly that they were unable to follow up their victory, but after collecting their scattered forces retired from the field.   It is said that at this moment Lord Gormanston proposed to Kildare that the English should "consummate their good fortune by slaughtering the remainder of the Northern army who had fought for them.†

The Earl of Kildare does not seem to have taken advantage of the weakened condition in which the Dalcasians must have been left after the battle of Knocktow; nevertheless, he felt that so long as this famous tribe remained supreme in the West of Ireland, there could be no security for his countrymen living within the Pale, and still less for extending their rule over the country.   In A.D. 1510 the Lord Deputy erected a fortress in the parish of Kilteely, co. Limerick, in spite of the opposition of the Irish, and having secured this place as a base for his operations, "attended by the chiefs of the English and Irish of Leinster, and O'Donnell from Donegal, Kildare advanced with his forces into South Munster," with the intention of weakening the power of the chiefs of Munster before striking his final blow at Thomond.   Having effected this object, the Lord Deputy passed into the county of Limerick, where he mustered all the English of Munster, Meath, and Leinster, and proceeded to the town of Limerick.

From "The Four Masters" we learn that "Torlogh O'Brien, Lord of Thomond, with all his forces, together with the Macnamaras and the Clanricardes, mustered another army to oppose Kildare.   The Earl—

---

* Ware states that it appears from the white book of the Exchequer that not an Englishman was slain or even wounded in this battle. (See "Memoirs of the O'Briens," p. 156.)

† "Memoirs of the O'Briens," p. 156; "The History of Ireland," by the Abbé Macgeoghegan, p. 378.

that is, the Lord Justice—marched with his army until he arrived at the
wooden bridge which O'Brien had constructed over the Shannon, and
he broke down the bridge." Kildare's object was to attack the
O'Carrolls of Ely and other clans of East Thomond before they could
unite their forces with those of O'Brien in Clare. Torlogh, however,
with his followers forded the Shannon, and coming up to Kildare's
army, encamped close to them, so that, as "The Four Masters" state: "the
two forces could hear each other's voices and conversation during the
night. On the morrow Kildare marshalled his army, placing the English
and Irish of Munster in the van, and the English of Meath and Dublin
in the rear. O'Brien's army attacked the English and slew the Barons
Kent, and Barnewall, with many other men of distinction. The English
only escaped by flight, and the army of O'Brien returned home in
triumph with great spoil."

Kildare made no further effort to conquer the Dalcasians west of the
Shannon, but in 1513 he laid siege to Leap Castle, the residence of the
O'Carroll's of Ely, and failing to take the place by escalade, "and being
unprovided with heavy ordnance, he was obliged to raise the siege for
the purpose of procuring artillery ; he was, however, taken ill, and died
in September 1513. Clare for some years enjoyed peace and hardly
appears on the pages of Irish history. We are told that in 1528 one of
the inhabitants of this province, O'Daly of Corcomroe, a poet, died ; he
was famed, among other qualities, in that he " kept a house of general
hospitality," p. 34. In the year 1522 Teigie O'Brien, while leading an
attack in support of the O'Carrolls, was killed " by the shot of a ball." *
We have already referred to the fact that Kildare had to raise the siege
of Leap Castle for want of artillery, which at this time seems to have
come into use in Ireland ; it was gunpowder and the cannon of the
early part of the sixteenth century that sealed the fate of that country,
for the native chiefs had no means of obtaining firearms, and as opposed
to such weapons their swords and spears were useless. The *last* battle
had been fought under the old style of warfare by the O'Briens and
Macnamaras against the English, and, as on so many previous occasions,
they had driven back their foes and so preserved their lands and homes
in Clare.

Torlough O'Brien died in the year 1538, and was succeeded by his son
Conor, who was married first to a daughter of Clanricarde, and secondly
to a Desmond. The condition of Ireland at this time is described in
the State Papers of the reign of Henry VIII., where it is stated that the
country was under the rule of some sixty chief captains or princes

* " Annals of the Four Masters."

"that only liveth by the sword, and obeyeth unto no other temporal person but only to himself that is strong"; the son of such chief "shall not succeed to his father without he be the strongest of the tribe, and by election." There be "also diverse petty captains, and every one maketh war and peace for himself, without licence of the chief captain." The English folks in Ireland "be of Irish habits, of Irish language, except in the cities and walled towns." But the English, it is argued, would gladly accept the king's laws and protection were it not for the "Irish enemies." No tribute could be collected. There were no bishops, priors, or vicars to preach the word of God; only "the poor friar beggars." Every semblance of English government had passed from Ireland. "The king had no army or ally, native or English, in Ireland, outside a few walled towns."

The question Henry VIII. had to decide was, should he bring Ireland under the English crown, or give her up completely to the control of her native chiefs. The king determined in favour of the former policy, and, A.D. 1541, in a Parliament assembled in Dublin, Henry was created *King of Ireland*, a title which was to descend to his successors; and it was enacted that it should be deemed high treason to impeach this title or oppose its authority. It is impossible to read Henry VIII.'s despatches without coming to the conclusion that, while he determined to strive and enforce law, and bring the Irish people into subjection, he wished to prevent violence and to meet their wishes as far as possible with reference to their religion, laws, and ancient customs. The king instructed Wolsey to direct "the Irish clergy to preach and to publish that the king only required to bring the country to order, not to make war against those who do their duty, nor to take anything from any man who is lawfully entitled to it, but to make a fair distribution of land at reasonable rents, seeing that they now lived without order, nor wealth, nor being assured to any succession to their lands."* Henry adopted this policy in spite of the recommendation of his Irish advisers to proceed to conquer the country, to exterminate its inhabitants, and replace them with "men born in England."†

The Irish chiefs must have felt at this time that it was useless for them to attempt to resist England, so that Henry VIII.'s opportunity for effecting a settlement of the Irish question was favourable; and, from documents in our possession, we must arrive at the conclusion that the king's acts did not falsify his intentions as expressed in the above extract from his message to the Church in Ireland. Before we can

---

* "Calendar of State Papers," Henry VIII. A.D. 1520.
† *Ibid.* vol. iv. pt. ii., May 20, 1526, p. 1075.

rightly appreciate the spirit of the agreement entered into between the Crown, and Sioda Macnamara and other chiefs regarding the tenure of their lands, we must revert to one or two points connected with the history of Clare.

The Earl of Kildare was at the time Lord Deputy, and, having been summoned to England, he left his son, Thomas FitzGerald, at the head of affairs. Soon after the earl's departure, rumours reached Ireland that he had been seized and executed by command of the king. Fitz-Gerald, without waiting to ascertain the truth of this rumour, threw up his office and renounced his allegiance to the Crown. He took up his quarters with his relations, the O'Carrolls of Ely, and was soon joined by other Irish chiefs; but Lord Grey, having arrived in Ireland with a considerable force, FitzGerald had to cross the Shannon and take refuge with the O'Briens at Clonroad. Lord Grey, however, attacked the Irish of Thomond east of the Shannon, and, having again destroyed the bridge at Killaloe, he completely isolated Conor O'Brien and the Dalcasians of Clare from the rest of the country. A still more severe blow was to fall on this tribe, for Conor's eldest son turned traitor, and entered into an alliance with the Earl of Desmond, whose daughter he had married. Donogh O'Brien's conduct may best be given in his own words, as they were reported at the time (6th of October 1535) by Lord Butler to Henry VIII.* Donogh is stated to have observed to Lord Butler that:

"I have maryd your syster, and for becaus I have maryd your syster, I have forsaken my father, myn unkle, and all my fryndes and my contrey, to come to you and to help to doo the Kyng's servys. I have been sore wounded, and have no rewarde nor nothing to leve upon. What wolde ye have me do? Iff that it wolde plese the Kyng's grace to take me into hys servys, and that you will come into the contrey, and bring with you a piese of ordnannce to wyn a castell, the whych castell is called Carygoguillin, and his Grace to give me that which never was none Inglishe man's 200 yere, and I will desyer the King no helpe nor ayde of no man but this Ynglishe captyn with his honderyth and od of Ynglish men to go with me upon my father and myn unkle, the which are the Kyng's enemies, and upon the Irish men that never Ynglish men were amongis, and for all land that I shall conquer, it shall be at the King's pleser to sett Ynglish men in yt, to holden of the King as his pleser schal be, and I to refewys all such Irish fasehions, and to order myselfe after the laws of Ynglish, and all that I can make conquer."

Lord Grey at once proceeded to attack the castle above referred to, situated near Limerick, and through means of Donogh's treachery it surrendered. This, together with the loss of East Thomond and the destruction of the bridge over the Shannon, was a heavy blow to the

* "O'Brien's Memoirs," p. 166.

Dalcasians, but they seemed determined to resist the invasion of their lands and homes in Clare, which were again threatened by the English under Lord Grey. The OBriens and Macnamaras took up their position in a castle belonging to one of the latter family, but the artillery of the English battered down the walls of the keep, and after a brave resistance the Dalcasians had to surrender the castle, and with it Clare; but their conduct on this occasion so favourably impressed Lord Grey that he entered on a truce with the Irish, which was to last for twelve months (A.D. 1537).

Conor O'Brien died in the following year, and was succeeded by his brother Morrogh, who, having joined O'Neill in a futile attempt to resist the English, returned to Clare prepared to give in his submission to Henry VIII.

In the year 1542, St. Leger, who was Lord Deputy of Ireland, summoned a Parliament to meet at Limerick, with the object of legalising an agreement with the chiefs of Thomond regarding the tenure of the land and other questions concerning the legal government of that part of the country. Morrogh O'Brien, and Sioda Macnamara came to Limerick to meet the Lord Deputy, with documents which they had prepared, stating the terms upon which they were willing to hand over their lands to the Crown, the basis of the understanding being that the landlords of Clare should receive their lands back with titles drawn up according to English law and procedure. The following is a copy of the agreement entered into between Sioda Macnamara, and Henry VIII. on this occasion :

PATENT 34, HENRY VIII., A.D. 1542, *December* 10.

This indenture made between the Rt. Honbl. Sir Anthony St. Leger Knight of the Most Noble Order of the Garter Gentleman of the King's Privy Council and Lord Deputy-General of Ireland for and behalf of his most high and tremendous Majestie of the one part and Sioda, son of Mac-con son of Sioda son of Mac-con son of Teigie son of (Lochlain) Mac-con Macnamara of Mountallon in the Principality of Thomond, Chief Captain elect of his name and sept called Clancuilein in the said principality for and on behalf of himself and of all the rest of the gentlemen and freeholders of the said sept in the Baronies of Dangan, Bunratty, and Tulla, in the said principality as authorised by the said gentlemen and freeholders under their deede and seale of the other partie.

Witnesseth that the said Sioda Macnamara doe for himself and all the rest of the said gentlemen and freeholders of the Baronies and places aforesaid for their heirs and assignes covenant, promise, grant, agree, and condescend to and with the said Rt. Hon. the Lord Deputy to surrender and give up in the King's Majesties and Hon. Court of Chancery within the Realm of Ireland to the use of the King Majestie his heirs and successors when he thereunto shall be required, all such manors, castles, rents, tenements, lands, reversions, and all other heredits that they and every of them have within the said baronies and places aforesaid within the Principality aforesaid, either in use or possession, and then the said Sioda and the rest aforesaid shall receive and take the same back by letter patent from his Majesty to have and to hold to them and their heirs for ever, yielding and paying unto his Majesty, his heirs and successors, such yearly rents, services, and reservations as shall be expressed, mentioned, and contained in the said letters patent and the said Rt. Hon. Lord Deputy for and in behalf of the King's most excellent Majesty doth promise and grant to and with the said Sioda, that the said Sioda and the said gentlemen, freeholders, their heirs and assignes, shall not only have letters patent made into them of the said lands, tenements, and heredita-ments according as before is expressed, but also shall from and after the date thereof be free and wholly discharged, acquitted, and exonerated of and from the boroughs accustomed to be paid out of the said baronies and places aforesaid by the sept aforesaid to his Majesty's gallowglasses, and of all cesses, charges, and exactions and impositions of soldiers, horses, and horseboy, and all other manner of cesses, charges, duties, and exactions whatsoever they be other than the rents, reservations, and charges hereafter specified ; in consideration of the discharge of which boroughs and other charges aforesaid, the said Sioda for and in the behalf of himself and all the rest aforesaid, hath given and granted like as he doth hereby give and grant to the said Rt. Hon. the Lord Deputy to the use of the King's Majestie, his heirs and successors, for ever one yearly rent charge of fifty marks of good and lawful money of Ireland, payable at the feasts of Michelmas and Easter by even portions, the first payment to begin at the feast of Easter, which shall be in the year of our Lord God one thousand five hundred and forty three, and so yearly for ever at the several feasts aforesaid, at his Highness his Exchequer within the said realm of Ireland, or into the hands of the Vice-Treasurer, or general receiver of the same realm for the time being, and if it fortune the said rent of fifty marks to be behind in parte or in the whole by the space of six months next after any of the said feasts, that then it shall be lawful for the said Rt. Hon. the Lord Deputy or other governor or governors of this realm for the time being to enter and distraine in all and singular, the lands, tenements, and hereditaments within the said baronies and places aforesaide, and the distress so taken to detain and keep till the said yearly rent be wholly satisfied and paid ; and further, the said Sioda doth for himself and the rest aforesaid, their heirs and assignes, covenant, promise, and grant to and with the said Lord Deputy, for and in behalf of the King's most excellent Majesty, his heirs and successors, not only to bear yearly for ever to all and general rodes, hostings, journies, and risings onto ten spearmen and forty kearmes as they have been accustomed, but also to pay and yield yearly to his Majesty, his heirs and successors, for ever such ancient rents, customs, and dewties as the same usually yielded heretofore ; that is to say, thirteen marks lawful money of Ireland, and thirteen bushels of ottes at such terms, tymes, and places as the same have been accustomed, and the said Rt. Hon. the Lord Deputy does promise and grante for and in the behalfe of the King's most excellent Majestie that the said Sioda and the rest of the gentlemen and freeholders aforesaid in none of their lands, tenements, and hereditament aforesaid, in no parte, parcel, or number thereof shall from henceforth be charged cessed, or imposed, or be contributory with any other parte or partes of the Principalitie of Thomond in any manner, cesse, charge, exaction, rising out or otherwise by any manner or means, but shall be and remain severed from them in the charge aforesaid, any custom or use heretofore to the contrary notwithstanding ; and the saide Rt. Hon. the Lord Deputie for and in the behalf of the King's most excellent Majestie doth promise and grant to and with the said Sioda and the rest of the gentlemen and freeholders of the baronies and places aforesaid, that if it shall fortune at any time hereafter any part or parcell of the lands, tenements, and hereditaments chargeable with the said yearly rent of fiftye marks, to be seized, recovered, or taken out of the lands or possessions of the said Sioda or of any of the rest of the gentlemen and freeholders of the baronies and places aforesaid, by due order and ceremony of the King's Majestie's laws, that then and for soe much of the yearly rent charge of fiftye marks as the same lands, tenements, and hereditaments were charged with to be defaulted and allowed in the said yearly rent of charge of fiftye-two marks anything hereinafter contained to the contrary notwithstanding.   In witness of this part of this indenture remaining in the custody of the said Sioda for him and the rest aforesaid, the said Rt. Hon. Lord Deputy, for and in the behalf of the King's most excellent Majestie, has hereunto put his seal at Dublin, the 10th day of December in anno 1542, and in the thirty-fourth year of the reign of our sovereign lord, Henry VIII., by the grace of God, King of England, France, and Ireland, Defender of the Faith, and so forth.

ANTHONY ST. LEGER.

PATENT 35, HENRY VIII., A.D. 1543.

The King etc. etc. to all those et cet., sends greeting.   Because as we are informed as to the submission of Sioda the son of Mac-con the son of Sioda son of Mac-con the son of Teigie the son of (Lochlain) Mac-con Macnamara, the elected chief and captain of the Clancuilein and other gentlemen of this clan because of their present submission to us and in submitting their lands to our representative and faithful servant in Ireland the Lord Deputy Sir Anth. St. Leger that the same Sioda shall remain Chief and Captain of the country of Clancuilein and all that pertains to it we decide declare and decree and confirm that he shall possess hold occupy and guard it with all that belongs to it in any way he pleases with regard to the ancient usages and customs of the country for as long as he lives and behaves as our subject and performs to us and our successors the rights of vassals and obeys in all things our Lieutenant in Ireland and the aforesaid Sioda in compliance with the law passed in the thirty-fourth year of the king's reign shall further comply with our Lieutenant in Ireland and with the Council existing at the time.

With these witnesses, Bourke Chief of Clanricarde, Morrogh O'Brien Chief of Thomond, Conor O'Brien Baron of Ibrickan and many others. In the presence of the King at Greenwich on the Second of July in the thirty-fifth year of his reign.   *By the special Command of the King.*

After receiving the submission of Morrogh O'Brien, Henry VIII. wrote as follows to the Lord Deputy: "We think it mete in case he shall repayer to our Parliament, as reason is he shude, that he shuld make humble sute to us to receive some estate and honour at our handes, mete to be placed in our Parliament; for he can neither stand with our honour, nor with state of our Parliament, to have any man placed there as a Pere, but he have indede the state of a Pere, by the right cours and ordre of our lawes." The Lord Deputy therefore recommended that Morrogh O'Brien should be created "Erle of Thomond," and Donogh O'Brien Baron of Ibrickan during Morrogh's lifetime, after which he was to succeed to his uncle's titles and estates. The O'Briens, Clanricardes, and others, went over to England, and on the 1st of July, A.D. 1543, received their titles from Henry VIII. at Greenwich. To cover O'Brien's expenses to England the Lord Deputy had to lend him "an hundred pounds sterling in harp grotes, in default of other money, for there ys no sterling money to be had within this your realme."

The day previous to recommending Henry to create Morrogh O'Brien an "Erle," the Lord Deputy addressed a letter to the king, in which, referring to Sidoa Macnamara's submission, he observes, "and that the said M'Nemarro ys a man whose anncestors have in those partes alwayes borne a grete swynge, and one that for himself is of honest conformities, whose landes lye holy on the farsyde the Shanan, we most humbly beseech your Majestie to regarde him according to your princly bounty to advance him to the honour of a baron by the name of Clancuilein, and that he may holde such landes and possessions as he now hathe." To this communication Henry VIII. replied, probably at the instigation of O'Brien, who was at the time at Greenwich, that "we have made the lord of Upper Ossery Macnamarrow a knight." * This title was never assumed by Sioda Macnamara. The Rev. D. White suggests it may have been lost or sent to some one else, for Sioda Macnamara died as he had lived, simply a landlord of Clare and chief of his sept.

Sioda Macnamara married a daughter of Desmond O'Shagnasie of Gort, and had four sons, the eldest, John, died in 1570, leaving an infant son, Sir John Macnamara, who died without issue. Shan, the second son of Sioda, died on March 31, 1587, leaving five sons his co-heirs under the law of gavelkind, which was still in force in Clare; the second of these sons, named Teigie, and his son Sioda, was made heir at law by his cousin Sir John Macnamara. It was from this branch of the family that James Macnamara, M.P. for Leicester, and his brother Admiral John

---

* "State Papers," vol. iii. p. 476 (Ireland). A similar honour was conferred on Denis O'Grady, head of the Clan Donghaile ("O'Brien Memoirs," p. 186).

Macnamara, were directly descended.   Sioda Macnamara, chief of the
sept above referred to as having entered into an agreement with King
Henry VIII., had a brother Rory, who married a daughter of Patrick
French, of Douras, co. Galway, and he inherited the property of Ballinacragga and Rathfolan, situated between the present town of Newmarket
and Ennis, co. Clare.   From this branch of the Macnamaras the family
of the writer of these pages is derived, as is shown in their registered
pedigree.

CHAPTER XI

Henry VIII.'s Irish policy just and liberal—Difficulties of working it in Clare—
The Macnamaras oppose the second Earl of Thomond in favour of Donald
O'Brien as their chief—Covenant between the O'Briens and Macnamaras,
A.D. 1558—Bribery of Governor of Connaught—O'Brien takes refuge in Sioda
Macnamara's castle of Rosroe—Rathfolan castle—Bastard sons of Bishop of
Killaloe—Sidney's report on Clare and the Macnamaras, A.D. 1576—His
efforts to persuade landowners to enter on fresh terms as to land tenure and
revenue.

WHEN Henry the Eighth accepted the terms proposed by Sioda Macnamara and the other landowners of Clare he directed the Lord Deputy
to take special care that " neany of them suffer any displeasure nor
damage hereafter for their submission, but you are to aid them and see
the same revenged as the case shall require." * Sir J. Davies, Mr. Lecky,
and other authorities state, under the provision of Henry the Eighth's
agreement it was assumed, in spite of immemorial usage, that the land
was to become the absolute hereditary property of the chiefs who agreed
to Henry's terms, to the detriment of their tenants and other landholders,
and was, therefore, a " burning grievance to the humbler clansmen." †
So far as our sept was concerned, however, it is clear that its chiefs urged
England to extend her laws to Ireland. They were perfectly well aware
of the nature of the agreement they entered into " on behalf of themselves and all the rest of the gentlemen and freeholders of the said sept
in the baronies of Bunratty, &c." It was in those baronies that the sept
originally obtained their tribal lands in the fifth century, and they were
in possession of these same lands in the year 1654, or a century after
entering into their agreement with Henry the Eighth. The object of
this arrangement was to bring the titles of the landed property from
under the Brehon laws, into such form that they could be held in
conformity with English law. The king thoroughly appreciated the difficulty that existed in granting negotiable titles to the owners of the old
tribal and other lands on equitable terms ; but whatever the technical

* " State Papers," vol. iii. p. 476.
† "A History of Ireland in the Eighteenth Century," by W. E. Hartpole
Lecky, vol. i. p. 16.

difficulty, Henry the Eighth was emphatic in his orders that the parties concerned were to lose nothing that was essential to their interests or customs ; he had no idea of making the transfer of the land from the old to the new law a means of confiscation or damage to the landowners of Ireland ; but then the question arose as to how the land in Clare, which was freehold, a part of the old tribal lands, could be brought under English law, for, as Edmund Spenser justly remarked, the " lawes ought to be fashioned into the manners and conditions of the people for whom they were meant, and not to be imposed upon them according to the simple rule of right, for then, instead of good, they might work ill, and prevert justice to extreame injustice." * This was the idea Henry the Eighth entertained, and it would have been well for Ireland had his policy been adhered to by England in her subsequent dealings with Ireland.

The new order of things established by Henry the Eighth was, however, hardly likely to run smooth, especially as regards the change from tanistry to hereditary succession ; for the system of tanistry was at the root of much that was most valued by the Irish ; it signified the right of families to elect their head, and of the people to choose their chief. On the death of Morrogh O'Brien this difficulty at once became pronounced, for he was a younger brother of Conor, the first Earl of Thomond, but by special arrangement, when Conor died, Morrogh, as having been his tanist, previously to the arrangement with Henry the Eighth, succeeded to the earldom, but on his death Conor's eldest son became, under English law, heir to the title. Conor, however, had been twice married, his second wife being a Desmond, and this family objected to the hereditary transmission of the title, which virtually barred them from becoming the head of the Dalcais, or rather Earls of Thomond. The tribe also were much in favour of establishing Donald O'Brien, the son of Conor's second wife, as their chief, in place of Donough the late lord's eldest son, who was, however, created third Earl of Thomond by letters patent after the death of his father. Donald, as the fittest man for the office, was supported by the Macnamaras, and they attacked the newly created Earl, drove him out of Clonroad, and so severely injured him that he died. Donald was elected as chief of the Dalcais, and he at once started on the old lines and led his tribe on a plundering excursion through Limerick and then into Connaught. This kind of game went on for two years, when the Earl of Sussex was appointed Lord Deputy of Ireland, and he determined to bring the O'Briens to order ; he therefore marched from Dublin towards Clare, but was met by Donald with so

* " View of the State of Ireland," by Edmund Spenser, p. 17.

large a force that the Lord Deputy thought it unwise to risk a battle, and so came to terms with the Dalcasian chief. In the following year, 1558, Sussex again entered Clare and speedily drove Donald O'Brien into exile, replacing him by the lawful heir to the property and title of the Earl of Thomond. When Donough, the third Earl, had thus been placed in a secure position he attended a solemn service in the Cathedral of Limerick, and publicly renounced the name of O'Brien as an appellation or title, promising to be faithful to the crown of England, and to rule the people of Thomond according to the laws of the realm. Important stipulations were on this occasion imposed on certain of the landlords of Thomond, and among them the representatives of one of the principal branches of the Macnamaras, who undertook on behalf of himself and his retainers to be faithful subjects of the English crown, and also to be true to their chief the Earl of Thomond.* A copy of this agreement has been preserved and translated into English by Mr. Hardmian, it runs as follows : †

These are the conditions and covenants entered into by Conor O'Brien, Earl of Thomond, and Macnamara, to wit, Teige, son of Cuvea, son of Cumara, who is the Macnamara. That he and his heirs for ever shall conduct themselves faithfully and without malice towards the earl and his heirs for ever, not only himself and his heirs, but that no one on their part shall act contrary to these conditions ; and particularly that he or his descendants shall never wage war against the earl or his heirs for ever. Moreover, Macnamara and his heirs shall be loyal and faithful to the country of Clancuilein, and not encroach upon them beyond the bounds of justice for ever. His father and grandfather to give guarantees, the four principal persons as well as the chief steward and marshal of Macnamara. The sureties for the performance of said covenant are: God and his angels, and Macnamara to swear by any oath the most sacred before the Chief Justice of Ireland in presence of the English and Irish of Ireland. Furthermore, Macnamara and his heirs shall be bound in a certain sum to be specified for the performance of those obligations, that neither he or his posterity shall be guilty of defection from the earl or his descendants for ever.

From this document it would appear that some of the Macnamaras, who had supported Donald O'Brien against Donogh Earl of Thomond, had been imprisoned, and that their release depended on their entering into a stipulation not to offend in this manner again. At the same time, it is only fair to state that the branch of the Macnamaras referred to in this deed were not the same as those to which Sioda Macnamara belonged, who had only a short time previously promised to remain faithful subjects of the Crown. This fact can be confirmed by reference to the pedigree of the family ; and we find the whole sept remained true to

* " Memoirs of the O'Briens," p. 191.
† " Transactions of the Royal Society of Antiquaries of Ireland," vol. xv.

their engagements, for when Donald O'Brien shortly afterwards returned to Clare, and obtained possession of Inchiquin Castle, the Macnamaras absolutely declined to support him any further in opposition to the Earl of Thomond.   On the other hand, we are told the sept suffered severely in an engagement fought at Spancihill against Donald, in June 1558, the year Elizabeth succeeded to the English throne.*

Henry VIII. had determined to establish courts of justice in Ireland, which were to be constituted of the bishop of the diocese and some of the principal landowners. The officers forming these courts were to be charged with extensive powers, embracing military operations; at the same time sheriffs were instituted, and a nucleus formed from which a regular system of judicial authorities might have developed to enforce law and order in the province.   Beyond this, free schools were established, to be maintained by local cesses raised for the purpose.   But there was as yet no adequate system provided for enforcing these salutary reforms; they were largely arrangements the outcome of good intentions, but wanting in material support to carry them into effect.   For instance, Sir E. Fitton had been appointed president of the province of Connaught, and in A.D. 1570 he proposed holding a court of eighteen days' duration, in the Monastery of Ennis, county Clare, "to administer justice," and to reduce Clancuilein and other Dalcasian septs to order. Teigie O'Brien was appointed the first sheriff of Clare, and he placed a quantity of food and drink in the monastery for the use of the president; and with that he seems to have been content.   For on the following day, when Sir Edward arrived, he sent off messengers to the Earl of Thomond to summon him to Ennis.   On receiving this message, the Earl, we are informed, "came to the resolution of making a prisoner of these officers of the law; and the English president, finding his monastery becoming rather uncomfortable, made his escape on foot from the place, and was fortunate enough to find a guide to conduct him through the narrow passes and wild, intricate ways of the district."†

Queen Elizabeth, however, who had just come to the throne, would not tolerate this kind of thing, and she directed the Earl of Ormond to proceed at once into Clare with a well-equiped force.   This action had the desired effect, and the Earl of Thomond not only had to abandon his forts, but to retire from Clare and take refuge in France.   He subsequently obtained pardon from the Queen, and returned to Ireland.   The following year the president of Connaught came to Ennis, accompanied by a strong force, "and established laws and rules, and abolished injustice and lawlessness."   To secure obedience to these laws, he

* " Annals of the Four Masters," A.D. 1559.   † Ibid. A.D. 1570.

carried hostages from the Macnamaras and other chieftains of Thomond along with him to his head quarters in Athlone. "The Four Masters" observe that it would be difficult "to calculate the hundreds of cows given to the president of Connaught, Sir E. Fitton, by the men of Thomond during the two years he remained in the territory"; in other words, he took such large bribes that, even in those lax times, the Government was obliged to recall him to England.*

In 1563 the Earl of Thomond was with Sioda Macnamara at his castle of Rosroe, a place to which Dineley refers in his "Diary," and has also left us a sketch of it as he saw it in 1680. He states "it was a fair seat, situated among good lands and orchards, with a very pleasant and profitable large port or lough on the one side thereof, abounding with large trout. Here are also plenty of wild fowl. About a mile and a half from hence by water, between the castles of Rathlahem and Rath-folan, the lough of Rosroe runs underground for half an English mile, being opposed by hills and rocks."† In this castle the earl had retreated to obtain protection from his relative, Donald O'Brien of Inchiquin; the latter, however, attacked the castle, but was driven back by Sioda Macnamara, and pursued across the river Fergus.‡ Donald O'Brien then betook himself to a place near Corcomroe in Burren, and we are informed that a ship containing "pirates" landed near Loop Head, and Donald O'Brien seized some of the unfortunate sailors, hung not a few, and burnt others, according to the measure of their crime.§ Acts of this description demonstrate the laxness with which English law and order was administered in Clare at this time. Another instance illustrating the condition of this part of Ireland in the year 1569 is afforded by a peti-tion which Sir H. Sidney received from Galway, stating that, "on the borders of Thomond certain outlaws, being bastard sons of the Bishop of Killaloe, robbed all travellers, and had put a raid on a castle which they meant to defend." This bishop was an O'Brien, and after his death, in 1569, the English Government appointed the first Protestant bishop of Killaloe, a young man, Morrogh O'Brien, recommended by

* Edmund Spenser refers to these corrupt practices in Ireland as very preva-lent in his day. Writing of military commanders he observes : " the captanie, halfe of whose souldiours are dead, and the other quarter never mustered, nor scene, comes shortly to demand payment of the whole accompt, where by good meanes of some great ones, and privy shareing with the officers and servants of other some, he receiveth his debt, much less perhaps than was due, yet much more indeede than is justly deserved " (" View of the State of Ireland," by Edmund Spenser, p. 154).

† Frost's "History of Clare," p. 543.   ‡ White's "History of Clare," p. 184.
§ "The Annals of the Four Masters."

the Lord Deputy to Elizabeth for this office, "because he was a Protestant, and had been educated at Oxford; and, further, his father is
dutifully affected to Her Majesty."* Elizabeth at this time created
another O'Brien Protestant bishop of Kilfenora, county Clare.†

The Lord Deputy Sidney made an official visit to Clare in the year
1571. One of the main objects he appears to have had in view was to
suppress the practice of landlords in charging their tenants with
"uncertaine cesses, cuttings, and spendings"; but this custom among the
Irish was of such long standing that even the Lord Deputy could do little
in the matter. He states that when he was at Limerick "two Lords of
Thomond, called Mac Nemarroes, came to him lamentinge the ruyn and
wast of their countries." The Lord Deputy adds "and ruyned they are
indede, craving to have the execution of English lawes and to have
Sheriffes planted amongst them."‡ Again, writing to the Council in
April 1576, Sir Henry Sidney observes "that he left Lymerick on the
27th of February, and entered Thomond attended by Earl of Thomond,
and several of the O'Briens, who had in former times been Kings of
Limerick, all so neire kinsmen and yet no one of them friende to
another." Sidney adds, " I also had with me the twoe MacNemarroghes,
by us called East and West Mac Nemarroghes, cheife gentlemen of that
countrey, which, if it were in quiet, they might lyve lyke principale
knights in England." Among all the chief men Sir Henry Sidney met
with in Thomond, he states he "could not find one descended in English
race. They all complained of the Obryens for the ruyne of their
countrey; and truly in such desolation and wast it is." Sir Henry, after
crossing the Shannon, marched through Clare in two days on his way to
Galway, so that he really could have seen very little of the country. The
Lord Deputy remained for some time in Galway, and bound the
O'Briens "by bonds of great sommes," and further he carried off the
earl's brother with him to Dublin, where he "still deteined hym in iron."
Sir Donell O'Brien of Ennistymon was made Sheriffe of Clare. Other
officers were appointed, such as a Provost-Marshal, with a proper force
to back his authority, and keep the idle people which swarmed in the
country in restraint. Sir H. Sidney states that "the root and origine of
all this trouble was the uncerteine grannte, and unstable possession of
their landes, whereupon grewe their warres." The Lord Deputy adds,

* White's "History of Clare," p. 197.

† "Tracts relating to Ireland" (vol. i. of "The Archæological Society of
Ireland").

‡ "Letters and Memorials of State," written by Sir Henry Sidney, K.G., four
times Lord Justice of Ireland, vol. i. p. 94; *idem*, p. 102.

" I brought them to agree to surrender all their landes into the Queene's handes, and to take it of her Highness agayne, and yeilde both rent and service, and therefore I have confidence to make a good reckninge for the Queene."

The meaning of this arrangement between certain of the principal landlords of Clare and Galway with the Lord Deputy was, that precision was to be given to the tenure of the land beyond that of the agreement which most of them had entered into with Henry VIII. Sir H. Sidney, however, had an eye to the revenue; it was clear if Ireland was to be governed the executive and the military must be paid otherwise than by a perpetual charge on the English exchequer. The Lord Deputy proposed therefore in place of the cesses and other burdens, that landholders should pay a fixed sum every year to their landlords, and that the latter were to yield to the Crown a definite amount per annum in proportion to the extent and value of their landed property; this, however, was an altogether different proposal to that contained in the agreement just before concluded between the Crown and the landowners of Clare; it meant the imposition of the land tenure of England for that which had existed from time immemorial in Ireland.

In the year 1570, the "Four Masters" referred to the death of "Macnamara, chief of Clancuilein, a noble and majestic man;" he was followed as head of the sept by his tanist, so that not only was this form of succession in force among the members of our sept at the close of the sixteenth century, but the old system of chieftainship of the clan was also a recognised condition of their social system.

L

CHAPTER XII

O'Neill's rebellion—Desmond, A.D. 1582—Confiscation of the greater part of land of Ulster and South Munster by the Crown—Terrible years of war and famine, 1551 to 1582—Clare and the Macnamaras remained at peace—References to members of the sept by "The Four Masters"—Commencement of trouble between O'Briens and Macnamaras, A.D. 1567—Sidney's remarks on the dispute—Important inquisition in connection with land tenure by Macnamaras, A.D. 1585—Borome tax existed in Clare at the end of sixteenth century—Macnamara, chief of Clancuilein, refuses to sign Sidney's new plan of land tenure and revenue—Abides by his contract of Henry VIII.'s time—Sir J. Perrott orders tenure of land and amount of rents to be taken in Clare before a Commission—The Macnamaras had to appear before the Commissioners—They decline all change for reasons given by the Lord Deputy who supported Macnamara's contentions—He reports to Lord Burghley that there were no better men or any like the Macnamaras in their country—Correspondence on this subject between Lord Deputy and the Privy Council—J. Macnamara's letter to Lord Burghley—Quin Abbey granted by Queen Elizabeth to an O'Brien—Close of the sixteenth century in Clare attended with inroads from the North and rising of O'Briens of Ennistymon against the Macnamaras.

SHAN O'NEILL's rebellion of 1551–67 hardly affected the history of our sept, but it is well to refer to the language used by a representative Irish chief like O'Neill as to the reasons which induced him to oppose the Government by force of arms. O'Neill, in one of his communications with the English Government, observed: " The Queen I confess she is my sovereign ; but I never made peace with her but at her own seeking. My ancestors were kings of Ulster, and Ulster is mine and shall be mine ; O'Donnell shall never come into the country ; with the sword I won it and with the sword I will keep it." * With sentiments such as these in his heart Shan O'Neill, and his rival O'Donnell flew at each other like wild beasts, and when they and their followers were thoroughly exhausted by the strife, her Majesty Queen Elizabeth and the Lord Deputy took possession and proceeded to confiscate the whole of Shan O'Neill's territory, which included more than half the province of Ulster. The natives were driven from their homes, which were then made over to Scotch and English settlers. The O'Neills had been

* Joyce's " Short History of Ireland," p. 416.

foremost among the Irish chiefs to urge the King of England either to govern Ireland or else leave the Irish to manage their own affairs, and the Supreme Pontiff's warning given on that occasion had now been fulfilled in a manner more disastrous to those concerned than even the Pope imagined (p. 134).

Queen Elizabeth's Government in the year 1582 had to meet with another rising in Ireland headed by the Earl of Desmond. From the proclamation which the Earl issued we learn that this was to a large extent a religious movement ; at any rate it was under this pretext that Desmond obtained the moral and material support of the Pope and of the King of Spain.* Desmond in the year 1582 was crushed by the Government, and the whole of his enormous estates, and those of one hundred and forty of his principal followers were confiscated, and so another million of Irish acres fell into the hands of the Crown. This property was offered in parcels to Englishmen ; some of them were allowed 12,000 acres upon which to settle eighty-six English families, and so on with smaller estates. Other portions of Desmond's lands were offered to Englishmen in fee simple at the rate of twopence per acre. But with respect to all these allotments, stringent clauses were introduced preventing the natives of Ireland from becoming either tenants or sub-tenants on any of the confiscated properties.

During the frightful years of war and famine, first in the north and then the south of Ireland, which lasted from 1551 to 1582, the inhabitants of county Clare enjoyed comparative peace. The O'Briens still held considerable influence among the members of the old Dalcasian tribe, and their chief was a staunch friend of the Earl of Ormond and so of the Queen ; the Abbé Macgeoghegan, therefore, may have been right when he stated that the Macnamaras were kept in check during these perilous times by the Earl of Thomond ;† but it is doubtful from the nature of the rising if the members of Clancuilein would have had much sympathy with the Earl of Desmond. At this time they were in full possession of their landed property and carried on their affairs according to their old laws and customs, and, as we shall subsequently learn, their chief source of anxiety at this period was not so much from the action of the English as from that of their relative and former chief the Earl of Thomond.

During this time we find more than one reference in the " Annals of the Four Masters " to members of our sept, mostly obituary notices, as

---

* "Carew Papers," 1515-74, p. 397 ; also Joyce's " Short History of Ireland," p. 425.

† " The History of Ireland," by the Abbé Macgeoghegan, p. 508.

follows: "The son of Macnamara of Western Clancuilein died, a man of all Clare the most dreaded by his enemies in the field of battle." *
This is the last of the many references made by the Annalists to the fighting qualities of the head of our sept.

Another entry, dated 1571, in the "Annals of the Four Masters" records the death of Teigie Macnamara (son of Sioda), regarding whom it is recorded that he was the " support of his adherents and friends, and the exterminator and destroyer of his enemies."

We hear of trouble between O'Brien (Earl of Thomond) and the Macnamaras in the year 1567. The former had been educated in England, his mother and grandmother having been Englishwomen ; the Macnamaras, on the other hand, were still pure Celts, bred and born in Clare. In a letter which the Lord Deputy, Sir Henry Sidney, sent to the Council in London, dated from Cork, February 1, 1567, he observes that he had written to "the Earl of Thomond regarding his letter complaining against the Macnamaras, that so soon as we came to Limerick we would consider the complaint and require him to remember your lordships' letter, and not tangle with the Macnamaras. In the mean we received the earl's answer declaring that he could not do so, for that Macnamara had done many things which he could not suffer." Sidney continues, the earl affirms that they (the Macnamaras) had not only taken cattle, but also "despatched some knaves," which, he observes, " God knoweth, they might spare enough, and her Majesty lose never a good subject " ; and, further, he charged those concerned in the matter to meet him at Limerick on the following Thursday; "he spared not to tell the earl of his lack of dutie in oure said letter to his lordship." †
There was, however, much more than a few cattle involved in this matter, for, as we shall discover from subsequent correspondence, the Earl of Thomond, presuming on his position had appropriated lands belonging to the Macnamaras, and on the latter appealing against these proceedings, the earl had attempted to carry the point with a high hand, conduct which the Lord Deputy was not disposed to permit. Matters however seem to have quieted down for the time, and Sir Henry Sidney passed through Clare to Galway. He gave orders to abolish " coyning and livery," and such like cesses, directing that the rules of English law should be substituted for the Brehon code ; and to aid him in effecting this purpose, Donald O'Brien of Ennistymon was made governor of Clare. The new ruler signalized his accession to office by hanging

---

* "Annals of the Four Masters," A.D. 1584.
† MS. State Papers (Ireland), vol. xxiii. No. 32, vi., Rolls Office.

refractory Irishmen and malefactors. Clare was at this time separated from Connaught and joined to Munster.

Before referring to the important steps taken by Sir Henry Sidney at Galway, in relation to the land belonging to the members of our sept, we may with advantage refer to an inquisition made at Galway, before Sir R. Bingham, on January 27, 1585, as it throws much light on the nature and scope of the Lord Deputy's proposal concerning the tenure of land.* This inquisition was made with reference to the property of John Macnamara, who had recently died. We learn in the first place that, although J. Macnamara was an extensive landlord, he had no idea of what his rental was, for it is stated in this document that "neither the owner of the land, nor any one else, knew for certain how much rent they had or ought to pay on any of the said quarters of land." In these circumstances the commission had to refer the matter "to those who knoweth best how much the said rent should be." The estates referred to belonged to one of the chiefs of our sept, the son of the Sioda Macnamara who had signed the agreement with Henry VIII. on behalf of a number of the freeholders of his clan. It would seem to us almost incredible that a person in this position, as late as the sixteenth century, should have been unable to state the amount of his rental. The truth was, he had never received any rent, according to our meaning of the term. Lands which he did not require for his own purposes he made over to his family or relations to cultivate, they supplying him with a certain quantity of stock and grain to enable him to keep open house, and live as one of the chief men of his sept. The management of the property was still conducted on the conjoint family principle, modified according to the necessities of the times. The out-turn of the soil was consumed by man and beast living upon the land which produced the stock and grain. There was no idea of sending gold and silver derived from the sale of stock to London or Dublin to be spent by individuals who had no personal interest in the land, and, in not a few instances, who had never even seen it. Englishmen, however, had discovered that land in Ireland was worth having, from their point of view, which was to make money out of it. When this fact had been realised a rush of all sorts and conditions of men passed into Ireland from the east, and the confiscated estates of Ulster and Munster offered them an opportunity of which they were by no means slow to avail themselves.

We find in the inquisition concerning J. Macnamara's property, some

* This inquisition was taken in the presence of the governor of the province and a jury, and was to inquire as to rents payable to John Macnamara's heirs and the title on which he held his property.

curious allusions to customs existing in his family in the year 1585; for instance, we learn that, upon "the marriage of his eldest daughter, the number of XX cows was received from each barrony," and, further, "that the towns and villages hereafter named [and they form a very long list] were bound to keep and beare the said Macnamara's horses and horse-boys with sufficient horse-meat and boys-meat every Christmas and Easter, when he kept any of the said feast at his house or town of Dengen *and not els*." It should be noticed that this cess of coyning and livery was only to be enforced at stated periods and when the lord of the estate came to reside amongst his landholders. Beyond this, it is stated in this inquisition that any one might compound with "Macnamara to pay him yearly sixteen pecks of otts in leiue of the said horse-meat and boy-meat which they were wont to give." Macnamara's kearntyes and huntsmen had "dutys upon certain quarters of lands in the barrony" (a long list of lands follow), which were "always freely acquitted and discharged free of all demands"; and, what is more remarkable, we find from this deed evidence to the effect that the ancient "Borome" tax was collected in county Clare. This tax consisted of a certain number of cows taken by compulsion, or for every cow XXX pence sterling. And lastly, that the "said Earl's ancestors had at all tymes when & at what tyme he wold goe to a torny against any of his enemies arysing out upon the said Macnamara's country onely of footmen, that is to say, one footman upon every quarter of land inhabyted in the said Barrony with victuals for ii days, but if they were to stay any longer than ii days then the said Erle was not only bound to finde them meate and drinke upon his own charge, but also to give Macnamara a lyinge for every such time; and further was bound to give him the third part of all booties and spoyles which he chanced to get."*

The contents of this document, therefore, prove that customs instituted among the Celts in Clare during the first century of the Christian era clung to them until the close of the sixteenth century. For the tax referred to as the "Borome" tribute was imposed in the time of Eochaid; it was abolished in the year A.D. 680, to be reimposed at the beginning of the eleventh century by Brian Boru, or "Boroimhé," for it was in consequence of Brian, after he became monarch of Ireland, having reimposed this tax, that he obtained his second or distinguishing name.† From the inquisition above referred to, we learn that Brian

---

* MS. Collection of Family Papers in possession of the late Colonel J. D. Macnamara. Copy of an Inquisition taken at Galway, January 27, A.D. 1585.

† "Manners and Customs of the Ancient Irish," by E. O'Curry, vol. ii. . 120.

Boru's descendants, in the person of the Earl of Thomond, continued to receive the Boromean tribute as late as the year 1585.

We shall now be in a better position to understand the importance of the proposals made by Sir H. Sidney regarding the estates held by the landowners of Clare. The scheme, as given in the Lord Deputy's own words at the end of the last chapter, was to supersede the settlement which the Macnamaras and other septs had agreed to seventeen years before, and to charge a fixed amount for the purposes of the Crown on the tribute paid by each occupier of the soil. A moment's consideration is sufficient to demonstrate that there was an essential difference contained in this proposal and that of Henry VIII.'s, which had been accepted by the Macnamaras in the year 1542. Under King Henry's scheme, Sioda Macnamara agreed, on behalf of himself and the freeholders he represented, to pay fifty marks a year towards the Irish revenue, in lieu of all other cesses and cuttings either to their chief or any one else. This plan consisted in the imposition of a local tax to be paid for Imperial purposes, those who had to pay assessing themselves and collecting the money in accordance with ancient customs and usages, the king supplanting the chief of the tribe only in respect to tribute. But Sir H. Sidney's first object was to increase the revenue of the Crown by raising the land tax. His meaning, as stated in his own words, was to "make a good reckining for the Queen," and, in order to bring about this end, the Lord Deputy found it necessary to persuade the landowners to cancel their deed of agreement with Henry VIII., and make a fresh one with Queen Elizabeth, on the understanding they should pay a tax on their rental. But out of this proposal arose two important considerations: first, how much rent each landowner received; secondly, the title under which he held his lands. These questions had not been raised under Henry VIII.'s scheme. Rent, as we have seen from an inquisition taken on the spot, was unknown in Clare, or, at any rate, no one "knew how much rent they had or ought to pay" in coin, which was what Sir H. Sidney meant. Further than this, the titles by which landed property was held, were in the greater number of cases based simply on possession. Estates had been carved out of the old tribal and common lands upon which the occupiers had lived for generations; beyond this, unless such as were granted by Henry VIII., these landowners possessed no title to their landed property according to English law. John Macnamara, as we shall subsequently explain, clearly comprehended the nature of Sir H. Sidney's move, and he refused therefore to have anything to say to it; but he was an exception to the rule, for the Earl of Thomond had still sufficient influence to persuade the other landowners to assent to the scheme of the Lord Deputy. The earl was probably alive to his position as a court favourite, and he realised the power it gave him in obtaining the estates of persons in Clare, who could not prove their title to the lands they held, for all such lands were to be confiscated, and consequently re-allotted by the Government. The first step the earl took was to write to Queen Elizabeth to obtain for himself "freedom from cesses on all his own lands within the said county of Thomond." At the same time he sought to have the "wardship of heires after the decease of the chief of every name."* The earl obtained no small part of what he asked, and a considerable grant of the confiscated lands.

Sir H. Sidney, after having brought the landowners of Clare as a body to accept his views regarding a tax on the rents under the new system, left Galway and returned to Dublin. He resigned office in 1567, and for the time being his arrangement with the landlords of Clare was allowed to drop.† Although Sir Henry returned to Ireland in the following year, his hands were so full of other matters that he had no time to follow up his land scheme in Clare; he ended his third deputyship in the year 1578. Passing over the important period of the Earl of Sussex's rule in Ireland, we find Sir John Perrott at the head of the government in the year 1584. After about a month's delay he visited Athlone, Galway, and then proceeded through Clare, remaining for one night at Quin, where he was met by the sheriff of the county with a prisoner, one Donogh Beg, who had been concerned in some plundering and rising in Connaught. The "Four Masters" inform us that this prisoner "was hanged from a car, and his bones were broken and smashed with the back of a heavy axe; and his body, thus mangled and half dead, was affixed, fastened with hard and tough hempen ropes, to the top of the steeple of Quin, as a warning and example to evid doers." Sir John Perrot, on his return to Dublin, then called a Parliament, at which, we are informed by the "Four Masters," that John Macnamara, the elected representative of county Clare, was present, as also was the Earl of Thomond and several other O'Briens, with the Bishop of Killaloe.‡ It is probable that the representations of the earl, regarding the affairs of Clare, led the Lord Deputy to take up the land question at the point at which it had been left by Sir Henry Sidney in the year 1567, however this may be, it is certain that Sir J. Perrott appointed a Commission to proceed to Clare and inquire into the nature of the titles by which the landowners held

* Rev. P. White's "History of Clare," p. 194.
† Joyce's "History of Ireland," p. 423.
‡ "Annals of the Four Masters," A.D. 1585.

their estates, and the rent they received. The Commission had power to call before them "all the nobility, spiritual and temporal, and all the chieftains and lords of the counties and baronies of Thomond, and in lieu of the uncertain cesses, cuttings, and spendings to which tenants had been subjected, to compound after their best description, and to lay down all things that tend to the real good and quiet of the country; which, after passing of the same by indenture, is meant to be ratified by Act of Parliament." The Commission commenced its labours in Clare with proposals to " the chieftains of countries, gentlemen and freeholders, to pass to the Queen's Majesty, her heirs, a grant of ten shillings, or a mark, upon every quarter of land containing 120 acres, manured, that bears either horn or corn, in lieu and consideration to be discharged from other cesses taxation or challenge, except the rising out of horse and foot, for the service of the prince and state as agreed on, and some certain days labour for buildings and fortefications for the safety of the people and kingdom."*

The representatives of the leading families of Clare were called on to appear before the Commission, and among them John Macnamara of West Clancuilein, and Donald Macnamara of East Clancuilein. An indenture was drawn up dated August 17, 1585, upon the above understanding, which the "Four Masters" state was agreed to and signed by "every head and chief of a sept, and every other lord of a barony throughout the whole country, except by John Macnamara, lord of West Clancuilein, who did not put his hand to the composition they made." †

John Macnamara's father was the son of the individual who had so shortly before come to an agreement with Henry VIII., and there was every reason why this compact should not be disturbed, so far as his sept was concerned. They declined therefore to fall in with the views put forward by Sir Henry Sidney in this matter; and they had cogent reasons for distrusting the purpose of the authorities in Clare with regard to this land question, a fact clearly elucidated on reference to various official documents of this period. In a letter written by Lord Deputy Fytzwylliam to Lord Burghley, dated Dublin, July 26, 1588, it is stated that "by the fault of some of the Commissioners the composition book of Connaught with a yearly quit rent to the Earl of Thomond, wherewithal Macnamara findeth himself greatly greeved, he and his ancestors having always held the lands and owing no duty to the said Earl—by this rent charge laid on Macnamara the Earl of Thomond will ease himself in the composition money he ought to pay for Thomond. Macnamara to be

* " O'Brien Memoirs," p. 218. † " Annals of the Four Masters," A.D. 1585.

free from the Earl offereth to pay for all his country after the rate of composition which is ten shillings for a quarter of land.   And if the Earl can prove that he ought to pay a quit rent he will pay it."   Fytzwilliam continues : " Macnamara hath always been a good subject and so deserveth favour.   This gentleman," the Lord Deputy observes, " during the space of these thirty years hath very dutifully carried and behaved himself," and so Fytzwilliam urges on Lord Burghley the justice of " affording Macnamara that favour as the equity of his cause shall to your Lordship seem good."*   Before writing this letter the Lord Deputy had referred the subject to the Governor of Connaught for his opinion, so that a full inquiry might be made on the spot as to the correctness of the complaint made by Macnamara, and in reply to this communication a statement of the matter at issue is given by the local governor of the province.

The fact must be borne in mind that the Lord Deputy expressly states that for thirty years past John Macnamara had been a dutiful and loyal subject ; that is, from the time he had entered into a compact with the Crown to that effect.   Further, it should be noticed that J. Macnamara in 1588 was ready to continue to pay a tax of ten shillings per quarter of land for all his country, he had still the power and the will to act as the representative of his sept.   To return to the correspondence, Sir R. Bingham, Governor of Connaught, writes as follows to Walsyngham (in London) :

ATHLONE, *July* 26, 1588.

At the making of the late composition between her Majesty and the lords and inhabitants of this province, Macnamara, chief of the barony of Denigenyriggin in Thomond, found himself greatly injured that such rents, duties, chiefries, and seignories as of right belonged to him and his ancestors, by lawful and ancient course of inheritance, and that they quietly enjoyed for a long time, were cut off and taken away, and a new rent charge and many other things set upon the said barony and the inhabitants of it his tenants, for the Earl of Thomond, which the said earl or his ancestors had not any time before within the same, to the utter undoing of the said Macnamara and his heirs and successors for ever, which indeed myself and others of the Commissioners did much impugn and withstand at that very instant, but the late Lord Deputy Perrett and Sir Nicholas White, who took much upon him in these matters, handled the matter so far in favour of the earl, *as after his coming to Dublin they made up the books according to their own pleasure, to the no little hindrance of many a man in the province.*   The said Macnamara had now of late put up a petition to the new Lord Deputy Fytzwylliam, craving to be freed of the earl, saving of such things as in past right he ought to yield him, and offering, nevertheless, to pay 10ˢ a quarter to her Majesty, so as he may have a reasonable freedom

* " State Papers " (Ireland), vol. for 1586–88, p. 577, and also July 31, 1588.

assigned to him and to satisfy the earl anything which of right he ought to have of him or his country, by inquiry made already, or which he shall be able to make title unto, either by matter of record, evidence, ancient monument, or honest indifferent witnesses not suborned, whereupon his lordship directed warrant unto me and the Council of the Province to examine the contents of the said petition, and take such order in it, for Macnamara's relief as should stand with right and equity, leaving the Earl to any reasonable course of justice whereby he may recover his own in manner aforesaid. And the party considering the Earl is now in Court as petitioner to Her Majesty to confirm the said composition, and that we cannot proceed to deal in it according to my Lord Deputy's Commission, till he repair to these parts, made earnest request unto me to write unto your honor to be a mean for Her Highness, that no such information be granted till a full examination be first taken of the matter within this realm, and certificate thereof returned to your honors, *which I could not deny in so honest and just a cause.* I have sent you the copies of the petition, and of the warrant to myself from my Lord Deputy, that upon receipt thereof your honour may deal further as you shall think fit, but thus much I must write in behalf of Macnamara, that he has always behaved himself like an honest gentleman and dutiful subject, and deserveth to be favourably dealt withal. It is given out here that the Earl of Thomond will make personal suit of Her Majesty to grant him all the composition rent of Thomond for increase of his living ; it would much hinder herself and her subjects if the same were passed on to him. I thought good to give your honor a caveat that nothing be granted to Her Highnesses own prejudice, and if he make any suit to be restored to any castle in Ireland, " Thomond," by virtue of any grant from Her Majesty, I beseech you that the same may be referred to trial and examination, otherwise it will be the undoing of many, for his father hath put many castles into his patent which are the lawful inheritance of others.*

Sir J. Perrott's commission took copious evidence concerning the ownership and tenure of land in Clare. Subsequently a number of inquisitions were instituted before the proper authorities, aided by a jury, as to the title under which much of the land in Clare was held. These inquisitions extend over a period of several years, and in his history of Clare, Mr. Frost has given us a *résumé* of the evidence then taken, so far as that county is concerned. Among these inquisitions no less than seventy-two referred to lands then held by some three hundred landed proprietors belonging to our sept, who at the time resided within the area formerly assigned to the Macnamaras as tribal lands, situated between the rivers Fergus and Shannon.† Much of this land was at the end of the sixteenth century, such as that which belonged to J. Macnamara, "freely acquitted and discharged from all rents and demands," in fact, freehold property.‡

* " State Papers " (Ireland), vol. for 1586–88, p. 576.
† Frost's " History and Topography of Clare," pp. 267, 337, 385.
‡ Very Rev. P. White's " History of Clare," p. 207.

That the Earl of Thomond took advantage of his position at the court of Queen Elizabeth is evident from a statement contained in a letter from one of our family to Lord Burghley (dated March 3, 1588) ; he writes :

I thought it necessary to acquaint you with the unkind dealing of the Earl of Thomond my cousin sheweth towards me.   He tries to encroach upon my living as well by procuring his grandmother, Dame Ellen Butler, to sue me, as in demand of her third, as in divers other sorts.   I will not mention the sundry orders passed for mollifying the dissentions between his lordship's father and my father, as also between his Lordship and me. If the said Earl, either now at Court (London) or in this land, after coming here, will begin any suit against me for land, or otherwise prejudice me, persuade him to be contented with the observation of such orders as formerly hath past as well between our fathers as ourselves, or else that the whole matter or controversy between him and me, and between the said lady and me, be referred to the Lord Deputy, the Lord Chancellor, and the Chief Justice, whereby the said Earl and Lady may leave their continued vexing of me.   For if it please your Lordship, the most and "famoustest" member of lawyers of this land are allied to the Earl of Thomond through marriage with the house of Kildare, and his kindred with the house of Ormond, whereby I am forced to take refuge in the conscience of her Majesty's ministers of the Council of Ireland.*

The Lord Deputy, in forwarding this letter to Burghley, urges him "to have the cause of Macnamara in favourable remembrance, on account of his faithful and dutiful course"; and adds, " *there are not two more like him in the whole province.*" †   The Earl of Thomond's mother was a daughter of the Chancellor, Sir Thomas Cusack, and his wife a daughter of Lord Nugent of Delvin ; he had been brought up in the Court of Elizabeth.   Another member of the O'Brien family, Sir Turlough of Ennistymon, received letters patent bearing date December 14, 1583, confirming him in fee of the dissolved Abbey of Quin and its appurtenances.‡   In 1541 Quin Abbey had been formally dissolved by Henry VIII. and granted two years later to O'Brien, Baron of Ibirkane, who protected the monks.   After Elizabeth's confirmation of this grant, the friars still remained in possession.   As Mr. Westropp remarks, well had the Franciscans kept their vow of poverty, for in 1541 they owned but one acre of land.   The Macnamaras, however, must have felt keenly the suppression of the abbey, which had been founded and built by their ancestors in the year 1420, and since then the head of the sept and members of the family for many generations had been buried within its walls, where their tombs remain to the present time.

The close of the sixteenth century was destined to witness more

---

* " State Papers " (Ireland), vol. for 1588-92, p. 129.   † *Ibid.* p. 130.
‡ " O'Brien Memoirs," p. 213.

trouble and bloodshed in Clare, for Hugh Roe O'Donnell, the Earl of Tyrone, was at war with England, and he carried his arms into the Pale and the newly settled province of Ulster. To resist O'Donnell's advance towards the south-west Sir Conyer Clifford, Governor of Connaught, in May 1597, called on the Earl of Thomond and also the Clanricardes to assist him with a contingent of Clare men; and so the natives of the North and West of Ireland were again to meet on the battlefield. At the opening of this campaign the Munster forces were victorious, but subsequently fortune favoured O'Donnell, and O'Brien had to retreat into Clare. The northern chief, however, determined to punish his enemies, for such he considered the Clare forces in consequence of their having espoused the cause of the Queen, he therefore marched into Clare in May 1598, and swept the whole country west of the Fergus of its cattle, which he drove off into Donegal. The following year O'Donnell repeated this practice and made a second raid into Clare; passing along the valley of the Shannon and then turning west he swept through Macnamara's lands and so on to the Fergus, as far as Clare Castle. He then returned home along the Gort line of road as he had done in the previous year.

Seeing the apparent ease with which a raid of this kind could be effected without any effort on the part of the Government to restrain the offending nobleman, some of the younger members of the O'Briens of Ennistymon seem to have thought it well to try on the same game, and so they organised a cattle lifting expedition against Clancuilein. Under command of young O'Brien, they ravaged the lands and farms on either side of the Fergus as far south as Ballyalley, but on their return journey, when laden with spoil, they were met by a "rising out of the country of two cantred of the Macnamaras whose flocks and herds they had robbed. Teigie O'Brien was killed, and the expedition was dispersed."

All this turmoil and bloodshed in Clare occurred without the slightest intervention on the part of the Government, who thus signally failed to fulfil the agreement they had made with the members of our sept in 1545, "to protect them against their enemies," and to preserve order and justice in Clare.

Queen Elizabeth died in the year 1603. During her reign two formidable efforts on the part of Ireland to destroy the power of England in that country had been suppressed. England had doubtless asserted her supremacy over Ireland in a manner unknown in previous reigns, but this assertion of power had been attended with unheard of and most iniquitous confiscations of the lands, and other terrible wrongs committed against a vast number of absolutely innocent people who inhabited the provinces of Ulster and South Munster. Beyond this, the persecution of the Catholic clergy and the suppression of their religion laid the foundation of far-reaching changes in the social and political life of the Irish. Treatment such as that which the Roman Catholic bishops and clergy received at the hands of the Government led a warm-hearted, sensitive people like the Celts to sympathise deeply with their persecuted countrymen, and to transfer to them that reverence which in former times they had lavished on their chiefs.* The Celt must be led by some one ; his weakness is want of self-confidence. When his chiefs and landowners had been removed, the priest, tried by the fire of persecution, gradually developed into the leader of the Irish, and he has retained his position up to the present day.

The confiscations of Elizabeth beyond destroying a number of the ancient landowners, laid the foundation of one of Ireland's greatest misfortunes, that is, the introduction of a middleman, who came between the newly created landlords and the native occupiers of the soil. These people were the instigators of " rack-rent " in Ireland, and many other troubles, not the least of which was the hatred of the landholder or tenant to the representative of his landlord. No sooner, in fact, had the Celtic landowners been turned out of their ancestral possessions than we find Lord Burghley (December, 1596) complaining that the Englishmen who succeeded to their estates made over their lands "to deputies, who take greater rents than that allowed by Her Majesty, and so they are forced to re-let the ground to the Irish without maintaining any English on the property " (State Papers of 1596-7, p. 182). Lord Burghley corroborates the accuracy of the statement made by the Earl of Kildare, that the middlemen demanded extraordinary cesses over the whole country, a practice which rapidly developed, and caused infinitely greater hardships than " coyning and livery " as practised by the former Celtic landowners.

* A vigorous effort was made by the Government to establish what were called free schools throughout Ireland ; the Protestant religion was to be made compulsory in these schools so as to spread the tenets of that form of faith over the country, to the exclusion of the ancient religion of the people. At the same time strict orders were issued against saying Mass in any church in Ireland, when only the ritual contained in the Book of Common Prayer was to be used. The revenue of the Church appears to have been very irregularly managed, and some of the Macnamaras seem to have been in no way indisposed to take advantage of this state of affairs ; for instance, Dr. Rider, Bishop of Killaloe, complained that his predecessor had let the rectory in the parish of Quin for three score years to D. Macnamara, on a rental of eighteenpence per annum, but that it was worth at least two pounds a year. We learn that Sir J. and Daniel Macnamara held considerable church property, and that another branch of the family had some twenty-two townlands derived from the same source (White's " History of Clare," pp. 233-234).

CHAPTER XIII

James I.'s treatment of Catholics—Sudden application of English laws to Ireland entirely opposed to wishes of the natives of the country, a wrong not yet adjusted—Sir J. Davis's report on Clare, A.D. 1606—The execution of two weak-minded men—Case of Sir J. Macnamara, as showing how lands were secured by Court favourites from Irish gentlemen in 1608—Sir J. Perrott's decision on this case—His praise of Sir J. Macnamara, who is appointed High Sheriff of Clare, A.D. 1623—O'Brien's successful scheme to possess himself of the Tulla estates belonging to the Macnamaras, A.D. 1585—Sir Thomas Wentworth's (Strafford's) confiscation of the greater part of Clare by the Crown, "a violation of the King's promise."

JAMES I. having Celtic blood in his veins, and being the son of the unfortunate Mary Queen of Scots, the Irish rushed to the conclusion that he must be a Roman Catholic, and, acting under this impression, so soon as he came to the throne they turned the Protestants out of their churches, and re-established the old services. The Lord Deputy, however, marched with a force of armed men to Wexford, and made provision for the Protestant services being read in all churches throughout Ireland. At the same time the gentry were commanded to take an oath of allegiance to the King, which they had no objection to do; but most of them refused to acknowledge him as head of the Church; for this reason they received the name of "recusants," and measures were taken to confiscate their lands. So great was the persecution of the recusants that many of them left the country, including such men as the Earls of Tyrone and Tyrconnell. It was in vain the Irish urged on the King that all they desired was to be allowed to "exercise in public the religion which they had always practised privately; and as their public prayers gave testimony to their loyal hearts, so they were no less careful to manifest their duty to God, in which they never would be dissembling." The only answer they got to this appeal was an order that every Popish priest must leave the country on pain of death or imprisonment.

Another effect of this coercive policy was to drive a number of Irish youths abroad to be educated for Holy Orders. Seminaries were established for their reception in almost every country of Europe, and there they lived until prepared to go forth to administer to the religious wants of their countrymen with death or imprisonment staring them in the face.* As the Government were unable to lay hands on these youths in their Continental seminaries, they proceeded to punish parents who sent their sons abroad with the object of entering the priesthood ; and the rules compelling Roman Catholics to attend Protestant services were rigidly enforced. But it was all to no purpose ; and the Government, in despair of converting the Irish to the Protestant faith by these means, gave up the attempt. The custom of tanistry and of gavelkind were abolished by law ; and from a judgment delivered in Dublin in the year A.D. 1605, all Irish customs appertaining to landed property were to be set on one side in favour of the common law of England ; but no means were taken to guard the interests of junior members of families who under the Brehon code would have inherited sufficient land to maintain them and their children in that grade of society to which they belonged. These people, having been deprived of their inheritance by the substitution of English for Irish law, were turned adrift impoverished and unable to gain a living. It was the sudden and untimely application of English law to the condition of the landed proprietors living under the old Brehon code that completely disorganised the land tenure in Ireland, and from which it has never recovered.† The Government soon afterwards re-enacted the law of gavelkind in Ireland, with the express object of sub-dividing the estates of Irish Roman Catholic landowners, so as to minimise their influence in the country, and this Act remained in operation until the time of George III.

It was necessary to refer thus briefly to matters affecting the general

---

* Macgeoghegan's " History of Ireland," p. 481.

† " Manners and Customs of the Ancient Irish," by Eugene O'Curry, vol. i. p. 184. This wrong was effected mainly through English lawyers, greedy themselves, and urged on by the mercantile classes and aristocracy of England, with the object of confiscating for their own use the estates of the ancient landowners in Ireland. Sir G. Campbell, who was formerly Lieutenant-Governor of Bengal, and intimately acquainted with our method of dealing with the land question in India, after his return home studied the land tenure in Ireland, and in his work on the subject gives his opinion to the effect that : " This introduction of English law and of purely English Courts was a cardinal mistake " with respect to Ireland, for, as he says " the law must constantly have run counter to the customs and practice" of the country ; words almost identical with those used by Edmund Spenser on this subject. Sir George adds : " Pettifogging lawyers were constantly picking holes in titles, and under Strafford general insecurity prevailed ; the legal rights of the Irish were extinguished, and their lands confiscated " (" The Irish Land Question," by George Campbell, p. 30).

Mrs Macnamara
Wife of
Mr John Macnamara, M.P.
from a miniature
G. Cosway.

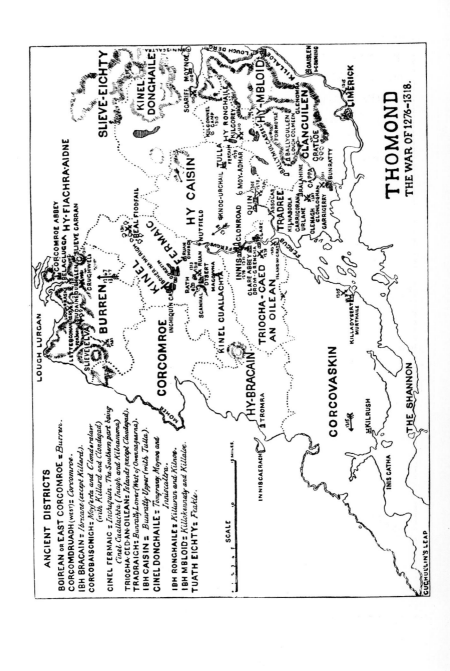

ANCIENT DISTRICTS

BOIREAN or EAST CORCOMROE = Burren.
CORCOMDRUADH (WEST) = Corcomroe.
IBH BRACAIN = Ibricane (except Killard).
CORCOBAISCNIGH= Moyferta and Clonderalaw
        (with Killard and Clondegad).
CINEL FERMAIC = Inchiquin. The Southern part being
        Cinel Cuallachta (Inagh and Kilnamona)
TRIOCHA-CED-AN-OILEAN= Islands (except Clondegad).
TRADRAICH= Bunratty Lower (West of Owennagarnia).
IBH CAISIN = Bunratty Upper (with Tulla).
CINEL DONGHAILE = Tomgraney, Moynoe and
        Inniscaltra.

IBH RONGHAILE = Killuran and Kilnoe.
IBH MBLOID = Killokennedy and Killaloe.
TUATH EICHTY= Feakle.

SCALE

LOUGH LURGAN

THOMOND

THE WAR OF 1276-1318.

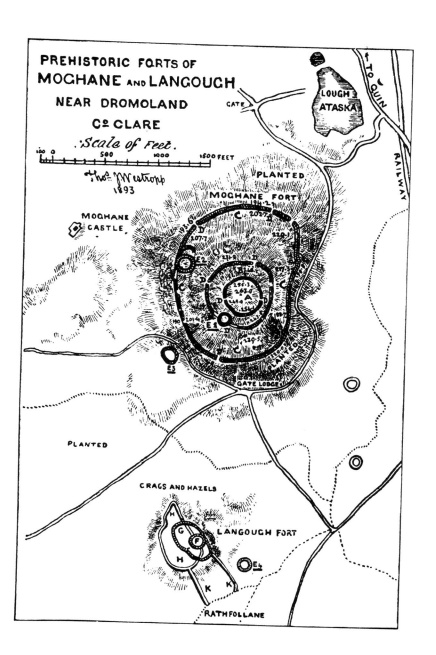

PREHISTORIC FORTS OF
MOGHANE AND LANGOUGH
NEAR DROMOLAND
Cº CLARE

Scale of Feet.
100 0   500   1000   1500 FEET

Thos. J. Westropp
1893

LOUGH ATASKA

f. TO QUIN

RAILWAY

GATE

PLANTED

MOGHANE FORT

MOGHANE CASTLE

GATE LODGE

PLANTED

CRAGS AND HAZELS

LANGOUGH FORT

RATHFOLLANE

Magh Adhar, near Quin, co. Clare, from the West.

Place of Inauguration of the Kings of Thomond.

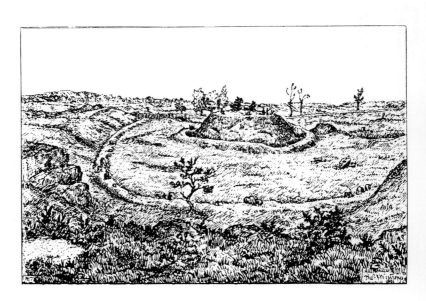

Magh Adhar from North-East.

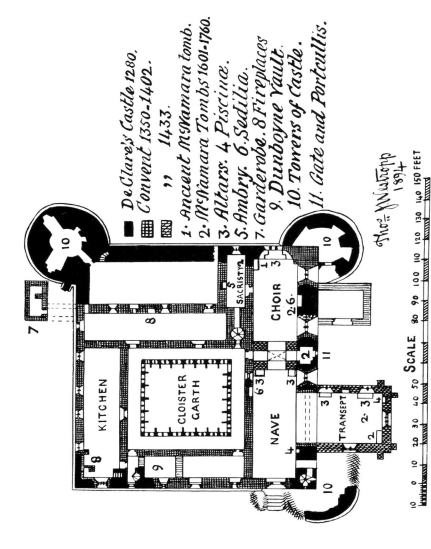

DeClare's Castle 1280.
Convent 1350-1402.
  ,,   1433.
1. Ancient McNamara tomb.
2. McNamara Tombs 1601-1760.
3. Altars. 4. Piscina.
5. Ambry. 6. Sedilia.
7. Garderobe. 8 Fireplaces
9. Dunboyne Vault.
10. Towers of Castle.
11. Gate and Portcullis.

Thos J Westropp
1894.

PLAN OF QUIN ABBEY AND FORT.

SCALE

10   0   10   20   30   40   50   80   90   100   110   120   130   140 150 FEET

7

8

KITCHEN

CLOISTER GARTH

8

9

NAVE

TRANSEPT

4

3

2·3

2

10

2

11

3

6·3

3

3

SACRISTY 2

5

CHOIR

2·6.

3

1

10

10

ENNIS ABBEY.

CRATLOERIAEL 1885

RALAHINE 1885

admie 9th 1803.

My Dear Mare—

I am extremely write to

Lord Ellenborough this very day, and what
I said of your yesterday is most perfect
correct that although you are the
more than we with an affront yet

one under the means to give an affront
If your antagonist had not told or
this statement his [ ] [ ] [ ] [ ] [ ] [ ] [ ]
have brought him into a [ ] of
[ ] [ ] [ ] on that subject
[ ] is [ ] [ ] to [ ] or [ ] [ ]
[ ] in your favour, [ ] my [ ] [ ]
[ ] in [ ] [ ] you must [ ] [ ]
[ ] [ ] [ ] [ ] [ ] Nelson Bronte
[ ] together [ ] —

CRATLOEMORE 1885 T.J.W.

DANGANBRACK 1885

QUIN ABBEY.

TOMB OF FOUNDER OF QUIN ABBEY
(LOCHLAIN MACNAMARA).

EAST WINDOW, QUIN ABBEY

THE CLOISTERS, QUIN ABBEY.

SECTION OF BALLYPORTREA KEEP.

A Entrance.

B Room, with a " murder-hole " commanding door.

C Rooms in staircase tower.

D Small room, from which passages run through spandrils of vault.

E Kitchen.

F Hall with stone floor.

G Room with wooden floor.

H Vaulted garret.

K Upper rooms.

L Fireplaces.

M Turret room.

N Machicolation.

O Enclosure.

P Flanking turret.

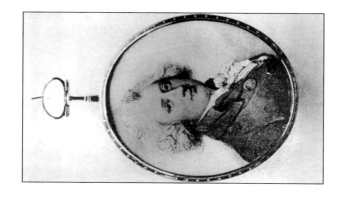

Mr John Macnamara, M.P.
from a miniature
G. Conway.

Admiral James Macnamara.

condition of the Irish in the early part of the seventeenth century in order to understand the history of our sept at this period. Sir John Davis was then Solicitor-General, and Speaker in the Irish Parliament; and in a letter to Lord Salisbury, dated May 4, 1606, he states that he had just returned from an official visit to Clare, "which is called Thomond," where he "beheld the appearance and fashion of the people. I would," he remarks, "I had been in Ulster again; for these are mere Irish as they, and their outward form not much unlike them; but when we came to dispatch business we found that most of them speak English, and understand the course of our proceedings well." Sir J. Davis continues as follows: "After the despatch of the gaol, which contained no extraordinary malefactors, our principal labour did consist in establishing sundry possessions of freeholders in the country, which had been disturbed in the time of the rebellion, and had not since been settled. The best of the freeholders next the O'Briens, are the Macnamaras, and the O'Lancyes, the chiefs of which families appeared in civil habit and fashion; the rest not so refined as some of the people of Munster." Sir J. Davis goes on to state that one of the provosts of Clare was brought before him on the charge of murder. This man's name was Downing, and Sir John writes: "It happened that an idiot fool belonging to the Earl of Thomond, with another of the same quality, a follower of J. Macnamara, a knight of Thomond, came straggling into the village where Downing dwelt; he, meeting them on a Sunday morning, took them immediately and hanged them both." Lord Thomond stated that Downing not only knew the men to be idiots, but also that one of them belonged to him, and so had executed him maliciously. Sir John Davis, however, forgave Downing, although the jury convicted him of murder, "upon which a few words of passion passed between the Earl and the Lord Deputy, Sir A. Chichester, and there the matter ended."*

This glimpse of social life in Clare during the year 1606 is instructive, for it confirms Sir H. Sidney's observation that the better class of landowners in that part of Ireland lived in much the same style as gentlemen of England of the period, and it further demonstrates how inadequately the laws were administered, for the two unfortunate men, hanged without trial by an underling like Downing, appear to have committed no greater offence than that of having crossed the path of this official on Sunday morning.

John Macnamara, mentioned in the above letter, was a grandson of Sioda, of Henry VIII.'s time, and son of John, who declined in the

* "Calendar of State Papers" (Ireland).

M

reign of Elizabeth to enter into a second agreement with the Crown as regards his estates. Sir John Macnamara was knighted in Dublin on the 29th of September 1603 ; he was a large landowner and a man of importance in his county. It would seem that the Earl of Thomond coveted his property, and from the following details appears to have organised a scheme for bringing Macnamara to grief and so obtaining possession of his estates.

We learn from the Protestant Bishop of Limerick that " Sir J. Macnamara was denounced for frequently harbouring an Irishman, Mac-Grath, Vicar-General of the Pope over the whole diocese, who took upon him to order priests and dispense in cases of matrimony and other cases as is shown and proved." This was a dangerous proceeding, and placed Sir John in jeopardy of having his property confiscated by the Crown.

In February 1608, Sir A. Chichester, the Lord Deputy of Ireland, received through some mysterious source a communication as follows : *

MONTALLION, 12 *February.*

Reverend father in God, my duty remembered. I understand there are shipping at Galway them that goeth for Spain, wherefore I heartily pray you, according to promise, to send this enclosed letter by the first trusty convenient messenger you may. Whereof I pray you not to fail, and so I commit you to God, and rest yours for ever to command. JOHN MACNAMARA.

Addressed to the Rev. Father in God Sir Owen, Preacher at Galway.
This deliver.

My honourable brother in Christ—I received your letter since the going away of O'Neale and O'Donnell, and am still according to my faithful vow and promise to you at our being last at Mockheins, wherein I will live and die. The Vicar-General, Mahoura Magralye, is with me still in these borders to perform these actions. And when the army cometh, according to your promise, either to the river of Limerick or the bay of Galwaye, I will presently come to them and take the Earl of Thomond's house of Bunrattie, for the better performance of my promise to you. I proposed to have gone thither when O'Neale and O'Donnell went away, but I altered my mind for the causes aforesaid. The Earl of Thomond is determined to go for England, and I cannot tell but that I may go with him to learn more news, and so write to you all.

The Baron of Delvin was taken prisoner and committed to the castle of Dublin, when he confessed all the secrets he had, and afterwards made an escape, and hope he is there with you ere now. Yours for ever confirmed,

JOHN MACNAMARA.

Directed to my honourable brother in Christ, Don Donaldos O'Sulivan. These delivered in Spain or elsewhere.

* " Calendar of State Papers " (Ireland, for 1606–8), pp. 428, 429.

The Lord Deputy on receiving these letters at once wrote the follow-ing dispatch to Earl Salisbury. His letter is dated :

DUBLIN, *February* 27, 1608.

Sends him copy of a letter intercepted at Galway, and states that Salisbury will perceive what are the plans shot at, and that there are many conspirators and favourers of these devilish intentions who pretend to be loyal daily familiar amongst them ; prays him to acquaint the king with the contents of the letters, and prays God may put it in his princely heart to root out all those that have been partakers in this treason, and to plant good and faithful subjects in their stead. None of his Majesty's predecessors have had like means of power to reform and settle this kingdom, nor greater cause given to use severe justice to the false-hearted and counterfeited subjects of the land. If this time and occasion be permitted, his Majesty's good subjects and servants may well despair of their safeties, for undoubtedly they will be taken unfounded, and suddenly cut off, perchance by those whom they are enforced to trust.

The Lord Deputy had written to the Earl of Thomond to come to him, and to bring the writer of the letter, who he believed was Sir J. Macnamara ; but for the more assurance, he willed him to bring all the John Macnamaras who are of any power or note in that country, to-gether with the priest, if he can light upon him. The Lord Deputy wrote as follows :

Has only a despatch to the Earl of Thomond since he received the letters from Galway, which came sealed to his hands, and he dared not impart the contents of them to any man until the party is secured, which makes him write all with his own hand. He keeps the original letters that he may therewith charge the writer when he comes unto him over with the Earl of Thomond or some other person of trust, for he doubts not getting him if the interceptors of the letters at Galway abuse him not.

P.S.—He may judge how needful it is to finish the work at Galway, and to strengthen Limerick, for if an enemy possess themselves of those places and the towns, it will be a hard matter to remove them.

In reply to this letter the Lords of Council wrote to Sir A. Chichester March 20th, 1608 :

Had received two letters of the 28th February and a copy of letter intercepted, from John Macnamara to Donald O'Sullivan in Spain, giving intimation of an attempt to be made by some foreign power and army in the Limerick river, or Bay of Galway. The party to whom the letter is addressed is better known than he who writes it. But he had given them hopes that he would be able to find him out and apprehend him, which he is requested to do, and having ensnared him to give them further intelligence. The Lord Deputy is praised for his carefulness ; but it is intimated to him that the same judgment they gave him in a former letter, that notwithstanding these alarms given by turbulent and sedisious spirits, there is no present fear of invasion."

In the letter following this it seems the Lord Deputy had been blamed not only for the escape of Lord Delvin from prison, but also that of " Coward, the sea captain and pirate." These charges Sir A. Chichester disclaims, and continues :

These imputations, together with the weakness of the persons and infidelity of officers and servants, proceeding for the most part from poverty, make him timorous to lay hands upon any great or active man, lest they should cause, after escape, greater harm than if they had never been apprehended at all. Besides, the juries are so partial that commonly the judges cannot possibly direct them aright, but they will many times give such a verdict as pleases themselves and the priests that govern them. Notwithstanding, he has within these few days caused the Earl of Thomond to apprehend Sir J. Macnamara for matter of treason, and has sent part of his troop of horse towards Limerick to bring him up to the Castle of Dublin, wherein he is driven to keep a continual guard of soldiers to attend that charge, over and above the ward of the castle, which he has committed to a costos, the constable being himself removed into the town jail. He proposes to send Sir John Macnamara over to their lordships, with the testimony of his treason written with his own hand, if it so pleases them.

Sir A. Chichester reported to the Lords of the Privy Council on the 2nd of April 1608, that "Sir John Macnamara was brought here yesterday, and he had committed him to the castle. For his maintenance there is no better case than the others, the wealth and greatness of these persons and many others like them being only in the dependence of men, of whose fortunes and affections they are the masters and disposers so long as they live in liberty amongst them and no longer; which inconvenience would be hereafter provided for, after their lands shall be confiscated to the Crown." Confiscation runs through the whole proceeding. Sir A. Chichester states that J. Macnamara :

denies writing the letter with which he is charged; he (the Lord Deputy) had compared them, and so have divers of the Council, with divers other letters and writings of his which he has gotten, and they agree in opinion that it is his own handwriting. He (Macnamara) seems to suspect one Lynch, a merchant of Galway, who (as he says) has long awaited to do him mischief, for counterfeiting his hand in this sort. Has sent for Lynch, together with the party who received the letters from the messenger that brought it, and for the messenger himself if he may be gotten.

Sir James Perrott, writing to the Earl of Salisbury in June 1608, refers as follows to Sir J. Macnamara : " Now in hold, as a more popular man than even the Earl of Thomond in his own country, and although he is married to the Earl's sister, yet has written letters to attempt his destruction unto some fugitives of Spain."* Sir James mentioned a

* " Calendar of State Papers " (Ireland, 1606–1608), p. 570.

number of the chiefs best known in Ireland as being under arms in Spain, and adds : " So that there never was so many men of note and experience in the wars of that nation at one time beyond the seas, ready to return and make parties in the several parts of this kingdom." *

Sir J. Perrott, having subsequently gone thoroughly into the evidence and circumstances of Sir J. Macnamara's case, arrived at the conclusion that he was innocent of the crime of which he was accused, and not only released him from confinement, but reinstated him in the full possession of his property ; he was appointed High Sheriff of Clare in 1623. Sir John lived until 1632, and we have a copy of his will leaving his estates to his three nephews ; he had no children. As already stated, it is probable this charge against Sir J. Macnamara was a plot to ruin him, and so lead to the confiscation of his property. It is to be observed that the Earl of Thomond's name appears more than once in the proceedings, and his influence would doubtless have been considerable with a Deputy such as Sir A. Chichester. That the Earl was capable of taking action of this kind is shown by his proceedings in the following case concerning the Macnamaras of Tulla.

The facts regarding this case have been drawn up from official documents, which are still in existence and were collected by the Chevalier O'Gorman in the year 1782. His original MS. is in the library of the Royal Irish Academy (24 D. 10). In this document O'Gorman traces step by step the evidence given before Inquisitions taken at Ennis in 1585, and subsequently as to the action of the Earl of Thomond in the year 1611 to gain possession of the estates of Fermoy, Tulla,† and Lissofin in Clare. O'Gorman wished to demonstrate by means of a well-authenticated case the process taken under the newly introduced English law for depriving an old Celtic family of their landed property.

It will be remembered that Lochain Macnamara, who was chief of Clanculien at the end of the fourteenth century, divided his territory into two portions, East and West Clanculien. At the same time he made over certain lands to a third son, Mahon ; this property was known as that of Tulla and Lissofin. O'Gorman states that Mahon Macnamara was " a religious man or priest " ; and from another source we learn that his son Donogh " at his own expense built the refectory and sacristy of the monastery at Ennis, and afterwards took the habit of the order " ; the landed property of Tulla and Lissofin, however, passed to his tanist, and from him to his successor, and so on without question until the year 1611.

---

* " Calendar of State Papers " (Ireland, A.D. 1608).

† See O'Gorman's MS. p. 80, for meaning of the word " Tarmore " lands ; also Sir J. Davis in " Letters of Earl of Salisbury," p. 260.

There was nothing remarkable in this, because the monks of the Celtic Church not only married, but their property in some cases descended from father to son, and in others was practically entailed upon members of certain families.*

In the year 1585 Sir John Perrott's Commission commenced its investigation as to the titles by which the landlords of Clare held their estates. The original titles were to be made over with the lands to the Crown, and to be received back by the owners with titles registerable in the Court of Chancery, and in conformity with English procedure. An inquiry of this kind made it necessary that the title deeds should be examined, and gave the agents of the Earl of Thomond an opportunity for discovering any flaw which might exist according to English law in those titles, with the object of upsetting them and having such lands confiscated, when they were either sold, or, as in this case, would most probably have been made over to the Court favourite, the Earl of Thomond.

The Commission discovered that the ancestors, Mahon and Donogh Macnamara, of the existing owners of Tulla and Lissofin, had been ecclesiastics of some kind about the year 1393. The plea was therefore put forward that these were Church lands, and must therefore be forfeited to the Crown under the statute of mortmain. The owner of the estates, Daniel Macnamara, argued that even supposing their ancestors had entered holy orders, there was nevertheless undoubted evidence to prove that the property had been held by members of their family for more than two hundred years. How was it possible, therefore, that these estates could be Church lands? Beyond this it was urged that the statute of mortmain could not apply to co. Clare in Richard II.'s reign, for at that period the Brehon laws alone were in force, and not an acre of land in Clare was then held by the English. The Commission who heard the case were aided by a jury; and as these refused to admit that there was any defect in the title, the matter was allowed to stand over, and Daniel Macnamara remained in possession of his property. But, as already explained, p. 170, the Governor of Connaught in a letter written to the English Minister, Walsyngham, states, with regard to the inquisition of Clare taken in 1585, that "the late Lord Deputy Perrott and Sir Nicholas White, who took much upon him in these matters, handled the matter so far in favour of the Earl of Thomond, as after their coming to Dublin they made up the books (regarding the inquisition) according to their own pleasure, to the no little hindrance of many a man in the province." These officials determined among other matters that the

* " Ireland and the Anglo-Norman Church," p. 355.

estates of Tulla and Lissofin should be confiscated, but it would have been too glaring a scandal to make them over to the Earl of Thomond direct; that nobleman therefore employed another person to purchase this property, which was then handed over to the Earl's agent. O'Gorman states their object in the first instance was "to get the benefit of the forfeiture—for could they only obtain possession of the property, from their power and strength in the country and by reason of the Earl's relations, that it would be a hard matter to dispossess them." An alderman of Dublin, named Weston, was put forward to buy the forfeited estates, which he did for the sum of £75, although one of them, Tulla, at that time was worth "at least £500 per annum" (A.D. 1611), the value of money then being much greater than it is at present. Alderman Weston made the estates over to Roland de le Hoyde, who was the Earl of Thomond's agent. The estate was then divided, the Earl retaining twelve quarters and De le Hoyde four, to compensate him for the part he had taken in the transaction.

The MS. of Chevalier O'Gorman contains the names of the Commission, the witnesses, quotations and references to original documents, which are too voluminous to insert in a work of this kind, and he concludes his paper with the following remarks : In fine, the "Earl of Thomond, had all the said lands under his control. He kept the whole of the Lissofin estate and other lands for himself, and his heirs now (1782) enjoy them. He left or gave to Sir Roland in fee form the castle and lands of Fornerly and other lands, part of the said territory, at a small yearly rent. Thus was the spoil divided, the ancient and lawful proprietors turned out of possession, and they and their heirs remained so. The Earl (as is reported for truth) turned out many other proprietors in both the said baronies, which shall not be particularised ; but that he had a great share is evident, for those deriving from him do now enjoy the same." O'Gorman proceeds to observe that "what induced me to treat in particular of this family of Macnamaras, who were the true and lawful inheritors of the estates of Tulla, was that I had only bare tradition relating to the ways and means used to deprive the rest of them of their inheritance ; but I have matters of record to prove how this same family and its posterity were ruined."

This account of the confiscation of the Tulla estates illustrates what was going on over the whole of Clare, and, in fact, in all those parts of Ireland which had not been already confiscated by the Crown ; but in the case above detailed the Government were not directly to blame : the plot seems to have been the work of a countryman and relative of the evicted family.

Donogh O'Brien, Earl of Thomond, in the year 1617 was appointed by James I. President of Munster. Clare was placed under his jurisdiction, and his example with reference to the appropriation of the properties above referred to was not likely to be lost on his contemporaries; as Governor of Munster, he became one of the principal officers of the Crown in Ireland. We are not therefore surprised to find that extensive schemes of confiscation of the properties of the landowners of Clare soon came to the fore, culminating, as Mr. Lecky observes, in the " most shameful passage in the history of the English government in Ireland."

We must again return to Sir J. Perrott's deed of composition entered into between him on the part of the Crown with the landowners of Clare. Under this agreement the landowners were to make good their titles held under the Brehon laws ; and having surrendered their lands to the Crown, were to receive deeds in exchange from the Crown for their lands, made out in such form and order as to be registerable under English law in the Court of Chancery. It was evident all this was something quite new to the Clare landowners ; they had no knowledge of the English procedure, which for the first time was then extended to the West of Ireland. The landlords trusted the Government, and as the action taken in this matter was the work of the Crown, and not theirs, they naturally supposed the Government officials in charge of the transaction would carry it through in a proper manner. After considerable delay, however, rumours reached Clare that matters were not progressing satisfactorily regarding the issue of the new title deeds. Two of the Macnamaras were deputed therefore to proceed to Dublin and ascertain what was amiss with regard to the documents in question. It then appeared that there was a hitch as to the procedure, which had not been all that was necessary according to law. These difficulties were, however, overcome, and the new title deeds were issued bearing the impression of the Great Seal. Nothing more was heard on the subject until A.D. 1632, when the Lord Deputy Wentworth discovered, that at the time of issuing these title deeds the landowners of Clare had one and all of them failed to enrol the documents in the Court of Chancery. Sir Thomas Wentworth (better known as Earl of Strafford), in consequence of this fault in the legal procedure, declared all these titles to be null and void ; and as the landlords had made their estates over to the Crown, to the Sovereign they belonged, and were accordingly to be confiscated without delay. It was conclusively shown that the Clare landowners had, before receiving their deeds paid the sum of £3000 into Court, for the express purpose of having the documents enrolled, and that the officials of the Government therefore were to blame and not the landowners. The Lord Deputy would listen to no plea of the kind, and seems to have been supported in his purpose by Henry, Earl of Thomond, who had succeeded his father Donogh to the titles and estates, as well as the Governorship of the Province of Munster.*

Mr. Lecky writes concerning this transaction : " In distinct violation of the king's solemn promise, after the subsidies that were made on the faith of that promise had been duly obtained, without provocation, or pretext, or excuse, Wentworth, who now presided with stern despotism over the government of Ireland, announced the withdrawal of the two principal articles of the Grace, the limitation of Crown claims by a possession of sixty years, and the legalisation of the Connaught (including Clare) titles. Inquisitions were made in order to preserve the show of justice, juries were summoned, and were peremptorily ordered to bring in verdicts vesting all the titles referred to them to the king." Every means was taken to insure compliance; men such as might give furtherance in finding a title for the king were carefully selected, and a grant of 4*s.* in the pound was given to the Lord Chief Justice and the Lord Chief Baron, out of the first yearly rent raised upon the commissions of defective titles, "which money," Wentworth, writing to Charles I. states " I find to be the best that ever was given. For now they (the Irish judges) do intend it with a care and diligence such as it were their own private property, and most certainly the gaining to themselves any 4*s.* once paid, shall better your Majesty's revenue ever after at least £5." These were words written by a Lord Deputy of Ireland to the King of England.† Mr. Lecky continues : "The sheriffs and the judges were the creatures of the Government, and Wentworth was present to overcome all opposition. The juries were assured that the project was for the advantage of the king and country ; that if they presumed to give unfavourable verdicts, those verdicts would be set on one side, and that, as Wentworth threatened, they might answer the king a round fine in the Castle Chamber in case they should prevaricate. In Galway the jury refused to give a verdict for the Crown, and the Lord Deputy at once imposed a fine of £1000 on the sheriff who had summoned this jury, and bound the jurors to appear in the Castle Chamber, where they were each sentenced to pay the heavy fine of £4000 (about £20,000 of our money), and to lie in prison till it was paid."‡

Charles I. approved of the action of his Lord Deputy in Ireland, for

* " O'Brien Memoirs," p. 258.
† " Strafford's Letters," vol. i. pp. 310–352, 442, 443, 451–454.
‡ " A History of Ireland in the Eighteenth Century," by W. E. H. Lecky, vol. i. pp. 31–32.

the royal approbation was conveyed to Wentworth in a letter from Secretary Coke, dated Whitehall, May 3, 1637, as follows: "You may take the opportunity the time offers to you to go on with the plantation in the county of Clare, and from his Majesty you may expect encouragement and support."* On the 23rd of August 1637, Wentworth wrote as follows from Limerick to Secretary Coke: "I must certify that his Majesty's title to the country of Clare and Limerick is found by inquisition with strange cheerfulness and contentment. I knew it privately by some intelligence. I have among them my Lord of Thomond, Lieutenant-Governor of that county, who had been exceeding diligent and forward in this service, not only leading himself, but persuading others into good conformity." It will be noticed the officer ruling Ireland in the name of the Sovereign stated that the inquisitions by which the titles to the lands of Clare were proved to be illegal, upon the plea above referred to, are said to have been found " with strange cheerfulness and contentment," whereas this same individual had imposed enormous fines and imprisonment on the sheriff and jurors who had attempted to gainsay his will or refused to sanction the wrong perpetuated in the name of law.

When the new patents were granted in 1610 to the Earl of Thomond, for the enormous grants of land he had already received from Government, J. Macnamara of Dangan laid claim to Cratlomore, and other estates which without question had belonged to his family for many centuries, but his claim was dismissed, and the property was granted to the Earl of Thomond.†

Charles I.'s troubles were now increasing in all directions, and he sent for Wentworth to come to his aid. The wrongdoing of this nobleman, however, was so great that the Parliament demanded his impeachment, and subsequently his execution. By Wentworth's death the confiscation of the landed property of Clare was postponed ; but what confidence could the landowners have had in the English Government after being treated as they had been by Wentworth, with the approval of the Crown ?

APPENDIX TO CHAPTER XIII.

An Inquisition of Indenture, taken at the town of Sixmilebridge, in the County of Clare aforesaid, on the tenth day of January, in the first year of the reign of King Charles, to inquire amongst other things, what lands and what holdings Shane ne Gilliagh MacNemarra, lately of Cuherbally-mullrony, in the aforenamed county, gentlemen deceased, hath held of the said Lord the King, in capite as well

* " Strafford's Letters," vol. ii. p. 76.   † Frost's " History of Clare," p. 411.

as in Dominico, as in Service, on the day he died. And how much he held of others, and by what service, and how much those lands and holdings are worth per annum, after deducting all charges. And at what time the same Shane ne Gilliagh MacNemarra died. And who was his immediate heir, and of what age; and if he were married or not; also concerning all alienations made to any person, of certain lands, tenements, or hereditaments in the aforesaid county, on the oath of upright and law-abiding men, of the above-mentioned county. Which jurors having been sworn, upon their aforementioned oath, declare that the aforesaid Shane MacNemarra was seized in his demesne as well as in his leased land and in a third part of one quarter of land in Ballymullroney. And being thus seized, he then died, on the last day of March 1587. And that all, and the several premises descended to certain persons, Donnogh, Maccon, Shane, Hugh, and Daniel MacNemarra, his sons and coheirs, according to a custom called Gavelkind, in use from ancient times in the said county. And from the day of the death of the said Shane ne Gilliagh MacNemarra, these remain seized of the premisses, in the following mode and form—viz., the aforesaid Donnogh remains seized of and in a third part of a quarter of land in Ballymullroney. And that the aforenamed Maccon MacNemarra remains in like manner seized of and in a third part of a quarter of land in Ballyrully. And that the aforementioned Shane MacNemarra is similarly seized in half of one quarter of land in Ballykelly aforesaid. And that the said Hugh MacNemarra is seized of and in half of a quarter of land in the aforesaid Carrowcore. And that the aforesaid Donnell MacNemarra is likewise seized of and in a quarter metre of land in the aforesaid Carrowcore. In testimony of which affair, the Commissioners, as well as the jurors, herewith place their seals, the day, year, and month aforesaid. Deliberated in the Chancery of Ireland, 24th July 1626.

CONNOR CLANCHY (Feodary).

John Evans, Deputy Exheator.

CHAPTER XIV

CHARLES I. has left us his opinion as to the causes which led to the Irish rebellion of 1641 in the following passage. He observes, " The extraordinary rigour and unjust severity made use of by some people in England caused the discontent which has long existed in Ireland to degenerate into rebellion. When discontent is turned to despair, and oppression into fear of extirpation, rebellion will naturally succeed, in order both to escape present tyranny and to counteract those evils which threaten, through the interested zeal or fanaticism of those who think that it is a proof of the truth of their religion to admit of none but their own.* James II. has also left his views of the causes which led to the rebellion of 1641 embodied in the preamble to the Act of the Repeal of Settlement, passed by the House of Parliament which sat in Dublin in 1689. The king states that this rising was caused by "the terror of Catholic subjects openly menaced by the Lords Justices with a massacre and total extirpation, thereby affrighting and compelling others, in

---

* " Memoirs of Castlehaven," pp. 20-21 ; " Ireland's Case," pp. 32-33.

despair of protection from their Government, to unite and take arms for their necessary defence and preservation of their lives."* In Clare the news of the rising in Ulster against the English was first heard at the fair held at Quin in 1641, and gave rise to such excitement that Barnabas, Earl of Thomond, considered it necessary to take immediate steps to prevent an outbreak against the English residents in his county. With the object of maintaining order he called a council of the principal landowners to meet him at Ennis early in January 1642, to consult as to the means best calculated to preserve peace. The Earl, at this meeting, invested Teigie and Donogh Macnamara with military authority over the civil population; he also appointed the latter gentleman as his chief captain and adviser. The militia of the county were enrolled, and a tax levied on the inhabitants for their support.

The English formed a very small proportion of the population of Clare, and were for the most part engaged as farmers on the estates of the Earl of Thomond. Hearing of the cruelties perpetrated by the Irish on their countrymen in the north, they naturally began to take measures for their own safety, and many of them assembled in a castle (Ballyallia) belonging to an Englishman, Mr. Maurice Cuffe. The Earl of Thomond was not trusted by the English; they accused him of favouring the Irish, and some time previously Wentworth had objected to the Earl being appointed Governor of Munster, because the Lord Deputy believed that he " merited nothing, as his brother, the late Earl, did." Lord Thomond issued an order to the effect that the English in Clare were to give up their arms for the use of the militia; but when men were sent to enforce this order, the English assembled at Ballyallia refused to obey it. Cuffe fortified and provisioned his castle, and the Irish then invested it, hoping to starve out the garrison rather than storm the castle, which, without artillery, would have been a risky proceeding, defended as it was by a body of well armed Englishmen.

Early in January, Donogh Macnamara, with a company of horsemen, was despatched by the Irish in Clare to confer with Phelim O'Neil as to the state of affairs in the West of Ireland; and further, if war was to be carried on, to procure the means for arming the people. Of cannon O'Neil had none to spare, and so Donogh Macnamara returned to Clare. He had an interview with Mr. Cuffe, offering to conduct him and the garrison of his castle to Limerick if they would give up the place. This they declined to do, and so Ballyallia remained closely

* " The Patriot Parliament of 1689," by T. Davis (edited by Sir Charles G. Duffy), p. 75.

invested by the Irish.* Not having any ordnance, the besiegers constructed a large wooden shed some thirty feet by nine in size; it was covered with layers of hides " so as to be impenetrable to musket bullets or arrows." This machine was moved up to the walls of the castle, and from it workmen commenced to undermine the foundations of the building. The Irish also made " a leather piece of ordnance about five feet long, which, being loaded with thirteen pounds of powder, burst at the first discharge." So matters went on until one of the Cuffes was taken prisoner by the Irish in an attempt to procure food for the garrison. The Irish then sent a message to the English that unless they consented to give up the castle, Cuffe junior would be hanged. Provisions and water were running short, and as no prospect of relief seemed probable, the garrison capitulated. Whatever the feeling may have been between the English and Irish in other parts of Ireland neither treachery or cruelty was shown them at this time in Clare. Donogh Macnamara and his followers conducted such of the garrison of Ballyallia as wished to leave the country to Bunratty, and they took ship to England ; others returned to their farms and remained in possession of them throughout the years of trouble which succeeded the surrender of Ballyallia.

During the year 1642 the distrust and disaffection of the Irish Roman Catholics to the English increased ; and there was good reason for this, because at this time numerous petitions were presented by Protestants, both to the Irish and to the English Parliament, calling on the Government to take steps to exterminate the Roman Catholics of Ireland. In these circumstances, as King Charles wrote, self-preservation led the Catholics to take up arms in self-defence. The Viceroy of Ireland at this time was the the Earl of Ormond, a Protestant. He stated that, in his opinion, it was " the publication of this design (on the part of the English) which led to the rising of 1641." The Irish Catholic Confederation was then inaugurated. We may learn the objects of the Association from the oath administered to its members on their joining the Society, as follows :

" I swear in presence of God, and of His angels and saints, to defend the liberty of the Roman Catholic and Apostolic religion, and the person, heirs, and rights of his Majesty King Charles, and the freedom and privileges of the kingdom against all usurpers, at the peril of my life and freedom."† The Confederation proceeded to form a supreme council, which met at Kilkenny ; Daniel Macnamara of Doon, and John Macnamara of Moyriesk, were elected as the representatives of

* Maurice Cuffe's " History of the Siege of Ballyallia Castle " (published by the Camden Society, 1841).

† " Vindiciarum Cath. Hiber.," lib. i. p. 6.

co. Clare.* Judges, sheriffs, and courts of justice were established by the Council, and at their request Charles I. directed the Earl of Ormond to fill the office of Lord Deputy of Ireland; nor was this appointment at the time objected to, for the confederates seem to have had full confidence in the Earl, although he differed from them in his views on the doctrines of religion.

Innocent X. was supreme pontiff at Rome, and in 1642 was kept informed of all that was going on in Ireland by Father Scarampi; but on an appeal for help from the Irish, the Pope, when sending them munitions of war, including considerable sums of money, thought proper to appoint one of the ablest ecclesiastics at his command as Nuncio to Ireland. The person selected for this mission was the Archbishop of Ferno, Monsignor Rinuccini; after considerable delay the Nuncio arrived in Cork in October 1644, with written orders from the Pope " not to go beyond the limits of pure benefit to the Catholic religion, to restore ecclesiastical discipline, and to reform the habits of Catholics relaxed by a long course of free living ; " he was " to have no thought of prejudicing the temporal dominion of any one ; " † but the Nuncio had no sooner arrived in Kilkenny than he found himself overwhelmed in politics and surrounded by a council engrossed in their own squabbles rather than uniting with fixed resolve to fight the battle of those who elected them to office.

About the time that Rinuccini appeared on the scene in Ireland a very different individual came to the fore. The young Earl of Inchiquir., an O'Brien, a man of wonderful energy, and a thorough soldier, but unstable as the wind : at one time a Protestant and Royalist, at another an officer under Cromwell's government, afterwards a Roman Catholic. He was carried by pirates to Morocco, but he escaped, and was soon heard of fighting, first in the cause of France, and then of Spain. Inchiquin commenced his military training as a lad in the Italian army, and, after active service in that country and in Spain, he returned to Ireland, and came to be on friendly terms with Strafford. He was, at the age of twenty-four, appointed to the command of Charles I.'s troops in Munster, and in that capacity was enabled to afford the king material aid.‡ Inchiquin, not content with being in command of the king's forces, aspired to become governor of the

* Frost's " History of Clare," p. 383; White's " History of Clare," p. 382.

† " The Embassy in Ireland, 1645-49 " (Rinuccini) (translated by Annie Hutton), p. 559.

‡ The king had already received from Ireland the sum of £120,000, a large amount in those days, on a promise to grant the Catholics religious liberty and that proprietorship of sixty years of land constituted a title (Sir C. G. Duffy, p. xxviii.).

province of Munster, he crossed over to England and met Charles I. at Oxford, in order to urge his claims to this appointment; the king, however, declined to accede to his request. Inchiquin, therefore, left England and at once offered his services to the Parliamentarians, who eagerly accepted his help and at the same time appointed him governor of Munster. This conduct on the part of Inchiquin was fatal to the Confederate cause. With a man of his energy and ability as leader in the south of Ireland, and with O'Neill, O'Donnell, and Macdonell in the north, the history of the country in the seventeenth century would probably have been different from that which has been handed down to us. The council of the Confederation at this time must have been hard up for a general, for they appointed the Archbishop of Tuam to lead their troops against the English garrison of Sligo. His name was O'Qucely, and he had, not long previously to taking command of the forces employed against the English garrison at Sligo, done battle in a very different cause, for he had gone over to the island of Aran, in Galway Bay, to destroy the image of "Mac Dara" (Dara meaning "oak"), which the people venerated with idolatrous superstition. It was in vain the Catholic clergy called on them to desist from worshipping this idol, and from swearing on it rather than on the Gospels; to put down this ancient superstition, which was evidently a remnant of the old Druidical worship, the Archbishop of Tuam, coming to the island, tore down the image and flung it into the sea.* He did not, however, long survive this proceeding, for in 1645 this unfortunate prelate, having only just assumed command of the Irish soldiers, was shot dead in his first encounter with the Parliamentary forces. In connection with this event, we find Daniel Macnamara and Sir D. O'Brien, of Ennistymon, appointed by the Irish to effect an exchange of prisoners with the commander of the English troops in Connaught.†

The Nuncio Rinuccini, on joining the council of the Confederation at Kilkenny, in October 1644, found that negotiations were being carried on with Charles I. which, in his opinion, were altogether unsatisfactory. He considered it absolutely necessary that any treaty with the king should include stipulations obliging the Government to appoint a Roman Catholic as Lord Lieutenant of Ireland, and granting the Irish Catholic bishops a seat in Parliament. Rinuccini questioned the right of the council to treat with a "heretic prince," and rather than

* " Proceedings of the Royal Irish Academy," 3rd series, vol. ii. No. 5, August 1893, p. 818.

† " Contemporary History of Affairs in Ireland from 1641 to 1652," by John T. Gilbert, vol. ii. p. 389.

accept the terms offered by the contracting parties, the Nuncio urged the necessity of war.* The ecclesiastics pressed their contention so strongly that Charles I., to conciliate them, recalled his Protestant Lord Deputy from Ireland.

In March 1646, some of the ships under orders of the Parliamentarians arrived in the Shannon, and anchored as near as possible to Bunratty Castle, which was then the residence of Barnabas, Earl of Thomond, he invited the officers of the fleet to visit him, and entertained them with great hospitality. Subsequently he handed the castle over to the English commander, and then took his departure for England; and joined his wife at her residence in Northamptonshire. With an English fleet obstructing the passage up the Shannon to Limerick, and Bunratty garrisoned by Parliamentary troops, the base of operations of the Confederates was so imperilled that it became necessary to dislodge the garrison of Bunratty from its position in Clare. The Confederate forces therefore surrounded the castle from the land side, and as the fleet could not pass up the river on which the castle stands, the garrison, after a brave defence, were compelled to surrender. During the siege the Pope's Nuncio joined the Irish army, and did much to expedite the military operations against the place. The Confederates found much valuable plate and vast quantities of military stores in the castle, "together with a splendid stud of horses." In his letter to Rome communicating the news of the fall of Bunratty, the Nuncio writes "that he had no hesitation in asserting that it is the most beautiful place he had ever seen. In Italy there is nothing like it, with its magnificent park and three thousand head of deer." We can well imagine this to be the case; the walls of this grand old castle, built by the De Clares in the thirteenth century, are still almost perfect, and are inhabited at the present time. Close beneath the castle is a fine stream, with the lower Shannon in the distance, and behind it undulating, park-like lands, beautifully wooded and covered with exquisite green turf.

In the year following the fall of Bunratty, that is in A.D. 1647, the Macnamaras were actively engaged in military operations. The leaders of the Confederate forces, in conjunction with the men of Ulster under Macdonell, determined to give battle to Lord Inchiquin, who was in command of the Parliamentary forces in the south of Ireland; the two armies met at a place called Knockmoness. The Irish of Munster behaved disgracefully. After firing a volley one of the regiments, commanded by Lord Castleconnel, threw down their arms and fled from the field of battle. They were followed by their comrades, and although their

* "The Embassy in Ireland of Rinuccini," p. 96.

N

officers entreated the men to stand by them, and this appeal failing, shot some of their panic-stricken soldiers, it was all in vain. About 1500 of the Confederate army were slain. Many of the officers remained on the field and were taken prisoners ; among them are mentioned the names of Lieut.-Colonel Macnamara, also Captains Brian, Daniel, and Patrick Macnamara, and Capt.-Lieut. Fitz Morris Macnamara.† The behaviour of the right wing of the Irish army was the reverse of that formed by the Munster men ; it was composed of soldiers from Connaught and Ulster, who, by their splendid behaviour in the early part of the engagement, drove back the whole of Inchiquin's left wing and captured his artillery : but being deserted by their Munster comrades, Inchiquin was able to direct the whole of his forces against the Connaught troops, and although they stood their ground and were almost annihilated, victory remained with the Parliamentarians.

The affairs of Charles I. and of the Irish Confederation were now reaching a climax ; the Kilkenny Council, in spite of the protests of Rinuccini, concluded a treaty with the King of England, by which it was agreed that the Irish Roman Catholics were to have freedom of religion so long as they remained faithful to the Crown ; but they were not to be compelled to take the oath of supremacy to the king as head of the Church. The Nuncio at this time was President of the Council of Kilkenny, and he gives an amusing account of a meeting of that assembly. It seems that as usual there was considerable difference of opinion on a certain subject under discussion, and after debating the question at issue with great animation, the parties concerned became much excited, so much so, that one-half of the assembly jumped up from their seats and rushed out of the council chamber.‡ The Nuncio discovered that he could neither manage his Council, nor persuade them to adopt his views regarding the treaty with Charles. He determined therefore to try what mild restraint would effect, and so he ordered the members of the Council to be shut up in Kilkenny Castle, and to be put on low diet for a time ; but they took their punishment rather as a joke ; and it had no effect whatever on their conduct.§

There was, however, one other measure left in the hands of the Nuncio, and that was to excommunicate those who refused to follow his advice regarding the government of Ireland. That this act might have full ecclesiastical authority, Rinuccini summoned a synod of the Irish bishops

* " The Embassy in Ireland of Rinuccini," p. 335.
† " Contemporary History of Affairs in Ireland, 1641–52," by John T. Gilbert.
‡ " The Embassy in Ireland in the Years 1645–49," p. 340.
§ *Ibid.*, p. 503 ; see p. 433.

to meet him in Kilkenny; after mature deliberation the following edict was issued by the synod:

"By authority of the Archbishops and Bishops of this realm, assembled before the illustrious and most Rev. Lord John Baptist Rinuccini, Archbishop and Prince of Fermo, and Apostolic Nuncio Extraordinary, it is declared that the cessation of the war to be evil and dangerous, and that no one can with safe conscience advocate the same."*

Matters, however, moved on. The Council of the Confederation neither heeded this edict nor the threat of excommunication, but they proceeded to conclude a treaty with King Charles upon the terms above referred to; and what in the eyes of the Nuncio was a still greater offence, they opened communications with Inchiquin, as a medium through whom they could treat with the Earl of Ormond, and persuade him to return as Lord Deputy to Ireland. Inchiquin had not long previously to these overtures forcibly entered the cathedral of Cashell, and slaughtered some of the priests; it was not therefore surprising that Rinuccini absolutely refused to have anything to say to him. As to Ormond returning as Viceroy to Ireland, the Nuncio urged that a step of this kind would cancel "the glory reaped by the clergy in expelling him from his office because he was a Protestant." The Earl of Ormond, however, consented to return, and was received by Inchiquin at Cork, and subsequently took up his residence in his castle of Kilkenny. Rinuccini, finding his mission to Ireland was hopeless, took ship at Galway in December 1648, and returned to the Continent.

The Irish were soon destined to pass under the hands of a very different man, Oliver Cromwell, backed by his veteran soldiers and the resources of England. On this subject Carlyle writes as follows:

One could pity this poor Irish people; their case is pitiable enough! The claim they started with in 1641 was for religious freedom. Their claim, we now all see, was just, essentially just, though full of intricacy, difficult to render clear and concessible—eight years of cruel fighting, of desperate violence and misery, left matters worse a thousandfold than they were at first. No want of daring or of patriotism, but without worth as armies; undrilled, unpaid, taking shelter in bogs where no cavalry can follow them, Ireland wasted, torn in pieces, till at last as in the torrent of Heaven's lightning descends liquid on it. Rose-water surgeons might have tried it otherwise; that was not Oliver's policy, not the rose-water one. They, "the Irish," chose to disbelieve him; could not understand that he, more than the others, meant any truth or justice to them.—They rejected his summons and terms at Iredah; he stormed the place, and, according to his promise, put every man of the garrison to death.†

* "History of the Confederation and War in Ireland," by J. T. Gilbert, vol. vii. p. 350; also "The Embassy," pp. 329-433.

† "Oliver Cromwell's Letters and Speeches," by Thomas Carlyle, vol. i. pp. 405-7.

On arriving in Ireland, Cromwell issued a proclamation to the inhabitants of the country as follows :

Such as have been formerly in arms may by submitting themselves have their cases presented to the State of England, when no doubt the State will be ready to take into consideration the nature and quality of their action, and deal mercifully with them. As for those now in arms, who shall come in and submit and give engagement for their future quiet and honest carriage, and submission to the State of England, I doubt not but they will find like merciful consideration. And as for such private soldiers as lay down their arms and live peaceably and honestly at their several homes, they shall be allowed to do so ; but as for those who, notwithstanding all this, persist and continue in arms, they must expect what the Providence of God, in that which is falsely called the chances of war, will cast upon them.*

Cromwell, upon the faith of this declaration, started to subdue those who resisted his government. The garrison of Kilkenny, after a stubborn defence, submitted, and were allowed to march out of the place " bullet in bouch." Drogheda resisted to the bitter end. It is said that Cromwell wrote to the governor of the place, warning him of the consequences of resisting, in the following words : " You may prevent effusion of blood " by submitting. " If, upon refusing this offer, that which you like not befalls you, you will know whom to blame." Admitting that Cromwell sent this message, it is more than doubtful if Aston, who commanded at Drogheda, ever received it. However that may be, on the 10th September Cromwell opened fire on the walls of the town, and by the following evening had made a sufficient breach to enable him to order a storming party to attempt to enter the place. This party was driven back by the defenders ; Cromwell then put himself at the head of another party, and fought his way into the streets of Drogheda. Aston, who was defending the breach, fell back and took up his position with three hundred followers on a mound in the town ; this was surrounded by Cromwell and his soldiers, and Aston and the whole of his men were slaughtered as they stood. Cromwell then ordered all who were found with arms in the town to be put to the sword ; a thousand men were thus butchered, and a small party of eighty took refuge in the steeple of St. Peter's Church. Cromwell first requested them to yield ; this they refused to do, and he then directed barrels of gunpowder to be placed beneath the edifice, and endeavoured to blow it up ; but failing in this, he ordered the church to be set on fire, and of the eighty unfortunate human beings in the steeple not one escaped ; many were burnt to death, and those who tried to escape the flames were killed by the Puritan soldiers. Cromwell had the letter of the law on his side. At any rate we have the Duke of

* "Oliver Cromwell's Letters and Speeches," by Thomas Carlyle, vol. ii. p. 45.

Wellington's authority for saying that a garrison or fortress which was taken by storm are not considered entitled to quarter.* Every friar found in Drogheda was knocked on the head and killed; and numbers of the defenders of the town were subsequently slaughtered in cold blood. "Not thirty of the whole number escaped with their lives," so Cromwell reported; and these, he adds, "are safe, with many oth rs, for Barbadoes."† And so with other places.

All this slaughter in cold blood was done by Cromwell's orders, and under his own eyes; he never denied his responsibility in these crimes, but was ready to justify the deeds he had committed, which in the seventeenth century, however, admitted of no possible excuse.‡

Ireland was speedily crushed; she had never before been treated in this way. But unutterably horrible as was Cromwell's passage through that country, it was no worse for the people that were left than the lingering death so many of them suffered from famine and pestilence. Cromwell at any rate had one good quality, he meant what he said, and he kept his word; he has left behind him a name in Clare, upon which the bitterest curses are heaped whenever it is mentioned. But all this misery had been foretold by Adrian IV. in Henry III.'s reign, as what must necessarily sooner or later follow, the policy pursued by England in Ireland; a policy which, terrible as were its results in Cromwell's time, was destined to cause yet more disastrous consequences in the latter half of the seventeenth, and in the first half of the eighteenth, centuries.

The headquarters of the Confederation, having been expelled by Cromwell from Kilkenny, took up their abode in Ennis, county Clare; but the Earl of Ormond felt the cause of the Royalists in Ireland was almost hopeless, and believed that Prince Charles alone could rouse the drooping spirits of his father's supporters; he, therefore, urged Charles to assume command of the attenuated Royalist forces; and the Prince, it is said, was actually on his road to Ireland, but was detained by a

---

* In the official "Manual of Military Law" (published by the War Office in 1894), chap. xiv. par. 14, we read: "The first principle of war is that armed forces, so long as they resist, may be destroyed by all legitimate means. The right of killing an armed man exists only so long as he resists; as soon as he submits, he is entitled to be treated as a prisoner of war."

† "Cromwell's Letters," by Thomas Carlyle, vol. i. p. 410; "History of the Commonwealth and Protectorate," by T. R. Gardiner, vol. i. p. 134.

‡ Ludlow served under Ireton, and informs us that a Colonel Axtell, "who was in command of some troops in Clare, had promised certain prisoners their lives; yet because some of his soldiers slew these unfortunate people, when Ireton heard thereof he deprived Colonel Axtell of his command, although he was a person of extraordinary qualities for the service" (Ludlow's "Memoirs," vol. i. p. 294).

French lady for three months, and then landed in Scotland. Charles almost immediately issued a proclamation cancelling his father's treaty with the Irish Confederation. In this proclamation he stated that the late king had no power to enter into negotiations with Papists; and he thus closed the door against freedom of religion to the Roman Catholics of Ireland. The Catholic Bishop of Killaloe endeavoured once again to arouse the Irish, and having collected a body of followers pitched his camp at Quin. This movement, however, was immediately suppressed by the Earl of Ormond, and the bishop and his followers sent to their homes. But Ormond found he could no longer serve Ireland with advantage, and he therefore left the country, having made over the remnants of the Royalist army to Lord Taaffe,* and Lord Castlehaven, and among them two hundred men of the Clare Brigade, commanded by Colonel D. Macnamara and Captain Sheda Macnamara.†

The Confederates still held Limerick, and Ireton considered it necessary to obtain possession of the city before disbanding the Parliamentary forces; to effect this object he had to cross the Shannon and so stop supplies reaching Limerick from Clare. The only place he could attempt to ford the Shannon was at Killaloe, where the steep wooded hills of Clare run down to the banks of the river; and it would have been easy for the Confederate troops to have resisted the passage of Ireton's army across the Shannon. No effort, however, was made to oppose the passage of the Parliamentary forces, and Ireton, to his surprise, crossed the river without difficulty, and marched unopposed along its Clare bank until he arrived opposite to Limerick; he then dispatched a force of some three thousand men under Ludlow to scour Clare and drive in supplies of cattle for his army. Ludlow and his men penetrated the county as far as Burren and returned to the main army with droves of cattle.‡

A passage from Ludlow's memoirs regarding Burren has already been referred to (page 2). He states that in spite of bad roads his men marched forty miles in twenty-four hours. At one place he came across a party of the natives and "he took a share with some of them in a pot of sour milk, which," he observes, "seemed to me the most pleasant liquor I ever drank." As a rule, the Irish kept out of his way,

---

* Lord Taaffe passed over to the Continent after the battle of the Boyne, and took service in the Austrian army. One of his descendants was the late Count Taaffe, Austria's most distinguished and successful minister. The Emperor of Austria spoke of the deceased statesman as "his trusted friend" and as "the self-sacrificing servant of the State"; "the people trusted and almost loved him; his simplicity and winning manners captivated them."

† "Contemporary History of Affairs in Ireland," by J. T. Gilbert, vol. vii. p. 265.
‡ *Ibid.*, vol. iii. p. 262.

retiring into dense woods and bogs, where it was impossible to follow them.*

Limerick was now completely surrounded by Ireton's troops, and so cut off from all supplies of food, and the plague which had broken out in the town some time previously to the commencement of the seige, began to commit terrible ravages among its half-starving population ; nevertheless, under the energetic leadership of Bishop O'Brien, the inhabitants of the city for several months refused to surrender. A party within the walls of Limerick, had from an early stage of the siege, considered that further opposition to the Parliamentary forces was hopeless ; and as time went on and the distress of the people became aggravated, this party led by one of the Burkes, Captain Teigie Macnamara, and Colonel Fennell, determined to open negotiations with Ireton. There was no hope of relief coming to the aid of the garrison, and their sufferings augmented day by day. In these circumstances the officers above named seized one of the gates of the city and proceeded to enter upon terms of capitulation with the beseigers ; although Bishop O'Brien and some of the principal citizens strongly opposed these proceedings, and endeavoured to drive Teigie Macnamara and his party from the post they had occupied ; the gates of the city were opened to the leader of the Parliamentary forces, and Limerick fell into their hands. The whole of the garrison were allowed to march out of the town, and its inhabitants, as had been agreed to by the beseigers before the capitulation, obtained permission to retain possession of their houses and property ; an exception, however, was made in the case of Bishop O'Brien and eleven other citizens, who were hung by order of the English general.†

In the April following the capitulation of Limerick a formal treaty was drawn up between the Parliamentarians and the officers of the Clare Brigade. Under this treaty, among other stipulations it was agreed that the troops forming the Brigade should deliver up their arms, but were to be allowed to retain their horses, and any real property they possessed, so long as they kept the peace. Provision was also made that any of the soldiers of the Brigade who desired to quit Ireland for the Continent should be enabled to do so at the expense of the Government. This document was signed on behalf of the Clare Brigade by Daniel Macnamara.‡ Ludlow informs us that in April 1652 " the number of Irish who submitted on condition of being transported into foreign service was so great, that they became a heavy burden to the State, before shipping could be provided to carry them all out of the country."

* Ludlow's " Memoirs," pp. 199 and 340.
† " Contemporary History of Affairs in Ireland," vol. iii. p. 262.
‡ *Ibid.*, vol. vi. p. 311.

Before passing on from this period in the history of our sept it is well to refer to matters connected with the Abbey of Quin, which had been founded by the Macnamaras, and although it had been dissolved by Henry VIII. in 1541, and made over by Queen Elizabeth to the O'Briens in 1578, the family whose ancestors built and endowed this monastery, and many of whose members were burned within its walls, still held it in loving memory. In the year 1617 Father D. Mooney visited Quin Abbey; at this time he found the choir and transept roofed, and two or three helpless old friars about the place. They remembered the monastery being suppressed, and that its gold and silver plate had been sent to Macnamara of Knoppogue,* and that after his death his widow retained it, but declined to give Mooney any information on the subject.

We learn from Mr. T. J. Westropp's interesting notes on Quin Abbey, that its community, taking advantage of the freedom of religious worship granted by the Roman Catholic Confederation of 1641, repaired and re-opened the college which had been connected with the monastery, and that in the course of a short time no fewer than eight hundred Irish youths were receiving instruction, under the guidance of the Franciscan fraternity of Quin. One of these scholars was the historian Anthony Bruodin, together with eighteen members of his family. From this author we learn some facts relating to the College of Quin, and further of its destruction by Cromwell's soldiers. There seems good reason to believe that a Major William, and Henry Stainer, seized the abbey while the monks were celebrating Mass, and the former attempted to drag the officiating priest from the altar, but the old friar with uplifted arm found time to curse his assailant, and foretell the extinction of his race. Stainer burnt down the building, and according to one account hanged the celebrant (T. J. Westropp's "History of Quin Abbey"). The Cromwellians seized the head of the college, Eugene O'Cahan, who they first scourged and then hung. Another of the community, Roger Macnamara, is referred to as follows: "This friar was a learned professor of the College of Quin Abbey, which his ancestors had built, and was ever a model of a simple and pious man. God determined to reward his piety, and so permitted him to be seized by soldiers, and by them taken to the town of Ennis, where, having refused to abandon his religion, he was first shot and then his head was severed from the body." The remaining monks of Quin fled to Drim, not far from their abbey, and aiding the parish priest, lived unmolested by the Government. One of the Quin monks clung to his old home till the middle of the last century, and wrote

* At present the seat of Lord Dunboyne. The keep of the old castle is still inhabited.

in the cloisters a beautiful poem to Lady O'Brien of Dromoland, who had befriended him. Capt. Teigie Macnamara in 1714 restored the tomb of the founder of the abbey, situated to the north side of the High Altar.

The eight years' turmoil and war carried on by the Confederation, followed by Cromwell's conquest of Ireland, had wrought frightful havoc among the inhabitants of the country; the misery and destitution to which they had been brought was appalling. For instance, in Clare in the year 1659, although many Irish Roman Catholic families from other parts of Ireland had been imported into the country, the total number of its population amounted to 16,474 Catholics, and 440 Protestants; its present population is about 141,475 people. The Government seems to have recognised the deplorable state to which the people of Clare had been reduced, for in May 1653, it is stated that " upon the serious consideration of the poverty and disability of the county Clare, and of the starving condition in which the few remaining inhabitants are, and the impossibility of getting in the monthly contributions charged upon the county, their whole substance being pledged for their arrears hitherto; it is ordered that the said county shall be charged with no sum until the further pleasure of the Commission in England for the affairs of Ireland shall be known therein." It was into this impoverished county, that Cromwell determined, if possible, to transplant the great bulk of the Irish who had not taken part in the late war.

Mr. Froude describes this act as a " masterly stroke of policy " on the part of Oliver Cromwell; this historian continues as follows : " The western province had a natural boundary in the Shannon. Beyond this deep and effectual barrier, the families of the chiefs—the middle and upper classes as we should call them, from whose ranks the worst elements of disorder arose—might receive an equivalent of lands of which they were deprived. There living among themselves, they might die out or multiply as their lot might be : a line of physical demarcation would then be drawn between the Teutonic and Celtic population." Mr. Froude adds that " the Catholic priests were judged guilty of high treason and ordered to depart—such of them as did not remove were put on vessels for Spain, and to the Barbadoes—finally, when the number arrested were too great to be provided for, they were removed to the islands of Arran, and Inis Bonfin. Romanism, sternly repressed, must have died out, and the lines of difference between the two countries, now as marked as ever, and almost as threatening, would have long ago disappeared."*

* " The English in Ireland " (Froude), vol. i. pp. 133 and 140; see Prendergast's " Cromwellian Settlement," 2nd edit. p. 246.

Under an Act of the English Parliament of September 1653, a large proportion of the confiscated lands of Leinster and Munster were granted in lieu of pay, and for services rendered to the Government by soldiers of the Parliamentary army in Ireland, numbering some 32,000 officers and men, with adventurers, settlers, and creditors of many kinds and classes. Certain of the City of London companies had lent money to the Government to carry on the war ; and in place of repaying the amount borrowed, the Government gave an equivalent out of the confiscated lands of Irish gentlemen. The individuals who had advanced money to the Government were called *adventurers ;* they held their first meeting, after the passing of the Act of 1653, in the Grocers' Hall, London, at " eight o'clock in the morning, to regulate, order, and dispose the drawing of lots for ascertaining to the said adventurers, where their dividends of lands shall be." By lots thus drawn, the houses and estates of numerous landed proprietors in Ireland passed into the hands of citizens of London, who had never even seen Ireland, and much less the estates from which their " dividends " were to be derived.*

County Clare was exempt from occupation by adventurers, for it was reserved as a kind of warren into which Irish Papists, who had not taken part in the military operations of the Confederate forces were to be banished. To make room for these innocent Papists, most of the landowners had to be expelled from these estates, including the Mac-namaras, who were turned out of house and home, and their lands made over by the Government to strangers.†

Mr. J. Frost, in his valuable work on the " History and Topography of County Clare," has compiled from the rolls of the Record Office

* The list of the adventurers is to be found at p. 48 of Prendergast's " Cromwellian Settlement." Their number was 1360, and the amount they subscribed came to £43,406 of the money of that period. See also " Life of Sir W. Petty," p. 65.

† Prendergast states that many of the ejected landowners of Clare " returned to the neighbourhood of their former homes, and took up their abode in offices attached to their mansions and tilled the land, their old homes being occupied by strangers, they being actually beggars, together with their wives and daughters." He adds : " On the 26th of September 1653, all ancient estates and farms of the people of Ireland were declared to belong to adventurers and the army of England, Connaught and Clare being assigned as an habitation of the Irish nation, to which their families were to be transferred by the 1st of May 1654, under penalty of death, if they were found east of the Shannon after that date ; the only exception to this rule were young labourers." " The gentry of Lymerick and Kerry were not to be transported into Clare, lest they should behold their native hills and be tempted to return home." " Ireland was to be divided into three parts—the pure English, pure Irish, and a mixed race " (see pp. 96, 133, 148, and 162).

in Dublin, abstracts of the inquisitions held in Clare under Cromwell's Act, concerning the forfeiture and distribution of these lands. Mr. Frost gives the names of the various landowners effected by this Act as they existed in the year 1641, that is, before the inauguration of the Irish Confederation. In another column he shows in detail, the names of the individuals to whom these lands passed after their confiscation.* From an analysis of these records the interesting fact is established, that the Macnamara sept in the year 1641, were living on precisely the same lands in Clare, which had been assigned to them as tribal lands about the year A.D. 420 (see pp. 36 and 67); that is, in the baronies of Upper and Lower Bunratty, and Upper and Lower Tulla.

From the inquisitions made during the years 1653-54, we find that various families of the Macnamara sept held in fee simple town lands, or portions of the ancient tribal lands, as follows :†

They possessed an interest in 37 town lands in Lower Bunratty.

,,	,,	53	,,	Upper ,,
,,	,,	36	,,	Lower Tulla.
,,	,,	46	,,	Upper ,,
,,	,,	4	,,	Clonderland.
,,	,,	0	,,	Burren.
,,	,,	0	,,	Inchiquin.
,,	,,	0	,,	Islands.
,,	,,	0	,,	Moyarta.
,,	,,	11	,,	Ibrickan.
,,	,,	0	,,	Corcomroe.

From this return it will be observed, that, in 1641, the Macnamaras only held town lands in four of the baronies into which county Clare was then divided, and practically no landed property in any of the surrounding baronies.

Sir W. Petty made a census of Clare in the year 1659, on behalf of Government; he also specifies the town lands, their owners and occupiers, before and after the confiscations; and from Sir William we learn that in the baronies of Bunratty and Tulla, Upper and Lower, there were one hundred and ninety-two "landowners of importance" of the name of Macnamara, holding their lands in what we should call fee simple.‡ These lands, as above stated, were the remains of the old

* James Frost, M.R.I.A.: "The History and Topography of County Clare," pp. 399 to 526.

† "Town lands" were a portion of land containing 120 Irish acres each, the Irish exceeding in size the English acre by five-eighths. Many of the Macnamaras had shares in twenty or thirty of these town lands; others possessed them to the exclusion of other holders.

‡ Frost's "History," pp. 227 and 384.

tribal lands of the sept, which were granted to their forefathers, the Celtic conquerors of Clare, early in the fifth century, and which had passed from one generation to another down to the year 1653. It is even more remarkable, that throughout the twelve hundred years the sept of Macnamaras had possessed the tribal lands, included in the four baronies above mentioned; with the exception of a few town lands in Ibrickan, members of this sept owned no lands whatever in any other part of Clare. Where they had first been planted on the soil, there they had grown and flourished for twelve centuries, without acquiring an acre of land in any other part of their own county, or of Ireland. Can we be surprised at these people having become rooted to the soil, and that a tenure of this kind, extending over centuries, had become a part of their being, and as such has to a large extent been passed on to their descendants, and so developed an intense love of their native land, however small the holding?

Of the two hundred principal families of the Macnamara landowners residing in the central part of Clare in 1641, within a radius of less than eight miles of Quin Abbey, all but six families were expelled from their lands and homes by an Act of Cromwell's Parliament of 1654; the reason given for this proceeding was that these unfortunate gentlemen had taken up arms in support of the King of England, who they and their fathers had sworn to serve, on the understanding that they were allowed religious freedom, and to hold their lands on the terms agreed to by their Sovereign* (page 150). The Macnamaras had fulfilled their part of the compact made with Henry VIII., and had gone so far as to decline absolutely and entirely to depart from it, when invited to do so by Queen Elizabeth's representative in Ireland.

Among the inquisitions held in Clare in connection with the sequestrated lands, reference is made to the properties of Ballinacragga and Rathfolan, the former situated about a mile from Newmarket on the left of the road to Ennis, and marked at the present time by a mound, the site of one of the Macnamara castles. The other, Rathfolan, situated almost opposite to Ballinacragga, although at some little distance from it, on rising ground to the right of the road leading from Newmarket to Ennis. The ruins of Rathfolan Castle enable us to comprehend the kind of building it originally consisted of, being more

---

* Mr. Frost, in his "History of Clare," writing of the confiscation of 1654–5, observes: "Of the numerous families constituting the Macnamara sept, only six obtained a grant of part of their possessions under the Cromwellian settlement, so complete was the ruin brought upon a race who for the space of 1360 years were powerful and prosperous owners of the lands of their inheritance" (p. 40).

like a country house of the present time, than one of the keeps, such as most of these Clare castles were in the fifteenth, and sixteenth centuries. Dinley, in his journal through Clare, dated 1680, in his sketch of Ballicar Castle, shows Rathfolan in the distance. Ballinacragga was built by Daniel Macnamara in the year 1607, and Rathfolan finished by his son John in the year 1641. Both properties had originally belonged to Lochlain Macnamara, who in the fourteenth century had divided Clancuilein into two branches, west and east, and these estates had descended from father to tanist, in regular succession for very many generations, until the seventeenth century.

The Rev. P. White, in his "History of Clare," observes, "that as a youth he had, from many sources, traditions relating to the disappearance of the Rathfolan, or the West Clancuilein family of Macnamaras, the lineal descendants of the founders of Quin Abbey." He adds, that having "made vain resistance, and killed some English troops who were out on a foraging expedition, the family had to fly precipitately to conceal themselves from coming vengeance." There is truth in this tradition. The Macnamaras of Rathfolan were dispossessed of their home and estates ; they sought refuge in Burren, a part of county Clare into which there was then only one road, and which is largely constituted of bare limestone mountains or hills. On an inlet of the Bay of Galway, Daniel Macnamara of Rathfolan, and his large family passed from their home in Lower Bunratty. They first settled at Dooras, on property belonging to their friends the Frenches. Some of the family lingered on in this locality, situated on the shores of Kinvarra Bay ; Daniel, however, moved westward to a place near Corcomroe Abbey, known as Balinacragga ; whether called after the old castle in Lower Bunratty or not we cannot tell, but this out-of-the-world locality still bears the name of Balinacragga.*

* Daniel Macnamara succeeded his father in 1665, and married the daughter of Keating, of co. Kildare.

CHAPTER XV

Importance of the study of the congenital character of individual members of the
sept, in order rightly to comprehend the past, present, and future social and
political condition of these people—The character of the members of Clancuilein derived from their history.

GOETHE observes, that the history of a people is their character ; it was
from a study of the history of the Celts, that the authorities referred to
in the first chapter of this work, formed their ideas regarding the congenital qualities of that race; and by means of a similar process, we
should now be in a position to arrive at some conclusions as to the
character of the members of our sept.* An inquiry of the kind is interesting, because it may not only give us the key by which to unlock the
secrets of the past social and political life of these people, but enable
us to follow their subsequent career with intelligence, and so perhaps,
without presumption, to forecast their future. In applying this principle
to the case of our sept we have the advantage of knowing, that until the
early part of the present century, many of them remained pure Iberio-
Celts, for they did not intermarry with other races. For instance, if we
refer to the pedigree of the Rathfolan branch of the family, we find that
from the earliest times, until the close of the nineteenth century the head
of the family always married into Celtic families. Further, these people,
for some twelve hundred years lived the life of agriculturists, and their
surroundings hardly varied throughout this long period. They were
never conquered until the time of Cromwell, and their physical conformation and character is at present, so far as we can judge, similar to
that which it was when they took possession of Clare in the fifth century.

They were a chivalrous people—that is, a generous, high-minded,
and brave set of men ; as an instance in point we may refer to one of
their remote ancestors, Connell. As the old historian observes, " his
integrity was such that he delivered up possession of a crown which he
was able to defend, because he had no right to it " (p. 66). It must be

---

* By congenital character is meant any individual peculiarities, whether structural or mental, with which an individual is born. As the old Celtic proverb has
it ; " If there is an amble in the mare, it will be in the colt."

remembered this was the action of a man who lived in times previous to the introduction of Christianity into Ireland.

Another example of the chivalrous character of these people may be referred to in the case of Sioda (Macnamara), who in the eighth century, having with his sept been deeply injured, and the sacred mound of Mag Adhair desecrated by the King of Ireland, Sioda, after three days' hard fighting, took the king prisoner. But so far from torturing or punishing the vanquished chief, we are told that Sioda treated him sumptuously, and then conducted him and the remains of his army homewards across the Shannon (p. 73).

If we pass on to the fourteenth century we are informed by Magrath that De Clare and his Celtic ally, Donough Brian Roe, sent certain of the relatives of Mac-Con (Macnamara) to that chief, with the object of inducing him to desert the cause of Mortough O'Brien, King of Thomond, in favour of the Anglo-Norman baron and his friends. Mac-Con, however, and his followers, without hesitation refused to listen to any treachery of this kind, and he and Clancuilein remained the staunch supporters of their acknowledged ruler ; in fact, it was by the assistance of our sept that Mortough retained his position as Chief of Thomond.* This incident occurred at a period when, according to Mr. Freeman, an English Ealdorman not only deliberately betrayed his country to the invader, but that "to do so now became the regular course in the part of royal favourites."†

In the year 1370 we find the Earl of Desmond in command of a force of English troops, bent on reducing the O'Briens and Macnamaras to subjection ; the Earl was however defeated, and having been taken prisoner by the Irish was conducted to Clonroad, in co. Clare. Desmond was so impressed with the life and state of society he met with in this distant part of Ireland, that he petitioned King Richard to be allowed to send his young son James (afterwards the famous Earl of Desmond) to be reared and educated by Turlough O'Brien, and his wife Slane Macnamara, in Clonrad.‡ The earl had to obtain the sanction of the king to this step, because at the time the O'Briens, and in fact all Celtic Irishmen, were accounted enemies of the English, to be hunted down and if possible destroyed like the wild beasts of the forest. We might refer to many other examples from the previous history illustrating the chivalrous character of the leaders of our sept, up to the time of their expulsion from Clare by the English in the seventeenth century. Shortly before that period, we have evidence bearing upon this point given by English officials, who had no love for the men they describe. The first of these

* See p. 118. † "History of the Norman Conquest of England." ‡ P. 139.

references is that of " Lord Deputy Sentleger," dated A.D. 1543. He wrote to Henry VIII. recommending the king to create Sioda Macnamara, Baron Clancuilein, because his " ancestors have in those parties alwayes borne a great swynge, and one that for himself is of honest conformatie whose landes lye holy on the farsyde the Shannon."*

Sir H. Sidney, in his tour through Clare in 1575, had the " two Macnamaras, chief gentlemen of their country, with him, who if the country were quiet might live like principal knights in England."† Sir H. Sidney adds "he could not find one descended in the English race amongst them." Sir A. Chichester again in writing to the Earl of Salisbury in June 1608, observes, that " John Macnamara now in hold is a more popular man than even the Earl of Thomond in his own country." In 1588 Sir R. Bingham, who as Governor of Munster had special opportunities of becoming acquainted with the people living in Clare, writing of Shane Macnamara, observes that he and his ancestors "quietly enjoyed these cesses and rents which were appropriated by the Earl of Thomond." Sir Richard continues, " This much I must write on behalf of Macnamara, that he has always behaved himself like an honest gentleman and a dutiful subject." In forwarding this communication, the Lord Deputy wrote to Lord Burghley, that the Macnamara referred to, had " during the space of these thirty years very dutifully carried and behaved himself," and adds "there are not two more like him in the whole province." The individual thus described was at the time the representative of Clancuilein in Clare.‡

Lastly I may quote a remark made by Mr. Frost, in his recent work on Clare. He states that among the members of the sept bearing the name of Macnamara many are still to be found in Clare, not a few of them labourers, but all derived from the old stock, and he has been struck by " the air of gentility and breeding observable in many humble members of this ancient family." In spite of adverse conditions, and a complete alteration in their environment, and after the lapse of many generations, the character of these people survives in their descendants, however humble their lot may be at present.

Brave to a fault were the members of this sept, foremost among a tribe whose pride was to lead the van of an advancing force, and who claimed equally as their right the honour of protecting it, and forming the rearguard in times of disaster and retreat ; and so we find them at Clontaf, and in many another hard fought battle.§ O'Donovan and others well versed in the history of Thomond, assert that had it not been for the personal bravery and devotion of the chiefs

* See p. 153.   † P. 160.   ‡ P. 171.   § P. 128.

of Clancuilein, the O'Briens could not have held their own in Clare, or prevented its falling into the hands of the English. The leaders of Clancuilein placed their lives absolutely at the service of their king as head of their tribe; they were ready to fight and to die in the defence of his interests, and in these old times war made men staunch and true to one another. We can hardly have a better instance of this than in the case of S. Macnamara, who, when a hostile army approached Quin in A.D. 1278, with a band of his relations entered the camp of the enemy at daybreak, with the object of engaging the leader of the hostile force in single combat. He fought his way onward with amazing vigour, his followers having all been slaughtered; still he strove to meet the leader of his king's enemies, but was overpowered and killed.*

Then again the action of Mac-Con (Macnamara) and his clan in the memorable battle of Corcomroe. In the neighbourhood of that beautiful abbey, surrounded by the wonderful hills of Burren, one of the most important battles in the history of Clare was fought, and the Macnamaras covered themselves with honour.† In the remarkably vivid description which Magrath has left us of this battle there is nothing ferocious or barbarous in the practice of war, for instance, with reference to the care of the wounded, he observes, they were "no longer foes but brothers in trouble," the burial of the dead, and other details referred to by this author, contrast favourably with scenes witnessed by the writer, in warfare carried on in our Eastern possessions in the early part of the second half of the present century. The Irish Celt, in his eager pursuit of pleasure, considered fighting as the noblest pastime; war was one of the chief duties of life, and it was thought honourable to die on the field of battle. The serious side of the subject seldom affected the soul of the gay, light-hearted Irishman.

So long as success in battle depended on a strong arm and individual prowess, the men of Clare held their own against domestic and foreign foes; but after arms of precision had been introduced these people completely succumbed. The truth was they had not then the means of purchasing guns, and if they had, there was no one to teach them how to use them, or to drill them as soldiers; they could act as individuals, man against man, but not against trained bodies of troops. As before remarked, after the introduction of powder and shot as destructive agents in war, the Celts of the West of Ireland disappeared as an independent people.‡

Loyal were the heads of this sept to their own chiefs, as also were their followers to them. However desperate the venture might be, the head of the sept could at any moment command the devoted services

* Page 106.   † Page 124.   ‡ Page 147.

of a trained body of his relations and dependants, who were prepared to
form round his person and enter the thick of battle; others have been
referred to who would not so much as listen to treachery.* When the
split took place in the thirteenth century among the O'Briens it became
necessary for the Macnamaras to choose which faction they should
support, and they elected to throw in their lot with Turlough O'Brien,
because he had married the daughter of their chief, Lochlain Macnamara,
and so in other cases their hereditary qualities bound them to one
another and to their rulers; the freedom of their families, their home and
lands were the objects for which they fought.† The devotion of the
followers to their chief was the keystone on which much of their action
rested.   These chiefs were elected by the sept as the fittest men to lead
and to rule its members, and so far as the history of Clare extends, we
know of no instance of the chief betraying the trust committed to his
care ; he had absolute power over the lives and liberties of his followers,
but during the twelve hundred years we have followed their history there
is no evidence of ill-treatment, tyrannical, or unjust dealing recorded
against any one of the heads of this sept.   These people were not only
loyal to their chiefs, but also to themselves ; they did their duty, and were
content to leave the issue to be judged of by its results, and in the hands
of their bards.‡   After English law had been imposed on the Irish, it is
true the O'Briens forsook their former rectitude of purpose, and took
advantage of the complicated enactments under the new order of things
to filch away the estates of their former devoted followers (page 181),
but these O'Briens were no longer Dalcasians.

Light-hearted and hospitable.§—These qualities seem to have been
marked features in the character of many members of our sept; in the
various annals of Ireland frequent references are made to members of the
family in terms such as the following : " Macnamara, chief of Clancuilien,
was a charitable and truly hospitable man, who established peace and
tranquility in his territory." Of another member of the family the " Four
Masters " state he "was renowned for his hospitality"; of a third, "he
was the best son of a chieftain of his time," and again of a head of the
Rathfolan branch of the Macnamaras, " he was a sumptuous, festive,
bounteous, and humane man "; lastly, we hear that another of the sept
was " a noble and majestic man and a favourite of women and children,
by reason of his gaiety and pleasantry." In selecting these, out of the
many references made to members of this sept, I have not chosen those
favourably noticed, and excluded unfavourable mention of members of

* P. 119.   † P. 121.   ‡ P. 30.
§ See appendix to this chapter, Sir J. Barrington's account of Donnybrook Fair.

the family : the latter, if they exist, so far as I am aware do not appear in the annals of Ireland.

The love of money was not a temptation to which Irishmen as a rule were exposed or into which they were likely to fall ; not that they were improvident, but the members of a sept like that of Clancuilien existed without money until the middle of the sixteenth century. The Pope's Nuncio, in one of his most remarkable reports on the people of the West of Ireland in the year 1648, observes that " they rarely touch money, and as rarely quarrell about it."

Imaginative.—Mr. Lecky states that Irishmen are endowed in an extraordinary degree with retrospective imagination, which quality he remarks is characteristic of these people. Too many Celts live habitually in dreams, largely drawn from the past, and of future honour and glory to which they have not sufficient perseverance to attain by steady applica- tion and hard work. If we refer to any of the able writers who portray the character of Irish men and women, we are struck with the frequent references they make to the scenes and customs of the ancestors of those who play a part in these narratives. The bards were full of this ancient lore, and nothing so much pleased the Irish people as to listen to their tales, concerning the part taken by their ancestors in the struggles and troubles through which their country had passed.* There are no people under the sun, in which the past plays so important a part in the daily life of those now living, as the Irish. Lover's song put into the mouth of that characteristic Irish servant, Mike, is hardly a burlesque, but rather a true picture of the retrospective imagination of these people.†

* Mr. A. J. Balfour has well expressed this fact when he stated, " Anybody who had not realised that the whole history of Ireland consisted of memories, not only of 250 years or 500 years old, he would venture to say had not begun to under- stand the history of that country " (speech delivered in the House of Commons, June 7th, 1895, in opposition to Mr. Morley's proposal to raise a statue to the memory of Oliver Cromwell).

> † " Oh ! once we were illigant people,
> Though we now live in cabins and mud ;
> And the land that we see from the hill-top
> Belonged to us all from the Flood.
> My father was then King of Connaught,
> My grand-aunt Viceroy of Tralee ;
> But the Sassenach came, and, signs on it !
> The devil an acre have we.
>
> " The least of us then were all earls,
> And jewels we wore without name ;
> We drank punch out of rubies and pearls—
> Mr. Petrie can tell you the same—

Sir J. Davis has recorded an interesting example of the devotion of the Brehons to their employers, and the great value they set upon the ancient documents committed to their care. Sir John writes, A.D. 1603, as follows: "Touching the certainties of the duties and provisions yielded to McGrath out of these lands, they referred to an old parchment roll, which was in the hands of one O'Brislau, a chronicler and principal Brehon of that country; whereupon O'Brislau was sent for, who lived not far from the camp, who was so aged and decrepid, as he was scarce able to repair to us; when he was come, we demanded of him a sight of this ancient roll. The old man seemed to be much troubled with this demand, made answer that he had such a roll in his keeping before the wars, but that in the late rebellion it was burnt among other papers and books by certain English soldiers. We were told by some present that this was not true; they affirmed that they had seen the roll in his hands since the wars. Thereupon my Lord Chancellor being present with us did minister an oath to him, and gave him a very serious charge to inform us truly of what had become of the roll. The poor old man, fetching a deep sigh, confessed that he knew where the roll was, but that it was dearer to him than life, and, therefore, he would never deliver it out of his hands unless my Lord Chancellor would take the like oath that the roll should be restored to him. My Lord Chancellor, smiling, gave him his hand and his word that he should have the roll re-delivered unto him if he would suffer us to take a view and copy thereof. And with tears in his eyes the old Brehon drew the roll out of his bosom, where he did continually bear it about him. It was not very large, but it was written on both sides in fair Irish characters; howbeit, some part of the writing was worn and defaced with time and ill-keeping. We then caused it to be translated into English, and perceived how many vessels of butter, and how many measures of meal, and how many

But except some turf mould and potatoes,
    There's nothing our own we can call;
And the English—bad luck to them!—hate us
    Because we're more free than them all!

"My grand-aunt was niece of St. Kevin,
    That's the reason my name's Mickey Free!
Priest's nieces—but sure he's in heaven,
    And his failin's is nothing to me.
And we still might get on without doctors,
    If they'd let the ould Ireland alone,
And if purple men, priests, and tithe proctors,
    Were crammed down the great gun of Athlone."

porkers, and such gross duties did arise unto McGrath out of the lands."*

Credulous.—It has been said with truth that the Celt is endowed with an intuitive appreciation of all that touches the mystic and supernatural ; as an instance in point one may refer to the faith displayed by Moncha, in her father the blind Druid (page 64). Stories of this kind fill many pages of early Irish legends, and they made a deep, and lasting impression on the people of the West of Ireland. The credulity of the chiefs and people of Clare during the fourteenth century, is well illustrated by the account which Magrath gives, in all seriousness, of the appearance of a supernatural being on three important occasions, twice to the leader of the Dalcasians, and once to de Clare.†

The Irish had, and to the west of the Shannon still have, a firm belief in their "banshees." The chief banshee of our tribe dwelt in the lovely wooded rocks overlooking the Shannon above Killaloe ; she accompanied the tribe to battle, "shreiking and fluttering over their heads, surrounded by satyres and spirits of the valley." The writer of these pages can well remember hearing his father describe the thrice-repeated wail of the banshee, which he had distinctly recognised, and which foretold the death of a dear friend ; nevertheless, he was a man who had seen much of men and the world.

The emotional or sensitive disposition of the Irish Celts, has been the obstacle above all others which has barred their progress as a people, and prevented them from joining hand in hand for that long and steady pull necessary for the establishment of a nation. The emotional side of their nature leads the Celt to arrive at rapid conclusions, which are by no means always lasting, and so he too frequently lends himself to carry through the schemes of designing or misguided men who, with fluent tongue, persuade him to follow on in the pursuit of social or political phantoms, in place of devoting his best powers of mind and body in a persevering effort to succeed in his calling in life. It has been fairly said that the creed of many Irishmen is, that "it ought to be —it must be—it is," and for no better reason, they too often waste their undoubted talents and energies in efforts wide of the mark at which they aim.

As individuals, the sensitive Irishman easily takes affront, and is apt to fancy himself injured by persons whose only fault is, that they are superior to himself in mental or physical acquirements ; the advancement

* "Tracts relating to Ireland," by Sir J. Davis, Attorney-General in Ireland ; also Vallaney, "Col. Hib.," vol. i. p. 161.

† See pp. 109, 123, 130.

of another person in life thus becomes tantamount with failure on his part, and so jealousy and unreal grievances are apt to add trouble and bitterness to the other burdens of life. The sensitive Celt cannot bear the hard blows of his more robust, but coarser neighbours, and is apt to shrink within himself, becoming shy and reserved in the presence of strangers. He can never forget a wrong, especially if perpetrated by one who has been his friend; for the bond of friendship with the Irish is something very real—one might almost say sacred—and, to him, in proportion is the offence of one who slights this tie. Among his own countrymen, and in polite society where the genius, wit, and vivacity of the Irish gentleman can have full play, he is seen to the best advantage from a social point of view. Beyond the confines of his own island, the Irishman's intense love of nature, deep human sympathy, and yearning for comradeship not unfrequently attract men with almost blind devotion to him. As soldiers and leaders of men, this quality is invaluable; we could hardly have a better example of this than in the person of the late Lord Mayo, and the remarkable influence he exercised over the native chiefs of India with whom he was brought in contact.

The exceeding brightness of Irish men and women is doubtless due to their emotional dispositions, and is eminently calculated to endow life with a charm, which has a marked influence for good in this careworn age. This element in the Irish character, we may hope, will long continue to throw its cheering light into many a household—a reasonable hope, seeing that Sir W. Petty calculated, in the year 1672, the world contained about a million Irish men and women; but they were said, as far back as the year 1849, to have increased to no fewer than twenty million people.* There is, however, another side to the picture: the qualities which render the Irishman light-hearted make him terribly alive to the pain and grief suffered by others. The anguish of mind thus caused is known only to himself, for the greater his grief the more he conceals his feelings in stolid silence; his sensitive nature too often shuns sympathy, and can best turn for relief to its own bitterness.

There is one alleged trait in the Irish which must be mentioned, and that is untruthfulness. With respect to this grave charge, we may, however, refer to the evidence of Englishmen who lived in the West of Ireland in the sixteenth century. For instance, R. Payne states that "the Irish keep their promise faithfully; nothing is more pleasing to

---

* "National Life and Character," by C. Pearson, p. 69. In the British Isles the Irish Celt constituted numerically 12 to 64 of the inhabitants in 1672. In 1849 they were 8 to 18 of the population, and at the present day exceed that proportion.

them than good justice." This statement was made in the year 1589. Sir J. Davis, writing a few years later, states that "there is no people under the sun that doth love equal and indifferent justice better than the Irish." We have despatches from English statesmen serving in Ireland, which bear independent testimony to the honourable and gentlemanly bearing of members of our sept in the sixteenth century; and there is everything in their history to prove that they entertained a high sense of honour, and nothing to show that they were an untruthful race. It is true that, as far back as the time of Henry III., the Irish chiefs stated that the people had been "remarkable for their candour and simplicity"; but they add, "from the oppression and cruelty they had experienced, they became artful and designing." This degradation in the moral character of a people follows, almost as a matter of necessity, when they are persecuted as the Irish have been until within recent times. We may admit that the character of the Irish Celt has suffered in this respect, and it is well they should realise this fact, and learn to correct the defect under which many of them labour. As the poorer classes become more independent and better educated, they will certainly grow more self-reliant, and, as of old, regain their character for "candour," if not of "simplicity."

Lazy.—The Irish are described as a lazy people. The Pope's Nuncio, writing of them in A.D. 1649, observes that they "feed only on what the earth produces without labour or trouble, and quietly accommodate themselves to the misery of the times";* but, he adds, "this does not prevent them, when instructed and placed in some post under rule and order, from liking and maintaining the course they have adopted." From one cause and another, including, perhaps, its laws, the population of Ireland had, until after the seventeenth century, never increased in excess of its food-producing power: the people, therefore, lived on the stock and crops raised on their own lands, that which was taken from the soil being consumed by persons tilling and residing on these lands. Habits engendered under many centuries of life in these conditions may have led to indolence, for subsistence in Ireland in those times required but little exertion on the part of the cultivator. Moreover, the forests were full of game, and abundance of fish lived in the rivers and lakes of the country, and these were for the most part open to the community. We have ample evidence, however, to prove that Irishmen of the present day, when well paid, fed, and under proper discipline, make first-rate labourers, both in their own and in foreign countries; they are to be trusted under circumstances of great trial and temptation,

* Rinuccini, "The Embassy in Ireland, 1645-49," p. 143.

as, for instance, in the case of the Irish constabulary, who, although enlisted in Ireland, have gone through the past ten years of excitement and trouble in that country, and thoroughly maintained the character of their forefathers. These men were born and bred in Ireland. Neither climate, soil, nor any other surroundings differ in their case from that of the civil population; but the constabulary are "instructed and placed in a post under rule and order, and so like and maintain the course they have adopted," with infinite credit to themselves and to the country. No doubt, regular habits and, above all, good food, have had much to do in developing the higher qualities inherent in many of these men.

The emotional side of the Irish impels them to a love of music, poetry, and painting, and last, but not least, to flowery language and brilliant ideas, often expressed in the most happy terms; we have examples of this in the case of Burke, Grattan, O'Connell, and many other distinguished statesmen, and not a few eminent preachers and barristers. A. Young, an Englishman, who had travelled over the continent of Europe, and observed much, writing from Ireland at the end of the seventeenth century, remarks that "the Irish are infinitely more cheerful and lively than anything we see in England; having nothing of that incivility and sullen silence with which so many enlightened Englishmen seem wrapt up, as if retiring within their own importance. The Irish love of society is as remarkable, as their curiosity is insatiable; and their hospitality to all comers, be their own poverty ever so pinching, merits never to be forgotten." ("Tour in Ireland," 1776, p. 147.)

At the commencement of this chapter it was stated that a study of the congenital characters of the members of a sept, or any other community of the kind, was not only interesting, but had its value from a practical point of view; for however much education may influence for good the character of young people, the better we understand our own dispositions, and the nature of the beings we have to train, the more likely we are to be enabled by example and precept to fit them to steer their course aright over the troubled sea of life. How many men are shipwrecked in their career, not from want of ability, but from a want of consistency of character. This infirmity shows itself as we advance from youth to manhood. Consistency of character is the strongest of all forces in moulding a man's career, since it is true to itself. It is character which inspires confidence among those we are brought in contact with, and is more potent in moulding an individual's destiny in his present, and future life than intellectual acquirements, or anything else that education, as tested by the modern standards of examination, can possibly bestow. If this be true, surely to know the character of the race to which we belong is something we should endeavour to learn. Beyond this, a right conception of the character of a people is the only rational standpoint from which to study their social and political condition. We may go a step farther, and state that sound knowledge of the congenital character of a people is necessary to those who take on themselves the offices of legislators and rulers, for without such knowledge they cannot wisely govern, any more than a surgeon can operate on the human subject without a knowledge of anatomy. It appears from the history of our sept, that from the fifth to the sixteenth century there had been no change whatever in the character of its members; their social and political relations had become modified, but not radically altered, because they had been guided by a succession of beings endowed with the same qualities; it was their disposition which, true to itself, was the force ruling their actions, and led to the development of their laws and other institutions, which to them were just and right, inasmuch as they were a reflex of the mind of the people; and among these people the brand of race is far deeper than the mark of nationality.

APPENDIX TO CHAPTER XV.

Regarding the light-heartedness of the Irish, we find them bright as ever in 1790, at which date Sir J. Barrington has given us a description of their sociality as witnessed at Donnybrook Fair. Sir J. states, at the outset of his narrative, that " he does not know any one trait of character conspicuous alike in himself and brother Pat, save that which is their common disgrace and incentive to all vices, *drinking;* and even in this the English far surpass the Irish."* There can be no question Irishmen (and for the matter of that, their terriers also) have an indigenous *goût* for fighting, and at Donnybrook there was no reserve in this matter. Numerous tents, composed of peeled wattles fixed in the ground at one end and bent over and tied together at the other, were covered with quilts of bedclothes and sheets, blankets, and so on; some of these tents were fifty feet long, and scattered over the green flat, through which a shallow stream runs drippling under a high bridge. The tent was furnished with a table and forms; these were not very steady, so that when the whisky got the mastery of some convivial fellow he was apt to fall over, and with him the row of men on his form, prostrating some ten or twenty gallant shamrock boys on their backs. After a certain amount of roaring, laughing, and not a little bad language, the whole party turned out into the open air and amused themselves with wrestling, leaping,

* Sir J. Barrington's " Personal Sketches," vol. iii. p. 232.

cudgelling, or fighting on the green.   But it was all a good-humoured proceeding.
" Men, to be sure, were knocked down now and then, but there was no malice in
it.   A head was often cut, but as quickly tied up by the man who had inflicted the
wound."   There was no brutal fighting, no cheats, gamblers, or even pickpockets,
perhaps for the very good reason that there was no money worth stealing.   Sir J.
Barrington states that the fair was " rich in all the glories of drinking, fighting,
kissing, making friends, dancing, singing, and joining sincerely in the dance as if
the clout tied round their heads were a Turkish turban.   Whatever happened *in*
the fair, neither revenge nor animosity went *out* of it with any of the parties."
All of which, Sir J. Barrington remarks, were incomprehensible features, and
therefore all wrong and barbarous to the " most egotistical animal in creation,
John Bull, who measures every man's coat according to his own cloth, and can
only fancy an Irish mob to be like a London rabble, and so that Donnybrook
Fair was a compound of all the vice, robbery, and swindling which is so dear to
St. Bartholomew."

CHAPTER XVI

Religious, political, and social life of people living to the west of the Shannon during the first half of the seventeenth century—Opinion of the Pope's Nuncio in A.D. 1658 concerning the state of the Church in Ireland—Sir W. Petty, and Edmund Spenser on this subject—Education—Payne and Champion's description of, A.D. 1589—Political state of the people changed but little for many centuries—Description of—Brehon laws still in force—Payne's account of how they worked—State of judicial proceedings under English rule—Social condition of the people of Clare—Land all in all to them—The family system still in force—Freehold and leasehold understood—Relations between the lord and landholder—Forest lands, and wolves—Agriculture—Dweilings—Furniture—Dress—Military system—Old customs prevailing in Clare—Description of country by Payne—Injustice of forcing English common law on the Irish—Treatment of women by the Irish—Relations of master and servant—Physical explanation of love of Irish for their lands and homes.

In the preceding chapter I have endeavoured from a study of the history of our sept to describe the individual character of its members, and we may now consider the religious, political, and social system which these people had developed before their final dispersion by Cromwell in 1654.

Religion.—With reference to the condition of the Church in Ireland during the latter part of the sixteenth, and the first half of the seventeenth century, we have the opinion on this subject of the highest authority, the Pope's Nuncio, Rinuccini. Writing from Ireland in the year 1658, he states "that the Catholics of Ireland, have from time immemorial been divided into two adverse factions ; one under the name of the old Irish," who, the Nuncio observes, "were tall, simple-minded, and unrefined in manner and living, and unskilled in negotiations ";* this party consisted of the Irish Celts, and included among its number the members of our sept, for they adhered to that form of Church discipline and order, which St. Patrick and his followers had founded throughout Ireland. Archbishop Lanfranc, has left us a brief sketch of the Celtic Church as it existed in the eleventh century, and we know that subsequently the Supreme Pontiff handed Ireland over to Henry II., in order that he might "root out from among them their foul sinnes and wickednesse, as also to yeeld

* Rinuccini's "Embassy to Ireland," pp. 49, 142, 486.

and pay yeerly out of every house a pension of one penny to Saint Peter" (p. 95).

The Irish Church in matters of discipline was ruled by its own authorities, largely under the tribal system. This "old Church" party were in matters of doctrine in accord with Roman Catholics throughout the world; but as in Henry II.'s time, so in that of Charles I., although they by no means declined the authority of the Roman Pontiff, they nevertheless adhered to their own ecclesiastical authorities and customs. On the other hand, the "new party" in the Irish Church, who met with the Nuncio's approval, consisted principally of English and French priests, who, as a rule, had been educated on the Continent and had returned to Ireland to minister to the Anglo-Normans, and the English settled in that country; they were directly under the orders of the Pope of Rome. The Nuncio was of opinion, that the "greatest obstacle to the progress of religion was the division between the old and new Irish parties in the Church," and adds that "with sorrow he found the bishops of the old party abhorring any form of dress or ceremonial, even administering some of the sacraments in secular dress." From a passage already quoted from contemporary history, it appears that a Bishop of Killaloe at the end of the sixteenth century, is referred to as having a large and turbulent family of bastard sons; and from Rinuccini we learn that the bishops of the old party, "for the most part were lukewarm, but the regulars are without comparison much more so; accustomed to live out of their convents, and acting as chaplains, with good stipends, to the barons of the island, not constrained by discipline to wear religious habit, they dare to preach almost seditious doctrines from the pulpit, some to prove that it is unnecessary to the support of faith to have churches, since in the Old Testament we are told the Hebrews were for centuries without a Temple; and that Christ instituted the Eucharist in a private house. To our scandal, on the very table from which the altar-cloth has been but just removed, playing cards, or glasses of beer, together with food for dinner, are at once laid." This account of the Church in Ireland by Rinuccini differs in no respect from that given by Archbishop Lanfranc, in A.D. 1070; and very much coincides with Edmund Spenser's observations made on this subject in 1596. He states that the Irish clergy were guilty of "gross simony, greedy covetousness, fleshly incontinency, careless slouth—saving that they have taken holy orders, they doe goe and live like lay-men, follow all kinds of husbandry and other worldly affairs as other Irishmen doe." Sir W. Petty, writing in 1658, states that the poorer classes in the West of Ireland "adhered to their religion from custom rather than dogma; they

seemed to obey the old lords and heads of septs rather than God."
However the fact is to be explained, it remains true that the Church in
Clare, and generally throughout the West of Ireland, from the earliest
time until it was suppressed by England, was such as is described by the
Pope's Nuncio, and by Edmund Spenser.

It is difficult to form an opinion as to what effect the Christian religion
may have had upon the lives of individual members of our sept. The
invasion of Ireland by the Danes and Anglo-Normans, together with the
subsequent war and turmoil going on in Thomond during the twelfth,
thirteenth, and fourteenth centuries, must have turned the minds of men
towards self-preservation rather than to the practice of religion. Even
in important ceremonies, such as the inauguration of the Kings of
Thomond on Magh Adhair, no reference is made to ecclesiastics or to
any religious observances ; the head of our sept officiated on these
occasions, and the function of making the king was a civil procedure.
The Macnamaras built Quin Abbey, and other churches on their estates,
but they never held Church preferments, as did some of the O'Briens,
O'Carrolls, and other Dalcasian families ; nevertheless, in the time of
persecution which fell upon the Irish Church in the seventeenth, and
eighteenth centuries, by far the greater number of the sept remained
staunch to their Church ; some of them, as, for instance, Roger Macnamara of Quin, rather than renounce their religion willingly yielded up
their lives.*

Education.—Sir J. Davis, writing of the Irish inhabitants of Clare in
the early part of the seventeenth century, describes them as being well
educated, and as both writing and speaking English with fluency. From
the original letter written by J. Macnamara to Lord Burghley, in March
1588, we find that not only was his handwriting and phraseology good,
but his style is independent and even dignified ; nevertheless, this
individual had probably never been east of the Shannon, unless on some
military expedition. He had learnt English as it was commonly taught in
the schools of the West of Ireland, long before Clare passed into the hands
of Englishmen. Robert Payne, writing in the year 1589, remarks,
that he had visited " a grammar school at Limerick in which a hundred
and three score scholars were assembled, most of them speaking good
and perfect English, for that they had been used to construe the Latin
language into English." Schools of a similar character existed at
Killaloe, and in various other parts of Clare ; it was here that the Macnamaras learnt to read the Classics, and gained a good knowledge of
English, and frequently of the French language. Champion, writing in

* Frost's " History of Clare," p. 634 ; and p. 200 of this work.

the second half of the sixteenth century, states : " Without either precepts or observation of congruity, they speak Latin like a vulgar language, learned in their common schools of *Leechcraft* and *Law*, whereat they begin as children, and hold on sixteen or twenty years, conning Groate, the 'Aphorisms of Hypocrates,' and the Civil Institutions, and a few other parings of those two faculties."* Champion continues : " I have seen them where they kept schoole, ten in some one chamber, upon couches of straw, their books at their noses, themselves lying flatte prostrate, and so chaunte out their lessons by peecemeale, being for the most part lustie young fellows." Such were the students of medicine and law in the West of Ireland in the year 1571. A system of secular education had existed there from the earliest times ; beyond this up to the period of the Reformation the clergy had excellent schools all over the country, and we have noticed (p. 200) that no sooner had the Confederate Government granted them freedom of religious worship, than they reopened their college at Quin Abbey, which we are told by one who studied there in A.D. 1646, was soon crowded with scholars.

The political condition of the people up to the middle of the sixteenth century was governed by their relation to the head of the sept, and through him with the chief of the tribe, and the provincial king ; it was very much what it had been from the earliest historical times. The Irish had never had a central government or established themselves as a united people ; their nearest approach to it was during Brian Boru's life, but then the provincial kings made war and peace without reference to any central authority ; all that they were expected to do in token of submission was to pay tribute to Brian. As we have seen from the history of our sept, they asserted their right to elect their own chief as late as the year 1557, and they did so on the understanding that he was " the most experienced, noblest, and most popular " leader they could secure ; in like manner they elected his tanist, so that they still held to their old customs in this respect.†

The provincial king was in the habit, up to the reign of Henry VIII., of meeting the chief landowners of his province in council, in order that they might consider changes in the distribution of the tribal lands, and probably also to revise, or add to the test cases contained in the Brehon code, so as to mould the laws to the wants of society. Other matters were dealt with by the heads of septs assembled in the house of the public hospitaller ; it must have been in some such meeting that Sioda

* " The Historie of Ireland," by E. Champion, p. 25.

† "A View of the State of Ireland," by Edmund Spenser (published 1596). pp. 11 and 12.

Macnamara, and the other freeholders of Tulla, in the year 1554, came to an agreement, as to the terms upon which to consign their lands to Henry VIII., a voluntary act on their part, for one and all of them were weary of the strife and misrule which the province suffered under the nominal rule of England.   There is no reason to suppose that the Brehon laws had failed to meet the wants of the people in the sixteenth century, but England had then assumed the responsibility of rulers without the means of enforcing the authority of the law; this, together with the quarrels of the Irish among themselves, led to great trouble and misery. The O'Briens being of the new party, probably despised their old supporters of Clancuilein, who were " unskilled in negotiations," and were therefore considered to be fit subjects to be plundered.

Sir J. Davis informs us that in his official tour through Ireland in James I.'s time, the Brehon laws still flourished.   He states that: " After arriving at any place he called the Brehons or scholars of the district before him, for they knew all the septs and families, and all their branches, and the dignity of one sept above another, and above what families or persons were chief of every sept, and next, and third, and fourth in rank, till they descended to the most inferior man in all the baronies."   Moreover, Sir John continues, " we looked to the Brehons to tell us what quantity of land every man ought to have by the customs of the country, which is of the nature of gavelkind."   If we compare this account of the work of a Brehon in the seventeenth century with that given in the Senchus Moir, we shall find that his duties in 1615, were precisely similar to that which they had been a thousand years before; and Robert Payne, an Englishman living in the West of Ireland, writing in 1589, has left us an account of his experience of the working of the Brehon code.   Payne states, that the law was ordered "with such wisdom and justice, as demanded worthy commendation. For I myself divers times have seen in several places within this jurisdiction, well near twenty cases decided at one sitting, with such justice that for the most part, both plaintiff and defendant hath departed contented."   One fails to understand why a system of this kind should have been suddenly swept away by English lawyers, ignorant of the language and customs of the people of Ireland; and in its place laws imposed on these people, many of which were foreign to their nature, and at variance with much they clung to with the deepest affection.   Edmund Spenser, writing at the time referred to, clearly comprehended the evils incident on a sudden, and radical change in the laws governing the Irish people.   He observes : " The condition of Ireland, how farre it differeth from England is apparent to the very least judgment; but to transferre the same lawes for the government of the realme of Ireland, was much more inconvenient and unmeete. Now then, if these laws (the common law of England) bee not likewise applied and fitted for Ireland, they sure for that country are very unjust." With reference to the criminal law the case was still stronger. However faulty the system of fines administered by the Brehons had been, it was so utterly different from that of imprisonment, and death as punishment for crime, that for many generations the newly introduced laws must have been deeply repugnant to the people ; especially in a case such as that to which reference has been made, in which an English official of small importance, took upon himself to hang two men one Sunday morning, because they were loitering about the place in which he resided.

The social condition of the people of Clare at the end of the sixteenth century was determined, as it had been from the time they settled in that part of Ireland, upon the amount of land which a family held. The original Ui-Caisin lands had become the freehold property of some three hundred members of our sept. They paid tribute for these lands to the head of the sept, and he in like manner to the chief of the tribe. Doubtless, the landowners made allotments to their kinsmen or friends of such lands as they did not require for their own purposes, and these lands were held in consideration of a tribute paid in kind and cesses, which were levied by the landlord on the landowner. But in all this there was nothing like the existing system of landlord and tenant. The tenure of land had doubtless altered from its primitive condition, but to this extent only, that the landlords, who originally held their land from the tribe, had come into permanent possession of these lands ; it had been converted into freehold. The conjoint members of the sept, however, had considerable control over the old tribal and common lands ; they could neither be bought, sold, or willed to an heir until after Henry VIII.'s time. The Brehons knew what lands belonged to each individual, and that was sufficient for the purposes of the community; any disputes on the subject were referred to the Brehons, and, as a rule, easily and amicably settled. These people did not know the amount of their rent, but they held possession of the land and gave tribute to their lord in the shape of stock, the amount being settled, if necessary, by the Brehon, and under these conditions the holding passed from father to tanist; but there was nothing approaching to tenant right or dual ownership in the soil, although in some few instances lands, especially ecclesiastic, were let on lease for terms of sixty, and even one hundred years.* Under the old system, however, the

* Frost's " History of Clare," pp. 279 and 283, also 286.

landholder received compensation for improvements he had effected on the land; if allowed to build a house, it became his property; land manured could not be changed until the crop on it had been worked off by the landholder, and so on.*

There can be no question, therefore, that the nature of freehold and of leasehold property was thoroughly understood by the Irish of the sixteenth century, but it is equally certain that in Clare the larger portion of the soil which was not cultivated by the landlord for his own domestic purposes was made over to other persons, generally members of his family, who employed it in like manner for their own use, and anything it yielded beyond this was virtually returned, directly or indirectly, to the landlord. The produce of the land was consumed by those who cultivated the soil, although doubtless, from the thirteenth century onwards, the export of cattle, and of horses from Galway, Limerick, and other parts had been effected in exchange for wine, silks, and other commodities from France and Spain.

Sir J. Davis made much of the hardship inflicted by cesses such as "coin and livery," imposed by landowner on the occupier of his soil. Doubtless, in the Pale, great wrong was done in this way;† but we have original documents bearing on this subject, one of which has been referred to, as it concerns the members of our sept, and there we find that the landlord's visits to his landholders were times of rejoicing, and strictly limited as to season and duration. Beyond this these visits were only allowed when the lord accompanied his servants to the house of the individual who had to entertain them. What is more to the purpose, this practice was the result of mutual obligations, for the landowner kept open house, not only for his immediate relations and friends, who were ever welcome, but also for those who occupied his lands, and, in fact, every one in the least degree dependent upon him. This generous, almost boundless, hospitality clung to the descendants of these landowners, and ruined not a few of them; nor has it as yet forsaken their sons and daughters, a survival, and that not the least pleasant, of those qualities which have made, and we trust will continue to make, Irishmen many friends, especially among their own countrymen.

Early in the seventeenth century much of the land in Clare was still covered with forest which abounded in game of all kinds, and was infested with wolves. As late as the reign of James I. we are informed that the king "understanding the great loss and hindrance which arose in Ireland by reason of the multitude of wolves in all parts of the

* "Manners and Customs of the Ancient Irish," vol. i. pp. clxxxix. and cxc.
† "A Short History of the Irish People," by A. G. Richey, p. 255.

country, did, by letters patent dated from Newmarket, 26th November, 1614, direct a grant to be made by patent to H. Tuttesham, who by petition hath made offer to repair to Ireland, and there use his best endeavours to destroy the said wolves, providing at his own charge men, dogs, traps, engines, and requiring no other allowance save only four nobles sterling for the head of every wolf, young or old, out of any county, and to be authorised to keep four men, and twelve couple of hounds in every county for seven years next after the date of this letter" ("Transactions of the Royal Society of Antiquarians," vol. xiv. page 62). The wolves, however, were to be exterminated by other means, for the forests in which they lived were speedily cut down, and the timber sold or burnt after the English took possession of the country.   Timber was required in Clare for smelting iron and working coal mines.   For instance, in the year 1605 we learn that King James granted to " J. Cutler and W. Phillips, certain grounds in Macnamara's country west of Shannon, with the right to open a coal mine." The Commissioners appointed by Parliament to inquire into the disposal of the confiscated estates observe, that " dreadful havoc has been committed on the woods ; for those on whom the confiscated lands have been bestowed, or their agents have been so eager after the smallest profit, that several large trees have been cut down and sold for sixpence each ; the destruction is still carried on in many parts of the country."* The Bishop of Kilmore, between the years 1699 and 1713, cut down and sold for his own profit, timber to the amount of £20,000.   The Bishop of Derry and many other Englishmen, who cared nothing for the lovely woods of Ireland, and feared lest a political change might deprive them of their confiscated estates, thought best to make the most of what they had, and cut down and sold all the valuable timber on their estates, and thus inflicted an irreparable injury on the country.† Of these woods Edmund Spenser in his " Faerie Queene "‡ wrote :

> Whylome when Ireland flourished in fame
> Of wealth and goodness, far above the rest
> Of all that bear the British Islands' name,
> The gods then used for pleasure and for rest
> Oft to resort thereto, where seemed them best ;
> But none of all therein more pleasure found
> Than Cynthia, that is soverine queene profest
> Of woods and forests, which therein abound
> Sprinkled with wholesome waters more than 'most on ground.

Canto vi. 38.

* Boates' "Natural History of Ireland " (1652), pp. 99, 100.
† Lecky's "History of Ireland," vol. i. p. 335.
‡ "State of Ireland," by Edmund Spenser, p. 200.

Rinuccini, who travelled over most of the West of Ireland, observes, that the "only bad road in the whole kingdom is that across the Munster mountains, and I had to pass them with a considerable suit and much baggage, I was furnished with vehicles for all, and an escort." *

Agriculture.—R. Paynes dilates on the profitable nature of investments in farming operations, carried on in Ireland in the latter part of the sixteenth century.   Horses, cattle, sheep, and swine, were the principal care of the Irish landowner.   Agriculture in some parts of Clare must have been of a very primitive description as late as 1680, for Dineley found in Burren "horses four abreast drawing the plough by their tails, which was the custom all over Ireland till by statute it was prevented ; yet they tolerate this custom here (Burren) because they cannot manage their lands otherwise, their plough gears, tackle, and traces being (as they are all over the rest of the kingdom) of gadds or withes of twigs twisted, which sure would break to pieces by the ploughshare so often jibbing against the rock, which gears being fastened by wattles or wisps to the horses' tails, the horses being sensible, stop until the ploughman lifts it over.   The garrons are seldom or never shood.   Here is but one narrow road on going out of it, and the land is marked by broad stones like slate, turned edgewise.   The common people use brogues made of raw hides or untanned leather."†   Those only who, like Dineley, have visited Burren can realise the rocky nature of its hill sides ; nevertheless, among these barren mountains there are numerous glades of marvellously fertile land, yielding herbage which is second to none in the country as pasturage for cattle.   A small quantity of oats, barley, and other cereals were grown with difficulty and in such quantities only, as was necessary for consumption by the few people, who in those times inhabited this desolate but most fascinating corner of Ireland.   It is to be observed that Dineley states, there was only one narrow road leading from the east of Clare into this district of Burren.   Produce was carried to fairs or from one place to another on the backs of horses, or dragged on rude sleighs over the roads ; there were no carts.

Dymmock, writing from Ireland, A.D. 1600, remarks that the country "yielded great stores beeffes and porkes, and excellent horses of a fine feature and wonderful swyftness, great plenty of wood except in Leinster, where being ready harbouring for the mear Irish, they have been cut down.   There is abundance of fish and fowle, mines of iron, lead, and copper.   The people are very glorious, francke, ireful, good

* "The Embassy to Ireland," p. 490.
† See also "Notes," Irish Archæological Society, vol. ii. p. 43.

horsemen, delighting in war, great hospitality, and kind-hearted, of exceeding love towards their foster brethren."

In Henry VIII.'s time the Earl of Thomond had to borrow money from the Lord Deputy in Dublin to pay his expenses to London, because "there was no money in his part of Ireland." All the dealings carried on by these people had been by barter, or the interchange of goods the products of their own lands and labour. E. Champion, in his History of Ireland, published 1571, observes, that "they exchange by commutation of wares for the most part, and have utterly no coyne stirring in any great lord's house. Some of them be richly plated; their ladies are trimmed rather with massive jewels than with garish apparell, and count it a beauty to be tall." In Galway and Limerick, however, a considerable trade had from the earliest times been established with France and Spain, wine, tin, silk, and other articles, being imported in exchange for wool, hides, and oak, together with other articles produced in Ireland.

Potatoes had been introduced into the country by Captain Hawkins as early as A.D. 1565; but nothing from the history of the period we are considering, would lead any one to suppose that potatoes would in subsequent years play so important a part in the food supply of the Irish. Tobacco had already gained a footing in the country, in spite of James I. having prohibited its use as "a loathsom custom." Venice was at this time the chief centre from which tobacco in a manufactured form was distributed through Europe.

Dwellings.—The people in Clare, up to the middle of the seventeenth century, lived for the most part in the old form of wicker and clay covered cabins. Keeps, or castles were scattered pretty thickly over Clare, and there are several rough sketches of these buildings in Dineley's Journal: most of them, however, were destroyed under the supervision of a commission appointed by Cromwell for that purpose.

Dineley has left us a sketch of one of the Macnamara castles, Roscoe. The keep or residence of the family was evidently surrounded by dwellings inhabited probably by the servants, retainers, and the stables, the whole being enclosed by a stone wall, which served not only as a means of defence against wolves, but within these walls was the inviolable refuge or home, a place which up to the time of Cromwell was sacred to the family, and into which, without permission of its head, neither the arm of the law nor any human being might enter. Sanctity of a precisely similar nature is in the mind of the Celt still connected with his house; a man, however deep his crime, is safe under the protection of his home. So strong is this feeling, that although the police often know who the criminal is, and although his evil deeds may have been perpetrated in open day, still it is often impossible to get his relations or near neighbours to give evidence against him.

E. Spenser states that as late as Queen Elizabeth's time many of the Irish " kept their cattle and lived themselves the most part of the year in cow-houses, pasturing upon the mountains and waste wild places, removing still to fresh lands as they have depastured the former." Many laws were passed to prevent indiscriminate grazing, but without avail, for the old custom of large tracts of common land clung to the people.

Furniture had improved somewhat, but was still, according to our ideas, very rough and inconvenient. Rushes covered the floor, and the windows were unglazed, but closed with a wooden shutter. Oil lamps and rushlights supplied light at night, such as it was. A chair or two, and as many stools, with an oak chest and a table, completed the furniture of the common room or hall, in the centre of which, or, it might be, at one end, the fire burnt, over which no small part of the cooking took place. Fingers were used in place of forks; in fact, Queen Elizabeth hesitated to adopt a fork for the use of her fingers; it was hardly, therefore, to be expected that her subjects in Clare would have been in advance of the court in matters of this kind.

Dress.—As late as 1584, in a Parliament convened at Dublin, the Lord President endeavoured to persuade the members from Clare to conform in dress to that of the other deputies of the Senate; but they declined, one of them replying, that the next thing would be to "give his chieftain petticotes to walk the streets in, so that the rabble might laugh at them both."* Some fifty years later Rinuccini stated, that most of the better classes of Irish wore the costume of their country. That the poorer classes of the West of Ireland had but few wants, living largely on trefoil and butter, their drink being milk, and for a great treat, whisky; nevertheless, he adds, " they have shoes, some few utensils, and woollen mantles which cover them, but they are much more careful of their swords and muskets than of their bodies."

The Military Force of the Irish has been described by J. Dymmock in his account of Ireland, written A.D. 1600. He states that " theire forces consist of Horsemen, Galloglasses and Kerne, the horsemen being armed with headpiece, shirtes of mayle, a sworde, a skayne, and a speare. They rode on paddes or pillowes without styrops, they beare the spear or lance by the middle and so encounter; every horseman hath two or three horses, and every horse a knave : his horse of service is allwaies led spare, and his knave, which caryeth his harness and speare, rydeth upon

* Macgeoghegan's " History of Ireland," p. 482.

the other, or els upon a hackney. The Galloglasses ar pycked and selected men of great mightie bodies, chosinge rather to dye than to yeelde ; armed with shirt of maile, a skull, and a skeine ; the weapon they must vse is a batle axe, six foot longe, the blade like a shomaker's knyfe, he hath a man for his harnesse bearer, and a boy to carry his provision. The Kerne is a kind of footman, sleightly armed with a sworde, a targett of woode, or a bow and sheafe of arrows with barbed heades, or els 3 dartes which they cast with wonderful facillity and nearness, a weapon more noysome to the enemy, especially horsemen, than yt is deadly ; within these few years they have practised the muskett and callyver, and are growne good and ready shott. The horseboys are the skumme and outcaste of the countrye serviceable for meatinge dressing of horses, and hurtfull to the enemy with their dartes."

Until the close of the sixteenth century we find some of the earliest forms of tribute still in existence among the members of our sept, as for instance, the Boromean tax. That these people should have continued to pay this tribute for so many centuries, and after it had long ceased to be imposed on other Irish communities, is very remarkable. The ancient system of what we may consider as a poor law, or rather provision for the sick and needy, had been preserved in Clare from the earliest times up to the seventeenth century (p. 33). Doubtless the work of charity had from the thirteenth century until the time of Henry VIII. been largely in the hands of the Church, but we have distinct references to the old system of poor-law relief, and to public hospitals in which provision was made for sick and wounded people, beyond that offered by the Church.

Payne, who lived and held land in the West of Ireland during the latter part of the sixteenth century, wrote of the Irish at this period as follows : " The Irish keep their promise faithfully, and are more desirous of peace than the English, nothing is more pleasing to them than good justice. They have a common saying, defend me and spend me, meaning from oppression of our countrymen (the English). You may travel through all their land without any injury offered of the very worst Irish, and be hospitably received by the best." This description of the Irish was written when there were practically no English landlords in Clare. Sir J. Davis travelled through the territories west of the Shannon in James I.'s time, and in the last paragraph of his famous work on Ireland, he sums up his opinion regarding the Celtic inhabitants of that country in the following words : "There is no people under the sun that doth love equal and indifferent justice better than the Irish, or will rest better satisfied with the execution thereof, although it is against themselves, as they may have protection and benefit of the law when upon just cause they do deserve it."

The Solicitor-General of Ireland could hardly write in these terms of the Celtic Irish at the present day. The county jail at Ennis is empty, not because there is no crime in co. Clare, but because it is well-nigh impracticable in the year 1895, to bring a certain class of agrarian offenders to justice in that country; and only a short time since many of the landed proprietors had to be guarded night and day in their houses by English soldiers. The reason for this is, that the character of the Irish in the nineteenth is precisely what it had been in the sixth century ; the people have not altered, but the laws which govern them have changed, and some of their provisions relating especially to that subject of paramount importance to an Irishman—the land—are foreign to the nature of the Celt. No one saw this with greater clearness than Edmund Spenser, who, as secretary to the Lord Deputy of Ireland, and residing as such afterwards among the people, knew them well ; in 1596 he wrote of the wrong England was doing to Ireland in forcing her laws on a people, whose nature and customs were so different from that of Englishmen.* This fact has been ignored by England with reference to the people of Ireland, but in India a different system was fortunately adopted, otherwise our hold on that country would have been an impossibility.

The Irish Celt held their women in tender regard, and so females were treated by them with consideration such as they then received among few other nations. Especially in the case of the lower classes, Irishwomen were never held to be the slaves of men ; they were employed in attending to their children, in weaving, looking after the domestic creatures belonging to the family, and such like occupations. These women were chaste as girls and as wives, and when young,

---

* Edmund Spenser, in A.D. 1596, writes of the application of the common law of England to Ireland, "that the law of itself is most rightful for the kingdom for which it was first devised: for this as it seems reasonable, that out of the manner of your people, and abuses of your country for which the law was invented, they take their first beginning, or else they should be most unjust ; for no lawes of man are just, but as in regard of the evils which they prevent, and the safety of the commonweal which they provide for, nor if these lawes of England bee not likewise applyed and fitted for the realme [Ireland] they are sure very inconvenient " ("A View of the State of Ireland," by Edmund Spenser, p. 32). In another place he observes : " The condition of it [Ireland] how farre it differeth from this of England is apparent to every least judgement, to transfer the same laws for the governing of the realme of Ireland was much more imminent " ("A View of the State of Ireland," p. 16).

endowed with taste, and an amount of refinement and manner to be seen among few others of their class in any part of Europe." *

> The wild sweet briery fence,
> Which round the flowers of Erin dwells.†

There are few amongst us who have resided in Burren, or in the agricultural district of Clare, who have not met with the typical Irish lass, with her winsome face, thick nut-brown hair twisted up round her small head, with those wonderful laughing blue-grey eyes, shaded with long dark lashes, high cheek-bones and finely moulded chin, with sweet firm lips and a captivating voice, her ankles and feet bare, and of perfect form—a wonderful thing is this Celtic foot. It may be we meet her sauntering along beside her young lover, a lad of seventeen, a creature with large grey eyes set in a brown face, with fine cut features, a pleasing voice and manner ; in truth, being an almost idyllically picturesque pair of human beings. Such, however, are many of the descendants of the old Celtic stock at the present day, in those parts of Ireland where there has been little if any adulteration of the race by intermarriage with other nationalities.

Under the native Irish or Celtic system, the landowner in Clare, in the sixteenth century, lived in his strong keep or castle, surrounded by the dwellings of his servants, horses, and cattle, the whole enclosed in a wall which formed the precincts or sanctuary, and woe to the enemy or intruder who attempted to force his way into this enclosure. The lord's time was spent in looking after his own property, which he farmed, in sport of every kind, and in hospitality.

The relations that existed between master and retainer in the Irish household has been a theme of never-ending satisfaction, not only to the parties concerned, but also to the writers of biography and fiction. Miss Edgeworth, in " Castle Rackrent," has drawn the character of an Irish servant which can hardly be surpassed. The tie that existed between the upper and lower classes was not unfrequently the result of that remarkable system of fosterage which prevailed among the Irish up to quite recent times. W. H. Maxwell, in his story of " Hector O'Halloran," has left us a well-drawn picture of the bonds of

---

* " Considerations for Promotion of Agriculture," by Lord Molesworth (signed by R. L. V. M.), published 1723, p. 31.

† Of the many pathetic stories having for their theme the terrible consequences of a fall from the standard of purity in the case of the Irish peasant girl, I know of none more tenderly or more beautifully told than Katharine Tynan's tale of the " Unlawful Mother," in her lifelike stories of " An Isle in the Water."

friendship, and intense devotion between Irishmen the result of fosterage, a system which has exercised a silent but untold influence on the social condition of the people, and which in its survival as a part of our being still plays a by no means insignificant roll in our social relations.

In the old Irish home dependants and tenants lived about the master's house, from boyhood—they came and departed as they pleased; much of the summer was passed in helping the old people in their own homes, in getting in the harvest, and tending cattle on the hills; the remainder of the year was devoted to the master, following him over the moors, or such of the forests as remained, in hunting expeditions; mixed with no small amount of dancing, drinking, and fighting, especially on holidays and festivals. These young Irish peasants of Clare were clean-limbed, light, active, and handsome fellows, perfect specimens of strength and symmetry, and as bold as they were handy in everything appertaining to snaring wild fowl, netting rabbits, and catching fish, and at all times ready to shed the last drop of their blood if necessary for the chief. When they married they obtained a patch of ground from their patron, on which to fix their own cabin, and settle down to cultivate such an amount of land as would feed them and their family, by the help of their pig and fowls, and, it may be, a cow; and with this they were perfectly contented and happy; when trouble came the chief was at hand to help them to the best of his ability. A system of this kind was in full operation in the West of Ireland two hundred and fifty years ago, in truth, existed there up till within the memory of living men, and it was a system which had flourished for certainly twelve hundred years previously.

It is difficult to realise a state of society such as that which existed among the members of our sept until the middle of the seventeenth century. Money was still practically unknown to these people, there was no such thing as wealth outside the possession of land and stock; no tenant, no tithes or taxes, beyond a fixed tribute on the land; no titles, the social scale being regulated by the amount of land a family possessed; there was no central government, no army, navy, or police; no poor laws, but the aged and sick were nevertheless cared for, as they are under the conjoint family system in India at the present day. The land was all in all to these people, not only was their social position ruled by it, but it had supplied them and their forefathers for many generations with the necessaries of life in the way of food and garments, and they had come to love it, and cling to it with an intensity of feeling such as that referred to by Mr. W. R. Le Faun, in his excellent retrospect of a long and genial life spent in Ireland; he remarks "that it is impossible for one who has not resided in Ireland, and been on intimate terms with the people, to realise the intense longing which animates them for the possession of land, no matter how small the holding."

It is beyond the scope of this work to discuss the various theories which have been advanced to explain the idiosyncrasy of individuals; the subject is one men have pondered over without avail. But I would venture, with diffidence, to express my own ideas as to the physical causes engendering that love of land which occupies the foremost place in the minds of every Celtic Irishman; my remarks on this subject, however, must be of the briefest possible nature, and in fact compressed into a single paragraph.

No one knows how conscious ideas and memory, or, as we commonly call it, the mind, is produced in the brain; but the fact remains clear that the brain is the principal organ of consciousness, and is the instrument through means of which expression is given to our thoughts. A definite form, structure, and connection of certain brain centres are probably necessary for the conception and retention of various ideas or sentiments. For instance, it may be that an individual possesses a love of music, or, as we say, has an accurate ear for harmony, because a certain area of his brain contains a special arrangement of nerve cells; and it is this arrangement of parts situated in a definite area of his sensorium which enables him with pleasure to listen to, and appreciate, music. This part of his brain is connected with the centre controlling the muscles of articulation, and so the individual not only enjoys music, but delights in talking about it to other people. Wherever a like arrangement of brain substance is present, the people so made are fond of music; and without this specialised form of brain matter they may strive ever so much to love harmony, but it is impossible for them to do so, although they may with some success learn to imitate those who possess the organisation above referred to. This specialised form of brain, like the features and build of people, is much a matter of hereditary transmission, and is doubtless gradually (that is, in the course of generations) developed, or the reverse, by surrounding conditions. Thus we can readily imagine that a community having no love for music might be located among a society who devoted much of their time to this art, and in the course of generations the brains of the former people would from constant exercise become so specialised that, like their neighbours, they might come to love music. If we apply this principle to the case of the Celts of Ireland, we can understand, from what has been said regarding their history, their intense desire to possess land.* The conditions under which their fore-fathers lived for centuries in dependence on the soil for their existence, and social and political status developed in their brains characters as marked as those of their features, giving to the mind of the being so constituted the intense longing for the possession of land to which Mr. Le Faun refers. Faculties of this description, once acquired, are doubtless hereditary, and so have been passed on from father to son up to the present day, faculties which can no more be controlled by Acts of Parliament than the natural colour of one's eyes or hair. English statesmen have hardly appreciated this fact, and the land question in Ireland has led to endless trouble, and will continue to do so until the nature of the Celt is changed, or the land system in Ireland is freed from the artificial encumbrances heaped on it by persons during the past three centuries in order to advance their own purposes. In place of this, a general scheme of purchase must be encouraged, through means of which the land may be bought on fair terms by those who, as of old, will till it and live upon it; the sooner this fact is recognised the better for the well-being of the inhabitants of Ireland and of England.

* The Greeks of old held that their "homos (law and custom) was king of all, exercising plenary power, spiritual as well as temporal, over individual minds; moulding the emotions as well as the intellect according to the local type, deter-mining the sentiments, the beliefs, and the predisposition in regard to new matters tendered for belief of every one; fashioning thought, speech, points of view, no less than of action, and reigning under the appearance of habitual, self-suggested tendencies" ("Plato and the other Companions of Socrates," vol. i. p. 249, by G. Grote).

CHAPTER XVII

In consequence of the confiscation of their lands, and the coercive measures of 1654, some forty thousand young Irishmen left their country and entered the military service of France, Spain, and Italy. At the same time, English slave dealers were given a free hand in Ireland, and a number of boys and girls shipped to Barbadoes, and sold to the planters.* As many as 6400 men, women, and children were sold in Barbadoes by one firm of Bristol merchants. During the year 1655 England added Jamaica to her possessions, and the Lord Protector applied to Lord H. Cromwell, then commanding in Ireland, to secure one thousand "Irish wenches" for the new possessions. Lord

---

* "History of Ireland in the Eighteenth Century," by W. E. H. Lecky, vol. ii. p. 104.

H. Cromwell, in reply, stated that there was no difficulty in executing this order, only "force would be required to take them," and Cromwell adds "that in addition to the 1000 young women, 1500 boys of from twelve to fifteen years of age should be included, for," he observes, "they can be well spared, and might be made Christians." This number of girls and boys were captured in Clare and Galway, and exported to the West Indies in October 1655.*

It was in connection with this proceeding that the rumours arose which are referred to by the Rev. P. White in his "History of Clare" (p. 205). A daughter of Daniel Macnamara, of Rathfolan, had married a young Captain O'Carroll, and it is reported that in an attempt to rescue some of the poor creatures who had been seized by Cromwell's soldiers, O'Carroll, having killed two of these Englishmen near Rathfolan, was himself shot dead. His young wife is said to have been seized, together with her little boy, and exported to Jamaica; the lad, in after-years, passed over to America, and subsequently became a person of note in Virginia.

On the restoration of Charles II. the hopes of many an Irish family rose high, for most of them had loyally supported his father; but they were doomed to disappointment, for the king could not be troubled with Irish grievances, but he appointed a commission to inquire into their claims. Mr. Frost has given us an abstract of most of the work done by this commission, so far as their investigations in Clare extended.† The Crown benefited largely by the confiscations; thus Charles II. bestowed no less than one hundred and seventy thousand acres of these lands on his brother James.‡ About two-thirds of the best lands in Ireland in 1641, which had belonged to Roman Catholics, in A.D. 1651 were made over to Protestants, most of them either Englishmen or Scotchmen. It seems that the commissioners appointed by Charles did their work in a very perfunctory manner, and three thousand cases were dismissed because there was not sufficient time to inquire into their merits.§ But the slight amount of concessions made to the old landowners of the country produced intense excitement, and disaffection among the English and Scotch adventurers; so much was this the case, that Pepys, in his Diary, informs us that "a plot was discovered in the north of Ireland among the Presbyters and others to secure Dublin

---

* Thurloe's "State Papers," vol. iv. p. 1000, and "Cromwellian Settlement," p. 92.

† Frost's "History of Clare," pp. 391, 526.

‡ "The English in Ireland," by J. A. Froude, vol. i. p. 141.

§ Lecky's "History of Ireland," vol. i. p. 15.

Castle and other places, and they debauched a good part of the army there, promising them ready money."

Some few of the Macnamaras managed to recover portions of their ancestral estates; for instance, Colonel J. Macnamara, of Cratloe, in a petition to King Charles, proved that his grandfather was possessed of large estates, and that when in exile he (Colonel Macnamara) was well known to his Majesty. We learn from the following document, the original of which is in possession of Mr. John Macnamara, together with a piece of the king's hair, presented by Charles II. to Colonel Macnamara when he was in Paris during the year 1654. This document runs as follows :

" I thank you for the affection you showed in making me your debtor, one hundred pounds, and do assure you that when my condition shall change I shall not fail to requite you.

"Witness my hand and seal this 25 day of March 1654.

[Seal]   CHARLES REX."

In spite of this assurance, but little could be done for Colonel Macnamara. The greater part of his lands had been made over to Peter Creagh, an Englishman, so detested by the Irish that he had to be provided with a considerable part of the Cratloe property, because it was situated not far distant from the garrison of Limerick.* In spite, however, of the loss of most of his estates, J. Macnamara was elected a Member of Parliament for his county in 1689; he was also appointed High Sheriff of Clare. A relation of his, Florence Macnamara, of Dromad, was Member of Parliament for Ennis.† Some other members of the sept also secured portions of their former estates, as, for instance, J. Macnamara, of Creeragh; Colonel Daniel; and John, of Moyriesk. Teigie Macnamara, the eldest son of Daniel, of Rathfolan (p. 205), was a distinguished officer in James II.'s army. Under the stipulations of the treaty of Limerick, he held the remnant of his father's property in lower Bunratty; but having mortgaged these lands to Sir D. O'Brien, under failure of redemption, the mortgage was foreclosed, and the last ancient property of Rathfolan passed from the Macnamaras into other hands (A.D. 1703). The castle, which had only been completed by Daniel Macnamara's father, is now a complete ruin.‡ After parting with the remainder of his former estates, Teigie Mac-

* White's " History of Clare," p. 267.

† " The Patriot Parliament of 1689," by Thomas Davis, edited by Sir C. Gavin Duffy, p. 159.

‡ " John Macnamara of Rathfolan " (Frost), pp. 239–416; and authenticated pedigree.

namara went to live at Smithstown, Burren, not far from Ballinacragga, where his father had settled some years previously.*

James II. appointed Tyrconnel as Lord Deputy of Ireland ; he was a Roman Catholic, and devoted to the king's policy. At the time of James' accession, the Irish army numbered some six or seven thousand men, all of them being Protestants. Tyrconnel, under the reserve or short service system of that period, increased the fighting men in Ireland to forty thousand, all of them being Roman Catholics, most of them descended from the old Celtic landowners. The Lord Deputy then dismissed all Protestants from the army ; he took the clothing of some four thousand of them, and sent them almost naked to gain a living as best they could. The disbanded Protestant officers, to the number of three hundred, mostly went to Holland, and appeared in the ranks of William's army at the Battle of the Boyne, and at Aughrim.†

King James landed in Ireland in March 1689, and on his arrival in Dublin issued a proclamation, requiring his absentee subjects to return to Ireland. He expressed his determination to suppress any civil disturbance in the country, and to grant religious freedom. Lastly, he summoned a Parliament to meet at Dublin on the 7th of May. The Irish had never abandoned the hope of obtaining a repeal or mitigation of the Acts of Settlement and Explanation ; as late as 1686 they had sent agents over to England to seek the repeal of these Acts ; but these agents were attacked by the London mob, and were glad to make their escape back to Ireland.

The Dublin Parliament of 1689, from an historical point of view, is of the greatest interest, but unfortunately the official transactions and Acts were ordered to be burnt by William Prince of Orange, and it was not until 1740 the Bills passed by this Parliament were reprinted. This Parliament was presided over by its legitimate king, and its members were freely elected by the inhabitants of the country. The members of the Upper House were the descendants of some of the former Celtic chiefs of provinces and tribes, the O'Briens, and so on, together with the heirs of Anglo-Norman noblemen, such as the Burkes, Butlers, and many others. The Commons contained representatives of the old septs ; for instance, of the four members elected by county Clare, and its borough (Ennis), two were Macnamaras. Many of the members of this

---

* The details above referred to have been collected from the original MS. papers of Mr. J. Macnamara, of Brighton, and the late Col. J. D. Macnamara, of Ayle. See also Frost's " History of Clare," note, p. 416.

† " The Life of John Churchill, Duke of Marlborough," by General Viscount Wolseley, K.P., vol. ii. p. 96.

Parliament, who then possessed the power to legislate for the country, had five-and-twenty years before lost by far the greater part of their estates under Cromwell's Act, and one of the first measures brought before the Dublin Parliament was the repeal of the Act of Settlement, which legalised the confiscations made by Cromwell and his officers.

Under Act 4, of James II.'s Parliament, it was settled that all persons entitled to any lands or whose ancestors possessed such lands on the 2nd October 1641, shall and may take action for recovering the same. Commissioners were appointed to determine the claims, and have power to award injunctions for putting such persons as shall appear to them to have established their claims in possession of such lands. The former proprietors were thus to be restored to their ancestral property; and "honest purchasers of lands under the Acts of Settlements" were to be compensated for the loss of their lands, from the lands held by persons in rebellion against their lawful Sovereign (James II.) since the 1st of August 1688; the commissioners were to allot and distribute such reprisals. If a purchaser had obtained lands in the province of Connaught, including county Clare,* other lands were to be provided from the estates of forfeited lands or otherwise. Tenants were not to be disturbed in their holdings by the change in the owners of their lands, unless in the case of the mansion-house of the old proprietor or his heirs and the demesne belonging thereto. The blot in this Act was that no provision was made for the families of these adventurers, who having been for twenty-five or thirty years in possession, and residing on the estates they had purchased, had rights to citizenship.

Another Act of this Parliament was "The Act of Attainder," which, as Mr. Davis observes, must be condemned; most of the persons attainted, and they formed a long list, were in arms against James II. Nevertheless, this Bill was on all fours with an Act introduced into the English House of Commons on the 10th June 1689, "to attaint of high treason certain persons who are now in Irelend or any other parts beyond the seas, adhering to their Majesties enemies, and shall not return into England by a certain day." The Bill introduced into the Dublin Parliament stated that the rebellion had broken out in the north of Ireland to dethrone their legitimate king, and bring in the Prince of Orange, and that full pardon having been offered and refused by the insurgents, they were attainted of high treason, and to suffer its penalties unless before the 10th August they came and stood their trial; their number amounted to 1270 individuals. By a second clause of this Bill, attainted persons who absented themselves from Ireland before or since the 5th November 1688, were to have all their goods and property confiscated.

* Connaught and Clare, as we know, had by Cromwell been set apart for Roman Catholic landowners from other parts of Ireland, who were *innocent*, that is, who had not joined the Confederate army.

Act 12 was an act for liberty of conscience and the representing of all acts inconsistent with the same.   Acts 13 and 15 provided payment of tithes by Protestants to the Protestant Church, and by Catholics to the Catholic Church. But it is beyond my purpose to enumerate the thirty and more important Acts which were passed by the Irish Parliament of 1789–90.

There is one Act, however, we must notice, and that is Act III., in which it is laid down that—

Ireland is and hath been always a distinct kingdom from that of His Majesty's Realm of England, always governed by his Majesty and his predecessors, according to the ancient customs, laws and statutes thereof.   No act passed in any Parliament held in England were ever binding in Ireland, excepting such of them as by Act of Parliament passed in this kingdom were made into laws in Ireland.

It is necessary to bear this Act in mind, for it was the first expression of the opinion of the landowners of Ireland on this important question : influenced no doubt by Molyneux, who was about this time an active Dublin politician.   The more carefully we study the Acts passed by James in the Dublin Parliament of 1689, the clearer it becomes that its members, most of them Roman Catholics and the direct descendants of the old landowners of Ireland, worked loyally, and strove to secure the rights of property and to do justice to all classes of society.   The gentlemen comprising this Parliament were, however, no mere party politicians ; many of them were officers in local regiments, such as Colonel J. Macnamara, who subsequently raised and commanded the Clare (Yellow) Dragoons.

It was necessary for Parliament to secure ways and means by which King James might be enabled to support his position, and for this purpose it was determined that a land tax should be imposed ; and a Bill was accordingly brought into the Irish landlord's Parliament ; in the preamble of this Bill it was stated that, " as it would be hard on tenants to bear any proportion of this tax, considering that it is difficult for them to pay rent," it was therefore enacted that in all cases where a tenant paid a full value for his lands, that he should be allowed to retain from his rent the whole amount of the tax charged on his holding.   If, however, the tenant paid half, or less than half, the value of the land which he held, then, and then only, was he to be called upon to pay one-half of the tax, so that the tenant in all rack-rented farms, or in fact in any holding in which he paid anything above the half value of the land in rent, was not to be called upon to pay any land-tax.   It was hardly possible to have devised better terms for tenants than those enacted by the Irish Parliament of 1689.   Three of the Macnamaras were appointed assessors under this Act for their county.   The members of the sept had

Q

been broken and brought very low in the world, as compared with their position up to 1654 ; but, though poor, their countrymen still respected and trusted them as their representatives in Parliament, and to act without appeal as land commissioners for their county.   King James appointed Florence Macnamara Deputy-Lieutenant of co. Clare, and John Macnamara of Cratloe, High Sheriff for the year 1689.*

A regiment of horse was raised, and also a regiment of infantry in Clare, for service under James II.   Among the list of cavalry officers we find the names Colonel J. Macnamara (commanding), also Captain Fineen and a second John Macnamara.   In the infantry were the names of Captains Donogh, and Teigie, and also Lieutenants John and Daniel Macnamara.   These regiments were enlisted during the spring of 1689, and in July of the same year they were called upon to take the field and fight against Dutch and English soldiers, who had served in military operations on the Continent.   Neither officers nor men of the Irish levies had the slightest knowledge of drill or the use of firearms ; they were raw recruits drawn from agricultural pursuits, and utterly unfit to fight on equal terms with veteran soldiers.   But such as they were, the Clare, among other levies, were directed in July 1689 to join Lord Mountcashel's troops, and attempt to drive the English out of the north of Ireland.   On July 30, a portion of these raw levies arrived within ten miles of Enniskillen, the force in that town being under the command of Colonel Wolseley, who sent Colonel Berry with a detachment of troops to watch the movements of the Irish army.   Colonel Berry came unexpectedly on a large body of Irish Dragoons and infantry, he retired therefore towards a place called Lismarkea, sending off an express to Wolseley for reinforcements.   Berry's road led him across a narrow causeway over a bog, at the further side of which was a quantity of thick brushwood ; here he drew up his forces, covering his men in the bushes to await the approach of the enemy, who were under the command of Colonel Hamilton.   As the Irish advanced over the narrow causeway Hamilton and his second in command were shot down by Berry's men, and as a number of the Irish fell they retreated from their position and fell back on the advance guard of their army ; this movement on the part of the Irish was effected about nine o'clock in the morning.   At eleven A.M. Colonel Wolseley arrived on the scene accompanied by a considerable force of cavalry and infantry.   The Irish took up a strong position on the side of steep wooded hills, through which the road passed to Newtown Butler, in front of them was a bog crossed by a causeway which was defended by the artillery of the Irish

* Frost's " History of Clare," p. 568.

army. Colonel Wolseley divided his troops into three bodies, one being ordered to pass over the causeway, and the others to the right and left were to make their way across the bog ; this movement was effected with all the dash and steadiness of well-trained English troops in face of the enemy's fire. The Irish cannon were captured, the commander of their cavalry and several other officers were killed, and the Irish Dragoons then turned their horses homewards and galloped off the field of battle ; the infantry followed their example, but were pursued by the English horse, and the greater number of them were cut to pieces or drowned in attempting to cross a lake.*

In the following year we again hear of the Clare Dragoons, at the Battle of the Boyne. It is not easy to follow this action, or to make out its details clearly ; of one thing we may be certain, and that is, that William of Orange's force was thirty-six thousand strong, those of the combined Irish and French troops numbered only twenty-six thousand, of these six thousand were Frenchmen.† But what is more important, the English army included the pick of William's veterans, whereas, with the exception of the French, the Irish army was constituted of troops such as those before referred to. It is beyond my province to attempt at length to describe the details of the Battle of the Boyne, in which not a few of the Macnamaras were engaged, and Teigie, for one, seems to have distinguished himself.

On the 1st of July, 1690, the Prince of Orange at daybreak detached a strong force, consisting of the right wing of his army, to cross the Boyne some miles above the position taken up by James II.'s army, and if possible by a flank movement to occupy the king's left wing, and also the road to Dublin. O'Neil's cavalry did good work on the part of the Irish, and for some time he prevented the English troops from crossing the river ; but O'Neil ultimately fell back and retired towards the main body of the Irish army. They were followed by the English, who, after advancing over very rough ground, found themselves brought to a stand by a bog which intervened between them and the left wing of the Irish. O'Neil's troops crossed the bog over a narrow passage, but it was impossible for the English to follow in the face of a strong opposing force. It would appear that James II. was to some extent ignorant of the ground to the left of his position, and he put himself, therefore, at the head of his French troops to oppose the advancing right wing of

* Rev. A. Hamilton : "The True Relation of the Action of Inniskilling men," published 1699 ; also "Memoirs of James, Duke of Berwick," written by himself, vol. i. p. 62.

† General Viscount Wolseley's "Life of the Duke of Marlborough," vol. ii. p. 136.

the English, which, as above stated had already crossed the Boyne some distance above the position occupied by the centre and left wing of the Prince of Orange's army. James II. having, like the English, arrived at the confines of the bog I have referred to, also came to a halt. After a time it would seem that the commanding officer of the English troops thought, as he could not advance, he had better retire, and this movement had an important bearing on the Battle of the Boyne; for James imagined, when he saw his opponents leaving their position on the other side of the bog, that they intended to occupy the road to Dublin, and so cut off his retreat on that city, and this he dreaded extremely.

While William's right wing and James' left were watching one another hard fighting had been going on between the centres, and right wings of the English and Irish armies. The old and famous soldier, Duke of Schomberg, commanded William's centre, and after a desperate fight managed to effect a landing on the opposite bank of the Boyne, in the face of the Irish centre. No sooner, however, had the Duke advanced from the river than his men were repeatedly charged by the Irish cavalry: the fighting between them and the Dutch infantry was very severe; we are told the Irish charged down on the English and Dutch no less than eleven times. Duke Schomberg was killed, and his men at length fell back and commenced to recross the river. In the meantime William had well-nigh lost his life while fording the Boyne at the head of the left wing of his army. After hard fighting he succeeded in forcing back the Irish right; they retired in perfect order; and had they and the centre at this critical moment of the battle been supported by King James with his French allies, the English must have been driven across the Boyne. In place of this, James, fearing that his communication with Dublin was imperilled, marched from the field of battle to Dublin. The Irish were directed to follow and cover the king's retreat; and this they did with unbroken ranks. But victory remained with the English, and James II. fled from Ireland a few days after the battle. In a memorandum, written subsequently to his arrival in France, the king stated that Lord Dungan, commanding the dragoons, was killed in one of the charges of cavalry at the Battle of the Boyne, after which this regiment could not again be brought to the charge; and he adds, " Clare's did not do much better." The king, however, describes "the right wing of horse and the Dragoons" advancing with undaunted bravery, and charging William's centre again and again, " evincing a gallantry and determination which would have done honour to the finest cavalry in Europe." And this they subsequently proved themselves to be, for when they had passed over to the service of France they covered themselves with glory in many a hard-fought battle. Lauzun, describing the Irish soldiers two months after the Battle of the Boyne, states that they were the finest to be seen anywhere.*

Mr. Standish H. O'Grady has kindly brought to my notice an address, written in Gaelic soon after the Battle of the Boyne, by Andrew Mac-Curtin, to Teigie Macnamara (see p. 238).† Mr. O'Grady has not only given me a translation of this address but also leave to publish it ; he is of opinion that the Epilogue contains a key to the name of Teigie's opponent at the Battle of the Boyne, which was no doubt plain enough to contemporaries. The word rendered " relic," Mr. O'Grady states, means also " an oath " (such being commonly sworn on some relic); also it signifies " a diadem " or " coronet." Evidently a man of mark therefore is referred to but not named by MacCurtin in the following address :

" (1) Triumphant, O Teigie, hath thine expedition been ; an easy task it is to speak of thy people : such their qualities, their excellence, their action, their violence [exercised] to protect the army. (2) [In thy house] many a feast, wine and music, habitually are under way with accomplished men; much old folk, many a simpleton pauper, at one time and another quietly slip into thy mansion. (3) Thou hast the hardihood of clan-Cas : not feeble thy performance in slaughter's execution ; wisdom in copious measure thou hast, and art a hospitaller that never basely turned back [from his function]. (4) What time the two kings were about to engage, thou wert a witness: numerous as were thy foemen, thine exploit at the Boyne was notorious. (5) . . . . [this quatrain wanting in MS.] (6) Till hand to hand by thee he fell in the mid-carnage ('twas sternly done); nor weariness nor slackness assailed thee, but amidst a host thou dealtedst death to him. (7) On Thomond's expanse again, thou wert the one to unremittingly check treachery; the rightful camp thou didst relieve, and hinder the pursuit . . . . (8) Alas that every mettled warrior [that every stout fellow] of the crew was not as he; [had they been so, then] neither Calvin nor his [brood] this day had been in the place of God's popula-

* " Lauzun's Letter of 3/9/1690 to Louvois " (Ranke), vol. vi. p. 143.

† MacCurtin was an Irish poet and was born in the parish of Kilmorry, co. Clare; he died in the year 1749. He belonged to the famous literary clan bearing his name, and who lived in and wrote of Thomond. He was the hereditary ollamh to the O'Briens, and a great authority on the pedigrees of the families of Munster ("Dictionary of National Biography," article signed by Norman Moore, M.D.).

tions. (9) [The deed was done on] the second day of July in that
year (no perishing indication 'tis) one thousand six hundred and bare
ninety—that without silence [*i.e.* I proclaim aloud] was Christ's age.

" EPILOGUE.

"Many as are [the other] good points to be told of Ranna's hero
[there is this too : that], in his valour no debility is discovered, and that
'tis coupled with abundant sapience ; moreover, that the relic which for
a season in Ireland the English had maintained in power, by his arm's
vigour and his members' lustiness he slew."

In December 1689 a part of the Yellow Dragoons were sent into
Clare to recruit, and Sir J. Butler, writing to the Sheriff of the county
regarding the return of the regiment, stated, that to avoid a repetition of
the complaints formerly made against the troopers, he directs Sir D.
O'Brien to take notice that " dragoons cannot hope to keep their horses
in proper condition on hay alone. The men were to be allowed to
purchase their own beef, mutton, and corn which the landlords must see
they are supplied with at a reasonable rate." * From this it would seem
that the previously alleged misconduct of the troopers arose from the
difficulty they had experienced in procuring proper food, and shelter for
themselves and their horses. In the following April Colonel J. Macnamara was employed under Lord Inchiquin to draw up a list of those
landowners in Clare who could supply horses for the Government ; and
he was directed to make use of his dragoons to seize such persons as
refused to comply with this order.

We must pass over the battle of Aughrim and the details of the second
siege of Limerick. Suffice it to remark that Teigie Macnamara (of Rathfolan), after the Battle of the Boyne raised a troop of his own and with
it garrisoned Clare Castle, which he held for King James until the capitulation of Limerick, under the provisions of which it appears that Teigie
retained possession of a portion of the Rathfolan estates.

After the surrender of Limerick a third confiscation of Irish property
took place. William had to serve his friends and followers, and he did
so as his predecessors had done, by seizing such Irish lands as he could
lay hands upon ; among these were Lord Clare's estates, to the extent
of some 86,000 acres, which William gave to his friend, Joost Van
Kepple, Earl of Albemarle. Lord Clare made his will in October 1690,
and among other bequests we find the following : " I leave to my brother
Colonel John Macnamara, two mares of the Neapolitan breed, and

---

* " Diocese of Killaloe," by Canon Dwyer, p. 377.

Whitefoot. I order that the widow of Daniel Macnamara shall be paid of my own cattle in as many as shall appear she had sorrowfully lost by me or mine ";* he directed Thomas Macnamara to "pay twenty pounds a piece to the friars of Quin and Limerick, and fifty pounds to the friars of Ennis." † His eldest son, Colonel Daniel O'Brien, succeeded to the title; but with his father ended the connection of the "Clare O'Briens," as they were called, with their native country, the family passed over to the Continent and settled in France. Many other families in Clare besides the O'Briens suffered for their loyalty to the man whom they regarded as their legitimate monarch; and after the surrender of Limerick they found themselves despoiled of everything, with no prospect before them but exile or poverty. In 1700 when the Court of Claims sat in Dublin to hear petitions from persons claiming exemption from attainder,

* Frost's "History of Clare," p. 609.

† The following note from the "Journal of the Royal Society of Antiquaries of Ireland" is from the pen of Mr. T. J. Westropp:

"*The Last Friars of Quin, co. Clare.*—Quin is one of the few Irish mediæval fraternities which prolonged its existence to the present century. Despite the execution of so many of its leading monks in 1651-2, the community had reassembled by the reign of Charles II. We find an excommunication, 7th April, 1670, in the names of Eugenius Callinan and Bonaventura Bruodin, guardians of Meelick and Ennis, against four friars who had rebelled against Moriartagh Ogrypha and Thady Broudin, guardians of Quin and Limerick priories (MSS., T.C.D., F. 4, 14), and later on, 18th November, 1689, Thady O'Brien, of Coolreagh, near Scariff, leaves by his will (now at Coolreagh), 'unto Father Daniel Macnamara, towards praying for the salvation of my soul, 5 shillings; to the friars of the Abbey of Quin 5 shillings'; and Daniel, Viscount Clare 20th October, 1690, bequeaths '£20 to the friars of Quin.'

"The burning of the Abbey by Colonel George Stamer, and his brother Henry, dispersed the monks, but at the time of Lady Chatterton's tour one of them still meditated, prayed, and wrote 'beautiful lines' to Lady O'Brien in the desolate cloister. I have known two persons who remembered the last monk, whose tombstone, a plain slab of limestone, in the east cloister walk, bears this inscription:

"'HERE LIES THE BODY OF THE | REV. JOHN HOGAN OF DRIM | WHO DEPARTED THIS LIFE A.D. 1820 | AGED 80 YEARS, THE LAST OF THE FRANCISCAN | FRIARS WHO HAD THEIR RESIDENTS (*sic*) | AT DRIM THE PLACE OF THEIR REFUGE | WHEN DRIVEN FROM THE ABBEY OF | QUIN. HE WAS SUPPORTED BY THE | PIOUS DONATIONS OF THE FAITHFUL | AND SERVED AS AN AUXILIARY TO HIS | NEIGHBOURING PARISH PRIESTS | IN THE VINEYARD OF THE LORD. HE | KNEW HOW TO ABOUND AND HOW TO SUFFER | WANT AS THE LORD WAS PLEASED TO | SEND. HE DIED IN HOLY POVERTY | RESPECTED FOR HIS STRICTNESS IN RELIGIOUS DISCIPLING (*sic*) | AND VENERATED | BY ALL. 'QUI SEMINAT IN LACHRYMIS EXULTATIONE METET.' | REQUIESCAT IN PACE, AMEN.'

"THOMAS J. WESTROPP,
"*Hon. Local Secretary, Royal Irish Society of
Antiquaries, North Clare.*"

a number of petitions were sent in from families who had lived for many generations in Clare, and among them several of the Macnamaras. Mr. Frost has given an abstract of these petitions in his history of Clare (page 570 to 602). In but few cases was the decision of the court favourable to the petitioners, and the court having soon dissolved, the lands confiscated from James's partisans were put up for sale at Chester House, Dublin, in the year 1703. All hope of restoration to their property having thus been destroyed most of the gentlemen concerned left Ireland, and struggled to eke out a miserable existence in the army and navy of foreign countries. Those who remained at home mostly sunk into the condition of peasants, and for a hundred years, under the baneful operation of the penal laws led a life of slavery and degradation.*

Under the treaty of Limerick it was agreed that the Irish troops who had fought for James II. were to be allowed to leave their country at the Government expense. The greater number of the men of the Clare Brigade assembled at the cavalry camp under the walls of Quin Abbey, and from thence marched to Limerick and embarked for France, among their officers were eight of the Macnamara family, who, together with their followers, entered the French service. The residue of St. Ruth's unfortunate army were shipped to France (1691). In all it is computed that some 19,000 splendid Irish soldiers under the gallant Sarsfield embarked at Cork.† The history of the Clare Brigade has yet to be written, and a most interesting one it would be, not only from a military but also from a social and political point of view. In the last battle the Brigade fought under the orders of Lord Clare, the French army in Piedmont was under the command of Catinat, who, we are told, at the battle of Marsaglia (October 1693), " to support and animate his troops by the example of the Irish soldiers, placed in the right wing of the first line the King's and Queen's Irish Dragoons, numbering some 1400 men. Clare's infantry, three battalions strong amounting to 2000 men were placed to the left of the line, and the Limerick regiment, 2800 strong, in the centre. Prince Eugene attacked and routed three of the French regiments posted in the first line. These giving way, their place was taken by Clare's three battalions, with two of the French from the second line, who charged the Germans with such fury that they in their turn were obliged to fall back. The battle was thus restored on the left wing, and the Irish dragoons being equally successful on the right, the day seemed lost to the Allies, when Eugene led up his centre,

* Frost's " History of Clare," p. 603.
† " Life of the Duke of Marlborough," by Viscount Wolseley," vol. ii. p. 239.

and with such effect as to have regained what had been lost on the wings. As this critical moment Wauchope, who commanded the Irish regiments of the centre (the Queen's and Limerick), led up his men to the charge. Three times he charged the allied centre without breaking it, but Eugene, after four hours' fighting, led his men off the field of battle, leaving the victory to the French. Among those killed was Daniel, fourth Lord Clare." * At the battle of Fontenoy again the Irish Brigade under Lally retrieved, by their coolness and courage at a very critical moment of the battle, what appeared to have been certain disaster to the French army.† In addition to the members of our sept who entered the French army with the Clare Brigade others passed over to the Continent and took service under the King of France, one of them afterwards became Vice-Admiral Macnamara in the French navy; he was a very distinguished officer and a great grandson of Sioda Macnamara, of Henry VIII.'s time (page 150); he belonged, therefore, to that branch of the family at present represented by John, and his brother Arthur Macnamara. We learn something of the history of the Macnamaras, who took service under the King of France, from the following letter patent of the title of Count in the kingdom of France, granted to Henry P. Macnamara, Captain of the King's ships, and Knight of the Order of St. Louis:

Louis, by the grace of God, King of France and of Navarre, to all salutation. Whereas it is right that a Sovereign should recognise the devotion and attachment of such of his subjects who unite to illustrious signal services, it shows his greatness to deck them with honours due to their highness of birth. Being informed of the distinction with which the late John Macnamara, Vice-Admiral of our kingdom, Commander and Grand Knight of our Order of St. Louis, and Commander of our port of Rochfort, as well as his brother Claud Matthew Macnamara, captain in our navy and Chevalier of our military order of St. Louis, have served in the navy and army of our most honourable grandfather, and being ourselves aware of the services equally distinguished which our well-beloved Henry Pantaleon Macnamara, captain of our fleet, and Knight of our military order of St. Louis, son of the said Claud Matthew, and nephew of the said John Macnamara, has rendered for a length of time, and yet continues to render to us great service; knowing also their attachment, and that of their ancestors to the Roman Catholic and Apostolic religion, on account whereof the House of Macnamara has ever the greatest trials. This house descends from Cassin, the second son of Cas, King of Limerick and of Thomond, the year of Jesus Christ, 434. It has had for appanage a territory or kingdom of Thomond, called the Principality of Hy-Cassin, from Cassin, its chief. This principality has been since called the Principality of Clann-Cullin, after *Coilean*, a descendant of Cassin.

---

* J. D'Alton's " Illustrations, Historical and Genealogical, of King James's Irish Army," p. 154.

† "Historical Memoir of the O'Briens," by J. O'Donoghue, p. 347–354.

Mac-Con Macnamara, prince of Clann-Cullin, constructed and founded, about the beginning of the fifteenth century, the noble and magnificent monastery of Cunnyeh (Quin), for the Observantine Brethren, and the Bull of Eugene IV. is seen bearing upon this point, under the year 1433. *" Dilecto filie nobito viro. Mac-Con-Macnamara Duci de Clann-Cullyan, &c. &c.*, i.e., to " His beloved son, to the noble man, Mac-con-Macnamara, Prince of Clann-Culin, &c. &c." This house hath never ceased to rule the Principality of Clann-Culin up to the middle of the sixteenth century, a time in which finding itself aggraved by the continuous incursions of the supporters of the English Reformation, and much enfeebled by the betrayal of its parent, the chief of the House of O'Brien to the common cause, in submitting himself as well as his estates to Henry VIII., and accepting from this Sovereign the title of Count of Thomond, it judged it prudent to submit likewise, as well as its principality, to Queen Elizabeth, and to receive from this princesss the Investiture thereof, with this difference, that it had rather, without altering its illustrious character, to hand down to its posterity the title of chief of this ancient house, than to receive it anew from the English Court, which up to that time was to it a stranger. At all times this illustrious house has made sacrifice of itself for the support of religion, and for the maintenance of the power to which it hath been attached, many of whose members have lost their life and their property in the service of Charles I., decapitated in 1649, for whom they raised two regiments at their expense. They made the same efforts for James II., and passed with him into France, where James III. gave them an authentic testimony of their services, and the antiquity and nobility of their birth, by a patent dated at St. Germain en Laye, the 7th of April, 1704. They have exhibited in our regards the same sentiments of honour and love for us personally; in a word, ever since that period of time, they have served us with the same zeal and distinction. Wishing therefore to give on all occasions the testimony of our satisfaction of the signal services which the brave Irish nobility has rendered to the kings who preceded us, and which it still continues to render to ourselves, we have resolved to adorn our well-beloved, the said Henry Pantaleon Macnamara, or Macnemara, with the title of Count of our kingdom, reversible for ever to the chief of the branch of this house, established in our said kingdom, as a distinctive mark due to his high nobility. For this purpose, &c.*

Henry P. Macnamara's eldest brother John was one of King Louis' pages from 1752 to 1754, and was then made " Page Dauphin," whence he passed into the French Navy, and was killed on board the *Theseus* in November 1758. His second brother, Claud, was also an officer in the French navy, and was killed in action on the 8th of September 1758.

We must, however, return to the Treaty of Limerick, for it had an important bearing on the history of the remaining families of our sept in Clare, and in fact on a large majority of the inhabitants of Ireland. Under this treaty, which was ratified, and signed by the Lords Justices of Ireland, on the part of their Majesties William and Mary, it was

* Authenticated copies of these documents are among Mr. John Macnamara's MS. collection of family papers; also in MS. Royal Irish Academy, 24 c. 20.

stipulated that Roman Catholics should enjoy such privileges in the exercise of their religion as they possessed in the reign of Charles II., and their Majesties undertook to summon a Parliament to endeavour to procure the Catholics of Ireland such further security as should preserve them from disturbance on account of their religion. The oath to be administered to Catholics was to be that of allegiance only, and no other oath; but no sooner had King William died than a series of measures, called the Irish Penal Code, were enacted, placing the Roman Catholics in Ireland under stringent coercive laws.

Mr. W. E. H. Lecky has classed their penal enactments under three heads :*

1. Those which were intended to deprive Catholics of all the advantages of civil life.

2. Those which were intended to reduce them to a state of brutal ignorance.

3. Measures taken to destroy the domestic happiness of Irish Catholics.

Under the first of these heads it was decreed that no Roman Catholic should be allowed to sit in Parliament; they were deprived of elective suffrage; they were not allowed to become magistrates, or members of the bench or of the bar; to enter the army, navy, or any of the Government services. They were not allowed to be employed as constables or as gamekeepers; in fact to possess guns or other such weapons, and were liable at any time to have their houses searched. No Roman Catholic might possess a horse worth more than £5, and any Protestant offering him that sum might take possession of his neighbour's steed.

Under the second set of enactments it was ordered that Irish Roman Catholics were to be excluded from the ministry; they were not to be permitted to be the guardians of a child, keep a school, or act as schoolmasters; they were prevented under heavy fine and penalty from sending their sons abroad to be educated.

Under the last set of enactments of the Penal Code, Roman Catholics were prevented from inheriting or buying any land; if they held land in mortgage for more than thirty years, on an information being given to that effect by a Protestant to the prescribed authority, the Roman Catholic was doomed to hand such land over to the informer. Many other enactments of this nature were ordered, setting children against their parents, and neighbour against neighbour. But sufficient has been cited to demonstrate what fearful penalties were imposed in the reign of Queen

* "History of Ireland in the Eighteenth Century," vol. i. p. 147; also A. Young's "Tour in Ireland," vol. ii. p. 271.

Anne on at least three-fourths of the population of Ireland, for this was about the proportion of Roman Catholics to Protestants in that country.

Beyond all this the law of banishment against Roman Catholic priests still continued, and a vigorous effort was made to educate a large proportion of the children of Roman Catholics in the doctrines of the Protestant faith.　Schools were established by Protestant clergymen with the object, it was alleged, of " rescuing the souls of thousands of the poor children from the dangers of Papist superstition."　These children were to be educated as Protestants, and were mostly taken from the homes of half-starving parents ; after being thus removed the children were prevented from communicating with their parents, and were brought up as Protestants ; a law was passed depriving Roman Catholic parents of the control of such of their children as had been brought into these chartered schools ; the Government expended £112,200 on this venture, which it is needless to say failed, and did a vast deal to raise bitter feelings in the minds of the poorer classes in Ireland against their rulers.*
Beyond this sum paid to the chartered schools, A. Young informs us that the amount given to Protestant bishops out of the ecclesiastical revenues of Ireland amounted to £74,000 per annum, and no less than £150,000 a year derived from the ancient endowments of the country was given to the clergy of a very small minority of the inhabitants of Ireland.†

As before explained, the Roman Catholic members of our sept, from the time of signing the agreement with Henry VIII., had remained loyal subjects, they had supported Charles I. and James II. as their lawful Sovereigns, and during William's reign no cause for provocation or for uneasiness was given to the Crown either by the Catholics of Clare or any other part of Ireland.　Subsequently, in Queen Anne's reign, and that of the first two Georges, the Roman Catholics of Ireland were not only loyal subjects, but in 1715 the English Government sent troops raised in Ireland to quell rebellion in Scotland.‡　And so again in 1722, and in 1747, England called to her aid Irish soldiers ; the penal laws therefore enacted against the Catholics of Ireland cannot be said to have been the result of disloyal or treasonable action on their part.

Mr. Lecky is of opinion that " the penal code as it was actually carried out, was imposed much less by fanaticism than by rapacity, and was directed less against the Catholic religion than against the property and industry of its professors."§ This was also the opinion of A. Young, who

* Sterne's " On the Chartered Schools of Ireland."
† Young's " Tour in Ireland," vol. ii. p. 112.
‡ " Memoirs of the Duke of Berwick."
§ Lecky's " History of Ireland in the Eighteenth Century," vol. i. p. 152.

was well acquainted with the Irish of the last century, he observes : " I have conversed on the subject with the most distinguished characters in the kingdom, and I cannot after all but declare that the scope, purpose, and aim of the laws of discovery as executed, are not against the Catholic religion, which increases under them, but against the industry and property of whoever professes that religion." *

In spite of their political, religious, and social disabilities, it is a remarkable fact that the population of Ireland increased from eight hundred and fifty thousand people in 1652 to a million in 1672, and that immediately before passing the Acts of 1664 (by the English House of Commons, and not by the Irish Parliament †), by which the export of cattle and of agricultural produce was prohibited, the revenues of the country had increased threefold. The walled towns were growing in size, the woollen manufactories were becoming famous, and signs of prosperity were visible in every direction.‡ It seemed natural that, in these circumstances, England would have been disposed to have given Ireland encouragement, and even help ; but we find the reverse was the case, and Sir Richard Davenant, a well-known financial authority of the eighteenth century, gives us the reasons why Englishmen should, in his opinion, insist upon a crushing export duty being levied on Irish cattle and all agricultural produce. Sir Richard argues that because living and labour were cheaper in Ireland than in England, and as the Irish had an abundance of cattle, they could afford to send stock over to England and undersell the farmers of that country. Rents in England had already begun to fall in value, and so this authority insisted on the necessity of preventing Irish cattle being sent either to England or to any of her dependencies in America or elsewhere ; for the same reason, in subsequent Acts, Irish bacon, butter, cheese, and other articles of consumption were practically prevented from being sent out of Ireland.§ At the time these Acts were passed, Irishmen had no possible means of obtaining a living unless by their cattle. This source of income having been cut off, they took to breeding sheep, so as to increase the production of wool. Thousands of Irishmen were employed in various branches of this trade, and their industry was rewarded, for we find in 1702 the balance of Ireland's revenue amounted to no less than £419,442. This bright ray of prosperity was destined, however, to be

---

* " A Tour in Ireland," by A. Young, vol. ii. p. 66.
† " The Case of Ireland," by W. Molyneux, p. 73 (edited by the Very Rev. Canon O'Hanlon).
‡ " Life of Sir W. Petty," by Lord E. Fitzmaurice, p. 239 ; also p. 140.
§ Hely Hutchinson : "Commercial Restraints of Ireland," p. 161.

extinguished, for reasons precisely similar to those which had ruined the cattle trade of the country. English noblemen, and merchants combined to urge on the King and Parliament the damage they were suffering from the importation of better and cheaper wool from Ireland than English farmers could produce. And so, in 1703, prohibitive taxes were placed by the English House of Commons * on Irish wool, and these taxes extended to the export of wool, not only to England, but to all her dependencies, and also to Flanders and other parts of the Continent.†

At the time these measures were passed against Irish trade, Englishmen were drawing annually no less than £732,000 in rents from that country, every penny of which would, under the old order of things, have been spent in Ireland. Beyond this, the Duke of Bedford estimated that in the year 1759 Ireland paid every year £85,591 to the Civil Pension List, most of this being granted to Court favourites and dependants of the first three Georges.‡ It is true that, six years after passing the various Acts referred to, and when the Government found that a vast number of the Irish people were in a starving condition, an effort was made to introduce the cultivation of flax into the country, the linen trade at the time being of no commercial value to England. The growth of flax, however, was a work of time, and was only suited to certain districts of Ireland.§

There would, therefore, seem to have been sufficient grounds for the indictment laid by Mr. Lecky, Arthur Young, and other authorities to the effect that the misery and suffering of the Irish in the latter part of the seventeenth, and first half of the eighteenth century was due to the hard, and selfish policy imposed by Englishmen on Ireland. Apparently without the slightest compunction the English commercial classes combined to destroy the trade of Ireland because it lowered their own profits. In the same way, and for similar reasons, the lands and woods of Ireland had been confiscated because they were of value to Englishmen, and the Irish were unable to resist the dominant race.

It may be well here to refer to the effects of this wrong on the inhabitants of Ireland, and first with reference to the poorer classes of landholders, or "cotters," as they were called, a specific and almost unique product of Irish industrial life.|| Throughout Clare, and in the

* This Act was not passed by the Irish Parliament, but by the English House of Commons ("The Cause of Ireland," p. 74).
† Hely Hutchinson: "Commercial Relations of Ireland," p. 94.
‡ Young's "Tour in Ireland," vol. ii. pp. 117, 273; note, p. 114.
§ Hely Hutchinson : "Commercial Relations of Ireland," p. 94.
|| Professor Cairnes' "Political Essays."

greater part of Connaught and Munster, the poorer classes were, to a man, Roman Catholics, and consequently under the penal code, and so without any educational advantages, and unable, unless by stealth, to engage in the offices of their religion. As a rule, the cotters possessed a pig or two, it may be a cow and some poultry; otherwise they had no property of any kind, and they depended entirely for subsistence upon what they could grow on the few acres of land which they rented. Eviction from this land in too many cases meant starvation, so that the cotter clung to his holding, and often paid a rent far beyond its value for the simple reason that he was helpless in the matter, and was, from his circumstances, compelled to give whatever rent was asked. The cotter got no agreement or lease; he was a tenant at will, and, as a rule, the landlord gave his land to the tenant who promised to pay him the highest rent. As Professor Cairnes observes, these cotters got no help from their landlords; they had to construct their own huts, half-naked, half-starved, utterly destitute, and ground to the dust by three great burdens: rack-rent paid, not to the landlord, but to the middle-man; tithes paid to the clergy, often absentees of a church to which the cotter did not belong; and lastly, dues paid to their own priests.

Bishop Nicholson, who seems to have been a hard, selfish Englishman, and not disposed, therefore, to spare much sympathy on the Irish, writes of the cotters as he saw them in the year 1728; he observes: "I never beheld, even in Picardy, Westphalia, or Scotland, such dismal marks of hunger and want as appeared among the poor of Ireland." The bishop states that one of his horses died on the road to Tuam; the carcase was immediately surrounded "by a number of poor Irish cotters, struggling desperately to obtain a morsel of flesh for themselves and their children." All this, be it remembered, occurred before the years of actual famine in Ireland 1729–40, and '44. Nicholson dilates on the evils springing from the practice of the middleman, and from rack-rent; he dwells on the starved, naked cotters in their mud cabins, unfit even for a pig to dwell in, much less a human being; but there the matter ends, they were Roman Catholics, and Irish men and women. Arthur Young states that the cotter "spoke a language that is despised, they professed a religion which was abhorred, and being disarmed, find themselves in many cases slaves even in the bosom of written liberty. The cotter is punished with the cane or horsewhip with perfect security, a poor man would in Ireland have his bones broken if he offered to lift his hand in his own defence."* Can we wonder at people in these conditions grow-ing deceitful or untruthful? Young was an Englishman who had visited

* See also Hely Hutchinson : " Commercial Relations of Ireland."

every part of the Continent, and has left us one of the most valuable
works on Ireland ever written.

The absentee English landlord necessitated the introduction into
Ireland of what are called middlemen, a class of individuals who are
described by a writer of the period as "a band of tyrants who were
formerly unknown in Ireland, and consists of a multitude of agents to
absentee landlords ; they take farms, and squeeze out a forced kind of
profit from the land by re-letting their holdings in small parcels to
cotters."* Poor as the tenants were, the middleman demanded from
them personal service of a far more grinding nature than that enacted by
the Irish landowners in days gone by.

Arthur Young found these middlemen not unfrequently the masters
of a pack of miserable hounds, with which they wasted their time and
money ; they were the hardest drinkers in the land, "and were the
most oppressive species of tyrants that ever lent assistance to the
destruction of a country."† They were relentless in collecting the rents
from the tenants to whom they had sub-let holdings ; and in case of
failure to pay had no more compunction in turning the unfortunate
cotter out on the road than they had of expelling a pig from his stye.‡
These were the men who in Clare had largely supplanted the heads
of the various families of Macnamaras and other septs living under a
system such as that referred to previously to 1641. Nor does this
description of the state of things complete the picture, for we must bear
in mind that the rule of these middlemen was exercised over a highly
sensitive people, full of retrospective imagination, and pride of race and
land. Arthur Young states, with truth, that many of these cotters were
the "lineal descendants of great families, once possessed of vast
property, but now in the lowest situation, working as cotters for the
great-great-grandsons of men, many of whom were of no greater account
in England than these poor labourers are at present, on that property
which was once their own." Young continues : "So entire an overthrow
and change of landed possession is, within the period, to be found in
scarcely any country of the world. In Ireland families were so
numerous, and so united in clans that the heirs of an estate are always
known ; and it is a fact, that in most parts of the kingdom the descendants
of the old landowners regularly transmit by testamentary deed, the
memorial of their right to those estates which once belonged to their
families."§

* "Inquiry into Causes of Popular Discontent in Ireland"; also Professor
J. E. Cairnes' "Political Essays."

† A. Young: "Tour in Ireland," vol. ii. p. 27.   ‡ Ibid., p. 59.   § Ibid., p. 59.

Passing from the cotter and middle men we may inquire, what changes had come over the resident landowners of Clare since the introduction of English law and government into that part of Ireland. Cumberland, who visited Ireland early in the eighteenth century, gives us what he states to have been a picture of the Irish gentleman of the period. This individual dwelt not far from the Shannon, in a spacious but dilapidated mansion, " from an early dinner to the hour of rest he never left his chair, nor did the claret ever quit the table. The slaughtered ox was hung up whole, and the hungry servitors supplied themselves with doles of flesh sliced from the carcase." This gentleman of Clare had no books in his house, he cared nothing for conversation, his chief pride was in his game-cocks. In such an establishment furious drunken quarrels often ended in duels.* Mrs. Delany, who visited Clare in 1732, dilates on the extravagant habits of the gentry ; at one residence she describes the house as being little more than a large cabin with spare furniture ; but the proprietor kept a man-cook. Mrs. Delany states she never witnessed such hospitality, and they not only treated her magnificently at the house, but on her departure stored her carriage with baskets crammed with good things for the journey.†

If we turn from the Celts of Clare to the Anglo-Celtic inhabitants of the Pale, we find them to have been a wild set of creatures at the end of the seventeenth century, for instance :

Sir J. Barrington informs us that his great aunt and uncle, Stephen and Elizabeth Fitzgerald, in the year 1690, held possession of the castle of Moret, in Queen's County ; the O'Cahils claimed the property from which they said they had been excluded by Queen Elizabeth, and they proceeded to attack the place, but were driven off by the Fitzgeralds. Stephen, however, went for a walk in his garden the following morning, when he was seized by a party of the O'Cahils and carried off in triumph ; after a time it struck them they might exchange their prisoner for the castle, and so they approached its walls and produced Stephen Fitzgerald, and a flag of truce was sent forward with a message to Elizabeth to the effect that " we have your husband in hault, yee's have yeer castle sure enough. Now we will change, if you please we'll render the squire and you'll render the keep ; and if yees wont do the same, the squire will be throttled before your two eyes in half an hour." To which Aunt Elizabeth replied, without hesitation—mark the words

---

* Cumberland's " Memoirs," vol. i. pp. 258–263. Duelling in those days was not confined to drunken country gentlemen ; for instance, the Lord Chancellor, the Earl of Clare, fought the Master of the Rolls, Curran ; the Chief Justice fought Lord Tyrawly and two others ; the Chancellor of the Exchequer fought H. Grattan ; the Baron of Exchequer, his brother-in-law and two others ; Chief Justice Norbury fought Fitzgerald ; and so on through a long list (Barrington's " Own Times, 1760," vol. ii. p. 4).

† Mrs. Delany's " Correspondence," vol. i. p. 351.

R

of Elizabeth Fitzgerald of Moret castle, they may serve for your own wives: " Flag of truce, indeed ! I won't render my keep, and I'll tell you why, Elizabeth may get another husband, but may never get another castle ; so I'll keep what I have, so be off." The O'Cahils kept their word, and in a short time old Stephen Fitzgerald was dangling in the air.*

Elizabeth subsequently took her only son to the top of the castle to behold his father's body, and made him swear to be revenged on his father's murderers. To make him remember his oath she ordered him there and then to be ducked in the horse-pond. In due time the lad fulfilled his promise and killed four of the O'Cahils.

Sir J. Barrington goes on to give us an extremely graphic description of a combination of the surrounding gentry to carry off his Aunt Elizabeth by main force and marry her to Cromarty O'Moore, who, it seems, drew her name in a raffle. This individual bribed one of Elizabeth's attendants, or rather thought he had done so, and prepared for an attack on her stronghold ; she was, however, too wideawake to be caught, and after a serious fight between her retainers and those of O'Moore, in which about a dozen men were killed, the enemy drew off and left Elizabeth in possession of her domicile, and there she continued to reside until " a very late period in the reign of George I."

Sir J. Barrington relates another story regarding his grandfather, a Mr. French and his wife, of co. Galway, a family whose name appears in our pedigree. This Mr. French was married to one of the Clare O'Briens, and having been frequently annoyed by a certain Mr. D. Bodkin, Mrs. French remarked one night before a large company that " she wished the fellow's ears were cut off ; that might quiet him." At supper Mr. Regan, the old butler, with joy in his eyes presented his lady with a huge snuff box, and on opening it, out fell a pair of human ears. On the lady's exclamation of horror, he exclaimed, " sure my lady, you wished that Dennis Bodkin's ears were cut off : so I told old Gahagan (the gamekeeper), and he took a few boys with him and here are his ears, my lady." Mr. French and his wife were tried at the Galway Assizes, but with his servants were acquitted on the plea that it was all a mistake from beginning to end.†

Barrington's description of an Irish party in his own younger days does one good to read, " a revel such as I never saw before, and shall never see again."‡ It shows us at any rate that we are made of different stuff from our grandfathers.

These people of Ireland, from the lowest to the highest, had indeed degenerated in their habits and customs in the course of half a century. Reference has been made to the regard which Irishmen had for the female sex, but as the following case demonstrates there were exceptions to this rule ; it illustrates also the depraved state into which society among the upper classes in Clare had fallen in the year 1707. It appears that on July 21, one Dame Margaret Macnamara, the widow of the late John Macnamara of Cratloe, petitioned the Parliament sitting in Dublin, to the effect that John O'Brien, aided by a band

---

* Barrington's "Own Times," vol. i. p. 22.

† Sir J. Barrington, Judge of the High Court of Ireland, " Personal Sketches of his own Times," vol. i. p. 46.   ‡ Ibid., p. 71.

of six followers, had attacked her house " in a most violent and notorious manner, and had forced away Margaret her daughter out of her custody." Dame Margaret had failed to regain her child, and petitioned the House to help her. Parliament ordered a Committee of the House to report on the matter, and with praiseworthy celerity they reported after three days' inquiry, that the facts mentioned in Dame Margaret's petition were true, and further that, " John O'Brien had forcibly gotten into his power Margaret Macnamara, and had barbarously treated her and threatened to ravish her if she would not consent to marry him : whereupon he procured John Machlin, a fryer, to marry him to the said Margaret against her consent." *

Another case, though not so directly bearing on our sept in Clare, is of interest as an illustration of the moral ruin which had fallen upon a son of one of the former landowners of the Ui-Caisin. Thomas Macnamara was the youngest boy of Daniel Macnamara of co. Clare.† At an early age Thomas thought "to advance himself by war," and so passed over to the Continent and entered the French army, and was therefore accounted "a rebel to the Crown of England." This youth had not been long in France before he fought several duels, and on one occasion at Fontainbleau, in an encounter of this kind, he killed two officers one after the other ; for this he was obliged to flee from France and take refuge in Flanders. Thomas Macnamara, we are informed, being "a good swordsman fought no less than thirty duels," and was never wounded, " and yet he had not then reached his twenty-first year of age." He had however to leave Flanders for the same reason as that which obliged him to quit France, and he came over to London, where it would seem he found an uncle who was evidently a man in good society, but Thomas fell among bad companions, and with them was concerned in a robbery "on the king's highway." The lad was taken, tried, and condemned to death. It seems, however, that he was such a remarkably handsome, fascinating young fellow, that "ten ladies dressed in white satin, and introduced by two ambassadors," presented a petition to the Queen in favour of Macnamara ; his companions in crime were reprieved but as Thomas was a rebel, no mercy was shown him.

One cannot but feel that Thomas had much of the Macnamara in him, nor can we help pitying an uneducated lad, for he was a Catholic, thrown on his own resources as a French soldier at the early age of eighteen,

* " Journal of the House of Commons of the Kingdom of Ireland for the Year 1707," July 21.

† " A Full Account of the Life of Thos. Macnamara," printed by E. Midwinter, West Smithfield, A.D. 1710.

and that, from no fault of his own, all opportunity for an honourable career either in the public services or professions having been closed to him by the laws of his country.

We have one more reference to make to a member of our sept who lived in the early part of the eighteenth century ; he was born in Clare in the year 1709, and named Ruadh Macnamara ; he was sent to the Continent to be educated for holy orders ; but the lad soon discovered that the Church was not his vocation, and he wandered from his seminary over the greater part of Europe, seeming to have learnt several languages with remarkable facility.   R. Macnamara subsequently returned to Clare and led a rollicking, roving life, half poet and minstrel ; lampooning the parish priest at one time, and making fun of all sorts and conditions of men, usually in verse ; he crossed over to America, and has left us an admirably written and most amusing account of his voyage, which has been translated from Gaelic into English verse by Mr. T. Hayes. R. Macnamara was best known for his songs, and among them an air and words of great beauty, "The Fair Hills of Holy Ireland." Thomas Moore set this fine air to his well-known words "Weep on, weep on, your hour is past ; " he wrote of it as the "song of sorrow." Ruadh Macnamara lived to the advanced age of 95 years, and died near his native village of Cratlow A.D. 1814.*

* "Adventures of Donchadh Ruad Mac-Con-Mara," by S. Hayes (Dublin : Y. O'Daly, 1853) ; also "Irish Music and Songs," by P. W. Joyce, LL.D.   In the "Gentleman's Magazine" for 1808, part i. p. 453, we find the following obituary notice : "October 6th, at Newtown, near Kilmacthomas, in his ninety-fifth year, Denis Macnamara, commonly known as Ruadh, or red-haired.   During seventy years at least, of such a rare course of longevity, this extraordinary man had been looked up to by his contemporaries in Irish literature as possessing that poetical eminence which ranked him among the most celebrated of modern bards."

CHAPTER XVIII

Smuggling in Ireland actively carried on in Burren in first half of the eighteenth century—Daniel Macnamara and members of his family took their share in these proceedings—The Doolin and Ennistymon branch of Macnamara's family of Rathfolan—Michel Macnamara and Eleanora O'Carroll—Character of people living west of the Shannon as shown by their combined action in the case of the Whiteboys—The object of this rising—The Roman Catholic Priests of A.D. 1763—Political feeling in Ireland—Molyneux, Swift, and Lucas—The Irish Volunteers first raised in Cork, A.D. 1744, Limerick and Galway 1766, throughout Ireland from 1776 to 1784 then disbanded—Their character—Loyal to the king and their country—Col. F. Macnamara commanded Clare Volunteers.

As far back as Henry VIII.'s time the Earl of Surrey had obtained the king's permission to destroy all the pirates he could capture in Ireland, the Earl having reported that these lawless freebooters swarmed round the coast of that country. During Elizabeth's reign matters had not improved in this respect; and in addition to the pirates a number of smugglers infested the bays and rivers of Ireland.* Stringent orders were issued to the local authorities to endeavour to put an end to smuggling, but as the officials participated in the profits of the contraband trade they rather encouraged than desired to stop traffic of this kind.†

The first occasion on which we hear of any of our sept being engaged in transactions connected with shipping was hardly of a creditable nature, although it was neither an act of piracy nor of smuggling. It seems that one of the vessels of the Spanish Armada had been driven up the Shannon and stranded on land belonging to one of the Macnamaras.

---

* " State Papers, Henry VIII.," 3. of A.D. 1521.

† Adam Smith describes the smuggler as "a person who though no doubt highly blamable for violating the laws of his country, is frequently incapable of violating those of natural justice, and would have been in every respect an excellent citizen, had not the laws of his country made that a crime which nature never meant to be so." Smuggling has never been regarded as a disgraceful crime by the community at large; with them the smuggler has been rather a popular character than otherwise, and if the conditions which shed a false lustre on his career were to recur he would again become a popular hero.

This vessel was the *St. John*, commanded by Admiral de Ricade.*
From State Papers of this period we learn that the owner of the land
upon which the vessel had stranded seized the ship and its contents,
and he not only appropriated them to his own use, but when ordered
by the Earl of Ormond to yield them to the Crown, " Macnamara
obstinately refused to do so "; and so tenaciously did this individual
hold to the *St. John*, that some of the furniture of this vessel is believed
to be still in the hands of his posterity.

The Government failing to prevent smugglers entering the rivers and
harbours of the West of Ireland, endeavoured through means of inland
defences to stop the passage of goods from the coast into the interior ;
but all their efforts were useless so long as excessive import duties were
levied on foreign produce.   Until the middle of the eighteenth century
the greater part of the wine consumed in Ireland was smuggled into the
country.   Galway Bay at that time was alive with smugglers.   Governor
Eyre complained that in the city large quantities of goods were landed
from vessels arriving from India and all parts of the world.†   Hardiman,
in his history of Galway, gives some details regarding the contraband
trade, which flourished in spite of revenue officers.‡   But we learn that
while complaints were being forwarded to the Government on the
increase of smuggling in Galway Bay, the chief officer of Munster, Sir
W. Hull, confessed to having landed some forty horseloads of pepper
on the coast of Clare, as well as silk, tobacco, gold, velvet and other
commodities.§

Such were the times as regards smuggling when Daniel Macnamara
of Rathfolan, having been expelled from his estates, found refuge in
Burren in the latter half of the seventeenth and the first half of the

* " Defeat of the Spanish Armada," edited by J. K. Langton, vol. ii. p. 218.
† Lecky's " History of Ireland in the Eighteenth Century," vol. i. p. 347.
‡ " History of Galway," p. 174.
§ " State Papers " (Ireland), A.D. 1620–25 ; also a Committee of the House of
Commons, appointed in June 1733, reported that no less than 958,945 lbs. of
tobacco were clandestinely landed and seized in England in six months ; beyond
this " large quantities were landed in Ireland."   Sir J. Cope's Committee
stated that " the smugglers had grown to such a degree of insolence as to
carry on their practices by force and violence, even in the City of London
going in gangs, armed with swords, pistols, and other weapons, to the number
of forty or fifty, and so defied the magistrates and revenue board.   His Majesty's
sloops were beaten off by the smugglers, often with considerable loss of life.
In fact, we find that these " freetraders " held their own along the Kent and
Sussex coast.   Sir E. Cope, in his report on the subject, asserted that they were
aided and abetted by the landed gentry residing along the coast and living
inland.

eighteenth century. In consequence of the crushing export duties levied by England on Irish wool and other agricultural produce, the temptation to smuggle was vastly augmented, and the profit to be derived from it greatly increased. The southern shore of Galway Bay, with its snug inlets for boats, such as Muckinish and Kenvarra Bays, which run up to the Burren hills, with their wonderful caves and dark hiding-places, would seem to be an ideal place for freebooters; and here Daniel Macnamara and his numerous family settled.* They were Roman Catholics, and therefore excluded from the army, navy, or any of the liberal professions ; but even in this world-forsaken Burren district they were not allowed to acquire land, for we find in 1690 and in 1701 that petitions were forwarded to the Government against them by *informers*, who claimed the lands which certain Macnamaras had acquired in Burren, because they had obtained these lands being Roman Catholics, and had consequently no right to them.†

Daniel Macnamara's eldest son, Teigie, after the capitulation of Limerick (p. 246) had retired to Smithstown, Burren, situated near the Atlantic coast, five miles east of Doolin, some thirteen miles south-east of his father's place at Ballinacragga.

In the year 1746 Antony McDonogh resided at Doolin, and from an account of the battle of Fontenoy, written by his grandson, and kindly lent to me by Dr. G. Macnamara of Corofin, we learn that McDonogh's son, a nephew of Dermot O'Brien, obtained a commission in the Irish Brigade through an introduction which his uncle had given him to Lord Clare, at that time living in Paris. This young McDonogh was subsequently sent to collect recruits in Ireland for the French army, and he returned for this purpose to Burren. Having enlisted the number of Irishmen he required, and who, we are informed, he was " obliged to collect by stealth, the recruits were sent to France in ships that came off the coast of Doolin, in Clare, with smuggled claret, and took back the wool of that part of the country and also recruits." Captain Mac-

---

* Daniel Macnamara succeeded his father in 1665; he owned the estates and castles of Ballinacragga and Rathfolan, close to Newmarket in Bunratty. It seems quite probable that after being driven out of his fertile estates in the south of Clare in 1654, he named his new home in Burren Ballinacragga, after that of his former residence in South Clare.

† Frost's " History of Clare," p. 613 ; also " State Papers, Ireland," Elizabeth, vol. cxxxviii.; White's " History," p. 214.

‡ Lecky states (" History of Ireland," vol. i. p. 419) that some 20,000 young men were in the course of a short time (1732) shipped for France and Spain ; " wild geese," as they were called, escaped in spite of Government from all the seaport towns of Ireland.

Donogh does not appear to have returned to France with his men, for in 1746 Lord Clare addressed a letter to him at Doolin ; this letter was dated Paris, October, 1746.*

Teigie Macnamara lived at Smithstown until he had attained an advanced age, he left a large family ; his grandson (William), born in 1714, married the daughter of Francis Sarfield, of Doolin Castle, and he succeeded to that property, containing some of the richest grazing lands in the country. William's grandson, who was for some time M.P. for county Clare, married the only child of M. Finucane, whose wife was the daughter of E. O'Brien of Ennistymon, in this way the Castle and estates of Ennistymon came into possession of the Macnamaras of Doolin, and are still held by William's grandson, H. W. Macnamara, Esq., High Sheriff of county Clare.†

Sioda Macnamara, of Henry VIII.'s time, had a brother Rory, and it was his great-grandson Daniel Macnamara, who in 1654 was expelled from Rathfolan and took up his abode at Ballinacragga, situated on the southern shore of Galway Bay.‡ Daniel's eldest son, Teigie, referred to above, had a younger brother named Daniel, who was twice married, his second wife being a daughter of Charles MacEnery of Castletown, county Kildare, this marriage took place in the year 1696 ; he had several children by his second wife, one of them, Michel, born in 1707, married the daughter of one of the Ely O'Carrolls in the year 1738. § Michel Macnamara's fourth son, Patrick, was born in 1752, and Patrick's

---

* DEAR MacDONOGH,—I congratulate you on your marriage, but trust it will not induce you to retire from the Irish Brigade. I hope you do not forget the memorable day they had at Fontenoy, and the other glorious days in which they had a share. Your promotion goes on, and all are wishing for your return. With your assistance and O'Brien's, the ranks are near filled up. I hope to see you soon. How does my old friend and relation Captain Dermot O'Brien get on ? Is he in good health and permitted to live and pray in peace ?—Yours, CLARE. To Mons. A. Mac Donogh, co. Clare, Ireland. (Rev. P. White's "History of Clare," p. 308.)

† William Macnamara, of Doolin, above referred to, had a younger brother Michel, whose son Timothy Nugent entered the Royal Navy with his cousin Burton, under their relative, Captain James Macnamara, to whom I shall subsequently refer. T. N. Macnamara died in 1870, and his son, Colonel Nugent Macnamara, formerly in the Sussex Militia, and subsequently of the Royal Marine Artillery, is living at Hove; his sister Florence and her husband, General C. Wallis, are at present residing at Ryde.

‡ Daniel Macnamara's father had possessed a house and property called Ballinacragga, close to Rathfolan, and my idea is that on his taking up his abode in his new home he called the place after his former home in Bunratty.

§ See the official pedigree of the family, registered in the office of the Ulster King of Arms, Dublin ; and also in the Herald's Office, London.

Cumea Mor (p. 89), from whom the Family of Macnamaras had their name, was son of Donald, who
was son of Menma (p. 80), who was son of Aodh,
son of Eana, son of Esida (pp. 73 and 75), son of
Sioda (p. 73), son of Maolchuile (p. 72), son of Culen,
son of Urethuile, son of Eoghan, son of Athluan,
son of Ardgal, son of Carthan (p. 70), son of Cassen
(p. 69), son of Cas (p. 69), son of Connal (p. 66).

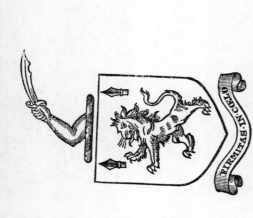

Arms on record in the College of Arms.
Gules, a lion rampant argent, in chief two
spearsheads or, a crescent argent for difference.
Crest.—A naked arm holding a scimitar, all
proper.
Motto.—Firmitas in cœlo.

FIRMITAS·IN·CŒLO

Donald (Macnamara) (p. 89).

Cumara Macnamara (p. 89).

Neil Macnamara (pp. 100-103).

Sioda Macnamara = Honora, dau. of Thady O'Carroll,
(pp. 100-102).   of Ely.

Covêha Macnamara (p. 107).

Donchardh Macnamara (p. 111).

Lochlain Macnamara = Honora, dau. of D. O'Conor,
(p. 118).   of Corcomroe.

Mac Con Macnamara, who was living when Magrath closed = Mary O'Brien, dau. of Mahon
his history of " The Triumphs of Tourlough," A.D. 1334.   O'Brien, of Inchiquin.
(p. 118).

Cumedha Macnamara (p. 133).

Hannah, dau. of Ouny O'Dwyre (first wife) = (Lochlain) Mac Con Macnamara = Anna, dau of O'Daly (second wife).
(pp. 133, 140, 150).

Sioda Macnamara,   Teigie Macnamara = Honora MacMahon   Mahon   Slane m. Brian   Hugh Macnamara, Lord
killed in Limer-   killed by his step-   of Carrigaholt.   Macna-   Catha an Aon-   of East Clanuilein (...
ick, A.D. 1369   brother, Hugh,   mara   aigh, king of

second son, Daniel, was the father of the writer of these pages. Michel was brought up at Ballinacragga, but spent much of his life at Ballena, county Mayo, where *free trade* was carried on up to the commencement of the present century. Carrick-on-Shannon seems to have been an inland depôt for contraband goods, and up to within recent times a few of the old inhabitants of that town could remember the arrival of smuggled stores in the place, and their subsequent transmission to various parts of the country.*

Michel Macnamara's wife (Eleanora O'Carroll) was not only a clever but a cultivated woman, and was held in the highest respect by all who knew her.† Other representatives of the leaders of the old sept are

---

* Michel left some silver plate which came into possession of his grandson, and is still in the hands of one of my brothers. This plate bears the O'Carroll and Macnamara crests. My father also possessed Michel's seals, which he constantly wore, until, to his great grief, they were accidentally lost; these seals were engraved with the Macnamara arms quartered with those of the O'Carrolls.

† The O'Carrolls of Ely were a branch of the old Dalcasian tribe (p. 36), and as far back as the year 1278 we find that the head of the Macnamara sept married a daughter of Thady O'Carroll, of Ely. I have referred on another page to the fact that a daughter of Daniel Macnamara, of Rathfolan (p. 237), married a young Captain O'Carroll, and it was in attempting to resist Cromwell's soldiers from carrying off some of the retainers of the family to be sold in the West Indies that he lost his life, and that his widow and son were then taken and sent off with many other young Irish men and women, to Jamaica and other West Indian islands. In consequence of the penal laws many families left Ireland and went over to America, and among them was Charles O'Carroll, afterwards of Carroltown, Virginia, U.S.; he was, I believe, a relation of Eleanora O'Carroll, the wife of Michel Macnamara. However this may be, Charles O'Carroll was a well-known person in his adopted country. It was by his orders that Stewart burned the obnoxious English vessels carrying tea at Annapolis, which was the culminating act of opposition on the part of our American cousins which led to the War of Independence ("Bird's-eye View of the History of Ireland," by Sir G. Duffy, p. 184). In signing the Act of Independence, O'Carroll, as he stated when putting his name to the document, risked vast landed possessions in Virginia. C. O'Carroll's granddaughter Marianne married the Marquis of Wellesley, and in consequence of this marriage the Marquis obtained permission to quarter the O'Carroll arms with his own. Charles O'Carroll lived to an advanced age (the pedigree, an account of C. O'Carroll, is to be found in the work of the "Royal Historical and Archæological Association of Ireland" for October 1883, by F. O'Carroll, A.B. T.C.D.), and before his death wrote as follows:—"I have lived to my ninety-sixth year; I have enjoyed continued health and been blessed with great wealth, prosperity, and most of the good things this world can bestow—public approbation, esteem, applause; but what I now look back on with great satisfaction to myself is that I have practised in freedom the duties of my religion." Eleanora O'Carroll, wife of Michel Macnamara, must have been a person very similar in character to her relative, Charles O'Carroll, of Virginia.

still living, among them the direct descendants of the eldest son of Daniel Macnamara, of Rathfolan, and subsequently of Ballinacragga, Burren, in the person of Colonel Nugent Macnamara, and his sister Mrs. Wallace ;* beyond this we have the more direct representatives of the chief of our sept in Henry VIII.'s time with us in the person of Mr. Arthur Macnamara of Caddington Hall, and Mr. John Macnamara, his twin brother; grandsons of John Macnamara, who in 1784–90 was Member of Parliament for Leicester.†

We must, however, return to the history of our sept, and by their actions in combination with their neighbours learn what kind of people they had developed into during the latter half of the eighteenth century ; to illustrate this point we may glance at the history of two very different organisations which flourished in the west of Ireland during the period referred to. The first of these combinations was known as the White-boys ; and the second as the Irish Volunteers of 1764–83. We may then pass on to consider the character of some of the individual members of our sept at the close of the last, and commencement of the present century.

The land in Ireland having practically been taken from its owners, and appropriated by those who in many cases had no interest in it beyond the amount of money they could make out of it. The question which naturally occurred to them was as to how they could best increase their rental. England had put a stop to the Irish trade in cattle and in wool, the landowners, therefore, came to the conclusion that it would be well to convert the grass plains of the country into wheat-growing lands. They succeeded in their efforts, for in 1767, an exceptional bad year, the value of the wheat exported from Ireland amounted to £447, and in ten years after this date the export of wheat had risen to £104,642 ; this increase raised the value of the farms on which the corn was grown. In promoting this object the Government in the year 1762 passed an Act, under which a bounty was to be paid out of the public purse upon the carriage of corn arriving in Dublin from all parts of Ireland. In the course of five years this bounty rose to be a charge of £60,000 a year on the revenue, besides this Ireland lost by the conversion of her splen-did pasture into bad tillage lands; no less than £53,000 a year in the produce of cows and bullocks, and £1,000,000 a year in sheep, in addi-tion to this there was the loss of labour on above, 25,000 stones of

* See note, p. 264.

† The pedigree and further references to these members of our sept will be found in the following chapter of this work.

woollen yarns annually.*   Nevertheless, the revenue increased, and for five-and-twenty years the country appeared to be improving ; then came the collapse of a rotten system, and so we find in 1778 the inhabitants of Ireland in a state of intense poverty and misery.†   Clare suffered from these causes less than some other parts of the country, for much of the soil was useless for arable purposes, and her people having adopted fair trade with the Continent and our West Indian and American colonies before that system had been sanctioned by law, her wool and other produce was sent in considerable quantities out of the country at a distinctly remunerative price.

Lord Weymouth writing from Dublin in May 1779 on the cause of the great distress at that time existing in Ireland, observes : " That the great and leading mischief is the rise of rents, the whole of which advance is, in addition to the former remittances, drawn from home by persons of property who never reside here. And these circumstances also operate in a degree, with regard to those in general settled in Ireland, who are very much disposed to expend the superfluity of their revenue in foreign countries " ; he adds, " there is reason to believe till quite lately

---

* A. Young's " Tour in Ireland," vol. ii. pp. 186, 261.

† A. Young has given us a summary of the causes which, in his opinion, had produced the misery which he witnessed among the lower and middle classes when he visited Ireland in the year 1778.   His remarks are so much to the point that it seems to me desirable to give an abstract of them in order that we may the better understand the nature of the social and political movement that occurred in Ireland towards the end of the eighteenth century.   Young observes that the causes which led to the miserable state of the people at the time referred to depended :

" 1. The oppression of the Catholics, which, by loading the industry of two millions of subjects, has done more to retard the progress of the kingdom than all other causes put together.

" 2. The bounty on the inland carriage of corn to Dublin, which, by changing a beneficial pasturage to an execrable tillage at a heavy expense to the public, has done much mischief to the kingdom besides involving it in debt.

" 3. The perpetual interference of Parliament in every branch of domestic industry, either for laying restrictions or giving bounties, but always doing mischief.

" 4. The mode of conducting the linen manufacture, which, by spreading over the north, has annihilated agriculture throughout a fourth part of the kingdom, and supplanted the great and flourishing woollen manufacture which had encouraged every branch of husbandry.

" 5. The stoppage of emigration for five years, which has accumulated a surplus population.

" 6. The ill-judged restrictions laid by Great Britain on the commerce of Ireland.

" 7. The great drain of rents of absentee estates being remitted to England."

considerable clandestine exports of goods were made from this country both to Portugal and also to the West Indies and to America."* It would appear that the rents paid to absentee landowners, and for civil pensions amounted to no less than.£2,223,000 per annum.

There were, however, other causes than those referred to by Mr. Young and Lord Weymouth which impoverished the small farmers and landholders, and that was the collection of tithes, for these had to be paid in the first place to the Protestant rector of the parish, and, in addition, there was the maintenance of the parish priest, which fell on the Roman Catholics. We have reference made to this subject by Mr. L. O'Brien (afterwards Sir Lucas) in a speech he delivered at Ennis in the early part of the year 1763, he referred to the lamentable neglect of the Protestant clergy to their duties in co. Clare, and stated that one of the bad consequences of this neglect of the clergy is those risings which have been mentioned to the violation of the law, for who can suppose that men will patiently suffer the extortion of a tithemonger when no duty for which the tithe is claimed has been performed in the memory of man. . . . ." He continues, " the insurrections, against which we are so eager to call out the terrors of the law, are no more than branches, of which the shameful neglect of the clergy and the defects in our religious institutions constitute the root." Mr. O'Brien was a Protestant, and subsequently Member of Parliament for Ennis ; the revolt he refers to was the organisation known as the Whiteboys. This organisation spread rapidly through parts of Ireland, its principal operations being carried on in the counties of Tipperary, Queens County, and Clare, where it continued to exist up to the year 1785 ; in truth, it exists there at the present time, being much more pronounced in seasons of distress. The Whiteboys from the first declared that their object was to relieve the cotters and small farmers from taxes imposed on the soil, and to restore the common lands to their owners, the people. The tithes were above all impositions the most obnoxious, paid as they frequently were to absentees, and to lay rectors, and too often collected by men who had undertaken to farm this tax as a speculation. In case of failure to pay calls made by tithe-collectors, tenants were evicted without mercy, and were unable to appeal to any higher authority for protection. The Whiteboys forbade any one to pay tithes or rent beyond a sum fixed by the members of the Society ; they would not permit any one to occupy land from which a tenant had been ejected for the non-payment of rent. Beyond this they pulled down numbers of walls, and broke down enclosures placed on the common lands, which, until the confiscations of

* " Life of Grattan," vol. i. p. 349.

Cromwell, and those who followed him, had formed a part of the ancient tribal lands.

Sir R. Aston, the Chief Justice of Common Pleas, was sent from Dublin to try a number of Whiteboys in Tipperary, and in reporting on this organisation he states, that it did not appear to him that there was the "least reason to impute those disturbances to disaffection to his Majesty, or his Government, but they took their rise from grievances of a private nature—Papists and Protestants were promiscuously concerned."[*]

The Whiteboys were frequently condemned, and even excommunicated from Catholic altars, with the effect of rather damaging the priest than the individuals concerned. In Clare if a priest took action of this kind, his congregation were apt to nail up his chapel door, and in one case they buried their priest up to his neck in brambles and thorns for having denounced the Whiteboys.[†]

Arthur Young visited Clare when this organisation exercised great power over the people, and he states that it had then been in existence for ten years in spite of every exertion of legal power; he further remarks that what struck him most was the surprising intelligence of these people; their system was such that one body of men almost "instantaneously" became aware of what their allies were doing in a distant part of the country. Young writes, "they all seem to be animated by one soul, and not an instance was known in that long course of time of a single individual betraying the cause; the severest threats and the most splendid promises of reward had no other effect but to draw closer the bonds which connected a multitude, to all appearances so desultory. *It was thus evident the iron rod of oppression had been far enough from securing the obedience or crushing the spirit of the people.*"[‡]

At the time the Whiteboys were extending so as to embrace a vast number of the Catholics of Munster, an outburst of popular feeling had been roused among the Presbyterian tenants of Lord Donegal, an absentee landowner of Ulster, who, when his leases fell due, in place of renewing them at a moderately increased rent, determined to raise £100,000 in fines on his tenants, and, as they could not pay this sum, they were ejected, and two or three rich Belfast merchants took their lands. The ejected tenants formed an organisation called the Steelboys; they proceeded to maim cattle and to break into the houses of the gentry. A large body of soldiers was sent against them, and several of

* "Burke's Correspondence," vol. i. p. 37.
† Rev. Father O'Leary's Works, p. 296.
‡ A. Young's "Tour in Ireland," vol. ii. p. 64.

the Steelboys were captured and tried at Carrickfergus, but no local jury would convict them; so that an Act was passed removing them for trial to Dublin. But in 1773 this obnoxious Act was repealed, and the organisation speedily subsided. Thousands of the Steelboys emigrated to America, and were afterwards found in the ranks of the American army.* Mr. Lecky observes this sudden subsidence of a formidable insurrection in the north of Ireland is a remarkable contrast to that of the persistence of the Whiteboys in the south. To my mind, however, the difference is to be accounted for in the diversity of character of the two peoples. The Catholic Celts of the south were a distinct race from the Presbyterians of the north of Ireland, who had not that intense love of land and brotherhood which characterised the agricultural population of Munster.

I wish, however, to draw special attention to Arthur Young's description of the Whiteboy movement, for if we analyse it we find it contains, in a concise form, as applied to a widely disseminated movement in the west of Ireland, the characters which we have seen specialised in the individual members of our sept before they had been driven from their old home in county Clare (see Chapter XV.).

During the second half of the eighteenth century various causes were at work in Ireland which, in the long-run, produced great changes in the political condition of the people. Among these was, first, the increasing influence of the Press in forming public opinion. Secondly, the action of America in throwing off the commercial restrictions imposed on her by England; and subsequently, in obtaining her independence, the effect of the French Revolution was also acutely felt in the north of Ireland. Thirdly, the spontaneous enrolment of Irishmen into volunteer corps at a time when England, under the pressure of urgent foreign complications, was compelled not only to withdraw her troops from Ireland, but also to obtain a large supply of men for her army and navy from that country. Acting under these influences, and in spite of English officials, the Irish Parliament of 1771 to 1789 gradually succeeded, first, in freeing the country from the commercial restraints under which she laboured. Secondly, in curtailing the duration of Irish Parliaments to a period of eight years, and in repealing Poyning's Act. Thirdly, in emancipating the Catholics from some of the most oppressive laws under which they laboured.

Molyneux led the way, in 1698, to open the minds of the people when he published his work, "The Case of Ireland," which produced a great impression on the Irish, and, for that matter, on Englishmen also.

* Benn's History of Belfast ("Gentleman's Magazine," 1772).

In this work, Molyneux tried to prove the independence of the Irish Parliament to legislate on all national concerns without control of the English Parliament. His essay is admirable in style, and in spirit, it was dedicated to the King of England. We find the premises contained in the work succinctly stated in the preamble of Act iii. of James II.'s Dublin Parliament of 1692 (p. 241). But if we admit the whole of Molyneux's argument to be unassailable, still the Acts of the Parliament which sat in Ireland, or, for that matter, in England, had practically no effect upon the inhabitants of the territory west of the Shannon from Henry II.'s time to that of James II. Molyneux's work, however, produced a marked influence on the people of Ireland; it was brought before the English House of Commons and condemned, and so the interest in the essay was increased, and procured for it a wide circulation.*

Dean Swift followed, in 1724, and in his famous Drapier letters reasserted the principles which Molyneux had laid down. He claimed for Ireland the right of self-government, and drew the line clearly between the prerogative of the Sovereign and the liberty of the people ; and urged that "government without the consent of the governed is simply the definition of slavery." A reward of £300 was offered by Government for evidence to bring the author of these letters to justice, and, although they were known to have been written by Swift, the grand jury refused even to find a true bill against the printers.

The work published by Dr. C. Lucas, made a greater impression on Irishmen than either of the above-named authors. He was a native of Corrofin, county Clare, and settled in Dublin. Leaving medicine, he took to politics. In 1741 Dr. Lucas published his ideas regarding the history and constitution of Parliament. This work brought down on him the anger of Dublin Castle, and he was compelled to seek refuge in England. In London, Lucas became acquainted with Dr. Johnson, who wrote of him as follows : " The Irish Ministers drove Dr. Lucas from his native country by a proclamation in which they charged him with crimes which they never intended to call upon him to answer, and oppressed him by methods equally irresistible by guilt or innocence. Let the man thus driven into evil for having been a friend of his country be received in every other place as a confessor of liberty, and let the tools of power be taught to learn that they may rob, but cannot impoverish such men." On the death of George I. Lucas returned to Dublin, and was received with great acclamation. He was elected

* " The Case of Ireland being Bound by Act of Parliament in England," by W. Molyneux. A new edition and excellent Preface to a Life of Molyneux has recently been published by Very Rev. John Canon O'Hanlon, P.P., M.R.I.A.

Member of the first Parliament of George III., and continued to represent the city until his death, which took place in 1771.*

Beyond the writings of these eminent Irishmen, the example set by America in resisting the taxes imposed on her commerce by England must have been an object-lesson of the deepest interest to the Irish. Men like Charles O'Carroll (p. 265) and many of his countrymen, who had been compelled to leave their homes and settle in America, were nevertheless keenly alive to what was going on in the old country, and spurred on the growing demand of the Irish to be relieved from the bondage under which their trade was placed by England.†

In the year 1744 England was engaged in war with France ; as a consequence our shores were seriously threatened by the French fleet, and so great was the danger at this time that the Government felt compelled in self defence to withdraw the greater part of her regular troops from Ireland. The coast swarmed with privateers, and cities like Limerick and Cork found it imperative for their own safety, after the withdrawal of the English troops, to raise regiments of volunteers to serve both as civil and military guardians of the people. In the year 1744 the inhabitants of Cork formed themselves into the "United Independent Volunteers." The regiment was dressed in blue uniform with buff facings, and was hence known as the "Cork True Blues." A medal was struck commemorating the first parade of this regiment at Cork.§ In February 1766 the citizens of Limerick raised a regiment of horse

---

* Lord Charlemont, who knew Lucas well, maintained that it was through his writing the spirit of Irishmen was raised to the point of determining that nothing should stand in the way of their obtaining such changes in the Government as would secure a limit being placed on the duration of the Dublin Parliament, of freeing the country from the commercial restrictions under which she then laboured, and other necessary reforms, so as again to give Irishmen some freedom of action in political life. Charlemont describes Dr. Lucas, with his "bodily infirmities, his gravity, his uncommon neatness of dress, his grey expressive eyes and hair, blending with a pale but striking countenance which attracted the attention of every stranger who entered the House. He raised his voice in support of his country when all around him was desolation and silence."

† Dr. Benjamin Franklin, one of America's most thoughtful and independent statesmen, visited the City and Parliament of Dublin in 1771. At the time of signing the treaty of American Independence he wished Ireland to be excluded from this agreement, because he observed "that country is much our friend"; the proposed agreement "was to be against England, to ensure change of measures, and not to hurt Ireland."

‡ Rockingham's "Life of Albemarle," vol. ii. p. 300.

§ On Some Medals of the Loyal Irish Volunteers, by R. Day, J.P., p. 459 ("The Journal of the Royal Society of Antiquaries of Ireland," 1891).

and foot; like the Cork troops, they wore blue uniform, they also had a medal bearing the motto "Amicta juncta," 1766, and on the reverse "Limerick Union." After the complete withdrawal of the king's troops from Limerick the volunteers mounted guard, and performed all the duties of the regular troops; but as in the case of the Cork regiment, they were from the first citizen soldiers, and their duties included the preservation of peace in the district to which they belonged, as well as its protection from foreign invasion. The Limerick Union regiment developed, and in the course of time (1782) had produced no less than twenty-six corps of well-trained "Loyal Limerick Volunteers."

In December 1776, the Dublin Parliament sent a Money Bill to England for the sanction of the Government. To the astonishment of the Irish Parliament it was discovered that English officials had altered the original Bill, and cut down the force to be retained in Ireland from twelve thousand men to four thousand, it having been previously stipulated that the minimum number of English troops to be retained in Ireland for the defence of the country should be not less than twelve thousand soldiers. This proceeding created an uproar in the Dublin Parliament, and led to the demand for a force of militia being at once raised; the Government declined this proposal, and Charles Ogle, Member of Parliament for Wexford, and other gentlemen, determined to follow the example set them by the cities of Cork, Limerick, and Galway, and to arm and enrol their tenants into volunteer corps. The uniforms of these corps were scarlet with buff facings. Many of the country gentlemen joined in the movement; and so, in the early part of the year 1777, the Kilkenny Rangers, and regiments of volunteers in Wexford and Wicklow, were brought into training under the orders of non-commissioned officers who, having passed through the Seven Years' War, were well acquainted with the details of drill and such like matters. It should be distinctly understood that this volunteer movement commenced in the South of Ireland, and spread to Clare and Connaught in 1766, and in the following ten years was well established over those parts of Ireland.* In fact, before the year 1777 the volunteers had done good work in the South of Ireland; for although drawn from the same class as the Whiteboys, when enrolled as soldiers they at once displayed a capacity for order, and a sense of duty which when brought to bear on the Whiteboys did more to suppress in a few months the excesses of that Society than the Government had been able to effect in as many years. The volunteers of the South of Ireland had

* O'Brien's "Memoirs," pp. 402, 3; also Sir J. Barrington's "Historic Memories of Ireland," vol. i. p. 49.

also been invaluable to the civil authorities in preserving the inhabitants of seaport towns from the depredations of pirates.*

The volunteers were at first confined to Protestants, but as their numbers increased no questions were asked concerning a recruit's religion, and some of the regiments were entirely formed of men professing the Roman Catholic religion.† Several of the Macnamaras commanded regiments of Clare volunteers; the privates were tenant-farmers and their sons.

The Right Hon. H. Grattan, who knew these men, especially those to the west of the Shannon, states that they were characterised by "their temperate zeal, their steady moderation, their sobriety, their alacrity to assist the civil powers ; and their readiness to march at a few hours' notice under orders of Government." He adds : "There was a serious, useful, irresistible principle, which seemed to be a part of their existence and success, something which reconciled the fears of the timid, and silenced the murmurs of those who wished their dissolution." ‡ Sir J. Barrington, writing on the same subject, remarks that the intercourse and military training of the Irish farmer and his lads seemed to transform them ; they became different creatures both in appearance and manner ; a striking revolution took place in their minds, and also in their external appearance."§ The men's minds, like their bodies, were brought under discipline, and elevated by coming into contact with their superiors.§ Francis Dobbs remarks that knowing the volunteers well he could not adequately "express his respect and admiration of what he beheld in this movement;" he continues: "It has been argued that volunteering wastes the men's time," but, he observes, "I venture to assert there is not a poor man in the kingdom the poorer for being a volunteer, the exercise of arms is his recreation, and no bad substitute for cock-fighting, horse-racing, and so on ; and, moreover, a saving rather than loss, for sobriety and discipline are necessary." ∥

Hardiman, in his history of Galway, writes of the volunteers in that town as having numbered four hundred well-armed troops, they had been in existence since 1776, and subsequently merged with the Galway, Tuam, and Loughrea Regiments, under command of the Earl of Clanricarde. Hardiman states that "after preserving the public peace they peaceably

---

* Francis Dobbs' "Thoughts on Volunteers," Dublin, 1780.
† Sir J. Barrington's "Memoirs," vol. i. p. 49, vol. ii. p. 123.
‡ "Life and Times of the Right Hon. H. Grattan," vol. ii. p. 180.
§ Barrington: "Rise and Fall of Ireland," p. 64.
∥ "Thoughts on Volunteers" (Dublin, 1780): a small pamphlet which in my opinion might with advantage be republished and largely circulated.

laid down their arms which they had voluntarily taken up, and again resumed their station with honour and applause amongst their fellow-men." * Much has been written of the Irish Volunteers, but they have received no higher praise than that contained in the few words quoted from the pen of the historian of Galway ; the men concerning whom he wrote were known to him, and they were all bred and born west of the Shannon, many of them grandsons of gentlemen whose lands had been confiscated by the English Government. Here in Clare and Galway the Roman Catholic Celts were, by Cromwell's directions, to be confined and separated from the rest of the world lest their influence should contaminate the Scotch and English, located over Ulster and Leinster. The descendants of these Scotchmen and Englishmen were at the end of the last century in open rebellion against England, but the Celt was true to his character, and when Ireland was invaded by England's enemies they loyally pressed forward to resist domestic traitors, and foreign foes. When the time arrived for the English to resume her functions, and replace the self-elected and organised volunteers of the West of Ireland by constituted authorities, the volunteers betook themselves, as was their ancient custom, without a thought of self or their own importance to their farms and agricultural pursuits ; and there they remained until in 1798, when the French attempted to land in Bantry Bay, and subsequently effected a landing in Killala ; on both these occasions the volunteers of Clare and Galway again sprang into existence, and the country was alive with them and the yeomanry, bent, as before, on trying to do their duty.†

In 1778 there was a well-founded report that the French had collected an expedition which was to effect a landing at Belfast, the town had been left almost without a garrison of regular troops, and this was the commencement of the volunteer movement in Ulster, the men at first being armed simply with scythes and other agricultural weapons. The volunteers rapidly increased in numbers, and in the year 1782 it is stated the force amounted in Ireland to no less than 100,000 officers and men, fairly armed, drilled, and taught to act in large bodies ; they also possessed a small force of artillery. England was powerless in the matter, her hands were more than full with rebellion in her American dependencies, and her shores threatened with the combined forces of France and Spain. It was at such a time the Irish volunteers came to the fore, having no idea of political independence or of ulterior possibilities ; their function was to maintain peace in Ireland, and if possible to save her from being overrun by a foreign army.

* Hardiman's " History of Galway," p. 189.   † Ibid., p. 191.

It was however impossible for an organisation such as the Irish volunteers to keep clear of politics; some of their officers such as Grattan, Flood, Dobbs, Lord Charlemont, and many others, were politicians of great weight, and must soon have felt the importance of 100,000 armed men at their command. A grand national Committee was formed in 1782, to be composed of delegates from all the volunteer regiments in Ireland ; Colonel Francis Macnamara was elected as one of the delegates from Clare ; but from the published minutes of the Committee it appears that he took no active part in this movement. Staunch friends of the volunteer's, such as the Duke of Leinster, objected strongly to having the force used for political purposes, or as the duke put it, in "having constitutional questions forced by the bayonet." Nevertheless, the fact remained, there were the volunteers, and with the example of America before them, those in power in England were not likely to turn a deaf ear to complaints regarding the harsh measures imposed on Irish commerce; but it was England's necessities alone which made her yield to Irish demands.

CHAPTER XIX

Ireland in the latter half of eighteenth century—Agitation for relief from English restrictions on trade—Meeting at Ennis, co. Clare—Action of volunteers—The Roman Catholic clergy—Relief of penal laws, A.D. 1793—Of Act 6 of George I. —Irish Volunteers of 1784-6 disbanded—Subsequent volunteers a different class of people—Character of original Irish volunteers—French revolutionary ideas in Ulster—Its inhabitants urge France to take possession and form a "national" government in Ireland—South and West of Ireland staunch to the Crown and country—They rise to a man to resist the French landing at Bantry Bay—This landing was on the invitation of Ulster and part of Leinster —Macnamaras in France refuse to join the revolutionary movement—Count Harry Macnamara—W. N. Macnamara of Doolin, High Sheriff of Clare, A.D. 1789—Landing of French at Killala—Volunteers of Clare, Galway, and West of Shannon march against them—Lord Cornwallis' order regarding volunteers —No higher praise could be given to any such body of men.

DURING the later half of the eighteenth century the Irish began to realise the nature of some of the causes which tended to produce the agricultural depression and consequent poverty in the country; the great majority of the people being Roman Catholics were unrepresented in the Irish Parliament, its members being restricted to Protestants who held a vast proportion of the landed property of the country, and naturally wished to maintain their own privileges. The Protestant landowners, and the Government had in the year 1753 come to the conclusion that so far as their interests were concerned, it was above all things necessary to prevent Irish Catholics from obtaining the franchise or seats in Parliament, otherwise the grip which the existing landowners held on the country might speedily disappear, and in order to prevent such a catastrophe measures were taken by the Government to secure a working majority in the Dublin legislative assembly. Bribes, in the form of titles, were offered to the aristocracy of Ireland, and in the way of pensions to the large landowners to induce them to place nominees of the Government in Parliament. This they were able to do as they commanded a considerable number of close boroughs in various parts of the country. The Duke of Bedford found that during his tenure of office, the Government spent no less than £28,000 a year out of the Irish

Treasury for the purpose of securing votes in the Dublin Parliament.*
An assembly packed in this way was a costly business, and the King,
therefore, held it together at his own pleasure, the Parliament of 1755
sat for no less than thirty consecutive sessions.   In this way the Government commanded the votes of one hundred and fifty-four members,
ninety-four of them being nominees of Protestant absentee landowners.

The first real effort made by the Irish people to disentangle the
political net by which they were surrounded, was to demand emancipa-
tion from the commercial restrictions imposed on the country; this
demand was the more urgent in consequence of the terrible agricultural
distress which existed throughout Ireland in the year 1778.   The Lord
Lieutenant went so far as to urge on the Government in London the
necessity for concessions in this direction, and after much hesitation the
House of Commons consented to allow the agricultural produce of
Ireland to be shipped to our colonies without, as heretofore, being first
sent over to an English port to be transhipped to America or the West
Indies.   But even this relief to the starving Irish was violently opposed
on the part of the mercantile classes and the landed proprietors in
England.   It was not, however, the time to heed clamour of this sort, for
public feeling was growing high in Ireland, and was soon likely to lead
to very decided steps being taken against the restrictions on trade.†
For instance, in an out-of-the-way place like Ennis, county Clare, at a
meeting held in June 1778, presided over by Colonel Francis Macnamara, High Sheriff of the county, resolutions were first passed expressing
the sincere loyalty of the meeting to the Sovereign ; after which it was
moved and carried that the meeting pledged itself, and all those it could
influence, not to purchase goods manufactured in England until such
time as that country chose to grant Ireland Free Trade ; similar meetings
were held throughout the country.‡   In October 1779, at an assembly of
the Dublin Volunteers, placards were exhibited inscribed with the words
" Free Trade or revolution."§   At the same time, Grattan, Sir Lucius
O'Brien, and other members of the Irish Parliament, pressed the matter
on the Government, and at length gained their end, for the restrictions
on the produce of agriculture were removed in the year 1780.   In the
same session Bills were passed relieving Dissenters in Ireland from the
Sacramental test; a habeas corpus Act was passed, in truth, England
found it necessary to yield to the claims of the Irish, for she was then

* O'Brien's " Memoirs," p. 391.
† Lecky's " History of Ireland in the Eighteenth Century," vol. ii. p. 179.
‡ O'Brien's " Memoirs," p. 412.
§ Ibid., p. 416; also Lecky's " History," vol. ii. p. 243.

not in a position to court resistance on the part of the inhabitants of the sister isle, having sunk into deep waters in America, where, in 1781, Lord Cornwallis was compelled first to march his force of four thousand troops through lines of American and French soldiers, after which the British had to yield up their arms to their enemies.

We must here refer as briefly as possible to the position of the Roman Catholic clergy in Ireland during the latter part of the eighteenth century. The penal laws were still in force against Papists, although practically they had become modified in the course of time, thus Roman Catholic priests not only lived without fear of molestation in all parts of the country, but they freely exercised their functions, and said Mass openly in their churches.   Nevertheless, Irish Roman Catholics were neither permitted to enter Parliament nor any of the Government services, nor could they legally purchase land.   We obtain an insight into the relative positions of the Protestant and Roman Catholic clergy in Clare at this period, from a speech delivered at Ennis by L. O'Brien (January 1764) ; he stated that the country had been divided into seventy-five parishes, but that there were only fourteen Protestant churches in these parishes, so that sixty-two of them were sinecures, and of the fourteen parishes with churches as a rule, the rectors were non-resident, leaving their work to curates who they paid at the rate of forty pounds per annum. L. O'Brien remarked that "to regret the non-residence of our clergy upon mere political grounds was similar to that of the sailor who, when his comrade's head was blown away by a round shot, regretted the up-setting of the tot of rum he was drinking at the moment he was struck." L. O'Brien stated that the Roman Catholic priest was diligent in pro-portion as Protestants were negligent, and he argued that neither by the laws of God nor man, should the nominal clergy be paid the tenth part of the produce of the land for doing nothing on behalf of those who worked the soil.*

With reference to the Roman Catholic clergy of this period, we not only have L. O'Brien's statement concerning them, but we know with what zeal and courage they had through terrible trial administered to the spiritual needs of their people.   At the latter end of the eighteenth century the majority of the priests residing in Clare were men of whom Irishmen might be proud.   As a rule, these priests were descended from the old Celtic landowners of the county, who had been sent over to France, Spain, and other parts of the Continent to be educated for their calling in life.   A contemporary, who knew these men well, describes them as having been "mild, amiable, and cultured gentlemen, uniting

* O'Brien's "Memoirs," p. 539.

the meek spirit of Christian pastors to the winning gentleness of the polished man of the world, the welcome guests at the tables of Catholics and Protestants." A few of these men have lived on to within recent times, and every one who has met them will thoroughly endorse O'Driscoll's account of them; they indicate to us what kind of beings the original landowners of Clare would have become, had they been permitted to develop under the influence of the advancing refinement of the times, and the gradual changes which were spreading over society at the close of the last century. We are told that these parish priests "in their own communion lent their influence to sooth the asperities of the times, and brought their knowledge of mankind, and their own, and foreign nations, to enforce their lessons of patience, fortitude, and for-bearance."* These men not only considered and gave due weight to the rights and feelings of other people, but also in their dealings with their neighbours practised what they inculcated, the spirit of charity. L. O'Brien observes, the priest was ever ready to attend his Protestant neighbour, and afford the best help in his power at the bed of sickness and death; he was not unfrequently called upon to marry Protestants, to baptize their children, and to bury their dead. These priests were loyal supporters of the Sovereign, and directly the oath of supremacy was so adjusted that the Roman Catholic Bishop of Killaloe could sub-scribe to it, he at once proceeded to Limerick and took the oath of loyalty to the Crown of England.† Persecution had done its work on these men; it had driven them from Ireland to study in continental seminaries, and to learn by trial and experience to take a broader view of the responsibilities of life than they were likely to learn at home. Moreover, young priests were, when abroad, brought into contact with men of refinement, which developed the good qualities natural to them; we may with confidence make a statement of this kind, because we have only to refer to the description given by the Pope's Nuncio of the Irish clergy in 1645, and compare it with that above quoted to appreciate the great change that had come over these men within a century.

In 1793 a Bill was introduced and carried through Parliament for the relief of the Catholics in Ireland; in the preamble of this Act it is stated that the Catholics had claims on the Government, in consequence of their "uniform peaceable behaviour for a long series of years." Under this Bill the forty-shilling freehold franchise was extended to Roman Catholics, but they were not allowed seats in Parliament until long after

* O'Driscoll's " Views of Ireland," vol. ii. p. 112.
† White's " History of Clare," p. 317.

this time. Under the Act of 1793, however, Roman Catholics were
allowed to enter the army and navy as officers, and most of the learned
professions were thrown open to them.*

With regard to the political aspirations of the Irish, we may learn
something from speeches made at a public meeting held at Ennis in
1782. The first resolution passed was a vote of thanks to the local
volunteers for their services and excellent conduct. It was then resolved
that "no power had any right to make laws to bind the kingdom save
the Lords and Commons of Ireland." This was going back to the
principle contained in Act iii. of James II.'s Dublin Parliament, and to
much that followed in the works of Molyneux, Swift, Lucas, and other
political writers. Opinions of this kind were urged on the Government
by Grattan, Flood, and others in the Parliament sitting in Dublin, and
in the House of Commons by Edmund Burke. It was largely through
their influence, backed by the people of Ireland, that C. Fox carried the
Bill by which Act vi. of George I. was repealed. This Act had
reasserted the right of England to legislate for Ireland. At the same
time, the duration of Irish Parliaments were curtailed from an indefinite
period to a term of eight years ; and it was further enacted that the Irish
Parliament was to have the same authority over local affairs in Ireland
as the English legislative assembly had over the affairs of that country.
A Mutiny Act was also passed; and for all these favours Ireland
willingly supplied England with some twenty thousand young fellows to
help to man the Royal Navy.

The Irish Volunteers came into existence in the year 1764, and by
1784–6 the original force had disbanded and settled down to their
farms and other occupations. During the period of the existence of
this self-constituted and self-elected force, we find that most of the
heavy restrictions laid on the productive resources of Ireland had been
removed. Her Roman Catholic population had been relieved from the
harshest penal laws, and a step forward had been made towards
obtaining political independence. All this was brought about to a great
extent by means of the volunteer organisation ; at any rate, we believe
that without the existence of this force Ireland might have waited a long
time for these measures of reform. Earl Carlisle, who was Lord
Lieutenant of Ireland from 1780 to 1782, referring to the Irish Volunteers
from his place in the House of Lords in 1788, stated "that nothing could
exceed the excellence of their conduct and discipline"; and he added,
"they had not done a single act for which they had not his veneration
and respect." These were the Irish Volunteers of 1764 to 1784,

* Lecky's "History of Ireland in the Eighteenth Century," vol. iii. pp. 122–141.

constituted of small landowners and farmers. This should be clearly understood, so as not to confound the original Irish Volunteers with the force subsequently enrolled, which took the name of volunteers, but were altogether a different class of men to those who had preceded them. The Duke of Rutland, who was Lord Lieutenant of Ireland in 1784, appreciated the difference between the volunteers before and subsequent to the time he took office, for he wrote as follows: "The old corps, who were very completely appointed, and piqued themselves on being gentlemen both in manner and appearance would not for a moment submit to be in the same regiment with such men as those enrolled now in Dublin," no longer called Loyal, but "Liberty corps of volunteers."* These men, we are told, were enlisted from the lowest classes of the people, and, through their officers, Napper Tandy, a Dublin ironmonger, and the like, opened communication with the revolutionary party in France to secure the landing of a foreign army in Ireland in order to establish a "*National* Government," Ireland being placed directly under the protection of France.† In Protestant Ulster this feeling was rampant, and Wolfe Tone took advantage of it, and instituted the Society of "United Irishmen," whose members were enrolled mainly with the object of clearing the English Government out of Ireland. In the pursuit of this object, religious differences were to be swamped. This Society, however, gained no hold on the Catholic population to the west of the Shannon, so that it was far from being what its founders proposed—an organisation in which all Irishmen could join for a common political purpose. The United Irishmen of Belfast, at their public meetings, were in the habit of drinking "Success to the Revolution," "Health and long life to Washington and Tom Paine." Resolutions were passed congratulating the leaders of the French Revolution in Paris on the capture of the Bastille. The volunteers removed the crown from their standards and replaced it with a cap of liberty. The Presbyterian and other Nonconformist ministers of Ulster, in their public services, prayed for the success of the French arms, and were cognisant of the fact that open rebellion was at the time being organised in Ireland, with the promised aid of an army to be landed in the country from France.‡

---

* The Attorney-General for Ireland stated at this time that the "original volunteers had hung up their arms and retired to cultivate the arts of peace, and their places were taken by men of the worst character."

† Lecky's "History of Ireland in the Eighteenth Century," vol. ii. pp. 394, 395, and 398; and Dr. Stock, on "Narrative of Landing of French at Killala," p. 8.

‡ Wolfe Tone's "Memoranda," vol. i. p. 268.

The Government were well informed as to the reckless and treasonable motive of the negotiations passing between the leaders of a section of the Irish people, and those of the French revolutionary party; and matters had come to such a pass in 1796 that the authorities considered it necessary to place Ulster and Leinster under martial law. In proposing these and other measures of a like nature in Parliament, the Attorney-General for Ireland stated he was convinced, that "in the South and and West of Ireland the Government might with confidence, and safety appeal to the gentry and farmers to act under commissions from the Crown;" he added, "it is evident to demonstration that the opinion of the people, and of all classes in the province of Munster and in Connaught has grown infinitely more loyal during the war." The Lord Lieutenant endorsed this opinion of his Attorney-General.* In these conditions corps of yeomanry, constituted of the old volunteer troops, were called out in the South and West of Ireland for the purpose of keeping under control the rising spirit of rebellion which was surging throughout the population of Ulster and Leinster, to such an extent that the Government ordered a search for arms to be made by the military authorities, and that troops should be quartered on the civil population of the disturbed districts.

In December 1796 an expedition of some thirty-eight vessels, carrying an army of 15,000 French soldiers for the invasion of Ireland, arrived on the south-west coast of Ireland, in Bantry Bay. A violent hurricane, however, swept the bay at the time, and not only prevented the French from landing, but compelled the commander of the transports to stand out to sea. The expedition returned to Brest, from whence it had proceeded.

No sooner had news arrived in Ennis, Galway, and Limerick, that a French force was about to land in Bantry Bay, than the yeomanry and volunteers turned out to a man to resist the enemy. The Clare troops were under command of Colonel Francis Macnamara, who with his cousins John, and William Macnamara of Doolin, had taken an active part in drilling, and in the equipment of the troops. The old martial spirit of the people was instantly in wild excitement, and from the accounts left us by those who witnessed the mustering of the Clare volunteers, under the descendants of the old Clancuilein chiefs, we are reminded of some of Magrath's descriptions of the rising of the men of our sept five hundred years previously. General Dalrymple, who was in command at Cork, reported that "all ranks of Irishmen rallied to his support, determined to resist the French from landing." He adds:

* Lecky's "History of Ireland in the Eighteenth Century," vol. iii. p. 122.

"From Mayo to Cork similar reports were received." * General Hutchinson reported from Galway that in the course of two or three days he could have raised an army from among the men of co. Galway, Clare, and Limerick, he stated that "all ranks of the people in these parts were equally zealous and well affected, I could not speak too highly to you of the loyalty of all this part of the kingdom." General Smith wrote from Limerick that "the country is reported to be infinitely more attached to Government than common report ever allowed of. Your yeomanry and volunteers are guardians, and infuse by their appearance and indefatigable activity and exertions the most loyal spirit throughout each barony. The cotters of every village are reported to me to be boiling their potatoes for the soldiers." † The force of regular troops in the Cork command when the French appeared in Bantry Bay only amounted to 4000 men and four guns.

Referring to this remarkable outburst of loyal feeling on the part of tenants, and farmers of Clare, and other parts of the West of Ireland, Mr. Lecky observes, "it is a remarkable fact that Cork, Galway, and Limerick, the great centres of Irish Catholicism, vied with one another in 1796 in proof of loyalty to the English Government when the French fleet was off the coast" of Ireland; we may add, at the invitation of the people of Ulster and of Leinster. But from the lessons to be derived from the preceding history, we may learn the true nature of the Irish Celt, and that their conduct in 1796 did not belie their character. If they had acted otherwise it would have been in defiance of their congenital qualities, which have been delineated in a former chapter of this work. There was no question with them as to Catholics or Protestants. It is true their environment had largely altered, but their inherent disposition was the force which led them on loyally to enrol in defence of their homes and their Sovereign. There can be no doubt that in this action they were influenced by their priests, and gentlemen representing the old Celtic families of Clare; they had been treated by Government in a manner few other people have been subject to; but when a threat of invasion menaced their hearths they were true to themselves. If further evidence were necessary in proof of this statement, we might refer to the fact that in the year 1796, there were many of the O'Briens, Macnamaras, MacMahons, and other descendants of Celtic Irish families serving as officers in the French army and navy, but none of them were found in the expedition sent by that country to invade their native land. "The same desperate fidelity with which their fathers had sacrificed

* Dalrymple to Pelham, December 24, 1796.
† General Smith to Pelham, December 30, 1796.

LOYAL TO CROWN AND COUNTRY

home and country, and fortune for their faith and their king still continued—they ranged themselves in France against the Revolution." *
According to my idea, because the "mind is the man" is as true in France
as in Ireland or any other part of the world, not a few of the old Irish
brigade returned to Ireland at the invitation of the Duke of Portland in
1794 ; abandoning France and her revolutionary measures, they entered
the English army at a time when the north and east of their own country
was full of disaffection to the Crown and deeply moved by French
sentiment. So strong was the feeling of loyalty impressed on the
character of the members of our sept, that we find one of them sacri-
ficing his life rather than abandon the cause of his king. From original
papers in the possession of Mr. John Macnamara it appears that King
Louis XVI. had created Henry Macnamara a Count (May 3, 1782).
Both Henry and the John Macnamara above referred to were direct
descendants of a common ancestor in the person of Sioda Macnamara
(p. 170), of Henry VIII.'s time. Henry was sent by Louis XVI. to
Madras in the year 1789 to negotiate a treaty with Tipu Sultan,† "which
negotiations he carried through with the most brilliant success." Returning home the following year, he retired to the Isle of France, where
he was killed in resisting a revolutionary outbreak in 1790 (November 4).
His brother succeeded to the title, and served with distinction in the
Prince of Condé's army ; he was severely wounded, and returned to
France with Louis XVI. ; being disabled from further active service he
obtained an appointment at Court.

In confirmation of the statements contained in these family papers
we learn from Colonel Wilks ‡ that, in 1789, shortly after Tipu Sultan's
departure from Travancore, " a French officer named in the Mysoorian
manuscripts Macnamara, who is represented as making a tour of inspection of the settlements of that nation in a frigate, touched at this part of
the coast, and took the opportunity of paying his personal respects to
the Sultan, by whom he was suitably received. Tipu affected to treat
with levity the serious admonitions of this officer regarding the formidable preparations of the English, in consequence of his proceedings in
Travancore ; and the Sultan invited M. Macnamara to a review of his
picked men, who were to drive before them the British Grenadiers.
Monsieur Macnamara spoke with distinguished courtesy of the appearance and performance of the troops, but it was specially observed by

* Lecky's " History," vol. iii. p. 525.
† " Rulers of India : Tipu Sultan," by L. B. Bowring, p. 137.
‡ " Historical Sketches of the South of India," by Lieut.-Col. M. Wilk
vol. ii. p. 155.

those present that his politeness did not go the full length of assenting to the Sultan's propositions. The repeated assurance of this officer that the English considered the war actually commenced somewhat quickened Tipu's departure from Travancore, and he took the opportunity of committing to the charge of M. Macnamara a letter addressed to Louis XVI. stating his confidence, and the necessity for immediate aid if these apprehensions should be realised." * Colonel Mallison states that in due course Tipu received a reply from Louis XVI.; this in all probability was conveyed by Count H. Macnamara, as we learn from the MS. papers above quoted.

The failure of the French expedition to Ireland, seemed to have augmented the bitterness of feeling against the English Government entertained by the people in the disaffected parts of Ireland ; murder and rapine increased, and the country was so disturbed that Grattan urged the yeomanry and volunteers of Munster and Connaught being called out to assist in maintaining order in the disaffected provinces. In March 1798, the leaders of the intended rising were assembled at their final meeting in order to mature their plans, when the place they were in was surrounded by an armed force, and the conspirators were secured. The yeomanry was at this time raised to 50,000 men, and these, with the regular troops, were quartered on the civil population of Ulster and Leinster, doubtless inflicting severe treatment and hardship on innocent as well as on guilty people in the proclaimed districts. The people of Ulster eagerly looked forward to the arrival of troops from France, and there was at the time no obstacle to their passage to the north of Ireland, for our fleet at the Nore was in a state of mutiny, but no foreign help came, and so the men of Ulster, with characteristic shrewdness, played a waiting game.† The brunt of the rebellion was left to the unfortunate people of Leinster; on the 24th of May 1798, a rebel force, armed with pikes and such like weapons, assembled at Naas ; they were, however, dispersed by the yeomanry. The inhabitants of counties Kildare, Queen's County, Carlow, and Meath then broke out into open rebellion, which terminated after much bloodshed and the massacre of ninety-seven women, children, and men on Wexford Bridge. The rebels were led by a priest, Father John Murphy, who had been educated in Spain—a curious example, it may be thought, of the Irish priest, described in the previous pages of this chapter, p. 279— but while Father Murphy was urging the unfortunate people into revolt and untold misery, the Archbishop of Dublin was emphatic and strong

---

* "Life of the Marquess Wellesley, K.G.," by Colonel G. B. Mallison, p. 15.
† Lecky: "History of Ireland during the Eighteenth Century," vol. iv. p. 340.

in condemning the rebellion; his Grace directed an earnest exhortation to be read from every altar in the country after Mass, expressing in strong terms the condemnation of the Church upon all those taking part in rebellion; and, further, exhorting Irishmen to remain loyal to the Crown. Bishop Stock, a Protestant, writing on this subject, stated that as the Roman Catholic priests depended absolutely on their people for subsistence, some of them drifted, almost against their will, into the ranks of the rebels.*

W. N. Macnamara, of Doolin, was high sheriff of county Clare during the year 1789, and throughout this memorable period the country west of the Shannon remained "perfectly peaceful."† In Munster, with the exception of some slight disorder near Cork and Limerick, it is stated that "there was no semblance of rebellion." One of the magistrates writing from Ennis at this time, observed that "county Clare had escaped the contagion, although he had discovered that agents from Ulster had frequently been sent to excite the people to rebellion, but beyond a few shepherds no one had been persuaded to join the Society of "United Irishmen."

In August 1798, two days after the Battle of the Nile had been fought, a second French expedition appeared off the west of Ireland; it formed the vanguard of the much larger army which was intercepted by Sir J. Warren at sea, and never reached Ireland.‡ A force of some 1500 French soldiers, however, landed at Killala, believing that the whole of Ireland would meet them with open arms, and rush to their standard; in place of this the French general found the people were indifferent to his movements, nor would they even help him unless paid for their services; some few of the natives, for the sake of the clothes and rations offered by the French, allowed themselves to be drilled. But Major-General Hutchinson, who commanded at Galway, on hearing that the French had landed in Mayo, instantly called out the yeomanry of Clare, Galway, and other Connaught regiments; they marched towards Mayo, and the General reported that he found along the whole of his route that the country was perfectly quiet, and the people hard at work on their harvest.§ It is unnecessary to follow the fortunes of the French expedition in Ireland farther than to observe that they landed at Killala on the 22nd of August, and that by the 9th of the following month Lord Cornwallis, who was in command of the English forces,

* "Narrative of what Passed at Killala in 1798," by an Eye-witness, p. 81.
† Lecky: "History of Ireland in the Eighteenth Century," vol. iv. p. 340.
‡ *Ibid.*
§ "A Narrative of what Passed at Killala in 1798," by an Eye-witness, p. 4.

had finished his work and returned to Dublin, the French force in the meantime having either been destroyed or taken prisoners. Lord Cornwallis, in his general order on this expedition, states that, with reference to the Irish troops, especially the yeomanry of Clare, and Connaught, that "They had rendered the greatest service, and are peculiarly entitled to the acknowledgment of the Government, from their not having tarnished their courage and loyalty by any act of wanton cruelty towards their enemies or their fellow-subjects."

We may look back with unmixed satisfaction to this description of our countrymen at the close of the eighteenth century : the farmers and landowners of the territory west of the Shannon, the home of the Irish Celt. Lord Cornwallis had seen much service, and he commanded the men he refers to at a time when, undisciplined as they were, we could readily have understood their giving vent to the feelings of their grosser nature, but as in 1316, at Corcomroe, so in 1798 they revelled in the prospect of active service, but they were no less anxious to assist the fallen, whether friend or foe; in fact, the latter existed no longer, they were brethren in arms (see p. 125). I have neither attempted to paint these people in borrowed garments or to describe them after some picture formed by imagination, but have given the evidence of unbiassed persons, often Government officials, who knew these Irish Celts, the opinion of such persons having been recorded at the time the incidents they describe occurred, and, farther, these witnesses had no motive for making any statements on the subject except such as were true.

CHAPTER XX

Colonel F. Macnamara, M.P., in Dublin Parliament voted for the Union—" Fire-ball " Macnamara—Mr. J. Macnamara, M.P. for Leicester, intimate with Mr. Pitt, and a strong Tory—Severely wounded in contested election—Pitt's letter to Mr. Macnamara—Married to Mary Jones at Gretna Green—His character and pedigree—Grandfather to Mr. Arthur and John Macnamara—Descended from head of sept in Henry VIII.'s reign—Admiral James Macnamara—His duel and trial—Letter from Lord Nelson—Another Macnamara a well-known person in London at end of last century—His character and that of other members of the old sept—Precisely the same qualities as their forefathers.

In the year 1792, William Pitt appears to have conceived the idea, that the solution of the Irish difficulty consisted in the union of the Dublin Legislative Assembly with the House of Commons; it is beyond my province to attempt to discuss the question of the Union;* but there is reason to believe that Mr. John Macnamara, M.P. for Leicester, was in favour of the Union, and also Colonel Francis Macnamara, one of the representatives of Clare in the Dublin Parliament, for he voted for the Act of Union passed in the year 1800.

* There can be no question as to the fact that Mr. Pitt carried his measure upon the faith of promises he could not fulfil. These consisted in the admission of Catholics as members into the new Parliament, the commutation of tithes, and the endowment of the Catholic priesthood. With reference to the means taken by the English Government to carry "the Union" Act, we may best give the sentiments expressed by Lord Cornwallis, who at the time was Lord Lieutenant of Ireland. He observes that "the political jobbing of this country (Ireland) gets the better of me; it has ever been the wish of my life to avoid this dirty business, and I am now involved in it beyond all bearing. . . . . How I long to kick those whom my public duty obliges me to court; my occupation is now of the most unpleasant nature, negotiating and jobbing with the most corrupt people under the sun. I despise and hate myself every hour for engaging in such dirty work, and am supported only by the reflection that without an Union the British Empire must be dissolved." He adds: " Nothing but conviction that the Union is abso-lutely necessary for the safety of the British Empire could make me endorse the shocking task which is imposed on me." It was for Lord Cornwallis to decide with his own conscience whether the end justified the means; but while confessing all this shame and contrition for the part he was taking in bribery and corruption, it is foolish to rile at those who received his bribes as being the most corrupt people under the sun.

T

Colonel F. Macnamara of Moyrisk was elected member for Clare in 1790; he had previously been an officer of the yeomanry and Clare volunteers, and held a prominent position in the county; he entered the Dublin Parliament as a supporter of the Government, and was a cotemporary of John Macnamara, M.P.; they were neighbours in Clare as boys, and probably on terms of friendship. Colonel F. Macnamara died in the year 1814, and was succeeded by his son Major Macnamara, who was Daniel O'Connell's second in the duel when he shot the unfortunate Mr. D'Esterre in 1815. Major Macnamara was urged to stand as Member of Parliament for county Clare, on Mr. Fitzgerald's promotion (he being member for Clare) to the Secretaryship of the Board of Trade; the major, however, declined the offer, in consequence " of his friendship for the Fitzgerald family."[*]

Major Macnamara's brother John, "Shawn Bwee," as he was called, or "Yellow John," on account of his swarthy complexion, lived at Moyrisk during his father's lifetime, and added much to the pleasure of the rollicking society which always crowded the rooms of that hospitable mansion. His father kept a pack of hounds, and more than one team of horses filled his stables, and with an establishment in proportion he ran up heavy debts, which ultimately led to the property being sold. But during the early part of this century the future was the last thing which Colonel Macnamara and his sons thought of. John, or as he was better known, *Fireball* Macnamara, was a great favourite throughout Clare; he is said to have fought fifty-seven duels during his early years, besides standing second in numerous affairs of honour. He is supposed to have fought incognito at the Battle of Vinegar Hill with the peasantry, and was then wounded in the thigh, and so was lame for the rest of his life. Fireball's name is at the present time a household word in Clare, and among the people numberless tales are told of his deeds; for he evidently exercised a fascinating influence over his neighbours and friends, and was overflowing with brave and generous sentiments; a keen lover of sport of every kind. The tender side of Fireball's nature was brought out in his chivalrous devotion to his charming sister, *Fair Mary of Moyrisk*, who seems not only to have been a remarkably beautiful young woman, but was also held in the highest respect by all who came under her influence. There was much in John Macnamara's character which reminds us of the qualities displayed by so many of his ancestors, who were chiefs of one of the principal families of our sept. Fireball was the last of the Moyrisk Macnamaras, and, like many of those who had preceded him he attached

[*] Very Rev. P. White, P.P., V.G.: " History of Clare," p. 337.

to himself the devotion of his countrymen, and could have led them anywhere he pleased. It would be quite possible to fill many pages with anecdotes concerning this individual, but want of space renders this impossible and must be reserved for other hands than mine ; but if properly arranged they would clearly bring out the qualities which have influenced the lives of so many of our clan. Fireball died in a small cottage close to Quin, and his tomb is to be seen in a corner of the oratory of the old abbey at the left-hand side of the high altar.*

Lord Cloncurry in his Memoirs states that when he first came to London, in the year 1795, he was invited to dinner by one of his countrymen, Mr. John Macnamara, who lived in Baker Street, and that on this occasion he met Mr. Pitt, England's great statesman and Prime Minister. Lord Cloncurry was a young man, and had come to study law at the Temple ; at this dinner-party he, for the first time, heard the subject of the Union discussed, and he remarks that " it acted like a ferment on him," and led him to publish a pamphlet which he observes "cost him a heavy price."†

Lord Cloncurry writes as follows : "This remarkable man, Mr. John Macnamara, was a noted high Tory politician, and upon the most intimate terms with Mr. Pitt." It would therefore seem that in the year 1795 Mr. Pitt and John Macnamara discussed the subject of the Union at the dinner table of the latter gentleman, so that it is probable Mr. Macnamara was one of those who had a good deal to say in bringing Mr. Pitt, to adopt this measure, which was consequently backed by a representative of one of the oldest Celtic families in the West of Ireland ; or more correctly, by two such representatives, that is, by

* " Lays and Legends of Thomond," by Michael Hogan, who knew Fireball, and mentions him frequently in his work. See notes to pp. 118, 223, 258, 345, and 363.

† Sir W. Petty had as far back as 1670 strongly advocated the " Union between England and Ireland." The arguments he used were that the Governments of both countries united would be safer and less expensive than if separated ; that the enrichment of Ireland and prevention of rebellion attainable by a union of Governments must be advantageous to both countries ; that the prerogative of King, Peers, or Commons in either kingdom need not be lessened ; that it would not hinder different laws, if necessary for the two countries, being enacted ; that as Wales and Scotland have profited by union, so might Ireland ; that union is strength. It was better without union to dispeople and abandon the land and bring all movables, including the English, out of the country. Sir William recites many other reasons for the union of the Governments of Ireland and England. He recognised the growth of Imperial questions and the construction of " a Grand National Council " to give advice and information on all Imperial subjects (" Life of Sir W. Petty," by Lord E. Fitzmaurice, p. 277).

Colonel F. Macnamara in the Dublin Parliament, and by Mr. John Macnamara, who had no conceivable object to gain in supporting Mr. Pitt as regards this measure; for he was essentially a gentleman, and consequently shrank from obtruding himself upon public notice: and this may have been one reason why Mr. Pitt trusted him in matters other than the Union, for among his papers we find copies of a correspondence regarding the terms of peace which France was prepared to offer England, in November 1797, but which Mr. Pitt was not disposed to entertain.   Lord Cloncurry mentions the fact that in the year 1788 Mr. J. Macnamara had been severely injured during a contested election for a seat in Parliament; this was one of the many violent fights between Whig and Tory for a representative for the City of Westminster.*   Mr. J. Macnamara was in the thick of the contest; and we have a copy of a letter he wrote on this occasion to his friend, Mr. Horne Tooke.   Mr. Macnamara had just been wounded, and states in this letter, that " Mr. Fox's friends have at length carried their point, so far as I am concerned.   Here I am, most terribly cut by some of their ruffians, doubtless properly instructed.   They first struck a poor woman with a child in her arms, and have, I fear seriously injured them both.   Do send first and enquire about this woman, and afford her any assistance in your power that she may require. I hope my wounds are not serious ; but lest they should prove to be so, I wish you and Mr. Vaughan to come here immediately to write relative to my wife and children.   Come directly, but first inquire about the poor woman at the top of the Haymarket." †   On receiving this letter Mr. Horne Tooke started off to see his friend, and on his return wrote an angry letter to Mr. Fox, in which he states that no less than two hundred and sixty wounded men were in the wards of the Middlesex, and other hospitals which he had visited, victims to the passions roused in this election.   Horne Tooke states that Mr. Earl, who was Mr. Potts' partner had been called to attend Mr. Macnamara, but was unable to state what might be the consequences of his wound on the head. The day he was injured Mr. Macnamara received the following letter from Mr. Pitt :

* Mr. Macnamara had been gazetted, in 1788, "Colonel of the Westminster Regiment of the Middlesex Militia."   "The London Packet," or "New Lloyd's Evening Post," April 4 to April 7; from the "London Gazette," April 5; St. James's, April 3.

† "A Pair of Portraits," London, 1789; Pamphlet, vol. cxxv. of Martin and Petts' Collection of Pamphlets, Athenæum Club Library.

DOWNING STREET, FRIDAY NIGHT,
June 25, 1788.

MY DEAR MR. MACNAMARA,—You will easily imagine the concern with which I learn the account of your having suffered so severely. I hope, however, that I shall have the satisfaction of receiving favourable news from you to-morrow. In the meantime I trust it is unnecessary to again assure you how sincere an interest I take in all that concerns you, and how anxious I shall be on all occasions to prove the regard with which I am your faithful friend,   W. PITT.

J. Macnamara, Esq.*

In 1780, Mr. J. Macnamara (who was born June 8, 1756) married an heiress, the only daughter of Mr. Arthur Jones, of Carmarthenshire. This gentleman was called to the Bar at the Middle Temple in March 1761, and was in extensive practice in London; he resided at Kensington.† In a letter written by Mr. J. Macnamara to his future father-in-law, dated Lincoln's Inn, December 6, 1779), he mentions his circumstances, and the settlement which he was prepared to make on his future wife. From this letter we learn that J. Macnamara's intimacy with Miss Jones had been a matter of some standing, but before broaching the subject of marriage he felt it to be his duty to obtain her father's consent. Whether Mr. Jones refused his sanction to his daughter's

---

* The original of this letter is among the MS. papers of Mr. John Macnamara. Lord Cloncurry mentions the fact that he had heard Mr. John Macnamara relate the circumstances of the death of a well-known actress, Miss Ray ; and on turning to the "General Advertiser and Morning Intelligencer " for the 17th of April, 1779, I find a detailed account of the trial of the Rev. J. Hackman at the Old Bailey for the murder of Miss Ray. Mr. John Macnamara was the first witness called, and stated that on the 7th of April, as he was leaving Covent Garden Theatre about eleven o'clock at night, he saw the deceased and another lady standing near the doorway, but unable to reach their carriage in consequence of the crowd. He went up to them and asked if he could be of any assistance to them ; they accepted his offer. Mr. Macnamara then cleared the way and took one of the ladies to her carriage. He went back for Miss Ray, and just as she reached the carriage the report of two pistol shots were heard. Miss Ray, who was leaning on Mr. Macnamara's arm, staggered, fell forward, and expired. Mr. Hackman stated at his trial that he had left his rooms fully intending to destroy himself, and letters were found on him confirming this statement. He had no knowledge of Miss Ray, and no possible motive for taking her life; a sudden madness seized him and he shot her. The judge ruled that, as at the time the prisoner shot Miss Ray he was about to commit an unlawful act, he was guilty of murder, although without premeditation. The jury returned a verdict of " Guilty " against Hackman.

† He was the only son of Mr. Thomas Jones, of St. Asaph.

marriage I know not, but it is certain John Macnamara, and Mary Jones were married on the 12th of January 1780, "by the way of the Church of England, and agreeable to the laws of the Church of Scotland," by Thomas Brown, at Gretna Green. Mrs. Macnamara was a charming and lovable woman, full of character and intellect, and highly esteemed by all who knew her. She was devoted to her husband and family; her mother was a member of the ancient Pembrokeshire family of Wogan; after their marriage, John Macnamara purchased Llangoed Castle, Brecon, where they resided for a considerable portion of the year, and when in London lived at 39 Baker Street, Portman Square. Mr. Macnamara was elected a Member of Parliament for Leicester in 1784, and held his seat until 1790; he seems to have been a popular member, but not to have taken any prominent part in the debates carried on in the House. Among his papers there is one marked in his handwriting, "A good sketch of myself," by a lady; my object in referring to this document is to show how true this man seems to have been to the character held by so many generations of his forefathers. (See Appendix to chapter.)

Mr. J. Macnamara died on the 3rd of May, 1818, and was buried in the grounds of Llangoed Castle. He has two grandsons living at the present time—Mr. Arthur Macnamara* and his twin brother, Mr. John Macnamara.† In the Appendix to this chapter I have given references to the original documents upon which the pedigree of this branch of the family is founded. Until the commencement of the present century, Roman Catholics in Ireland could neither register their births, deaths, or marriages, so that it is only from deeds, and private papers that a pedigree can be filled up in the case of many Irish families during the seventeenth, and early part of the eighteenth centuries.

Mr. A. Macnamara, and his brother John are descended from the second son of Sioda Macnamara of Henry VIII.'s time, and through him from Mac-con-Macnamara of 1334 (p. 133), and backwards to the founder of our sept. Sioda's son John, had several children; the eldest became Sir John Macnamara (p. 153); he died without issue, and his younger brothers passed over to France, and became the progenitors of Vice-Admiral Macnamara, of the French navy, and of Count H. Macnamara (p. 249). So that this French branch of the family, and Mr. John Macnamara and his brother, have a common ancestor in Sioda Macnamara above referred to.

* Of Caddington Hall, Hertfordshire.

† Mr. John Macnamara had one son, Arthur, who was accidentally killed by a fall on the Alps on the 16th of August 1890; he has two daughters, both living.

look ; like lightning are his opinions formed on the merits of the picture; if the defects predominate woe unto the object, *particularly* if one of his *own sex*, who flies before the arrow of his satire ; but he is merciful to the weaker sex: he is more, he is kind, he is generous, indulgent. Nature formed his head for the crown of a drum, to command an army, to rule a senate ; but his heart in a softer mould was made—*it* will be ever found in " My Lady's Chamber."

" A Good Sketch of Myself ":
Words written in J. Macnamara's handwriting.

CHAPTER XXI

Conclusions drawn from the preceding history regarding some of the leading
questions affecting Ireland—Arthur Macnamara, the last representative of
one of the chief families of Clancuilein.

MR. PRENDERGAST, the author of a well-known book, " The Cromwellian
Settlement of Ireland," arrived at the following conclusion from a study
of Irish history.   He observes that :

> Now the " Irish enemy " (or in other words, Irishmen living beyond the Pale)
> was no nation in the modern sense of the word, but a race divided into many
> nations and tribes, separately defending their lands from the English barons in
> their immediate neighbourhood.   There has been no ancient national dynasty
> overthrown ; the Irish had no national flag, nor any capital city as the metropolis
> of their common country, nor any common administration of law ; nor did they
> ever give combined opposition to the English.   The English, coming in the name
> of the Pope, with the aid of the bishops and with superior organisation, which
> the Irish easily recognised, were accepted by the Irish ; neither King Henry II.
> nor King John ever fought a battle in Ireland.

From this passage it would seem Mr. Prendergast was under the
impression that before the inhabitants of a country such as Ireland could
enter the family of nations, it was necessary for her to possess an abiding
dynasty, a recognised flag, central government, and a metropolis.   But
people may exist without one or other of these institutions, and yet form
a Nation according to the right meaning of the word, which is "a race
of people, an aggregation of persons of the same ethnic family, and
speaking the same language." *   Without question the Irish people
spoke the Gaelic or Celtic language until, of their own free will, they
learnt English.   They were from the early part of our era up to the
present time an Iberio-Celtic race; who have adhered to the Roman
Catholic form of religion from the fifth century ; they existed until the
reign of James I. under their Brehon laws ; and last but not least
they are linked to one another by hereditary qualities which have
moulded their characters and ideas into close concord.   The right,
therefore, of the Irish to be acknowledged as a Nation rests on solid

* " The Century Dictionary."

grounds, and in controverting this fact Prendergast was at fault, but he was quite right when he states that the people of Ireland, as far back as Henry II.'s reign, recognised the necessity that existed for English rule and law being introduced into their country. They understood how hopeless it was to attempt to govern the inhabitants of Ireland by two codes of law, which differed from one another in principle. It was the inappropriate suddenness, and the way in which the Common law of England was imposed on the Irish which led to such unmitigated evil.

Prendergast was correct when he stated that the Irish had always been divided into many tribes who were frequently at war with one another, or fighting with the object of preserving their lands from invasion by foreigners. But this constant pressure from without had the effect of welding these tribes and septs into firmly homogeneous societies, complete in themselves for social and political purposes. In this way the mind of these people became intently fixed on retaining possession of their homes and lands ; their thoughts being constantly focussed on these objects to the exclusion of all other important matters; and it was in these circumstances that our sept for upwards of a thousand years became rooted to Ui-Caisin, their tribal inheritance. An existence of this kind incapacitated them from combining to form a Nation in Prendergast's meaning of the term, and what is more important it engendered in them an inherited inability to associate in a permanent and broad sense for either political or social national life.

From the fifth until the middle of the sixteenth century Ireland was nominally ruled by four or five provincial kings, who were constantly at war with one another in order to gain supremacy over the country. Brian Boru, by dint of hard fighting became monarch of Ireland about the year 1002, and as such received tribute from the provincial kings. We have the details of the procedure followed by the various chiefs at Brian's table; the amount of tribute which each had to supply ; but we hear nothing of a National Council. After Brian Boru's efforts to free his country from the Norsemen, the King of Ossory refused to permit his wounded soldiers to pass through his territory on account of some old standing grudge he had against the Dalcasians, and at the battle of Clontarf the King of Leinster declined to assist Brian. Once only the provincial kings met in Council, with the object of devising means by which they might combine for the defence of their country against foreigners : but when they came together the question arose as to which of the kings was to take precedence at the Council-table ; they could not arrive at a satisfactory conclusion on this point, and so the meeting broke up, and there was an end to anything approaching

U

concerted action between the kings of Ireland for the defence of their country.*

If we refer to the history of the various invasions of Ireland, we find incontrovertible evidence of the incapacity of her leaders to sacrifice their own interests for that of their country. The first invasion of Ireland during historical times took place in the third century ; it was led by Mac-Con, a chief of Munster, who had been expelled from his country and taken refuge in Scotland ; he brought a large force of foreigners over to Ireland, and by their aid fought his way to the throne. The second invasion of Erin was by the Norsemen ; there was no combined effort on the part of the Irish to expel these foreigners for nearly two centuries ; and during that period they overran the greater part of Ireland. The third invasion was effected by Anglo-Normans at the solicitation of the King of Leinster, who had been driven from Ireland by his own subjects and taken refuge in England. The fourth invasion was by the Scotch, led by the Bruces, who were brought over to Ireland by Donough Brian Roe. Three of these four invasions were led by Celtic chiefs who sought, and obtained the assistance of foreigners to regain their position among their own people, regardless of the wrong they inflicted on Ireland, and with the object of recovering a position from which they had been driven by their countrymen. The landing of the Spaniards on the coast of Ireland in the year 1579, and of the French in the year 1798, was brought about by the people of the South, and of the North of Ireland on account of religious or political disabilities which led them to seek the aid of foreigners against the English Government.†

When first the Anglo-Normans entered on the conquest of Ireland her provincial kings were so deeply engrossed in their own quarrels that they failed to resist the common enemy, although it was well within their power had they acted with the ruler of Connaught to have driven the English from Dublin. The King of Connaught, finding he could not enforce his position as head of the provincial chiefs, entered into a compact with Henry II. by which he engaged to make Ireland over to the Crown of England, provided Henry would recognise him as head of the four provincial kings of Ireland. Brian Roe again, to expel the O'Briens and Macnamaras from their lands entered into an alliance with De Clare, and so brought about war to the west of the Shannon which involved its inhabitants for half a century in bloodshed and untold suffering. Almost the last battle fought by the Irish Celts under the old order of things was the culminating point of the nation's madness; for in this fierce engagement the inhabitants of the North and South of Ireland were

* See p. 82.   † See p. 282.

brought into the field under commanders of Anglo-Norman extraction, with a force of armed Englishmen standing by to watch the Celts tear one another to pieces, which they did until both parties were well-nigh annihilated.* True, this is somewhat ancient history, but if we are to gain any advantage from a study of this subject it is necessary carefully to consider facts of this kind; and the conclusion we must draw from these facts is, that our forefathers were incapacitated from the nature of their dispositions, to perseveringly combine with one another in order to advance the political interest of their country. This is a lesson taught us not only by the history of the Irish Celt, but the same conviction forced itself on the historians Mommsen and Thierry, from a study of the Celt during the period in which this race overran the greater part of Western Europe.†

The thing that hath been, it is that which shall be; and that which is done is that which shall be done.

Without entering on a discussion as to the political state of the Celtic population of Ireland at the present day, it is certain the same obstacles which prevented their forefathers from uniting for a long and uninterrupted attempt to form a nation, in Prendergast's meaning of the term, are as insurmountable now as ever they were. Nevertheless, the great majority of Irishmen, if we may judge from the Members they return to Parliament, are in favour of establishing a National Assembly in Dublin to regulate the affairs of Ireland. If, however, we refer this opinion to the judgment of history, and the character of the Irish, we are drawn to the conclusion that the idea of a Dublin Parliament of this kind is not Celtic, and that the opinion which the majority of Irishmen appear to hold on this subject is founded on premises, some of which are perfectly true, mixed with a large proportion of error.

In the first place, with regard to a Dublin Parliament, it is doubtful from recent experience in other countries, if parliamentary government is the best form of government to control the affairs of people who inherit a considerable amount of the Celtic nature. Parliaments are certainly not indigenous productions of the Irish race; on the other hand, they were imported from England, and their action was for long confined to the English Pale. The first that we hear of a Parliament in the West of Ireland was in the year 1542, when Sidney assembled his Parliament in Limerick to legalise the proposals of the O'Briens, Macnamaras, and other septs with regard to the titles of their lands being made conformable to English procedure. The first approach

* See p. 146.   † See p. 11.

to a National Council in comparatively recent times in Ireland was convened by the Confederates in the year 1648. This Assembly was certainly
wanting in administrative power, and soon became utterly disorganised,
as described by the Pope's nuncio, who states that on one occasion the
Council being assembled, the matter under discussion produced so much
excitement among the members present that half of them jumped up
from their seats, and rushed out of the hall in which the meeting was
being held.* How many similar meetings, including those in recent
times, have been reported as occurring among Irish politicians?

Mr. Thomas Davis, who has written an admirable account of the
Dublin Parliament of 1689, remarks that this Assembly " was the first, and
the last which ever sat in Ireland since the English invasion possessed
national authority, and complete in all its parts." † He further
observes that the Dublin House of Commons was "a sort of sept repre-
sentation"; for instance, the members for county Clare were an O'Brien
and a Macnamara, and for its borough (Ennis) another Macnamara and a
Butler : of the 224 members constituting the Lower House, six were
Protestants.

James II. entered Dublin on March 24, accompanied by D'Avaux as
ambassador from France, and with a splendid Court. On May 7 his
Parliament had assembled, and the king, " with robe and crown,"
addressed the Commons ; he pronounced his policy to consist in " liberty
of conscience, and against invading any man's property." The king
stated he had come to Ireland, " to venture my life with you in defence
of your liberties and my own rights." The conditions under which the
Parliament of 1689 met therefore were exceptional, the King of Ireland
was there to guard and control the deliberations of Parliament, Dublin
was predominated by his Court, and full of his English and French
friends and supporters. The members of this Parliament met, but
many of them had other urgent duties to attend to ; for example, John
Macnamara was soon to be Colonel of the " Yellow Dragoons," which
he raised in Clare, and led at the Battle of the Boyne ; Florence Macnamara, another member of the Dublin Parliament, was engaged in
organising a regiment of infantry raised in his own county. In these
circumstances, with the exception of the Act of Attainder, the Dublin
Parliament of 1689 did good work, and in a thoroughly business-like
manner. Among other matters it laid down the principle that "the
English Parliament had not, and never had, any right to legislate for

* See p. 194.
† " The Patriot Parliament of 1689." by Thos. Davis, edited by C. G. Duffy,
p. 39.

Ireland, and that none save the King, and Parliament of Ireland could make laws to bind Ireland." Mr. Molyneux took an active part in politics, but was not in Dublin during James II.'s Parliament; in his famous work, " The Case of Ireland," which he published in February 1697, and addressed to King William, he argued strongly in support of the proposition laid down by James's Parliament as above quoted; this work is frequently referred to by those who advocate a repeal of the Union; Molyneux, however, observes : "If from the last-mentioned records it be concluded that the Parliament of England may bind Ireland, it must also be allowed that the people of Ireland ought to have their representatives in the Parliament of England. And this, I believe, we would be willing enough to embrace, but this is a happiness we can hardly hope for."* Nevertheless, Ireland has now been close on a century governed by a Parliament of Irish and English members such as Molyneux advocated but hardly dared to hope for.

Apart from all political considerations what has been the practical outcome of the union of the Irish and English Parliaments? In the first place, we find that during the past century all classes of people in Ireland have benefited by the £50,000,000 which England has advanced for public works and other improvements in that country ; these advances have been made on the security of the political union that exists between the two islands. As a test of the progress made in Ireland we may refer to the amount which the inhabitants of that country had as a reserve fund at their disposal in cash, in June 1894, as follows :

The deposits and cash balances in the Irish Joint Stock Banks, which, comparing June with June, had gradually increased from £29,223,000 in June 1886, to £35,430,000 in the corresponding period of 1894, further rose to £37,491,000 in June of the present year, being the highest amount yet reached for June, and showing an increase of £2,061,000 or 5.8 per cent., as compared with the amount in the middle of last year, and an increase of £8,268,000 or 28.3 per cent, as compared with the amount in June, 1886. The balance in the Savings Banks in June last amounted to £7,371,000, or £744,000 in excess of the balance in June 1894, and this increase is £128,000 higher than that for the year ended June 30th, 1893, which was equal to double the highest annual increase in any of the twenty years preceding. The amount of Government Funds, Indian Stocks, and Guaranteed Land Stock on which dividends are payable at the Bank of Ireland was in June 1895, £25,824,000, compared with £25,375,000 in June 1894, being an increase of £449,000, following an increase of £92,000 at that date as compared with the amount in June 1893. The year 1894 was the first year since 1887 in which there

---

* " The Case of Ireland," by W. Molyneux, p. 70. A new and admirable edition of this work, with preface and life of the author, by the Very Rev. John Canon O'Hanlon, P.P., M.R.I.A.

was an increase under this heading in June as compared with the amount for June in the preceding year.   There has been an increase of £241,000 in the note circu lation as compared with the year 1894, the value having risen from £6,007,000 in June 1894, to £6,248,000 in the corresponding period of 1895.   The amount for June 1894, was £81,000 under that for June 1893.   The total receipts of the Irish railways for the first half of 1895 were in excess of those for the first half of any previous year, and show an increase of £25,441, or 1.6 per cent., as com pared with the first six months of 1894, the receipts for which period were £43,474 above those for the first half of the year 1893.

The banking and railway statistics for the year 1895, compiled by the Registrar- General, show that the deposits and cash balances in the Irish Joint Stock Banks, exclusive of £1,383,000 Government and other public balances in the Bank of Ireland, stood in December last at £39,008,000, being an increase of £1,401,000 over the corresponding period of 1894.   The estimated balance in the Post Office Savings Bank amounted to £5,603,000, being an increase of £626,000.   The accumulation of small savings in Post Office and Trustee Banks showed a very large increase during the year.   The railway receipts for the year were the highest on record.

If we desire further evidence as to the change effected by the Union we may call to mind the fact, that it is hardly a century since Irish Roman Catholics were prevented from practising as barristers or as physicians, they could neither obtain commissions in the army or navy; whereas at present the Lord Chief Justice of England is an Irish Roman Catholic; the Commander-in-Chief of the British army, Field- Marshal Viscount Wolseley, is an Irishman, as also is Field-Marshal Lord Roberts, in command of her Majesty's forces in Ireland.

To comprehend therefore the meaning of the demand made by Celtic Irishmen for a Dublin Parliament, we must seek for an explanation in the predominant components of their character.   From the commencement of our history the centre round which the life of the Irish Celt revolved was the possession of land ; his social and political existence depended on the land ; for centuries he considered neither life or anything else too great a sacrifice to spend in the defence of his ancestral property, however small it might be.   In fact, the possession of land was, and is the supreme desire of every Irishman, land upon which he and his family may enjoy life in their own way; he has no wish to heap up riches to spend on himself or leave to others ; he cares not to wander over the globe in search of recreation or pleasure; he dislikes a city life ; and, strange to say, Irishmen never for an instant doubt that Ireland is not the best of all countries, and their home the dearest spot on earth.   And what does history teach these people ? that their ancestors in defence of their lands, their king, and their religion, resisted as best they could the power of England, and having failed in their efforts, the English Government took by force the whole of their land, and gave or sold it to Englishmen and Scotchmen over the heads of its original proprietors, whose descendants still live on the land and love it with all the strong affection of their forefathers.* They have been taught that, as in the case of the crushing duties imposed on the produce of Ireland by the English landed, and mercantile interests during the last century,† that it was only through the efforts of a Dublin Parliament, and England's necessity, that these cruel taxes were repealed; so in the case of the land they are taught that through means of a Dublin Parliament alone can they obtain possession of the soil from existing English landlords, very many of whom are absolute strangers to Ireland, and of a different race and religion from its people.   This, to a great extent, explains the statement already made that the desire for a Dublin Parliament among Celtic Irishmen is founded on a mixture of truth and error; it is true broadly that Englishmen will grab everything they can lay their hands on, and having possessed themselves of land or anything else they hold to it with bulldog-like tenacity; but it is an error to believe that through means of a Dublin Parliament the Irish land question can be settled.   The times, however, are favourable for such a settlement, because landed property is not at present a very profitable investment, especially to non-resident landlords, who might therefore be disposed to sell their estates on reasonable terms, and invest the profits elsewhere.   Irish landholders now have their opportunity, and if they can obtain an advance of money on the land at a low rate of interest they would be able to purchase much of the confiscated soil of Ireland.   An arrangement of this description, however, can only be carried through by aid of the House of Commons and the English taxpayers, who, if they thoroughly understood the story of Ireland would provide the necessary funds to carry out this work.   Among other reasons, because from the knowledge we possess of the Irish character we may with safety rely on their paying back the purchase money, and interest due on loans advanced on the land, which, as of old, would become the property of the farmer.

The land is far and away the most prominent question with reference to Ireland, but it by no means involves the desire on the part of Irish farmers to drive resident landlords and private gentlemen out of the country.   Far, indeed, is this from being the case; the landholders know perfectly well, and thoroughly appreciate, the advantages to be derived from the presence of country gentlemen residing among them. They also recognise the fact that for many years to come there must be

* See p. 256.   .   .   † See p. 276.

a number of tenant-farmers in the country, for the process of re-purchasing the land can only be gradually proceeded with; any sudden change in a matter of the kind would necessarily be attended with unsatisfactory results.

With reference to tenant-farmers, we must bear in mind that the old system of land tenure in Ireland had much in common with the rest of Europe, and was almost identical with that of India. It was the English system which was peculiar in its nature, and differed from that of other nations; and it is this exceptional land tenure which the Government has for three centuries vainly endeavoured to impose on the Irish Celt. These people have never accepted the capitalist as the rightful owner of the land—the tenant cultivating it under contract, and the labourer working for hire. And when the landlord handed his estates over to the middleman, and spent his rents in England open war was declared by the Irish against the landlord. This hostility showed itself in the "Whiteboy" rising, which commenced more than a hundred and fifty years ago, and, in spirit, is just as pronounced in many parts of Ireland to-day as it was in the year 1745.

There can be no doubt that, until the year 1870, the position of tenants throughout the West and South of Ireland was most unsatisfactory; and, further, that Irishmen are under a deep obligation to Charles Parnell, and the Land League for their successful exertions in improving the condition of tenant-farmers in Ireland. The mistake was in the Government allowing the Irish tenants to remain for so long a time without relief, necessitating the intervention of the Land League. It was precisely the same with the tax on Irish produce during the last century, the Government being completely under the control of capitalists, the most selfish class of persons in the country.* What is now urgently required is the re-establishment of the former relations between the landlord and the farmer or tiller of his lands, a fixed rent being settled once and for all, if necessary, by the Land Commissioners; and, in case of the non-payment of rent, the tenant to be made a bankrupt, his farm sold, and any excess above the amount due as rent to go to the bankrupt. Under existing conditions, many landlords are now in a worse plight than their tenants were five-and-twenty years ago.

A Board of Agriculture, and the institution of technical schools might do a vast deal to improve the system of agriculture and all that pertains to it in Ireland. Here again we should do well to take a lesson from our ancestors, who in precept and practice insisted on the fact, " that discipline, obedience to superiors, and the work which a boy or girl

* See pp. 251–254.

would have to follow in their future career" were, as they still should be, the primary objects of education.*

But, after all, the gradual transfer, by means of a voluntary process of the land in Ireland to the resident occupier and tiller of the soil is the right and only real way to settle the land question. With the transference of the land to the farmers it is essential they should also obtain a thoroughly good title to their property; the re-establishment of the Brehon system of compulsory registration of deeds connected with land would be invaluable. A system of this kind, commencing with a clear title would limit, as of old, the necessity for lawsuits and endless trouble in all matters connected with the transfer of the soil, and much that belongs to it. A plan of compulsory registration might readily be carried out in Ireland, especially with the aid of the perfect survey maps which have been completed for the whole of that country.

There will, however, be sudden and vehement outbursts of dissatisfaction among the agricultural population of Ireland in spite of all that the Government can do, for it is the nature of Celts to let off their pent-up feelings in this way. We are informed that, as far back as the year 1064, in consequence of "much inclement weather in Ireland, its corn, milk, fruit, and fish were destroyed, and the people grew discontented; there was no safety for any one."† In these circumstances, coercive laws were enacted by the ruler of Ireland, "to restrain every injustice great and small." These measures were successful, and it is much to be wished that the historians of the period had left us the scope and bearing of these laws. The character of Irishmen has not altered; and the conditions which caused this outburst of discontent under the Government of Torlough O'Brien, will stir up precisely the same spirit under the Government of Queen Victoria.

We may learn another important lesson from our history, and that is, the respect and strong feeling of affection entertained by the people of the West of Ireland for their Sovereign; loyalty to their rulers is a deeply impressed character in the mind of the Irish Celt; it existed under the old tribal system, and, so far as our sept is concerned, was transferred from the Kings of Thomond to Henry VIII. of England when he assumed paramount power over Ireland. One might write many pages filled with evidence showing that these people have faithfully adhered to the sentiments of their forefathers in loyalty to the Crown. In the period of their great distress, and when urged by the inhabitants of Ulster to revolt against their Sovereign, they rose with enthusiasm as volunteers and yeomanry to resist the enemies of their king, in precisely

* See p. 23.   † See p. 86.

the same way as they had done in support of their chief Torlough O'Brien in the thirteenth century. The Earl of Ormonde in the year 1649 appreciated this quality in the Celts; he knew that if Charles II. could then have been persuaded to leave France and land in Ireland that the people would have rushed to his support. But, failing to secure the presence of Charles in Ireland, Ormonde gave up the royal cause as hopeless, for the condition of things was desperate, and the presence of the King was necessary to revive the well-nigh exhausted feeling of loyalty which existed among the Irish. There is much in this, the inherited principle of devotion to the Sovereign is deeply implanted in the Irish Celt, but human nature requires something more than a principle to worship. It is much to be wished that a royal castle were provided on Loch Derge, near the site of Brian Boru's beautiful habitation, in which some of the members of our Sovereign's family might from time to time take up their abode; nothing would conduce more to advance the social and political condition of the West of Ireland than the residence of one of the royal family of England in that part of the country for a certain portion of the year. These people have not only been loyal, but numbers of them, as sailors and soldiers, have fought and died for England in every part of the world; and in these times the devotion of a thoroughly loyal, brave, and essentially chivalrous people is something worth cultivating. Our agricultural population in the various divisions of the United Kingdom have formed the backbone of England, and they may be relied upon in the future as in the past; nowhere are they to be found in greater perfection than among the people of the West of Ireland.

Another Irish problem seems capable of explanation through means of history, and that is, the development of some of the Irish priests into political agitators. The clergy of the seventeenth century, until the heavy hand of persecution was laid upon them were, in the West of Ireland lax in discipline, and certainly did not inspire that implicit devotion on the part of the people which exists at the present time. At the end of the last century, however, the Irish priests were, as a rule, thorough gentlemen, and earnest pious men, loved and respected alike by their own flock and the Protestants in their neighbourhood, they were loyal and devoted servants of their Sovereign, and seemed to be the one peaceful and most cherished element in a rude, almost wildly reckless, state of society.* At a distance we now hear of the Irish priest principally as a political agitator, often the leading spirit on the platform and at the polling-booth, and the most verbose and acrimonious spirit at political

* Pp. 219, 280.

meetings; following most certainly a different line of conduct to that laid down by His Holiness Pope Innocent X. in his memorable charge to Monsignor Rinuccini before he left Italy for Ireland. Nothing but harm can follow the interference of the priest in politics, for it will inevitably sooner or later depress their sacred office in the minds of the people, and undermine the reverence and devotion of Irishmen to their religion. This is so clearly the teaching of history that to explain the existing state of things we must turn to the nature of the predominant qualities of the Irish people.

There can be no question that a majority of the Irish priests at the present day are not only very much of the people, but are derived from the class of landowners; born, therefore, to an irresistible longing to possess land, or rather that it should be brought back into their families, some of whom are descended from the former landlords of the country. Many of the priests have had this feeling intensified rather than otherwise during the course of their education, associating only with men possessed of similar sentiments; in this respect their predecessors were at an advantage, for the Continental seminaries in which most of them were educated were frequently governed by polished Frenchmen or Austrians, and the whole atmosphere of these establishments developed the chivalrous sensitive nature of the Irish Celt; he returned therefore to his native country to spread wide the religion, loyalty, and culture which he adorned.* The land question is at the root of the action taken by the political priest of the present day; once let that question be settled, and we shall hear little more of politics among the clergy, or of a Dublin Parliament among the laity.

The question of a thoroughly efficient Roman Catholic University in Ireland is second only to that of the land problem. We must remember that the Irish Celt, and the Saxon look at this question through very differently tinted glasses, and we may surely admit that the former are right on so vitally an important matter as that of the education of the rising generation. The efforts of the Government in this respect has so far been a failure, because they have never dealt with it in a complete and comprehensive manner, or thoroughly appreciated the opinions held by Roman Catholics on this subject. What is required is a university governed by well-balanced ecclesiastical and lay authorities, in which young men, under conditions acceptable to Roman Catholics, can receive a complete and high-class education. In such a university and its affiliated colleges lads preparing for the priesthood might receive their preliminary training, together with companions of the same

* Pp. 279–280.

religion who propose entering the medical and other professions; arts, science, and literature would there find a congenial home, and doubtless flourish, for the Irish are a highly intellectual race. The university must be enabled to grant degrees, means being taken to secure that the educational standard is on a level with that of older institutions. One cannot help feeling that a university of this description would draw out and refine the character of many young men whose career in after-life would very much tend to influence the tone of society, and no class could do this to greater advantage than the priesthood; the religious zeal and devotion of these Irishmen to their sacred calling is beyond all question; but not a few of them are deficient in that refinement and culture which the training they would receive in a well-ordered university is capable of developing, and which was so conspicuous an element in the lives of their predecessors in the last century. A university of this kind can only rise gradually, and by aid of the State, for Ireland is by no means a rich country: opposition there would certainly be to endowing an institution of this description from the National Exchequer, but in all fairness, if the story of Ireland could only be brought home to Englishmen, they would meet their fellow-subjects upon equitable terms, and with a liberal hand in so important an object as that of founding and endowing at least one Roman Catholic University in Ireland.

The knowledge to be acquired from our history renders it extremely problematical as to whether Irishmen are likely to profit by, or even to appreciate, the advantages claimed by Englishmen for elected county and parish councils to manage local affairs; at any rate it would be wise to wait until they ask for institutions of this description. The grand jury system has worked well in Ireland; it is an old and tried form of local government, and may with advantage be entrusted with greater powers than it now possesses. A system of this kind is better adapted to the nature of the Irish Celt than county and parish councils, which will certainly give rise to much and repeated excitement at the time of elections, and such councils when formed will probably engender corruption in the local administration, elements which in Ireland certainly do not require stimulating to greater action.

With these general remarks on some of the leading questions of the future, based on the story of an old Irish sept, we must conclude this work. But before doing so I would refer in few words to the character of one of the direct descendants of the former chiefs of Clancuilein, who has only recently passed from among us in the full vigour of early manhood.

In the preceding chapter reference was made to the career of Mr. John, and his brother, Admiral Macnamara, with the object of demonstrating how closely their lives were in conformity with congenital qualities precisely similar to those which had characterised so many of their ancestors. Two of Mr. John Macnamara's grandsons are living at the present time, and Arthur, the son of one of them (Mr. J. Macnamara), was the last of the male representatives of S. Macnamara, chief of his sept in the first half of the sixteenth century, and through him descended from the progenitor of our clan.* I was on terms of intimate friendship with Arthur Macnamara, and it was our wish to have worked out the history of Clancuilein conjointly. We had, however, hardly formed this idea when by a fall on the Alps my friend was killed; and so, amidst the interruptions of a busy life the work fell into my hands : it would have been a far more complete history of our sept had Arthur Macnamara been spared to write it; but I was impelled to go on with the work, not only because the subject was one of much interest, but also because I feel sure its completion would be in accordance with the wishes of my friend.

Arthur Macnamara was true to the character of his progenitors, he was chivalrous, brave, and a loyal friend, endowed with high mental qualities, and full of Celtic sensitiveness and brightness, qualities which endeared him to every one who knew him; to this there could be no better testimony than the words of one who watched his career as a schoolboy at Harrow, and an undergraduate at Cambridge, with the closest and warmest interest, and who wrote of him as follows in the "Harrovian" of the 2nd of October, 1890 : †

"Arthur Macnamara came to Harrow in the spring of 1875, when he was a candidate for an Entrance Scholarship. After a brilliant examination he won the first Scholarship. His school career was an almost unbroken series of triumphs. But perhaps the most striking incident in his Harrow life was his winning the Gregory Scholarship, the blue ribbon of the School, in April 1877, within two years of his coming to Harrow. There are some who can remember with what mingled amusement and astonishment, wholly devoid of self-assumption or conceit, the young boy of not yet sixteen years, standing somewhat aloof in the school-yard, heard his name read out by the examiner as the foremost scholar in the school.

"He was elected to a Minor Scholarship at Trinity College, Cambridge, and left Harrow for the University in July 1879. After obtaining in due time his First Class in the Classical Tripos he devoted himself

---

* See pedigrees, pp. 264, 294.

† Arthur Macnamara was killed in a fall when descending the Dussistock on August 16, 1890; his body was buried in the cemetery at Lucerne.

assiduously to work for the Bar, and was already, in the opinion of well-qualified judges, marked out for future distinction.

" But it is not on his exceptional abilities, nor even his attachment and services to Harrow, that the memory of those who loved him (and who that knew him well did not love him ?) will now most fondly dwell. It was the sweetness of his nature, his tenderness and unselfishness, his unaffected modesty, his childlike simplicity, his sunny humour and love of fun, his affectionateness and sincerity, that endeared him so deeply to his friends."

In the " Alpine Journal " for November 1890, we find the following statement regarding Arthur Macnamara : " His love for the mountains and his unbounded energy made it probable that he would soon have reached the first rank of English climbers. His energy was apparent in every pursuit in life. On one occasion, when an undergraduate at Cambridge, he walked from Cambridge to Oxford in a single day. And I have known of his running the last six miles home after a long day's walk in order to meet some friends at a Welsh inn. To walk from his rooms near Piccadilly down to Harrow for breakfast, was at one time almost a frequent practice on his part. Indeed, his affection for his old school was very great, and he was never happier than when in his old haunts."*

One who knew him intimately has truly observed, that " it was a privilege to have met a really unselfish man, and we may try to repay the debt we owe him by following, to some small degree, the example of his true and almost perfect life." To which expression of genuine feeling we can heartily say, So be it ! and hope that many members of our sept, and of Irishmen, scattered over the face of the earth, may cheer the lives of those among whom their lot is cast, by a display of qualities which shone so brightly in one of the last of the direct representatives of the old chiefs of Clancuilein.

* From the police report of the " Times " for November 1884, we learn that a man of the name of Roney, one of the roughs and terrors of Drury Lane, was quarrelling with a woman near the corner of Great Queen Street. He knocked her down and sat upon her. A number of roughs stood looking on, but an elderly gentleman pushed his way through the crowd, and begged the man to desist from ill-treating the woman. The ruffian turned on the old gentleman and struck him in the face, the woman rose and endeavoured to screen her protector. At this point a young gentleman, a student of Lincoln's-Inn, seeing what was going on, jumped out of a cab in which he was passing : he was evidently a master of the science of self-defence, and in spite of Roney's great size, and strength he received in the course of a few minutes such well-deserved punishment as not only surprised him much, but also those who were looking on ; the young gentleman who administered this summary justice to Roney was Arthur Macnamara.

INDEX

x